GW00673331

BMW Owners Workshop Manual

A K Legg T Eng MIMI

Models covered
BMW 525 & 525 Auto; 2494 cc
BMW 528 & 528 Auto; 2788 cc
BMW 528i & 528i Auto; 2788 cc

Does not cover revised range introduced October 1981

ISBN 1 85010 430 1

Printed in England (632–9N1)

ABCD

THE BOOK

Haynes Publishing Group
Sparkford Nr Yeovil
Somerset BA22 7JJ England

Haynes Publications, Inc
861 Lawrence Drive
Newbury Park
California 91320 USA

British Library Cataloguing in Publication Data
Legg, A. K.
BMW 525, 528 & 528i owners workshop manual.
– (Owners Workshop Manuals).
1. Automobiles – Maintenance and repair
I. Title   II. Series
629'28'722   TL152
ISBN 1-85010-430-1

Acknowledgements

Thanks are due to the Champion Sparking Plug Company who supplied the illustrations showing the various spark plug conditions. Castrol Limited kindly supplied the lubrication data, and Sykes-Pickavant Ltd provided some of the workshop tools. Special thanks are due to all those people at Sparkford who helped in the production of this manual.

About this manual

Its aim

The aim of this manual is to help you get the best value from your vehicle. It can do so in several ways. It can help you decide what work must be done (even should you choose to get it done by a garage), provide information on routine maintenance and servicing, and give a logical course of action and diagnosis when random faults occur. However, it is hoped that you will use the manual by tackling the work yourself. On simpler jobs it may even be quicker than booking the car into a garage and going there twice, to leave and collect it. Perhaps most important, a lot of money can be saved by avoiding the costs a garage must charge to cover its labour and overheads.

The manual has drawings and descriptions to show the function of the various components so that their layout can be understood. Then the tasks are described and photographed in a step-by-step sequence so that even a novice can do the work.

Its arrangement

The manual is divided into thirteen Chapters, each covering a logical sub-division of the vehicle. The Chapters are each divided into Sections, numbered with single figures, eg 5; and the Sections into paragraphs (or sub-sections), with decimal numbers following on from the Section they are in, eg 5.1, 5.2, 5.3 etc.

It is freely illustrated, especially in those parts where there is a detailed sequence of operations to be carried out. There are two forms of illustration: figures and photographs. The figures are numbered in sequence with decimal numbers, according to their position in the Chapter — eg Fig. 6.4 is the fourth drawing/illustration in Chapter 6. Photographs carry the same number (either individually or in related groups) as the Section or sub-section to which they relate.

There is an alphabetical index at the back of the manual as well as a contents list at the front. Each Chapter is also preceded by its own individual contents list.

References to the 'left' or 'right' of the vehicle are in the sense of a person in the driver's seat facing forwards.

Unless otherwise stated, nuts and bolts are removed by turning anti-clockwise, and tightened by turning clockwise.

Vehicle manufacturers continually make changes to specifications and recommendations, and these, when notified, are incorporated into our manuals at the earliest opportunity.

Whilst every care is taken to ensure that the information in this manual is correct, no liability can be accepted by the authors or publishers for loss, damage or injury caused by any errors in, or omissions from, the information given.

Introduction to the BMW

The BMW models covered by this manual are soundly constructed and mechanical components are engineered to fine limits. A buyer contemplating the purchase of one of these cars will be reassured by the knowledge that they are absolutely conventional in design and should cause no problems in overhaul or repair.

The fact that BMW models have enjoyed such long production runs over many years provides a hedge against depreciation and ensures the availability of both new and second-hand spare parts.

All models described in this manual are easily identified by having only four-door saloon bodywork.

Contents

BMW 525

BMW 528

General dimensions, weights and capacities

Dimensions
Overall length
UK models .... 4620 mm (181.9 in)
USA models .... 4823 mm (189.9 in)

Overall width
UK models .... 1690 mm (66.5 in)
USA models .... 1708 mm (67.2 in)

Overall height
UK models .... 1425 mm (56.1 in)
USA models .... 1420 mm (55.9 in)

Ground clearance (loaded) .... 136 mm (5.4 in)

Wheelbase .... 2636 mm (103.8 in)

Turning circle .... 10.5 m (34 ft 5 in)

Weights
Kerb weight (with full fuel tank)
UK models:
    525 .... 1350 kg (2976 lb)
    528 (carburettor) .... 1385 kg (3053 lb)
    528 (injection) .... 1410 kg (3108 lb)
Note: *Add 20 kg (44 lb) for automatic transmission*
USA models:
    528i (manual) .... 1495 kg (3296 lb)
    528i (auto) .... 1510 kg (3329 lb)
    530i (manual) .... 1497 kg (3300 lb)
    530i (auto) .... 1517 kg (3344 lb)

Maximum towing weight (up a gradient of 1 in 8 with a braked trailer) .... 1800 kg (3968 lb)

Maximum roof rack load .... 75 kg (165 lb)

Capacities
Engine oil
Without filter .... 8.8 Imp pt; 5.2 US qt; 5.0 litre
With filter .... 10.1 Imp pt; 6.1 US qt; 5.75 litre

Cooling system (including heater) .... 21.1 Imp pt; 12.7 US qt; 12.0 litre

Fuel tank
UK models .... 15.5 Imp gal; 18.5 US gal; 70 litre
USA models (pre-1978) .... 15.5 Imp gal; 18.5 US gal; 70 litre
USA models (1978-on) .... 13.6 Imp gal; 16.4 US gal; 62 litre

Manual gearbox
4-speed .... 1.9 Imp pt; 1.2 US qt; 1.1 litre
5-speed .... 2.8 Imp pt; 1.7 US qt; 1.6 litre

Automatic transmission .... See Chapter 6

Final drive .... 2.82 Imp pt; 1.7 US qt; 1.6 litre

LCS-13-44-SP Amended June 1985

Use of English

As this book has been written in England, it uses the appropriate English component names, phrases, and spelling. Some of these differ from those used in America. Normally, these cause no difficulty, but to make sure, a glossary is printed below. In ordering spare parts remember the parts list may use some of these words:

English	American	English	American
Accelerator	Gas pedal	Locks	Latches
Aerial	Antenna	Methylated spirit	Denatured alcohol
Anti-roll bar	Stabiliser or sway bar	Motorway	Freeway, turnpike etc
Big-end bearing	Rod bearing	Number plate	License plate
Bonnet (engine cover)	Hood	Paraffin	Kerosene
Boot (luggage compartment)	Trunk	Petrol	Gasoline (gas)
Bulkhead	Firewall	Petrol tank	Gas tank
Bush	Bushing	'Pinking'	'Pinging'
Cam follower or tappet	Valve lifter or tappet	Prise (force apart)	Pry
Carburettor	Carburetor	Propeller shaft	Driveshaft
Catch	Latch	Quarterlight	Quarter window
Choke/venturi	Barrel	Retread	Recap
Circlip	Snap-ring	Reverse	Back-up
Clearance	Lash	Rocker cover	Valve cover
Crownwheel	Ring gear (of differential)	Saloon	Sedan
Damper	Shock absorber, shock	Seized	Frozen
Disc (brake)	Rotor/disk	Sidelight	Parking light
Distance piece	Spacer	Silencer	Muffler
Drop arm	Pitman arm	Sill panel (beneath doors)	Rocker panel
Drop head coupe	Convertible	Small end, little end	Piston pin or wrist pin
Dynamo	Generator (DC)	Spanner	Wrench
Earth (electrical)	Ground	Split cotter (for valve spring cap)	Lock (for valve spring retainer)
Engineer's blue	Prussian blue	Split pin	Cotter pin
Estate car	Station wagon	Steering arm	Spindle arm
Exhaust manifold	Header	Sump	Oil pan
Fault finding/diagnosis	Troubleshooting	Swarf	Metal chips or debris
Float chamber	Float bowl	Tab washer	Tang or lock
Free-play	Lash	Tappet	Valve lifter
Freewheel	Coast	Thrust bearing	Throw-out bearing
Gearbox	Transmission	Top gear	High
Gearchange	Shift	Torch	Flashlight
Grub screw	Setscrew, Allen screw	Trackrod (of steering)	Tie-rod (or connecting rod)
Gudgeon pin	Piston pin or wrist pin	Trailing shoe (of brake)	Secondary shoe
Halfshaft	Axleshaft	Transmission	Whole drive line
Handbrake	Parking brake	Tyre	Tire
Hood	Soft top	Van	Panel wagon/van
Hot spot	Heat riser	Vice	Vise
Indicator	Turn signal	Wheel nut	Lug nut
Interior light	Dome lamp	Windscreen	Windshield
Layshaft (of gearbox)	Countershaft	Wing/mudguard	Fender
Leading shoe (of brake)	Primary shoe		

Buying spare parts
and vehicle identification numbers

Buying spare parts

Spare parts are available from many sources. BMW have many dealers throughout the UK and USA, and other dealers, accessory stores and motor factors will also stock BMW spare parts.

Our advice regarding spare part sources is as follows:

Officially appointed vehicle main dealers – This is the best source of parts which are peculiar to your vehicle and are otherwise not generally available (eg complete cylinder heads, internal transmission components, badges, interior trim etc). It is also the only place at which you should buy parts if your vehicle is still under warranty. To be sure of obtaining the correct parts it will always be necessary to give the storeman your vehicle's engine and chassis number, and if possible, to take the 'old' part along for positive identification. Remember that many parts are available on a factory exchange scheme – any parts returned should always be clean! It obviously makes good sense to go straight to the specialists on your vehicle for this type of part, for they are best equipped to supply you.

Other dealers and auto accessory shops – These are often very good places to buy materials and components needed for the maintenance of your vehicle (eg oil filter, spark plugs, bulbs, fan belts, oils and greases, touch-up paint, filler paste etc). They also sell general accessories, usually have convenient opening hours, charge lower prices and can often be found not far from home.

Motor factors – Good factors will stock all of the more important components which wear out relatively quickly (eg clutch components, pistons, valves, exhaust systems, brake cylinders/pipes/hoses/seals/shoes and pads etc). Motor factors will often provide new or reconditioned components on a part exchange basis – this can save a considerable amount of money.

Vehicle identification numbers

Modifications are a continuing and unpublicised process in vehicle manufacture. Spare parts manuals and lists are compiled on a numerical basis, the individual vehicle numbers being essential to identify correctly the component required.

The engine number is located on the crankcase just above the starter motor (photo).

The vehicle identification plate is located within the engine compartment on the side wheel arch (photo). The vehicle identification number is also repeated on the centre of the bulkhead.

On North American cars, the vehicle identification number is repeated on the top surface of the instrument panel just inside the windscreen.

The gearbox type and model number is stamped on the gearbox casing.

The engine number is stamped on the crankcase

The vehicle identification plate

Tools and working facilities

Introduction

A selection of good tools is a fundamental requirement for anyone contemplating the maintenance and repair of a motor vehicle. For the owner who does not possess any, their purchase will prove a considerable expense, offsetting some of the savings made by doing-it-yourself. However, provided that the tools purchased meet the relevant national safety standards and are of good quality, they will last for many years and prove an extremely worthwhile investment.

To help the average owner to decide which tools are needed to carry out the various tasks detailed in this manual, we have compiled three lists of tools under the following headings: *Maintenance and minor repair, Repair and overhaul,* and *Special*. The newcomer to practical mechanics should start off with the *Maintenance and minor repair* tool kit and confine himself to the simpler jobs around the vehicle. Then, as his confidence and experience grow, he can undertake more difficult tasks, buying extra tools as, and when, they are needed. In this way, a *Maintenance and minor repair* tool kit can be built-up into a *Repair and overhaul* tool kit over a considerable period of time without any major cash outlays. The experienced do-it-yourselfer will have a tool kit good enough for most repair and overhaul procedures and will add tools from the *Special* category when he feels the expense is justified by the amount of use to which these tools will be put.

It is obviously not possible to cover the subject of tools fully here. For those who wish to learn more about tools and their use there is a book entitled *How to Choose and Use Car Tools* available from the publishers of this manual.

Maintenance and minor repair tool kit

The tools given in this list should be considered as a minimum requirement if routine maintenance, servicing and minor repair operations are to be undertaken. We recommend the purchase of combination spanners (ring one end, open-ended the other); although more expensive than open-ended ones, they do give the advantages of both types of spanner.

Combination spanners - 10, 11, 12, 13, 14 & 17 mm
Adjustable spanner - 9 inch
Gearbox/rear axle drain plug key
Spark plug spanner (with rubber insert)
Spark plug gap adjustment tool
Set of feeler gauges
Brake bleed nipple spanner
Screwdriver - 4 in long x $\frac{1}{4}$ in dia (flat blade)
Screwdriver - 4 in long x $\frac{1}{4}$ in dia (cross blade)
Combination pliers - 6 inch
Hacksaw (junior)
Tyre pump
Tyre pressure gauge
Oil can
Fine emery cloth (1 sheet)
Wire brush (small)
Funnel (medium size)

Repair and overhaul tool kit

These tools are virtually essential for anyone undertaking any major repairs to a motor vehicle, and are additional to those given in the *Maintenance and minor repair* list. Included in this list is a comprehensive set of sockets. Although these are expensive they will be found invaluable as they are so versatile - particularly if various drives are included in the set. We recommend the $\frac{1}{2}$ in square-drive type, as this can be used with most proprietary torque wrenches. If you cannot afford a socket set, even bought piecemeal, then inexpensive tubular box spanners are a useful alternative.

The tools in this list will occasionally need to be supplemented by tools from the *Special* list.

Sockets (or box spanners) to cover range in previous list
Reversible ratchet drive (for use with sockets)
Extension piece, 10 inch (for use with sockets)
Universal joint (for use with sockets)
Torque wrench (for use with sockets)
'Mole' wrench - 8 inch
Ball pein hammer
Soft-faced hammer, plastic or rubber
Screwdriver - 6 in long x $\frac{5}{16}$ in dia (flat blade)
Screwdriver - 2 in long x $\frac{5}{16}$ in square (flat blade)
Screwdriver - 1$\frac{1}{2}$ in long x $\frac{1}{4}$ in dia (cross blade)
Screwdriver - 3 in long x $\frac{1}{8}$ in dia (electricians)
Pliers - electricians side cutters
Pliers - needle nosed
Pliers - circlip (internal and external)
Cold chisel - $\frac{1}{2}$ inch
Scriber
Scraper
Centre punch
Pin punch
Hacksaw
Valve grinding tool
Steel rule/straight-edge
Allen keys (inc. splined/Torx type if necessary)
Selection of files
Wire brush (large)
Axle-stands
Jack (strong scissor or hydraulic type)

Special tools

The tools in this list are those which are not used regularly, are expensive to buy, or which need to be used in accordance with their manufacturers' instructions. Unless relatively difficult mechanical jobs are undertaken frequently, it will not be economic to buy many of these tools. Where this is the case, you could consider clubbing together with friends (or joining a motorists' club) to make a joint purchase, or borrowing the tools against a deposit from a local garage or tool hire specialist.

The following list contains only those tools and instruments freely available to the public, and not those special tools produced by the vehicle manufacturer specifically for its dealer network. You will find occasional references to these manufacturers' special tools in the text of this manual. Generally, an alternative method of doing the job without the vehicle manufacturers' special tool is given. However, sometimes, there is no alternative to using them. Where this is the case and the relevant tool cannot be bought or borrowed, you will have to entrust the work to a franchised garage.

Valve spring compressor (where applicable)
Piston ring compressor
Balljoint separator
Universal hub/bearing puller
Impact screwdriver
Micrometer and/or vernier gauge
Dial gauge
Stroboscopic timing light
Dwell angle meter/tachometer
Universal electrical multi-meter
Cylinder compression gauge
Lifting tackle
Trolley jack
Light with extension lead

Buying tools

For practically all tools, a tool factor is the best source since he will have a very comprehensive range compared with the average garage or accessory shop. Having said that, accessory shops often offer excellent quality tools at discount prices, so it pays to shop around.

There are plenty of good tools around at reasonable prices, but always aim to purchase items which meet the relevant national safety standards. If in doubt, ask the proprietor or manager of the shop for advice before making a purchase.

Care and maintenance of tools

Having purchased a reasonable tool kit, it is necessary to keep the tools in a clean serviceable condition. After use, always wipe off any dirt, grease and metal particles using a clean, dry cloth, before putting the tools away. Never leave them lying around after they have been used. A simple tool rack on the garage or workshop wall, for items such as screwdrivers and pliers is a good idea. Store all normal wrenches and sockets in a metal box. Any measuring instruments, gauges, meters, etc, must be carefully stored where they cannot be damaged or become rusty.

Take a little care when tools are used. Hammer heads inevitably become marked and screwdrivers lose the keen edge on their blades from time to time. A little timely attention with emery cloth or a file will soon restore items like this to a good serviceable finish.

Working facilities

Not to be forgotten when discussing tools, is the workshop itself. If anything more than routine maintenance is to be carried out, some form of suitable working area becomes essential.

It is appreciated that many an owner mechanic is forced by circumstances to remove an engine or similar item, without the benefit of a garage or workshop. Having done this, any repairs should always be done under the cover of a roof.

Wherever possible, any dismantling should be done on a clean, flat workbench or table at a suitable working height.

Any workbench needs a vice: one with a jaw opening of 4 in (100 mm) is suitable for most jobs. As mentioned previously, some clean dry storage space is also required for tools, as well as for lubricants, cleaning fluids, touch-up paints and so on, which become necessary.

Another item which may be required, and which has a much more general usage, is an electric drill with a chuck capacity of at least $\frac{5}{16}$ in (8 mm). This, together with a good range of twist drills, is virtually essential for fitting accessories such as mirrors and reversing lights.

Last, but not least, always keep a supply of old newspapers and clean, lint-free rags available, and try to keep any working area as clean as possible.

Spanner jaw gap comparison table

Jaw gap (in)	Spanner size
0.250	$\frac{1}{4}$ in AF
0.276	7 mm
0.313	$\frac{5}{16}$ in AF
0.315	8 mm
0.344	$\frac{11}{32}$ in AF; $\frac{1}{8}$ in Whitworth
0.354	9 mm
0.375	$\frac{3}{8}$ in AF
0.394	10 mm
0.433	11 mm
0.438	$\frac{7}{16}$ in AF
0.445	$\frac{3}{16}$ in Whitworth; $\frac{1}{4}$ in BSF
0.472	12 mm
0.500	$\frac{1}{2}$ in AF
0.512	13 mm
0.525	$\frac{1}{4}$ in Whitworth; $\frac{5}{16}$ in BSF
0.551	14 mm
0.563	$\frac{9}{16}$ in AF
0.591	15 mm
0.600	$\frac{5}{16}$ in Whitworth; $\frac{3}{8}$ in BSF
0.625	$\frac{5}{8}$ in AF
0.630	16 mm
0.669	17 mm
0.686	$\frac{11}{16}$ in AF
0.709	18 mm
0.710	$\frac{3}{8}$ in Whitworth; $\frac{7}{16}$ in BSF
0.748	19 mm
0.750	$\frac{3}{4}$ in AF
0.813	$\frac{13}{16}$ in AF
0.820	$\frac{7}{16}$ in Whitworth; $\frac{1}{2}$ in BSF
0.866	22 mm
0.875	$\frac{7}{8}$ in AF
0.920	$\frac{1}{2}$ in Whitworth; $\frac{9}{16}$ in BSF
0.938	$\frac{15}{16}$ in AF
0.945	24 mm
1.000	1 in AF
1.010	$\frac{9}{16}$ in Whitworth; $\frac{5}{8}$ in BSF
1.024	26 mm
1.063	$1\frac{1}{16}$ in AF; 27 mm
1.100	$\frac{5}{8}$ in Whitworth; $\frac{11}{16}$ in BSF
1.125	$1\frac{1}{8}$ in AF
1.181	30 mm
1.200	$\frac{11}{16}$ in Whitworth; $\frac{3}{4}$ in BSF
1.250	$1\frac{1}{4}$ in AF
1.260	32 mm
1.300	$\frac{3}{4}$ in Whitworth; $\frac{7}{8}$ in BSF
1.313	$1\frac{5}{16}$ in AF
1.390	$\frac{13}{16}$ in Whitworth; $\frac{15}{16}$ in BSF
1.417	36 mm
1.438	$1\frac{7}{16}$ in AF
1.480	$\frac{7}{8}$ in Whitworth; 1 in BSF
1.500	$1\frac{1}{2}$ in AF
1.575	40 mm; $\frac{15}{16}$ in Whitworth
1.614	41 mm
1.625	$1\frac{5}{8}$ in AF
1.670	1 in Whitworth; $1\frac{1}{8}$ in BSF
1.688	$1\frac{11}{16}$ in AF
1.811	46 mm
1.813	$1\frac{13}{16}$ in AF
1.860	$1\frac{1}{8}$ in Whitworth; $1\frac{1}{4}$ in BSF
1.875	$1\frac{7}{8}$ in AF
1.969	50 mm
2.000	2 in AF
2.050	$1\frac{1}{4}$ in Whitworth; $1\frac{3}{8}$ in BSF
2.165	55 mm
2.362	60 mm

Jacking and towing

The jack supplied with the car tool kit should only be used for changing roadwheels (photos). When carrying out repairs to the car, jack up the front end under the crossmember or the rear under the differential/final drive unit. Always supplement these jacks with axle stands placed under the bodyframe members.

Eye brackets are provided at the front and rear of the car (photo); primarily these are fitted to the body as points whereby the car can be lashed down during transportation. If these eye brackets are used for towing in an emergency, do not tow vehicles which are considerably larger in size and weight than your own car. If your car is equipped with automatic transmission, it must only be towed if the speed selector lever is first placed in the N position and the road speed does not exceed 30 mph (48 kph). The total distance covered must not exceed 30 miles (49 km) unless an additional 2 Imp pints (1.1 litres) (2.4 US pints) of fluid are added to the transmission unit, or the propeller shaft disconnected, otherwise lack of lubrication may damage the internal components. Always reduce the fluid level again when the car is ready to operate normally. Tow starting or starting the car by running it down an incline is not possible with the type of automatic transmission fitted.

Jacking the car

Spare wheel compartment

When changing a wheel always chock the diagonally opposite roadwheel

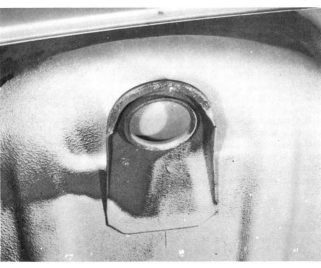

Rear towing eye

Safety first!

Professional motor mechanics are trained in safe working procedures. However enthusiastic you may be about getting on with the job in hand, do take the time to ensure that your safety is not put at risk. A moment's lack of attention can result in an accident, as can failure to observe certain elementary precautions.

There will always be new ways of having accidents, and the following points do not pretend to be a comprehensive list of all dangers; they are intended rather to make you aware of the risks and to encourage a safety-conscious approach to all work you carry out on your vehicle.

Essential DOs and DON'Ts

DON'T rely on a single jack when working underneath the vehicle. Always use reliable additional means of support, such as axle stands, securely placed under a part of the vehicle that you know will not give way.

DON'T attempt to loosen or tighten high-torque nuts (e.g. wheel hub nuts) while the vehicle is on a jack; it may be pulled off.

DON'T start the engine without first ascertaining that the transmission is in neutral (or 'Park' where applicable) and the parking brake applied.

DON'T suddenly remove the filler cap from a hot cooling system – cover it with a cloth and release the pressure gradually first, or you may get scalded by escaping coolant.

DON'T attempt to drain oil until you are sure it has cooled sufficiently to avoid scalding you.

DON'T grasp any part of the engine, exhaust or catalytic converter without first ascertaining that it is sufficiently cool to avoid burning you.

DON'T allow brake fluid or antifreeze to contact vehicle paintwork.

DON'T syphon toxic liquids such as fuel, brake fluid or antifreeze by mouth, or allow them to remain on your skin.

DON'T inhale dust – it may be injurious to health (see *Asbestos* below).

DON'T allow any spilt oil or grease to remain on the floor – wipe it up straight away, before someone slips on it.

DON'T use ill-fitting spanners or other tools which may slip and cause injury.

DON'T attempt to lift a heavy component which may be beyond your capability – get assistance.

DON'T rush to finish a job, or take unverified short cuts.

DON'T allow children or animals in or around an unattended vehicle.

DO wear eye protection when using power tools such as drill, sander, bench grinder etc, and when working under the vehicle.

DO use a barrier cream on your hands prior to undertaking dirty jobs – it will protect your skin from infection as well as making the dirt easier to remove afterwards; but make sure your hands aren't left slippery. Note that long-term contact with used engine oil can be a health hazard.

DO keep loose clothing (cuffs, tie etc) and long hair well out of the way of moving mechanical parts.

DO remove rings, wristwatch etc, before working on the vehicle – especially the electrical system.

DO ensure that any lifting tackle used has a safe working load rating adequate for the job.

DO keep your work area tidy – it is only too easy to fall over articles left lying around.

DO get someone to check periodically that all is well, when working alone on the vehicle.

DO carry out work in a logical sequence and check that everything is correctly assembled and tightened afterwards.

DO remember that your vehicle's safety affects that of yourself and others. If in doubt on any point, get specialist advice.

IF, in spite of following these precautions, you are unfortunate enough to injure yourself, seek medical attention as soon as possible.

Asbestos

Certain friction, insulating, sealing, and other products – such as brake linings, brake bands, clutch linings, torque converters, gaskets, etc – contain asbestos. *Extreme care must be taken to avoid inhalation of dust from such products since it is hazardous to health.* If in doubt, assume that they *do* contain asbestos.

Fire

Remember at all times that petrol (gasoline) is highly flammable. Never smoke, or have any kind of naked flame around, when working on the vehicle. But the risk does not end there – a spark caused by an electrical short-circuit, by two metal surfaces contacting each other, by careless use of tools, or even by static electricity built up in your body under certain conditions, can ignite petrol vapour, which in a confined space is highly explosive.

Always disconnect the battery earth (ground) terminal before working on any part of the fuel or electrical system, and never risk spilling fuel on to a hot engine or exhaust.

It is recommended that a fire extinguisher of a type suitable for fuel and electrical fires is kept handy in the garage or workplace at all times. Never try to extinguish a fuel or electrical fire with water.

Note: *Any reference to a 'torch' appearing in this manual should always be taken to mean a hand-held battery-operated electric lamp or flashlight. It does NOT mean a welding/gas torch or blowlamp.*

Fumes

Certain fumes are highly toxic and can quickly cause unconsciousness and even death if inhaled to any extent. Petrol (gasoline) vapour comes into this category, as do the vapours from certain solvents such as trichloroethylene. Any draining or pouring of such volatile fluids should be done in a well ventilated area.

When using cleaning fluids and solvents, read the instructions carefully. Never use materials from unmarked containers – they may give off poisonous vapours.

Never run the engine of a motor vehicle in an enclosed space such as a garage. Exhaust fumes contain carbon monoxide which is extremely poisonous; if you need to run the engine, always do so in the open air or at least have the rear of the vehicle outside the workplace.

If you are fortunate enough to have the use of an inspection pit, never drain or pour petrol, and never run the engine, while the vehicle is standing over it; the fumes, being heavier than air, will concentrate in the pit with possibly lethal results.

The battery

Never cause a spark, or allow a naked light, near the vehicle's battery. It will normally be giving off a certain amount of hydrogen gas, which is highly explosive.

Always disconnect the battery earth (ground) terminal before working on the fuel or electrical systems.

If possible, loosen the filler plugs or cover when charging the battery from an external source. Do not charge at an excessive rate or the battery may burst.

Take care when topping up and when carrying the battery. The acid electrolyte, even when diluted, is very corrosive and should not be allowed to contact the eyes or skin.

If you ever need to prepare electrolyte yourself, always add the acid slowly to the water, and never the other way round. Protect against splashes by wearing rubber gloves and goggles.

When jump starting a car using a booster battery, for negative earth (ground) vehicles, connect the jump leads in the following sequence: First connect one jump lead between the positive (+) terminals of the two batteries. Then connect the other jump lead first to the negative (–) terminal of the booster battery, and then to a good earthing (ground) point on the vehicle to be started, at least 18 in (45 cm) from the battery if possible. Ensure that hands and jump leads are clear of any moving parts, and that the two vehicles do not touch. Disconnect the leads in the reverse order.

Mains electricity

When using an electric power tool, inspection light etc, which works from the mains, always ensure that the appliance is correctly connected to its plug and that, where necessary, it is properly earthed (grounded). Do not use such appliances in damp conditions and, again, beware of creating a spark or applying excessive heat in the vicinity of fuel or fuel vapour.

Ignition HT voltage

A severe electric shock can result from touching certain parts of the ignition system, such as the HT leads, when the engine is running or being cranked, particularly if components are damp or the insulation is defective. Where an electronic ignition system is fitted, the HT voltage is much higher and could prove fatal.

Routine maintenance

Maintenance is essential for ensuring safety and desirable for the purpose of getting the best in terms of performance and economy from the car. Over the years the need for periodic lubrication – oiling, greasing and so on – has been drastically reduced if not totally eliminated. This has unfortunately tended to lead some owners to think that because no such action is required the items either no longer exist or will last forever. This is certainly not the case; it is essential to carry out regular visual examinations as comprehensively as possible in order to spot any possible defects at an early stage before they develop into major expensive repairs.

Every 250 miles (400 km) or weekly – whichever comes first

Engine
Check the level of the oil and top-up if necessary (photos)
Check the coolant level and top-up if necessary (photo)
Check the level of electrolyte in the battery and top-up if necessary (photo)

Removing the engine oil level dipstick

Topping up the engine oil level

Topping up the coolant level

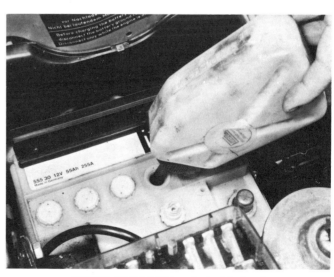

Topping up the battery electrolyte level

Clutch and brakes (as applicable)

Check the level of fluid in the clutch/brake hydraulic fluid reservoir, and top-up if necessary (photo). However if topping-up is necessary on a regular basis the leak should be located and rectified

Tyres

Check the tyre pressures (photo)
Visually examine the tyres for wear and damage

Lights and wipers

Check that all the lights work
Clean the headlamps
Check the windscreen washer fluid level and top-up if necessary (photo).

Every 5000 miles (7500 km) on UK models or every 6250 miles (10 000 km) on USA models

---

Engine

Change the engine oil and renew the filter (photo)

Steering

Check the power steering oil level and top-up if necessary

Every 10 000 miles (15 000 km) on UK models or every 12 500 miles (20 000 km) on USA models

---

Engine

Change the engine oil and renew the filter
Check the coolant antifreeze/inhibitor concentration and adjust if necessary
Check and adjust the valve clearances
Check and adjust drivebelt tension
Check all engine nuts and bolts for tightness
Renew the spark plugs
Renew and adjust the distributor contact points (if applicable)
Lubricate the throttle linkage
Renew the air filter element
Check the exhaust system for leaks and deterioration
Check the fuel tank sender unit filter and the fuel pump filter (if applicable)
Check the emission control components for security and deterioration
Check the cooling system and hoses for leaks

Transmission

Check the manual gearbox oil level and top-up if necessary
Check the automatic transmission fluid level and top-up if necessary
Check the final drive oil level and top-up if necessary

Clutch/brake hydraulic fluid reservoir

Checking the tyre pressure

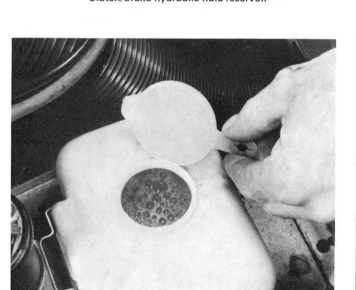

Checking the windscreen washer fluid level

Engine sump drain plug location

Check the driveshaft bellows and final drive oil seals for leaks
Check the propeller shaft universal joints for wear

Brakes
Check the front brake pads and discs for wear
Check the rear brake pads and discs, and adjust the handbrake
Visually check the hydraulic lines for damage, deterioration and leaks
Check the brake servo hose for condition and security

Steering and suspension
Check the steering gear oil level and top-up if necessary
Check the steering gear and joints for wear, and adjust the steering gear if necessary
Check the power steering oil level and top-up if necessary
Check the suspension joints and mountings for wear and damage
On USA models check and if necessary adjust the front wheel bearings

Body
Lubricate the door locks and hinges
Check the seat belts for security and condition
Lubricate the foot pedal pivots

Every 20 000 miles (30 000 km) on UK models or every 25 000 miles (40 000 km) on USA models

---

Engine
Renew the in-line fuel filter
Renew the oxygen sensor and EGR filter and check emission control components (if applicable)

Transmission
Renew automatic transmission fluid filter screen
Change the manual or automatic transmission oil/fluid

Change the final drive oil
Check the clutch wear (if applicable)

Brakes
Check the operation of the servo unit

Electrical
Check and if necessary adjust the headlamp alignment

Every 40 000 miles (60 000 km) on UK models or every 37 500 miles (60 000 km) on USA models

---

Brakes
Check the handbrake linings for wear

Steering and suspension
Renew the power steering filter and check the operation of the power steering
Check and if necessary adjust the front wheel bearings

Every 12 months

Clutch and brakes
Renew the hydraulic fluid in the clutch and brake circuits

Every 24 months

Engine
Drain the cooling system and flush it, then refill with new antifreeze solution

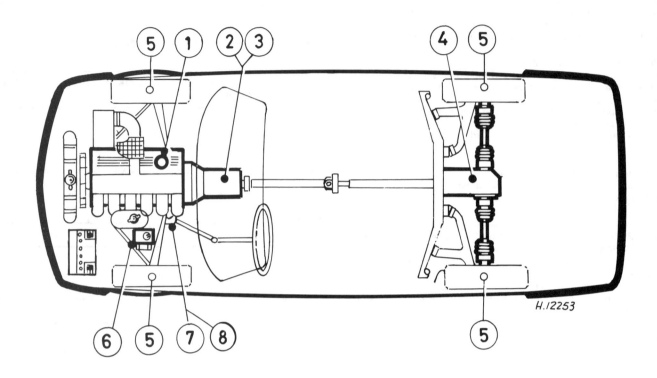

H.12253

Recommended lubricants and fluids

Component or system	Lubricant type or specification
Engine (1)	SAE 15W/40, 15W/50 or 20W/50 multigrade engine oil to API SE or SF
Manual gearbox (2)	SAE 80 gear oil to MIL-L-2105-A or API-GL4
Automatic transmission (3) ZF transmission Borg-Warner transmission	 Dexron ® II automatic transmission fluid Type F automatic transmission fluid
Final drive (4) Normal differential Limited slip differential	 SAE 90 hypoid gear oil to API-GL5 plus 6% additive content (eg Esso Gear Lube B 80W-90, Mobil Final Drive Gear Lube BM, Shell Final Drive Oil BMW or equivalent) Fuchs Renogear LS90
Wheel bearings (5)	High melting-point general purpose grease
Brake and hydraulic systems (6)	Hydraulic fluid to SAE J1703, DOT 3 or DOT 4
Power steering system (7)	Dexron® automatic transmission fluid
Manual steering system (8)	SAE 90 hypoid gear oil

Note: *The above are general recommendations only. Different operating territories require different lubricants. If in doubt, consult the driver's handbook supplied with the vehicle, or your nearest BMW dealer*

Fault diagnosis

Introduction

The vehicle owner who does his or her own maintenance according to the recommended schedules should not have to use this section of the manual very often. Modern component reliability is such that, provided those items subject to wear or deterioration are inspected or renewed at the specified intervals, sudden failure is comparatively rare. Faults do not usually just happen as a result of sudden failure, but develop over a period of time. Major mechanical failures in particular are usually preceded by characteristic symptoms over hundreds or even thousands of miles. Those components which do occasionally fail without warning are often small and easily carried in the vehicle.

With any fault finding, the first step is to decide where to begin investigations. Sometimes this is obvious, but on other occasions a little detective work will be necessary. The owner who makes half a dozen haphazard adjustments or replacements may be successful in curing a fault (or its symptoms), but he will be none the wiser if the fault recurs and he may well have spent more time and money than was necessary. A calm and logical approach will be found to be more satisfactory in the long run. Always take into account any warning signs or abnormalities that may have been noticed in the period preceding the fault – power loss, high or low gauge readings, unusual noises or smells, etc – and remember that failure of components such as fuses or spark plugs may only be pointers to some underlying fault.

The pages which follow here are intended to help in cases of failure to start or breakdown on the road. There is also a Fault Diagnosis Section at the end of each Chapter which should be consulted if the preliminary checks prove unfruitful. Whatever the fault, certain basic principles apply. These are as follows:

Verify the fault. This is simply a matter of being sure that you know what the symptoms are before starting work. This is particularly important if you are investigating a fault for someone else who may not have described it very accurately.

Don't overlook the obvious. For example, if the vehicle won't start, is there petrol in the tank? (Don't take anyone else's word on this particular point, and don't trust the fuel gauge either!) If an electrical fault is indicated, look for loose or broken wires before digging out the test gear.

Cure the disease, not the symptom. Substituting a flat battery with a fully charged one will get you off the hard shoulder, but if the underlying cause is not attended to, the new battery will go the same way. Similarly, changing oil-fouled spark plugs for a new set will get you moving again, but remember that the reason for the fouling (if it wasn't simply an incorrect grade of plug) will have to be established and corrected.

Don't take anything for granted. Particularly, don't forget that a 'new' component may itself be defective (especially if it's been rattling round in the boot for months), and don't leave components out of a fault diagnosis sequence just because they are new or recently fitted. When you do finally diagnose a difficult fault, you'll probably realise that all the evidence was there from the start.

Electrical faults

Electrical faults can be more puzzling than straightforward mechanical failures, but they are no less susceptible to logical analysis if the basic principles of operation are understood. Vehicle electrical wiring exists in extremely unfavourable conditions – heat, vibration and chemical attack – and the first things to look for are loose or corroded connections and broken or chafed wires, especially where the wires pass through holes in the bodywork or are subject to vibration.

All metal-bodied vehicles in current production have one pole of

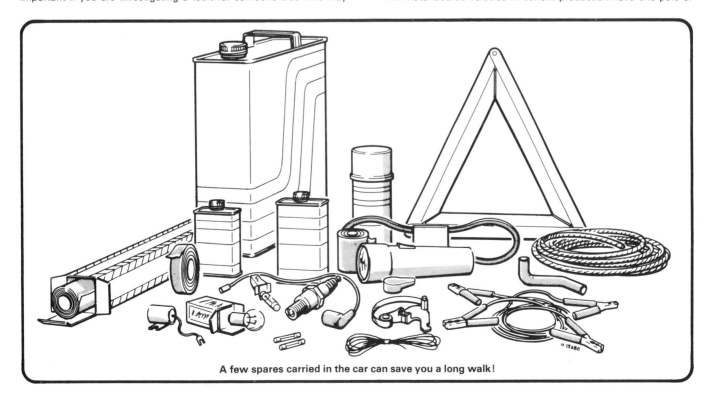

A few spares carried in the car can save you a long walk!

the battery 'earthed', ie connected to the vehicle bodywork, and in nearly all modern vehicles it is the negative (−) terminal. The various electrical components – motors, bulb holders etc – are also connected to earth, either by means of a lead or directly by their mountings. Electric current flows through the component and then back to the battery via the bodywork. If the component mounting is loose or corroded, or if a good path back to the battery is not available, the circuit will be incomplete and malfunction will result. The engine and/or gearbox are also earthed by means of flexible metal straps to the body or subframe; if these straps are loose or missing, starter motor, generator and ignition trouble may result.

Assuming the earth return to be satisfactory, electrical faults will be due either to component malfunction or to defects in the current supply. Individual components are dealt with in Chapter 10. If supply wires are broken or cracked internally this results in an open-circuit, and the easiest way to check for this is to bypass the suspect wire temporarily with a length of wire having a crocodile clip or suitable connector at each end. Alternatively, a 12V test lamp can be used to verify the presence of supply voltage at various points along the wire and the break can be thus isolated.

If a bare portion of a live wire touches the bodywork or other earthed metal part, the electricity will take the low-resistance path thus formed back to the battery: this is known as a short-circuit. Hopefully a short-circuit will blow a fuse, but otherwise it may cause burning of the insulation (and possibly further short-circuits) or even a fire. This is why it is inadvisable to bypass persistently blowing fuses with silver foil or wire.

Spares and tool kit

Most vehicles are supplied only with sufficient tools for wheel changing; the *Maintenance and minor repair* tool kit detailed in *Tools and working facilities,* with the addition of a hammer, is probably sufficient for those repairs that most motorists would consider attempting at the roadside. In addition a few items which can be fitted without too much trouble in the event of a breakdown should be carried. Experience and available space will modify the list below, but the following may save having to call on professional assistance:

Spark plugs, clean and correctly gapped
HT lead and plug cap – long enough to reach the plug furthest from the distributor
Distributor rotor, condenser and contact breaker points (where applicable)
Drivebelt(s) – emergency type may suffice
Spare fuses
Set of principal light bulbs
Tin of radiator sealer and hose bandage
Exhaust bandage
Roll of insulating tape
Length of soft iron wire
Length of electrical flex
Torch or inspection lamp (can double as test lamp)
Battery jump leads
Tow-rope
Ignition waterproofing aerosol
Litre of engine oil
Sealed can of hydraulic fluid
Emergency windscreen
'Jubilee' clips
Tube of filler paste

If spare fuel is carried, a can designed for the purpose should be used to minimise risks of leakage and collision damage. A first aid kit and a warning triangle, whilst not at present compulsory in the UK, are obviously sensible items to carry in addition to the above.

When touring abroad it may be advisable to carry additional spares which, even if you cannot fit them yourself, could save having to wait while parts are obtained. The items below may be worth considering:

Throttle cable
Cylinder head gasket
Alternator brushes
Fuel pump repair kit
Tyre valve core

One of the motoring organisations will be able to advise on availability of fuel etc in foreign countries.

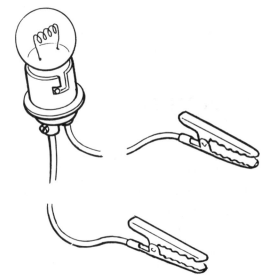

A simple test lamp is useful for tracing electrical faults

Tool tray in luggage compartment

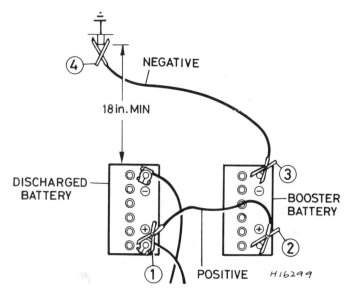

Jump start lead connections for negative earth vehicles – connect leads in order shown

Engine will not start

Engine fails to turn when starter operated
Flat battery (recharge, use jump leads, or push start)
Battery terminals loose or corroded
Battery earth to body defective
Engine earth strap loose or broken
Starter motor (or solenoid) wiring loose or broken
Automatic transmission selector in wrong position, or inhibitor switch faulty
Ignition/starter switch faulty
Major mechanical failure (seizure)
Starter or solenoid internal fault (see Chapter 10)

Starter motor turns engine slowly
Partially discharged battery (recharge, use jump leads, or push start)
Battery terminals loose or corroded
Battery earth to body defective
Engine earth strap loose
Starter motor (or solenoid) wiring loose
Starter motor internal fault (see Chapter 10)

Starter motor spins without turning engine
Flat battery
Flywheel gear teeth damaged or worn
Starter motor mounting bolts loose

Engine turns normally but fails to start
Damp or dirty HT leads and distributor cap (crank engine and check for spark)
Dirty or incorrectly gapped distributor points (if applicable)
No fuel in tank
Excessive choke (hot engine) or insufficient choke (cold engine)
Fouled or incorrectly gapped spark plugs (remove, clean and regap)
Other ignition system fault (see Chapter 4)
Other fuel system fault (see Chapter 3)
Poor compression (see Chapter 1)
Major mechanical failure (eg camshaft drive)

Engine fires but will not run
Insufficient choke (cold engine)
Air leaks at carburettor or inlet manifold or in injection system
Fuel starvation (see Chapter 3)
Ballast resistor defective, or other ignition fault (see Chapter 4)

Engine cuts out and will not restart

Engine cuts out suddenly – ignition fault
Loose or disconnected LT wires
Wet HT leads or distributor cap (after traversing water splash)
Coil or condenser failure (check for spark)
Other ignition fault (see Chapter 4)

Engine misfires before cutting out – fuel fault
Fuel tank empty
Fuel pump defective or filter blocked (check for delivery)
Fuel tank filler vent blocked (suction will be evident on releasing cap)
Carburettor needle valve sticking
Carburettor jets or injectors blocked (fuel contaminated)
Other fuel system fault (see Chapter 3)

Engine cuts out – other causes
Serious overheating
Major mechanical failure (eg camshaft drive)

Engine overheats

Ignition (no-charge) warning light illuminated
Slack or broken drivebelt – retension or renew (Chapter 2)

Ignition warning light not illuminated
Coolant loss due to internal or external leakage (see Chapter 2)
Thermostat defective
Low oil level
Brakes binding
Radiator clogged externally or internally
Electric cooling fan not operating correctly (where applicable)
Engine waterways clogged
Ignition timing incorrect or automatic advance malfunctioning
Mixture too weak

Note: *Do not add cold water to an overheated engine or damage may result*

Low engine oil pressure

Warning light illuminated with engine running
Oil level low or incorrect grade

Checking for a spark while cranking the engine

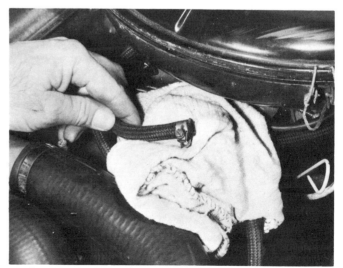

Checking for fuel delivery on a carburettor engine while an assistant cranks the engine

Defective sender unit
Wire to sender unit earthed
Engine overheating
Oil filter clogged or bypass valve defective
Oil pressure relief valve defective
Oil pick-up strainer clogged
Oil pump worn or mountings loose
Worn main or big-end bearings

Note: *Low oil pressure in a high-mileage engine at tickover is not necessarily a cause for concern. Sudden pressure loss at speed is far more significant. In any event, check the warning light sender before condemning the engine.*

Engine noises

Pre-ignition (pinking) on acceleration
Incorrect grade of fuel
Ignition timing incorrect
Distributor faulty or worn
Worn or maladjusted carburettor or injection system

Excessive carbon build-up in engine

Whistling or wheezing noises
Leaking vacuum hose
Leaking carburettor or manifold gasket
Blowing head gasket

Tapping or rattling
Incorrect valve clearances
Worn valve gear
Worn timing chain
Broken piston ring (ticking noise)

Knocking or thumping
Unintentional mechanical contact (eg fan blades)
Worn fanbelt
Peripheral component fault (generator, water pump etc)
Worn big-end bearings (regular heavy knocking, perhaps less under load)
Worn main bearings (rumbling and knocking, perhaps worsening under load)
Piston slap (most noticeable when cold)

Chapter 1 Engine

For modifications, and information applicable to later models, see Supplement at end of manual

Contents

Specifications

General

Type	....	Six-cylinder, in-line, single overhead camshaft
Bore	– 525/528	86.0 mm (3.386 in)
	– 530	89.0 mm (3.504 in)
Stroke	– 525	71.6 mm (2.819 in)
	– 528/530	80.0 mm (3.150 in)
Capacity	– 525	2494 cc (152.13 cu in)
	– 528	2788 cc (170.07 cu in)
	– 530	2986 cc (182 cu in)
Firing order	....	1–5–3–6–2–4
Compression ratio	– 525	9.0 to 1
	– 528 (UK)	9.0 to 1
	– 528 (USA)	8.2 to 1
	– 530	8.1 to 1
Maximum power output – BHP (kW)		
	– 525	150 (110) at 5800 rpm
	– 528 (carburettor)	170 (125) at 5800 rpm
	– 528i (UK)	177 (130) at 5800 rpm
	– 528i (USA)	169 (125) at 5500 rpm
	– 530i	176 (129) at 5500 rpm
Compression pressure	....	142 to 156 lbf/in^2 (10 to 11 bar)

Crankshaft

Main journal diameter (standard)	60.00 mm (2.3622 in)
Main bearing running clearance:	
Red code	0.030 to 0.070 mm (0.0012 to 0.0027 in)
Blue code	0.030 to 0.068 mm (0.0012 to 0.0026 in)
Main journal diameter undersizes	Three, in increments of 0.25 mm (0.0098 in)
Crankpin journal diameter (standard)	48.00 mm (1.8898 in)
Crankpin running clearance	0.023 to 0.069 mm (0.0009 to 0.0027 in)
Crankpin journal diameter undersizes	Three, in increments of 0.25 mm (0.0098 in)
Endfloat	0.085 to 0.174 mm (0.0033 to 0.0068 in)

Connecting rods
Length between centres .... 135.0 mm (5.315 in)
Small-end bush diameter .... 22.0 mm (0.8661 in)

Pistons
Oversizes available .... 0.25 and 0.50 mm (0.010 and 0.020 in)
Clearance in cylinder (new) .... 0.045 mm (0.0018 in)
Maximum difference in weight between all pistons .... 10g (0.35 oz)

Piston rings
Clearance in groove:
    Top compression .... 0.060 to 0.092 mm (0.0024 to 0.0036 in)
    2nd compression − except KS .... 0.030 to 0.062 mm (0.0012 to 0.0024 in)
                    − KS .... 0.040 to 0.072 mm (0.0016 to 0.0028 in)
    Oil control   − except KS .... 0.020 to 0.052 mm (0.0008 to 0.0020 in)
                    − KS .... 0.030 to 0.062 mm (0.0012 to 0.0024 in)
End gap:
    Top compression .... 0.30 to 0.50 mm (0.012 to 0.020 in)
    2nd compression − 528 .... 0.30 to 0.50 mm (0.012 to 0.020 in)
                    − 530 .... 0.20 to 0.40 mm (0.008 to 0.016 in)
    Oil control .... 0.25 to 0.50 mm (0.010 to 0.020 in)

Gudgeon pins
Clearance in piston .... 0.001 to 0.005 mm (0.00004 to 0.00020 in)

Cylinder block
Bore diameter (standard):
    525/528 .... 86.015 mm (3.3864 in)
    530 .... 89.015 mm (3.5045 in)
Oversizes .... Two, in increments of 0.250 mm (0.010 in)
Maximum wear clearance between piston and bore .... 0.10 to 0.15 mm (0.004 to 0.006 in)

Cylinder head
Valve guide bore diameter .... 14.0 mm (0.5512 in)
Valve guide oversizes .... Three, in increments of 0.1 mm (0.004 in)
Valve guide protrusion:
    UK models .... 15.0 mm (0.590 in)
    USA models .... 13.5 mm (0.531 in)
Head thickness (standard) .... 129.0 mm (5.079 in)

Flywheel
Minimum friction surface thickness .... 13.5 mm (0.531 in)

Camshaft
Bearing running clearance .... 0.034 to 0.075 mm (0.0013 to 0.0029 in)
Endfloat .... 0.030 to 0.180 mm (0.0012 to 0.0071 in)
Timing chain tensioner spring free length .... 155.5 mm (6.122 in)

Valves
Valve clearance (cold) .... 0.30 mm (0.012 in)
Valve timing (at valve clearance of 0.5 mm/0.020 in):
525
    Inlet opens .... 6° BTDC
    Inlet closes .... 50° ABDC
    Exhaust opens .... 50° BBDC
    Exhaust closes .... 6° ATDC
528 (UK) and 530
    Inlet opens .... 14° BTDC
    Inlet closes .... 54° ABDC
    Exhaust opens .... 54° BBDC
    Exhaust closes .... 14° ATDC
528 (USA)
    Inlet opens .... 7° BTDC
    Inlet closes .... 51° ABDC
    Exhaust opens .... 51° BBDC
    Exhaust closes .... 7° ATDC
Valve stem diameter .... 8.0 mm (0.3150 in)
Valve head edge thickness (new):
    Inlet .... 1.5 mm (0.059 in)
    Exhaust .... 2.2 mm (0.087 in)
Valve head edge thickness (minimum):
    Inlet .... 1.3 mm (0.051 in)
    Exhaust .... 2.0 mm (0.079 in)
Valve seat angle .... 45° 30'

Valve stem-to-guide maximum clearance .... 0.15 mm (0.006 in)
Valve spring free length .... 43.5 mm (1.712 in) or 46.0 mm (1.811 in) depending on manufacturer

Lubrication system

Oil pump:
    Type .... Bi-rotor, chain-driven from crankshaft
    Idling oil pressure .... 26 to 28 lbf/in^2 (1.8 to 2.0 bar)
    Relief valve opening pressure .... 68 to 74 lbf/in^2 (4.8 to 5.2 bar)
    Outer rotor-to-body clearance .... 0.150 to 0.275 mm (0.006 to 0.011 in)
    Inner-to-outer rotor clearance .... 0.150 to 0.275 mm (0.006 to 0.011 in)
    Rotor endfloat .... 0.035 to 0.095 mm (0.0014 to 0.0037 in)
    Relief valve spring free length .... 68.0 mm (2.677 in)
Warning light switch operating pressure .... 2.8 to 7.1 lbf/in^2 (0.2 to 0.5 bar)

Torque wrench settings

	lbf ft	Nm
Main bearing caps	42 to 45	58 to 63
Cylinder head bolts (engine cold):		
Stage 1	26 to 32	34 to 44
Stage 2	49 to 52	67 to 71
Stage 3	56 to 59	77 to 80
Sump drain plug	44 to 47	60 to 65
Sump bolts	6.5 to 8.0	9 to 11
Upper to lower timing cover	6.5 to 8.0	9 to 11
Flywheel/driveplate	72 to 83	100 to 115
Vibration damper to crankshaft	318 to 333	440 to 460
Big-end bolts	38 to 41	52 to 57
Timing chain tensioner plug	22 to 29	30 to 40
Camshaft flange	101 to 108	140 to 150
Oil pump relief valve	25 to 29	35 to 40
Oil filter housing	22 to 25	30 to 34
Engine mountings — M10	31 to 35	43 to 48
— M8	16 to 17	22 to 24

1 General description

The engine is of the six cylinder, in-line, single overhead camshaft type. The combustion chambers are hemispherical with inclined overhead valves.

The crankshaft has seven main bearings, and the lubrication system is based on a rotor type oil pump which is chain driven from the crankshaft. A full-flow oil filter is incorporated in the system.

All the engines fitted to this range of models are mechanically similar, variations in capacity ratings being obtained by changes in the bore and stroke measurements, as will be evident in the Specifications.

The cylinder block is of cast iron construction, while the cylinder head is of light alloy. Valve seats and guides are renewable and are shrunk fitted into the cylinder head.

The engine is inclined at 30° to lower the centre of gravity, and to reduce the bonnet line.

A fully closed crankcase ventilation system is employed, and piston blow-by gases are drawn into the inlet manifold via a hose from the valve cover to the air cleaner body.

2 Major operations possible with the engine in the car

The following components can be removed and refitted while the engine is still in the car. Where more than one major internal component is to be removed, however, it will probably be quicker and easier to first remove the engine complete.

(a) *Cylinder head and rocker shafts*
(b) *Sump (after removing the front stabiliser bar)*
(c) *Oil pump (after removal of sump)*
(d) *Upper and lower timing gear covers*
(e) *Timing cover oil seal*
(f) *Crankshaft rear oil seal (after removal of the gearbox and flywheel or automatic transmission and driveplate)*
(g) *Piston/connecting rod assembly (after removal of the cylinder head and sump), although engine removal is to be preferred*
(h) *Camshaft (after removal of the cylinder head)*
(i) *Timing chain and sprockets*
(j) *Flywheel (or driveplate — automatic transmission) after gearbox removal*
(k) *Engine mountings*

3 Major operations only possible after removal of the engine from the car

The following operations can only be carried out after removal of the engine from the car:

(a) *Removal of the crankshaft*
(b) *Renewal of the crankshaft main bearings*

4 Method of engine removal

Although the manufacturers recommend the removal of the manual gearbox or automatic transmission as necessary before the removal of the engine from the car, on the automatic transmission model used as our project car the engine was easily removed leaving the transmission in the car. However, on manual gearbox models, it is recommended that the gearbox is first removed since additional clearance is required for the clutch.

Removal of the engine together with the transmission is not recommended considering the total weight involved and the additional work necessary to remove the front suspension crossmember.

5 Engine — removal

1 Remove the bonnet as described in Chapter 12.
2 Disconnect the battery negative lead.
3 Remove thhe radiator (Chapter 2) and air cleaner assembly (Chapter 3).
4 Remove the fan blades and coupling from the water pump as described in Chapter 2.
5 Place a suitable container beneath the engine, remove the sump drain plug, and drain the engine oil. When completed, refit and tighten the plug.
6 Loosen the clip and remove the top hose from the cylinder head outlet (photo).
7 Disconnect the heater and water hoses from the cylinder head and inlet manifold as applicable. Note the location of the heater hoses on the bulkhead, then disconnect and remove them.
8 Disconnect the cable from the starter motor and remove it from the mounting grommet (photo).

5.6 Removing the top hose

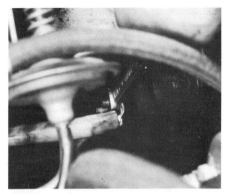

5.8 Disconnecting the starter cable

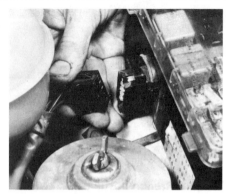

5.9 Disconnecting the fusebox multiplug

5.10 Disconnecting the engine earth wire

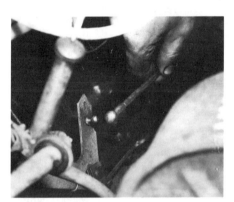

5.12 Throttle relay and rod

5.15 Power steering pump bracket on the engine

9   Disconnect the multiplug(s) from the fusebox (photo), unclip the loom, and place it on the engine. Leave the loom connected to the various components.
10   Disconnect the small wire from the battery positive (+) lead, and the earth wire from the cylinder block (photo).
11   Note the location of the fuel supply and return hoses then disconnect them.
12   Disconnect the throttle linkage from the relay arm beneath the inlet manifold (photo).
13   Disconnect the brake servo vacuum hose from the inlet manifold. If the clip is crimped, prise it apart with a screwdriver, and obtain a new screw type clip.
14   Pull the HT lead from the coil then disconnect the LT leads after identifying them for position. Note that the double wire is connected to the positive (+) terminal.
15   Where applicable remove the power steering pump and drivebelt with reference to Chapter 11, but place the pump to one side without disconnecting the fluid hoses. Unbolt the hose bracket from the cylinder block (photo).
16   Where applicable remove the air conditioning compressor as described in Chapter 12 together with the drivebelt.
17   Disconnect the exhaust pipe(s) from the exhaust manifold with reference to Chapter 3.

Fuel injection models
18   Remove the air flow sensor as described in Chapter 3.
19   Lift the windscreen washer fluid reservoir from its bracket and place it to one side. Disconnect the multiplug from the electronic ignition control unit, and the wires from the resistors. Unclip the wiring loom.
20   Disconnect the multiplugs from the relays on the side of the engine compartment, and unclip the wiring loom.
21   Open the glovebox, depress the spring, and disconnect the multiplug from the control unit. Disconnect the small wire then pull the wiring loom into the engine compartment.
22   On USA models only, disconnect the hose from the carbon filter where applicable. Note the location of all emission control vacuum

hoses then disconnect them. Disconnect the fuel hoses from the pressure regulator and injection tube.

Manual gearbox models
23   Remove the gearbox as described in Chapter 6.
24   Remove the reversing light switch wires and the clutch hydraulic hose from the retaining clips.

Automatic transmission models
25   Jack up the front of the car and support it on axle stands. Apply the handbrake.
26   Unbolt the oil cooler pipe bracket from the cylinder block. If necessary disconnect and plug the oil cooler pipes at the transmission.
27   Disconnect the downshift cable from the throttle arm and bracket with reference to Chapter 6.
28   Unscrew and remove the bellhousing bolts noting that one retains the fluid level dipstick tube.
29   Remove the transmission front cover (3 bolts) then unscrew the driveplate bolts while holding the crankshaft stationary. It will be necessary to turn the driveplate in order to position each of the four bolts at the bottom in turn.
30   Prise the plastic vent from the bottom of the bellhousing.
31   Lower the front of the car to the ground, and support the transmission with blocks of wood or a trolley jack.

All models
32   Unscrew and remove the left and right engine mounting upper nuts (photos).
33   Attach a suitable hoist to the engine hangers at the front and rear of the engine. For better access to the front hanger remove the water pump to cylinder head outlet by-pass hose (photo).
34   Lift the engine from the mountings.
35   On automatic transmission models separate the engine from the transmission and torque converter while keeping the torque converter fully engaged with the transmission. If the torque converter is seized in the end of the crankshaft use levers to release it, but make sure that the engine is correctly aligned with the transmission.

5.32A Removing the top nut from the right-hand engine mounting

5.32B Right-hand engine mounting lower nut

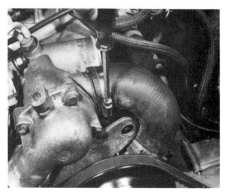
5.33 Removing the by-pass hose

5.36 Removing the engine

7.1A Showing engine wiring cable bracket on block

7.1B Oil pressure switch location (arrowed)

36 Turn the engine slightly anti-clockwise then check that everything has been disconnected and lift the engine from the engine compartment (photo). Take care not to damage any component mounted on the bulkhead or engine compartment panels.

37 Lower the engine onto a workbench or large piece of wood placed on the floor.

6 Engine dismantling – general

1 If possible mount the engine on a stand for the dismantling procedure, but failing this, support it in an upright position with blocks of wood.

2 Cleanliness is most important, and if the engine is dirty, it should be cleaned with paraffin while keeping it in an upright position.

3 Avoid working with the engine directly on a concrete floor, as grit presents a real source of trouble.

4 As parts are removed, clean them in a paraffin bath. However, do not immerse parts with internal oilways in paraffin as it is difficult to remove, usually requiring a high pressure hose. Clean oilways with nylon pipe cleaners.

5 It is advisable to have suitable containers to hold small items according to their use, as this will help when reassembling the engine and also prevent possible losses.

6 Always obtain complete sets of gaskets when the engine is being dismantled, but retain the old gaskets with a view to using them as a pattern to make a replacement if a new one is not available.

7 When possible, refit nuts, bolts, and washers in their location after being removed, as this helps to protect the threads and will also be helpful when reassembling the engine.

8 Retain unserviceable components in order to compare them with the new parts supplied.

7 Ancillary components – removal

If a complete engine strip-down is to be carried out, now is the time to remove the following ancillary components (as applicable) from the unit. The removal operations are described in detail in the appropriate Chapters of this Manual. As the wiring harness has been removed with the engine, the first job to do is to systematically identify the leads with labels, and remove the complete harness from the engine (photo).

> *Alternator and drivebelt (Chapter 10)*
> *Starter motor (Chapter 10)*
> *Inlet manifold (Chapter 3)*
> *Exhaust manifold (Chapter 3)*
> *Water pump (Chapter 2)*
> *Fuel injection equipment (Chapter 3)*
> *Oil filter, filter head, and dipstick (Chapter 1)*
> *Clutch mechanism (Chapter 5) on manual gearbox models*
> *Emission control equipment (Chapter 3)*
> *Fuel pump (Chapter 3)*
> *Distributor and spark plugs (Chapter 4)*
> *Thermostat (Chapter 2)*
> *Oil pressure switch (photo)*

8 Cylinder head – removal

Note: *If the engine is still in the car, first carry out the following operations:*

(a) *Disconnect the battery negative lead*
(b) *Drain the cooling system (Chapter 2)*
(c) *Remove the air cleaner and carburettor or fuel injection equipment, and emission conntrol equipment where applicable (Chapter 3)*
(d) *Disconnect all hoses, wiring, and throttle attachments together with all vacuum connections*
(e) *Remove the inlet and exhaust manifolds (Chapter 3)*
(f) *Remove the distributor and spark plugs (Chapter 4), and the fuel pump (Chapter 3)*

8.2A Removing the valve cover ...

8.2B ... and gasket

8.3A Thermostat housing and TDC bracket

8.3B Removing the thermostat housing

8.4 TDC timing marks on the crankshaft pulley and timing cover

9.2A Compress the valve springs and remove ...

9.2B ... the retainer ...

9.2C ... and valve springs ...

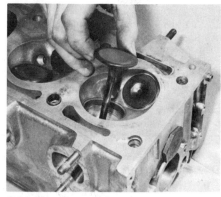
9.3A Removing an inlet valve

9.3B Removing an exhaust valve

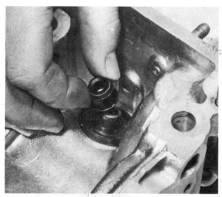
9.4A Removing a valve seal ...

9.4B ... and spring seat

1 Unscrew the two nuts on the valve cover and withdraw the plug lead holder and distributor cap.

2 Unscrew the bolts and lift off the valve cover and gasket (photos).

3 Unscrew the nuts from the thermostat housing, remove the TDC sensor bracket from the top stud, and withdraw the housing and gasket from the cylinder head (photos).

4 Check that the TDC timing mark on the crankshaft damper is aligned with the lug on the timing cover and that both valves on No 1 cylinder are closed (photo). This will have been checked when removing the distributor.

5 Unscrew the bolts from the upper timing cover then withdraw the cover and remove the distributor driveshaft. Remove the gasket.

6 Unscrew the timing chain tensioner plug from the lower timing cover and extract the spring and piston. Note that the spring has considerable pressure.

7 Flatten the tab washers on the front of the camshaft gear, unscrew the bolts and remove the gear from the camshaft and chain.

8 Ease the timing chain over the front of the camshaft so that it rests on the guide.

9 Unscrew the cylinder head bolts half a turn at a time in the reverse order to that shown in Fig. 1.8. Remove the bolts.

10 Lift the cylinder head from the block. If it is stuck, tap it free with a wooden mallet. Do not insert a lever into the gasket joint as you may damage the mating surfaces.

11 Remove the cylinder head gasket from the cylinder block.

9 Cylinder head – dismantling

1 Remove the camshaft as described in Section 10.

2 Using a valve spring compressor, compress each valve spring in turn until the split collets can be removed. Keep all components identified for position. Release the compressor and remove the retainer and spring (photos). If the retainers are difficult to release, do not continue to tighten the compressor, but gently tap the top of the tool with a hammer. Always make sure that the compressor is held firmly over the retainer.

3 Remove each valve from the combustion chambers keeping them together with their respective springs, retainers, and collets (photos). Number the valves starting with No 1 from the front of the cylinder head.

4 Prise the valve seals from the guides and remove the spring seats (photos).

10 Camshaft – removal

1 Remove the cylinder head as described in Section 8.

2 Extract the fuel pump pushrod from the cylinder head (photo).

3 Unbolt the camshaft oil supply pipe noting the location of the copper washers (photos). Mark the front of the pipe to ensure correct reassembly – an arrow is stamped on the front on later models.

4 Unbolt the camshaft rear cover and remove the gasket. Note that the exhaust side bolt is fitted with a fibre washer (photos).

5 Flatten the tab washer on the front of the camshaft, then unscrew the retaining nut and withdraw the flange while holding the camshaft stationary with a lever inserted between the cylinder head and the special flat on the camshaft (photo).

6 Unbolt the camshaft thrust plate (photos).

7 If available use BMW service tool No 111060 to open all the valves then withdraw the camshaft from the cylinder head (photo). If this tool is not available, or if the rocker arms and shafts are to be removed, proceed as follows.

8 Note the location of all the rocker arms, shafts, springs, circlips, washers, and spacers. Keep the components in their exact order of removal in the subsequent procedure.

9 Turn the camshaft to close the valve on the first rocker arm, then push the arm and spacer to one side and extract the circlip. Remove the remaining circlips on all four shaft sections using the same procedure.

10 Using a soft metal drift carefully tap the shafts from the cylinder head at the same time removing the various components. When removed reassemble the shafts and wire them together to ensure correct reassembly.

10.2 Removing the fuel pump pushrod

10.3A Removing the camshaft oil supply pipe

10.3B Underside of the camshaft oil supply pipe showing oil spray holes

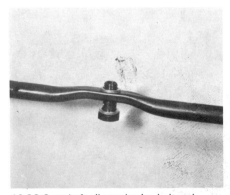

10.3C Camshaft oil supply pipe bolt and copper washers

10.4A Removing the camshaft rear cover

10.4B Note the fibre washer on the camshaft rear cover bolt (arrowed)

10.5 Removing the camshaft flange

10.6A Removing the camshaft thrust plate bolts ...

10.6B ... and thrust plate

10.7 BMW service tool No 111060 being used to remove the camshaft

10.11 Removing the camshaft from the cylinder head

11.1 Removing the crankshaft pulley nut

11.2 Removing the crankshaft pulley and damper

11.3A Separating the crankshaft pulley ...

11.3B ... and hub from the damper

12.2A Removing the driveplate (automatic transmission) ...

12.2B ... and flywheel

13.1 Removing the alternator and power steering pump brackets

11 With the rocker components removed, withdraw the camshaft from the cylinder head (photo).

11 Crankshaft pulley and vibration damper – removal

Note: *If the engine is still in the car, first carry out the following operations:*

(a) *Remove the radiator, and fan blades and coupling as described in Chapter 2*

(b) *Remove the air conditioning compressor drivebelt (Chapter 12), and power steering pump drivebelt (Chapter 11), as applicable*

1   Hold the flywheel/driveplate stationary with a lever inserted into the starter ring gear (remove the starter or transmission front cover if necessary), then unscrew the pulley nut (photo). The nut has a standard right-hand thread, but is tightened to a very high torque (see Specifications).
2   Lower the pulley and damper from the front of the crankshaft (photo).
3   Mark the hub in relation to the pulley and damper then unscrew the bolts and separate the components (photos).

12 Flywheel/driveplate – removal

Note: *If the engine is still in the car, first carry out the following operations:*

(a) *Remove the clutch as described in Chapter 5 (manual gearbox models)*

(b) *Remove the automatic transmission as described in Chapter 6 (automatic transmission models)*

1   Hold the flywheel/driveplate stationary with a lever inserted into the starter ring gear then unscrew the retaining bolts. The bolts are installed with a liquid locking agent so they will be very tight.
2   Withdraw the flywheel/driveplate from the crankshaft – note that it is located by a dowel pin. Remove the square plate on automatic transmission models (photos).

13 Sump – removal

Note: *If the engine is still in the car, first carry out the following operations:*

(a) *Remove the front stabiliser bar as described in Chapter 11*

(b) *Remove the alternator (Chapter 10) and power steering pump (Chapter 11) if applicable, but do not disconnect the hoses*

(c) *Drain the engine oil*

1   Unbolt the alternator and power steering pump brackets from the cylinder block and sump (photo).
2   Unscrew the retaining bolts and remove the sump and gasket (photo). If the engine is still in the car, turn the crankshaft until No 6 crankpin is above the sump joint face, then lower the front of the sump and withdraw it to the right.

3   If the engine is on the workbench, support it on its side.

14 Timing chain and cover – removal

Note: *If the engine is still in the car, first carry out the following operations:*

(a) *Disconnect the battery negative lead*

(b) *Remove the air cleaner (Chapter 3)*

(c) *Remove the distributor and spark plugs (Chapter 4)*

(d) *Remove the radiator and bottom hose (Chapter 2)*

1   Unscrew the bolts and lift off the valve cover and gasket.
2   Turn the crankshaft until No 1 piston is at TDC and the timing marks on the crankshaft pulley and timing cover lug are aligned.
3   Remove the crankshaft pulley (Section 11) and sump (Section 13).
4   Unscrew the bolts from the upper timing cover then withdraw the cover and remove the distributor driveshaft (photos). Remove the gaskets.
5   Unscrew the timing chain tensioner plug from the lower timing cover and extract the spring and piston (photos).
6   Flatten the tab washers on the front of the camshaft gear, unscrew the bolts and remove the gear from the camshaft and chain (photos).
7   Ease the timing chain over the front of the camshaft so that it rests on the guide.
8   Unscrew the lower timing cover bolts noting that the TDC sensor bracket (if applicable) is located on the two right-hand upper bolts (photo) and the engine hanger on the left-hand bolts.
9   Withdraw the lower timing cover and gaskets from the dowels (photo).
10 Release the timing chain from the crankshaft sprocket and withdraw it from the guide. If the cylinder head is still in position take care not to damage the protruding section of the cylinder head gasket.
11 Extract the circlips and remove the timing chain guides (photos). If the cylinder head gasket is still in position it will be necessary to remove the water pump (Chapter 2).

15 Oil pump and chain – removal

1   If the oil pump chain is to be removed, first remove the timing chain and cover (Section 14) then unbolt the sprocket from the oil pump and remove the chain from the crankshaft (photos).
2   If the oil pump only is to be removed, first remove the sump (Section 13).
3   Unbolt the sprocket from the oil pump, then unbolt the oil pump from the crankcase and the centre main bearing cap (photos). Note the location of any shims for the adjustment of the chain tension.

16 Oil filter and head – removal and refitting

1   Place a suitable container beneath the oil filter then unscrew the centre bolt (either on top of the filter head or at the bottom of the bowl) and lower the bowl from the head (photos).
2   Extract and discard the filter element, clean the bowl with paraffin, and wipe dry (photo). On the type with a bottom centre bolt take care

13.2 Removing the sump

14.4A Removing the upper timing cover ...

14.4B ... and distributor drive shaft

14.5A Unscrew the plug ...

14.5B ... and remove the timing chain tensioner spring and piston

14.6A Camshaft gear and retaining bolts location

14.6B Removing the camshaft gear. Note dowel pin (arrowed)

14.8 Removing the TDC sensor bracket

14.9 Removing the lower timing cover

14.11A Extract the circlips ...

14.11B ... and remove the timing chain guides

15.1A Remove the oil pump flange bolts ...

15.1B ... and withdraw the sprocket

15.3A Oil pump to centre main bearing cap bracket mounting plate

15.3B Removing the oil pump

16.1A Unscrew the oil filter centre bolt ...

16.1B ... and remove the filter bowl and element

16.1C Oil filter bowl as viewed from under the car

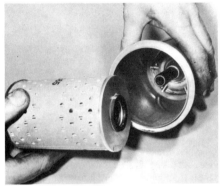

16.2 Removing the oil filter element

16.3A Oil filter head and dipstick holder

16.3B Removing the oil filter head

16.4 Oil filter bowl rubber O-ring location

17.3 Removing a big-end bearing cap

17.4A Removing a piston and connecting rod

not to lose the spring and plate.

3   If necessary unbolt the filter head from the cylinder block and remove the gasket. Note that one bolt retains the dipstick holder – the dipstick tube can be removed from the cylinder block with a pair of grips (photos).

4   Refitting is a reversal of removal, but fit a new filter and gasket, and filter bowl rubber O-ring (photo).

17 Pistons and connecting rods – removal

Note: *If the engine is still in the car, first carry out the following operations:*

> *(a) Remove the cylinder head (Section 8)*
> *(b) Remove the oil pump (Section 15)*

1   Check the big-end caps for identification marks. If necessary use a centre punch on the caps and connecting rods to identify them in relation to the cylinder number and for the fitted position.

2   Turn the crankshaft so that No 1 crankpin is at its lowest point, then unscrew the big-end bearing nuts noting that the machined end of the nuts faces the cap.

3   Withdraw the cap complete with the bearing shell (photo).

4   Using the handle of a hammer, tap the connecting rod and piston from the bore and withdraw them from the top of the cylinder block (photos). Keep the bearing shells in the cap and connecting rod noting that the locating tabs are on opposite sides.

5   Repeat the procedure given in paragraphs 2 to 4 on the remaining pistons and connecting rods.

18 Crankshaft and main bearings – removal

1   With the engine removed from the car (Section 5) follow the procedure for removing the pistons and connecting rods described in Section 17, but it is not necessary to completely remove them from

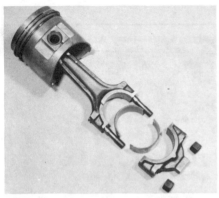

17.4B Piston, connecting rod, and big-end bearing components

18.3A Crankshaft rear oil seal and housing

18.3B Removing the crankshaft rear oil seal housing

18.5 Checking the crankshaft endfloat with a feeler blade

18.6A Removing the centre main bearing cap

18.6B Removing the front main bearing cap

18.7A Removing the crankshaft ...

18.7B ... an intermediate main bearing shell ...

18.7C ... and centre main bearing shell

18.7D Showing both types of main bearing shell

20.1A Unscrew the oil pump cover bolts ...

20.1B ... remove the cover and strainer ...

the cylinder block.

2   Remove the flywheel/driveplate (Section 12), timing chain and cover (Section 14), and oil pump (Section 15).

3   Unbolt the rear oil seal housing from the cylinder block and remove the gasket. The housing is located on two dowels (photos).

4   Check the main bearing caps for identification marks, and if necessary use a centre punch to mark them.

5   Using a feeler blade between the centre crankshaft web and thrust washer check that the crankshaft endfloat is within the specified limits (photo). If not, new centre main bearing shells will be required (ie a complete set).

6   Unscrew the bolts and remove the main bearing caps complete with bearing shells. Note that the top and bottom shell locating tabs are on the same side, and that the centre main bearing shells are flanged (photos).

7   Lift the crankshaft from the crankcase, then extract the bearing shells from their recesses keeping them identified for location (photos).

19   Examination and renovation – general

With the engine completely stripped, clean all the components and examine them for wear. Each part should be checked, and where necessary renewed or renovated as described in the following Sections. Renew main and big-end shell bearings as a matter of course, unless you know that they have had little wear and are in perfect condition.

20   Oil pump – examination annd renovation

1   Unbolt the cover and strainer from the oil pump body and remove the intermediate plate (photos).

2   Unscrew and remove the plug from the oil pressure relief valve and extract the plunger and spring (photo).

3   Using feeler blades check the following clearances:

(a)   Between the outer rotor and pump housing
(b)   Between the tips of the inner and outer rotors
(c)   Between the rotor face and the cover mating face of the pump housing

Where these tolerances are not within those specified, renew the components as necessary (photos).

4   If the drive flange must be removed, use a two legged puller. Press on the new flange so that the distance between the outer faces of flange and rotor is 1.744 in (44.3 mm).

21   Crankshaft and main bearings – examination and renovation

1   Examine the bearing surfaces of the crankshaft for scratches or scoring and, using a micrometer, check each journal and crankpin for ovality. Where this is found to be in excess of 0.001 in (0.0254 mm) the crankshaft will have to be reground and undersize bearings fitted.

2   Crankshaft regrinding should be carried out by a suitable engineering works, who will normally supply the matching undersize main and big-end shell bearings. Note that the crankshaft journals and bearing shells are identified for size with paint markings. A crankshaft of original size has red or blue dots on the web edges. Undersize crankpins are identified by an adjacent painted line, one line for first undersize, two lines for second undersize, etc. Undersize main journals are identified in a similar way, but the line is on the counterweight side of the web.

3   Where applicable, check the spigot bearing in the rear of the crankshaft – it is either of ball bearing or needle bearing type. To remove it pack the space behind it with thick grease then drive a close fitting dowel rod through the centre of the bearing.

4   When fitting the bearing lubricate it with high melting point grease. The felt ring on the ball bearing type should be soaked in hot tallow prior to refitting and tapping the cap into position. Refer to Fig. 1.2 for the needle bearing fitted dimension.

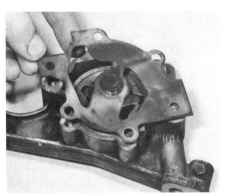
20.1C ... and the intermediate plate

20.2 Removing the oil pump relief valve spring and plunger

20.3A Checking the oil pump outer rotor to housing clearance ...

20.3B ... inner to outer rotor clearance ...

20.3C ... and rotor end clearance

20.3D If the oil pump outer rotor is removed, refit it with the dot facing the cover

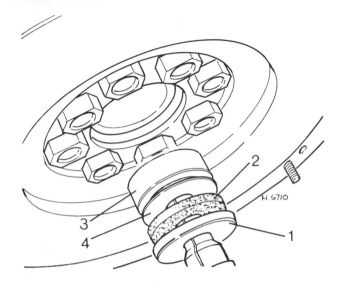

Fig. 1.1 Crankshaft spigot bearing (ball bearing type) components
(Sec 21)

1	Retainer	3	Ball bearing
2	Felt ring	4	Cover plate

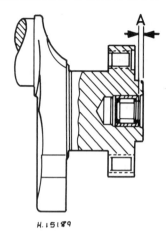

Fig. 1.2 Crankshaft spigot bearing (needle bearing type) fitted
position (Sec 21)

$A = 3.0 \, mm \, (0.118 \, in)$

22 Pistons and piston rings – examination and renovation

1   The piston rings are very brittle and will break easily if opened too
far during removal. Two or three old feeler blades or strips of tin may
be inserted behind each ring at equidistant points to facilitate removal.
Use a twisting motion and pull the rings from the top of the piston. The
feeler blades will prevent a lower ring dropping into an empty groove
as it is withdrawn.
2   Clean all carbon off the rings and grooves, taking care not to
scratch the aluminium surface of the pistons.
3   Before fitting the rings to the pistons, check the ring gap. Place the
ring in the cylinder bore and press it down to the bottom of the cylinder
with a piston, and using a feeler gauge, check that the endgap is as
given in the Specifications at the beginning of this Chapter. If the ring
gap is too large the ring will have to be renewed, if too small the gap
can be increased by filing one end of the ring with a fine file. Be careful
not to break the rings as they are very brittle. Ensure that the gap is not
less than that specified; if it closes under normal operating
temperatures the ring will break.
4   Check that each ring gives a side clearance in the piston groove
according to the Specifications (photo). If the gap is too large, new
pistons and rings will be required if BMW spares are used. However,
independent specialist manufacturers of pistons and rings can
normally provide the rings required separately. If new BMW pistons
and rings are being obtained it will be necessary to have the ridge
ground away from the top of the cylinder bores. If specialist oil control
rings are being obtained from an independent supplier the ridge
removal will not be necessary as the top rings will be stepped to
provide the necessary clearance. If the top ring, of a new set, is not
stepped it will hit the ridge made by the previous ring and break.
5   If new pistons are obtained the rings will be included, so it must
be emphasised that the top ring be stepped if fitted to a cylinder which
has not been rebored, or had the ridge at the top removed.
6   The groove clearance of new rings on old pistons should be within
the specified tolerance. If it is not enough the rings could stick in the
grooves, causing loss of compression and oiling-up. If it is too loose,
this accelerates wear on the side of the ring grooves.
7   The gudgeon pin should be a push fit into the piston at room
temperature. If it is slack, both the piston and gudgeon pin should be
renewed. The pin is retained by circlips.
8   Make sure that, when new pistons are fitted, the weight group
stamped + or – on the piston crown is the same on each piston and
that the piston rings are fitted with the correct faces upwards. Correct
installation of the piston rings is important if they are to function

22.4 Checking a piston ring side clearance

correctly; the upper face is usually marked 'top' as shown in Fig. 1.3.
Arrange the ring gaps at 120° to each other.
9   Note that the small end lubrication hole in the connecting rod
must face the same direction as the arrow on the piston crown
(photos).

23 Connecting rods and bearings – examination and renovation

1   Big-end bearing failure is indicated by a knocking from within the
crankcase and a slight drop in oil pressure.
2   Examine the big-end bearing surfaces for pitting and scoring.
Renew the shells in accordance with the sizes given in the Specifications. Where the crankshaft has been reground, the correct undersize
big-end shell bearings will be supplied by the repairer.
3   Should there be any suspicion that a connecting rod is bent or
twisted, it must be replaced by one of similar weight. Without bearing
shells, the new rod must be within ± 0.14 oz (4 gm) of the weight of
the other rods.
4   Connecting rods can be supplied with ready-machined small-end
bushes, but, if an adjustable reamer can be obtained, the small-end
bush alone can be renewed. Press out the old bush. When pressing the
new bush into place, make sure that the seam in the bush is at 90° to

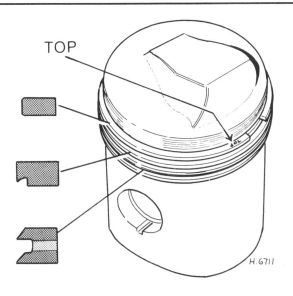

TOP

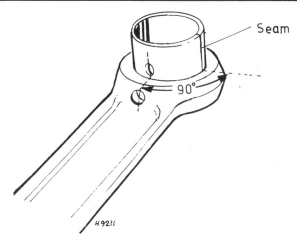

Seam

90°

Fig. 1.4 Correct installation of small end bush (Sec 23)

Fig. 1.3 Piston ring cross sections (Sec 22)

22.9A Oil lubrication hole location in the connecting rod

22.9B The arrow on the piston crown must face the front of the engine. Note piston weight group marking (–) near the arrow

the small oil hole to provide correct alignment of the oil drilling (Fig. 1.4). Drill and deburr the oilway and then ream out the small-end bush. The gudgeon pin should slide through the bush with light pressure applied when it has been lubricated with a little engine oil.

24 Cylinder block – examination and renovation

1   The cylinder bores must be examined for taper, ovality, scoring and scratches. Start by carefully examining the top of the cylinder bores. If they are at all worn a very slight ridge will be found on the thrust side. This marks the top of the piston ring travel. The owner will have a good indication of the bore wear prior to dismantling the engine, or removing the cylinder head. Excessive oil consumption accompanied by blue smoke from the exhaust is a sure sign of worn cylinder bores and piston rings.
2   Measure the bore diameter just under the ridge with a micrometer and compare it with the diameter at the bottom of the bore, which is not subject to wear. If the difference between the two measurements is more than 0.01 mm (0.0004 in) then it will be necessary to fit special pistons and rings or to have the cylinders rebored and fit oversize pistons. If no micrometer is available remove the rings from a piston and place the piston in each bore in turn about $\frac{3}{4}$ in (2 cm) below the top of the bore. Check the clearance with a feeler gauge, and then recheck the clearance at the bottom of the bore, comparing the difference with the tolerance in the Specifications. Oversize pistons are available as listed in the Specifications.
3   These are accurately machined to just below the indicated measurements so as to provide correct running clearances in bores machined out to the exact oversize dimensions.
4   If the bores are slightly worn but not so badly worn as to justify reboring them, then special oil control rings and pistons can be fitted which will restore compression and stop the engine burning oil. Several different types are available and the manufacturer's instructions concerning their fitting must be closely followed.
5   If new piston assemblies are being fitted and the bores have not been reground, it is essential to slightly roughen the hard glaze on the side of the bores with fine glass paper so the new piston rings will have a chance to bed in properly. It is important that a stepped top ring is used in this instance – a standard type ring would hit the ridge at the top of the bore (see paragraph 1) at its upper extent of travel and shatter.
6   Thoroughly examine the crankcase and cylinder block for cracks and damage and use a piece of wire to probe all oilways and waterways to ensure they are unobstructed.

25 Camshaft – examination and renovation

1   Carefully examine the camshaft bearing surfaces in the cylinder head for wear. If there is any pitting, scoring or wear, the cylinder head will have to be renewed unless a specialist firm is available to build up the worn bearings and in-line bore them to the specified diameters.
2   The camshaft itself should show no signs of wear, but, if very slight scoring on the cams is noticed, the score marks can be removed

by very gentle rubbing down with a very fine emery cloth. The greatest care should be taken to keep the cam profiles smooth.

3   Examine the distributor drive gear which slots into the forward end of the camshaft. There should be no chipped teeth or other damage to the skew gear and no slackness radially between the camshaft slot and the drive gear shaft.

4   If the camshaft endfloat is excessive the thrust plate should be renewed.

26 Valves and valve seats – examination and renovation

1   Examine the seating surfaces on the heads of the valves for pitting and burring, especially the heads of the exhaust valves. The valve seatings in the cylinder head should be examined at the same time. If the pitting on valve and seat is very slight the marks can be removed by grinding the seats and valves together with coarse, and then fine, valve grinding paste. Make sure the valve rim thickness is not reduced below the specified limits.

2   Where bad pitting has occurred to the valve seats it will be necessary to recut them and fit new valves. If the valves seats are so worn that they cannot be recut, then it will be necessary to fit new valve seat inserts. These latter two jobs should be entrusted to the local BMW dealer or motor engineering works. In practice it is very seldom that the seats are so badly worn that they require renewal. Normally, it is the valve that is too badly worn for refitting, and the owner can easily purchase a new set of valves and match them to the seats by valve grinding.

3   Valve grinding is carried out as follows. Smear a trace of coarse carborundum paste on the seat face and apply a suction grinder tool to the valve head. With a semi-rotary motion, grind the valve head to its seat, lifting the valve occasionally to redistribute the grinding paste. When a dull matt even surface finish is produced on both the valve seat and the valve, wipe off the paste and repeat the process with fine carborundum paste, lifting and turning the valve to redistribute the paste as before. A light spring placed under the valve head will greatly ease this operation. When a smooth unbroken ring of light grey matt finish is produced on both valve and valve seat faces, the grinding operation is complete.

4   Scrape away all carbon from the valve head and the valve stem. Carefully clean away every trace of grinding compound, taking great care to leave none in the ports or in the valve guides. Clean the valves and valve seats with a paraffin-soaked rag then with a clean rag, and finally if an air line is available, blow the valves, valve guides and valve ports clean.

27 Valve guides – examination and renovation

1   Test each valve in its guide for wear. After considerable mileage, the valve guide bore may wear oval. This can best be tested by inserting a new valve in the guide and moving it from side to side. If the stem of the valve deflects by over 0.006 in (0.15 mm) then it must be assumed that the tolerance between the stem and guide is greater than the permitted maximum as listed in the Specifications Section.

2   New valve guides are available in several oversizes if necessary. The fitting of new valve guides should be entrusted to an engineering works or BMW dealer..

28 Timing chain and gears – examination and renovation

1   Examine the teeth on both the crankshaft gear wheel and the camshaft gear wheel for wear. Each tooth forms an inverted V with the gear wheel periphery, and if worn the side of each tooth under tension will be slightly concave in shape when compared with the other side of the tooth. If any sign of wear is present the gear wheels must be renewed.

2   Examine the links of the chain for side slackness and renew if necessary. It is a sensible precaution to renew the chain anyway if the engine has covered over 30 000 miles (50 000 km). The rollers on a very badly worn chain may be slightly grooved.

3   A puller is required to remove the gear from the crankshaft.

29.2 A rocker arm showing valve clearance adjusting eccentric and camshaft pad

29 Rocker arms and shafts – examination and renovation

1   Thoroughly clean the rocker shafts and then check the shafts for straightness by rolling them on a piece of plate glass. It is most unlikely than any will deviate from normal, but any which do should be discarded and new ones obtained. The surface of the shafts should be free from any wear ridges caused by the rocker arms. If any wear is present renew the shafts.

2   Check the rocker arms for wear of the rocker bushes, for wear at the rocker arm face which bears on the valve stem, and for wear of the pad face (photo). Wear in the rocker arm bush can be checked by gripping the rocker arm tip and holding the rocker arm in place on the shaft, noting if there is any lateral rocker arm shake. If shake is present, and the arm is very loose on the shaft, a new bush or rocker arm must be fitted.

3   Check the adjuster wheel eccentric which bears on the end of the valve stem, also the pads which bear on the cam lobes for looseness and renew as necessary.

30 Cylinder head – decarbonising and examination

1   With the cylinder head removed unscrew the spark plugs. Use a blunt scraper to remove all trace of carbon and deposits from the combustion spaces and ports. Remember that the cylinder head is made of aluminium alloy, which is relatively soft, and can be damaged easily during the decarbonising operation. Scrape the cylinder head free from scale or old pieces of gasket or jointing compound. Clean the cylinder head by washing it in paraffin and take particular care to pull a piece of rag through the ports and cylinder head bolt holes. Any dirt remaining in these recesses may well drop onto the gasket or cylinder block mating surface as the cylinder head is lowered into position and could lead to a gasket leak after reassembly is complete.

2   With the cylinder head clean, test for distortion if a history of coolant leakage has been apparent. Carry out this test using a straight edge and feeler gauges or a piece of plate glass. If the surface shows any warping in excess of 0.0039 in (0.099 mm) then the cylinder head will have to be resurfaced, which is a job for the specialist engineering company. The thickness of the cylinder head must not be reduced by more than 0.012 in (0.3 mm) and the depth of the upper timing cover must be reduced by an equivalent amount to compensate.

3   Clean the pistons and top of the cylinder bores. If the pistons are still in the block, it is essential that great care is taken to ensure that no carbon gets into the cylinder bores between bore and piston, as this could scratch the cylinder walls or cause damage to the pistons and rings. To ensure this does not happen, first turn the crankshaft so that two of the pistons are at the top of their bores. Stuff rag into the four other bores or seal them off with paper and masking tape to prevent particles of carbon entering. Do the same for the water jacket holes to

prevent carbon entering the cooling system and damaging the water pump. Pack the space between the pistons and bores of the two cylinders being worked on with grease. When decarbonisation on those two cylinders is complete, the grease can be carefully removed with a small screwdriver, bringing any particles of carbon with it.

4   Rotate the crankshaft and bring the next two pistons up to the top of their respective bores and repeat the carbon removal operations.

5   Rotate the crankshaft and bring the last two pistons up to the top of their bores and complete the carbon removal operations.

6   Thoroughly clean all particles of carbon from the bores and then inject a little light oil round the edge of the pistons to lubricate the piston rings.

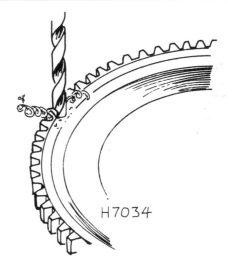

Fig. 1.5 Drilling the starter ring gear – manual gearbox models only (Sec 31)

31 Flywheel/driveplate and starter ring gear – examination and renovation

1   If the teeth of the starter ring gear are badly worn, the ring gear will have to be renewed on a manual transmission flywheel. On automatic transmission models, the complete driveplate will have to be renewed.

2   To remove a ring gear from the flywheel, drill a hole $\frac{1}{4}$ in (6 mm) diameter at the root of one tooth. Do not drill right through the ring gear into the flywheel; a hole of 0.3 in (8 mm) depth will be sufficient (Fig. 1.5).

3   Split the ring gear with a sharp cold chisel (see Fig. 1.6) taking precautions to avoid flying fragments.

4   Place the new ring gear in an oven and heat it to between 200°C and 230°C (392°F and 446°F).

5   Place the heated ring gear on the flywheel (chamfer towards engine), and tap it squarely into position using a brass drift. Do this as quickly as possible because the ring gear will cool quite rapidly.

6   Where the machined face of the flywheel is scored or shows surface cracks, it should be surface ground, but the thickness of the friction face (A) must not be less than 0.532 in (13.5 mm) as shown in Fig. 1.7.

7   The ring gear renewal procedure is not particularly easy, and some owners may prefer to entrust the job to their local dealer.

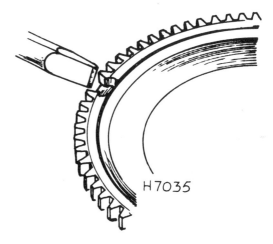

Fig. 1.6 Splitting the starter ring gear – manual gearbox models only (Sec 31)

32 Crankshaft oil seals – renewal

1   At the time of major engine overhaul, always renew the crankshaft front and rear oil seals.

2   The front seal, which is located in the timing chain lower cover, can be extracted using a hooked tool after the crankshaft pulley has been removed, or, if the timing cover has been removed, the seal can be removed with a piece of tubing used as a drift.

3   The rear seal is housed in a retainer accessible after the clutch and flywheel (or driveplate – automatic transmission) have been removed. If the retainer is removed, take care not to damage the sump gasket.

4   After pressing the new seals into position, pack grease into the seals between the sealing lips, before refitting them to their respective components (photos). If the crankshaft pulley has a scored groove on its sealing face, fit the timing cover oil seal so that its sealing lips locate on the unworn part of the pulley. Apply sealing compound to the sump gasket if the rear retainer has been removed, and always fit a new gasket to the retainer.

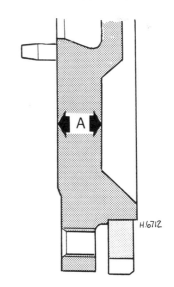

Fig. 1.7 Flywheel friction face minimum thickness checking point A (Sec 31)

33 Engine reassembly – general

1   To ensure maximum life with minimum trouble from a rebuilt engine, not only must everything be correctly assembled, but it must also be spotlessly clean. All oilways must be clear, and locking washers and spring washers must be fitted where indicated. Oil all bearings and other working surfaces thoroughly with engine oil during assembly.

2   Before assembly begins, renew any bolts or studs with damaged threads.

3   Gather together a torque wrench, oil can, clean rag, and a set of engine gaskets and oil seals, together with a new oil filter element.

32.4A Installing a crankshaft front oil seal in the timing cover

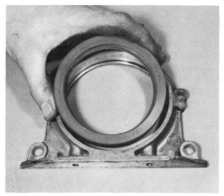

32.4B Installing a crankshaft rear oil seal in the retainer ...

32.4C ... using a length of wood

34.4 Fitting the oil pump bracket to the centre main bearing cap

34.5 Tightening the main bearing cap bolts

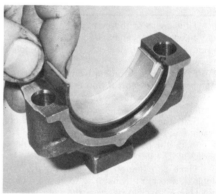

35.2 Inserting a big-end bearing shell in the cap

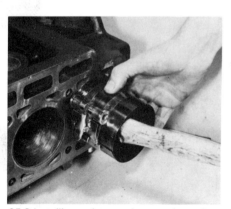

35.3 Installing a piston and connecting rod using a piston ring compressor

35.6 Tightening the big-end nuts

37.3 Make sure that the tensioner rail (arrowed) is located in the pocket

37.8 Checking that the camshaft is positioned at TDC No 1 cylinder using a steel rule

39.2A Applying a liquid locking agent to the driveplate bolts

39.2B Tightening the driveplate bolts – note the lever in the starter ring gear

34 Crankshaft and main bearings – refitting

1   If the timing gear has been removed, insert the Woodruff key and press the gear onto the front of the crankshaft – heating the gear beforehand will assist in this operation.

2   With the crankcase inverted, insert the bearing shells into their crankcase recesses, making sure that both sides of each shell are absolutely clean before fitting. Number 4 main bearing shells incorporate the thrust flanges.

3   Oil the bearings liberally and carefully lower the crankshaft into position.

4   Fit the bearing shells to the main bearing caps and install them in their correct sequence as previously identified. Remember that No 4 main bearing cap carries the bracket support for the oil pump (photo).

5   Screw in and tighten the main bearing cap bolts evenly to the specified torque (photo).

6   Check that the crankshaft turns smoothly with hand pressure, and then fit the rear oil seal retainer complete with new oil seal and gasket.

7   Using a feeler blade at the centre bearing, check that the crankshaft endfloat is within the specified limits.

35 Pistons and connecting rods – refitting

1   Turn the crankshaft so that No 1 crankpin is at its lowest point.

2   Insert the bearing shell into No 1 connecting rod (photo). Apply oil liberally to the bearing and the piston rings and smear some up and down the cylinder bore. Fit a piston ring compressor to the piston.

3   Insert the connecting rod into the cylinder bore taking care not to scratch the bore surfaces. With the compressor standing squarely on top of the cylinder block and the piston rings well compressed (but not tight), place the wooden shaft of a hammer on the piston crown and then give the head of the piston a gentle but firm tap with the wooden shaft to drive the piston/connecting rod assembly down the bore (photo). Do not force anything or the piston rings will break. Remove the compressor.

4   Oil the crankpin then pull the connecting rod onto it taking care not to displace the bearing shell.

5   Insert the bearing shell in the big-end cap then fit the cap to the connecting rod making sure that the previously made identification marks are correctly positioned. Recheck that the piston crown arrow faces the front of the engine.

6   Fit the nuts (machined end first) and tighten them to the specified torque (photo). Check that the crankshaft turns smoothly.

7   Repeat the procedure in paragraphs 1 to 6 on the remaining pistons and connecting rods.

8   If the engine is in the car, reverse the preliminary procedures given in Section 17 with reference to Sections 36 and 43.

36 Oil pump and chain – refitting

1   Loosen the mounting plate nuts on the oil pump.

2   Position any adjustment shims on the cylinder block noting that the thickness must be the same at the two mounting bolt surfaces.

3   Locate the oil pump on the dowels, insert the bolts and tighten them. Now insert the rear mounting bolts in the centre main bearing cap bracket and tighten them together with the mounting plate nuts.

4   If the oil pump chain has been removed locate it on the crankshaft gear.

5   Locate the sprocket in the chain, position it on the oil pump flange, then insert and tighten the bolts using a liquid locking agent.

6   Check the chain tension and if excessive add shims between the oil pump and block.

7   Refit the timing chain and cover (Section 37) and sump (Section 38) as applicable.

37 Timing chain and cover – refitting

1   Locate the chain guides onto the pins and insert the circlips.

2   Fit the timing chain to the gear and at the same time insert it into the guide.

3   Position the timing cover gaskets on the cylinder block, then fit the lower timing cover making sure that the tensioner rail is located in the tensioner pocket (photo).

4   Insert the bolts together with the TDC sensor bracket (if applicable) and engine hanger and tighten them.

5   If removed refit the cylinder head as described in Section 43.

6   Ease the timing chain over the front of the camshaft.

7   Refit the crankshaft pulley as described in Section 40 and the sump as described in Section 38.

8   Check that the crankshaft and camshaft are positioned at TDC No 1 cylinder. The camshaft flange dowel pin must face to the bottom right – see photo 14.6B – and the upper screw hole must be aligned with the camshaft lubrication tube (photo).

9   Insert the camshaft gear in the chain so that it can be located on the flange dowel pin without moving the camshaft or crankshaft.

10 Fit the tab washers and bolts. Tighten the bolts and bend the tab washers to lock them.

11 Insert the timing chain tensioner piston and spring in the lower timing cover and screw the plug and washer on two or three threads.

12 With the engine upright, fill the tensioner pocket with engine oil, then lever the tensioner rail back and forth until oil emerges at the plug. If difficulty is experienced, dismantle the tensioner and check that the internal vent slots are clear.

13 Tighten the tensioner plug.

14 Position the upper timing cover gaskets on the cylinder head and fill the holes in the cylinder head gasket with sealing compound. Note that early gaskets may not incorporate the holes.

15 Locate the distributor driveshaft in the camshaft with the oil hole uppermost.

16 Fit the upper timing cover and insert the bolts finger tight. Semi-tighten the inter-cover bolts, then fully tighten the remaining bolts followed by the inter-cover bolts.

17 Fit the valve cover together with a new gasket and tighten the bolts evenly in a diagonal sequence.

18 If the engine is in the car, reverse the preliminary procedures given in Section 14.

38 Sump – refitting

1   Check that all mating faces are clean, then fit a new gasket to the cylinder block, lower timing cover, and rear oil seal housing using jointing compound.

2   Offer the sump into position and insert the bolts finger tight. Tighten the bolts to the specified torque evenly and in diagonal sequence.

3   Fit the alternator and power steering pump brackets to the cylinder block and sump and tighten the bolts.

4   If the engine is in the car, reverse the preliminary procedures given in Section 13.

39 Flywheel/driveplate – refitting

1   Fit the flywheel on the crankshaft and over the dowel pin. On automatic transmission models locate the square driveplate on the flywheel.

2   Coat the threads of the bolts with a liquid locking agent, then insert them and tighten them to the specified torque while holding the flywheel stationary with a lever inserted into the starter ring gear (photos).

3   If the engine is in the car, reverse the preliminary procedures given in Section 12.

40 Crankshaft pulley and vibration damper – refitting

1   Locate the hub in the vibration damper, and the pulley on the hub making sure that the previously made marks are aligned. The keyway in the hub must align with the TDC notch in the damper.

2   Insert the bolts and tighten them.

3   Locate the hub on the crankshaft and key, and drive it fully on using a block of wood.

4   Fit the pulley nut and tighten it to the specified torque while holding the flywheel/driveplate stationary with a lever inserted into the starter ring gear (photo). If a suitable torque wrench is not available use a metal tube on the socket to tighten the nut.

5   If the engine is in the car, reverse the preliminary procedures given in Section 11.

40.4 Tightening the crankshaft pulley nut

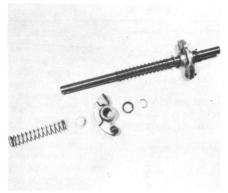

41.4A A rocker shaft and components

41.4B Installing a rocker shaft ...

41.4C ... spacer ...

41.4D ... rocker arm ...

41.4E ... washer ...

41.4F ... and spring

41.5 Fitting a circlip to the rocker shaft

41.7A Tightening the camshaft flange nut – note the position of the lever

41.7B Locking the camshaft flange nut

42.1 Using a metal tube to fit a valve seal

43.1A Cylinder head ready for fitting to the block

41 Camshaft – refitting

1 If the BMW service tool No 111060 is available the rocker shafts can be refitted prior to inserting the camshaft, otherwise proceed as follows.

2 Lubricate the camshaft journals with engine oil then insert the camshaft into the cylinder head taking care not to damage the head with the camshaft lobes.

3 Locate the thrust plate over the front of the camshaft, then insert and tighten the bolts.

4 Have the rocker shafts and components ready in their correct order. Using a soft metal drift, tap each shaft into the cylinder head, at the same time fitting the spacers, rocker arms, washers, and springs. Note that the grooves in the shafts must align with the cylinder head bolt holes in the head when the shafts are fully inserted. It will be necessary to turn the camshaft as the shafts are being inserted so that the rocker arms are not under pressure from the valve spring. Note that the chamfered side of the spacers must face away from the rocker arms (photos).

5 With all of the shafts installed push each arm and spacer to one side and fit the circlips. The camshaft must first be positioned to close the relevant valve (photo).

6 Locate the flange on the front of the camshaft so that it engages the Woodruff key.

7 Fit the tab washer and nut, and tighten the nut to the specified torque while holding the camshaft stationary with a lever inserted between the cylinder head and the special flat on the camshaft. Lock the nut by bending the tab washer onto one of the flats (photos).

8 Fit the camshaft rear cover to the head together with a new gasket. Insert and tighten the bolts evenly noting that the exhaust side bolt is fitted with a fibre washer.

9 Fit the bolts and copper washers to the camshaft oil supply pipe, locate the pipe on the cylinder head and tighten the bolts. Note that the oil spray holes must direct oil between the inlet and exhaust rocker of each cylinder.

10 Insert the fuel pump pushrod in the cylinder head.

11 Refit the cylinder head as described in Section 43.

42 Cylinder head – reassembly

1 Fit each spring seat over the valve guide and install the valve seals using a suitable metal tube (photo).

2 Lubricate each valve stem with engine oil then insert the valves into their respective guides.

3 Working on each valve in turn fit the spring (close coil end first) and retainer, then compress the spring with the compressor and insert the split collets. Release the compressor and remove it. Tap the end of each valve stem with a non-metallic mallet to settle the collets.

4 Refit the camshaft as described in Section 41.

43 Cylinder head – refitting

1 Make sure that the faces of the cylinder head and block are perfectly clean, and that the bolt holes in the block are clean and clear of oil. Clean the threads of the bolts and lubricate them with engine oil. Check that the locating dowels are correctly positioned in the block – remove them from the head if necessary (photos).

2 Check that the crankshaft and camshaft are positioned at the TDC No 1 cylinder position.

3 Locate the new gasket over the dowels on the block (photo). Do not use jointing compound.

4 Lower the cylinder head onto the gasket (photo).

5 Insert the cylinder head bolts and tighten them to the specified stage 1 torque in the order shown in Fig. 1.8 (photo). Tighten them again to the stage 2 and 3 torques using the same sequence then repeat stage 3 – only turn the bolts in the tightening direction.

6 Follow the procedure given in Section 37, paragraphs 6 to 16 omitting paragraph 7.

7 Fit the thermostat housing together with a new gasket and the TDC sensor bracket, and tighten the nuts.

8 Adjust the valve clearances as described in Section 44.

9 Fit the valve cover together with a new gasket and tighten the bolts evenly in a diagonal sequence.

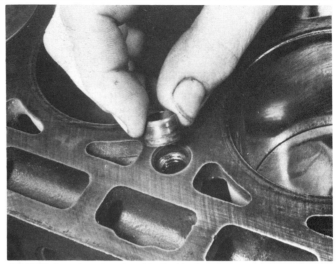
43.1B Fitting a locating dowel in the block

43.3 Fitting the head gasket

43.4 Lowering the cylinder head onto the block

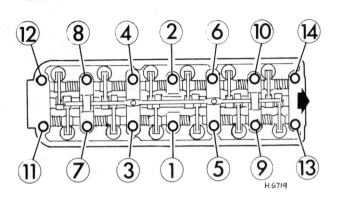

Fig. 1.8 Cylinder head bolt tightening sequence (Sec 43)

10 Fit the plug lead holder ot the valve cover and tighten the nuts.
11 If the engine is in the car, reverse the preliminary procedures given in Section 8.

43.5 Tightening the cylinder head bolts

44 Valve clearances – adjustment

1   The valve clearances must be adjusted with the engine cold.
2   Remove the valve cover and gasket, and the spark plugs.
3   Turn the engine until No 1 piston is at TDC on compression and both No 1 valves are closed. Use a spanner on the crankshaft pulley nut or on manual gearbox models engage top gear and pull the car forward; the compression stroke commencement can be ascertained by placing a finger or palm of the hand over No 1 spark plug aperture. Check that the TDC marks on the pulley and timing cover are aligned.
4   Both valve clearances for No 1 cylinder can now be adjusted. Loosen the locknut on the rocker arm and insert a thin angled rod into one of the holes in the eccentric adjuster. Turn the adjuster until a feeler blade of the correct thickness is a firm sliding fit between the adjuster and the valve stem. Do not insert the feeler blade between the camshaft and rocker arm. Tighten the locknut without moving the adjuster, then recheck the adjustment (photo).
5   With the valve clearances on No 1 cylinder adjusted, turn the engine until No 5 piston is at TDC on compression – the engine must be turned $\frac{1}{3}$rd of a revolution in its normal direction of rotation. Repeat the adjustment procedure for No 5 cylinder valves followed by No 3, 6, 2 and 4 cylinders.
6   Check the valve cover gasket for damage and renew it if necessary. Refit the valve cover and gasket, and the spark plugs.

45 Ancillary components – refitting

Refer to Section 7, and refit the listed components with reference to the Chapters indicated, where applicable.

46 Engine – refitting

Reverse the removal procedure given in Section 5, but note the following additional points:

(a) On automatic transmission models refer to Chapter 6 to check that the torque converter is fully engaged with the transmission and also to adjust the downshift cable. Top-up the automatic transmission fluid as described in Chapter 6
(b) Refill the engine with oil
(c) Refill the cooling system as described in Chapter 2

47 Engine – adjustment after major overhaul

1   With the engine refitted to the car, make a final check to ensure that everything has been reconnected and that no rags or tools have been left in the engine compartment.

44.4 Adjusting the valve clearances

2   If new pistons or crankshaft bearings have been fitted, turn the slow running screw in about half a turn to compensate for the initial tightness of the new components.
3   Remove the spark plugs and turn the engine over on the starter motor until the oil pressure warning light goes out. This procedure will ensure that the entire engine lubrication system is primed ready for starting; on carburettor engines the fuel will be pumped to the carburettors.
4   Refit the spark plugs and start the engine. Once the engine has fired keep it running until normal operating temperature has been reached and then check for oil and water leaks and rectify if necessary.
5   Due to the altered characteristics of the engine by the removal of carbon and valve grinding, the adjustment of the carburettor, ignition, fuel injection and emission control systems should all be checked as described in the relevant Chapters.
6   After the engine has been run to operating temperature, carry out the final tightening of the cylinder head bolts. (This can be done with the engine warm or cold.) Tighten each bolt through a further 25° ± 5°. Make up a cardboard template if necessary to indicate the angle required. There is no need for any further retightening.
7   If a number of new engine internal components have been fitted, it is recommended that the engine oil and filter are also changed at the end of the first 600 miles (1000 km) running. The engine and road speeds should be restricted for the initial period to assist in bedding-in the new components.

48 Fault diagnosis – engine

Symptom	Reason(s)
Engine fails to start	Discharged battery Loose battery connection Loose or broken ignition leads Moisture on spark plugs, distributor cap, or HT leads Incorrect spark plug or contact points gap (as applicable) Cracked distributor cap or rotor Blocked fuel supply Empty fuel tank Faulty fuel pump Faulty starter motor Low cylinder compressions Faulty transistorized ignition system (528i)
Engine idles erratically	Intake manifold air leak Leaking cylinder head gasket Worn valve gear and timing chain Incorrect valve clearances Damaged or loose crankcase ventilation hoses Idling adjustment incorrect Uneven cylinder compressions
Engine misfires	Incorrect spark plug or contact points gap (as applicable) Faulty coil or condenser (as applicable) Dirt or water in fuel Burnt out valve Leaking cylinder head gasket Cracked distributor cap or rotor Incorrect valve clearances Uneven cylinder compressions Faulty transistorized ignition system (528i)
Engine stalls	Idling adjustment incorrect Intake manifold air leak Ignition timing incorrect
Engine lacks power	Ignition timing incorrect Low cylinder compressions Excessive carbon build-up
Engine backfires	Idling adjustment incorrect Ignition timing incorrect Incorrect valve clearances Intake manifold air leak Sticking valve
Excessive oil consumption	Worn pistons and cylinder bores Worn valve guides and valve stem seals Oil leaking from valve cover, timing covers, crankshaft front or rear oil seal, head gasket or sump gasket

Chapter 2 Cooling system

For modifications, and information applicable to later models, see Supplement at end of manual

Contents

Specifications

System type .... Pressurized with belt driven pump, friction or viscous coupling fan (and auxiliary electric fan on models with air conditioning), crossflow radiator (incorporating oil cooler in right-hand tank on models with automatic transmission), and expansion tank

Expansion tank cap opening pressure .... 14.2 lbf/in^2 (1.0 bar)

Thermostat opening temperature
UK (manual) .... 84°C (183°F)
UK (automatic) and all USA models .... 80°C (176°F)

Viscous fan cut-off speed .... approximately 2300 rpm

Water pump impeller clearance .... 0.9 mm (0.035 in)

Fanbelt tension .... 5 to 10 mm (0.197 to 0.394 in) deflection midway between water pump and alternator pulleys with firm thumb pressure

System capacity (including heater) .... 21.1 Imp pt; 12.7 US qt; 12.0 litre

Torque wrench settings

	lbf ft	Nm
Radiator	6	8.5
Temperature transmitter	16	22
Expansion tank – M6	7	9.5
– M8	19	26.5
Oil cooler hose to radiator	10	13.5
Temperature switch (radiator)	23	32

1 General description

The cooling system is of the pressurized type and includes a cross flow radiator, belt driven water pump, and a friction or viscous coupling fan. The thremostat is located in a housing on the front of the cylinder head. Models equipped with air conditioning additionally have an electric fan, and on models with automatic transmission the right-hand radiator tank incorporates the transmission oil cooler. On early models, the radiator incorporates a drain plug, but this is disconnected on later models. A drain plug is however provided at the right-hand rear of the cylinder block.

The system functions as follows. Cold water in the water pump is forced around the water passages of the cylinder block and head, and after cooling the cylinder bores, combustion surfaces, and valve seats, emerges into the outlet branch at the front of the cylinder head. Initially the thermostat is closed and the water passes over the thermostat bellows, through the inlet hose to the water pump. Water

also circulates from the rear of the cylinder block through the heater, carburettor automatic choke (where fitted), and inlet manifold. It is then returned to the cylinder head output branch just below the thermostat. When the coolant reaches the predetermined temperature (see Specifications) the thermostat opens and water is drawn through the radiator bottom hose, past the thermostat, and into the water pump. The action of the thermostat also closes the bypass hole in the outlet branch so that hot coolant emerging from the cylinder head is drawn through the radiator top hose, through the radiator where it is cooled by the in-rush of air when the car is in forward motion and also by the cooling fan(s). It is then returned via the thermostat housing and inlet hose to the water pump.

The friction coupling fan incorporates a temperature sensitive element and piston; when the air around the element (ie leaving the radiator) reaches a predetermined temperature, the piston deflects a circular spring, and a friction lining locks the fan to the water pump hub.

The viscous coupling fan incorporates a fluid film drive which is engaged by centrifugal force (ie when the engine is running). The fluid film drive has the effect of limiting torque output so that the fan is governed to a maximum speed (see Specifications). This reduces fan noise and unneccessary power absorption.

The auxiliary electric fan on models equipped with air conditioning is controlled by a temperature switch located in the right-hand radiator tank at the bottom.

Water temperature is monitored by a sender unit on the cylinder head outlet branch.

2   Cooling system – draining

1   It is preferable to drain the cooling system when the engine has cooled. If this is not possible place a cloth over the expansion tank filler cap and turn it slowly in an anti-clockwise direction until the first stop is reached then wait until all the pressure has been released. Remove the filler cap.

2   Set the heater control to the 'warm' position.

3   Place a suitable container beneath the right-hand side of the radiator.

4   Unscrew the drain plug in the bottom right-hand side of the radiator and drain the coolant. If no drain plug is provided, loosen the clip and ease the bottom hose from the radiator outlet.

5   Drain the coolant from the cylinder block, by placing a suitable receptacle beneath the rear of the engine, and then unscrewing the hexagon plug, located at the right-hand rear side of the cylinder block (photos). If after removing this drain plug no coolant emerges, then prod the orifice gently with a suitable instrument to clear any obstruction.

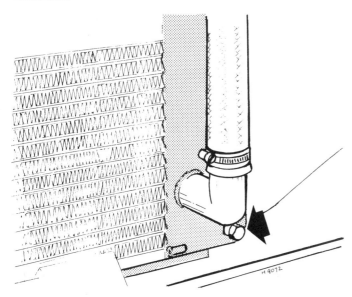

Fig. 2.1 Radiator drain plug location on early models (Sec 2)

3   Cooling system – flushing

1   The radiator and waterways in the engine may become restricted or even blocked with scale or sediment which reduces the efficiency of the cooling system. When this condition occurs, or the coolant appears rusty or dark in colour, the system may be flushed. In severe cases reverse flushing may be required as described later.

2   Remove the expansion tank pressure cap and move the interior heater control lever to the 'warm' position. Drain the coolant from the radiator as described in Section 2. Disconnect the top hose (and bottom hose if still in position) from the radiator.

3   Insert a hose in the radiator inlet and allow water to circulate through the radiator until it runs clear from the bottom outlet. Also insert the hose in the expansion tank to clear any sediment from the vent and supply hoses.

4   Remove the cylinder block drain plug then insert the hose in the radiator top hose and allow the water to circulate through the cylinder head, water pump, and cylinder block until it runs clear from the cylinder block outlet.

5   In severe cases of contamination the radiator should be reverse flushed. To do this remove the radiator as described in Section 6, invert it, and insert a hose in the outlet. Continue flushing until clear water runs from the inlet.

6   Disconnect the heater/inlet manifold return hose from the cylinder head outlet branch, then disconnect the heater supply hose from the rear of the cylinder head and insert a hose. Continue flushing until clear water runs from the return hose.

7   The use of chemical cleaners should only be necessary as a last resort, and the regular renewal of the antifreeze/inhibitor should prevent the contamination of the system.

4   Cooling system – filling

1   Refit the radiator if removed, and reconnect all the hoses. Refit and tighten the cylinder block drain plug. Check that the heater control is set to the 'warm' position.

2   Loosen the bleed screw located on top of the thermostat housing (photo).

3   Pour coolant into the expansion tank until it reaches the level mark. Water and air bubbles will emerge from the bleed slot at first, but when the water is free of bubbles, tighten the bleed screw.

4   Top-up the coolant level then refit the filler cap.

5   Run the engine at a fast idling speed until it reaches the normal operating temperature then stop it. After approximately one minute restart the engine and run it at a minimum of 4000 rpm for half a minute. Allow the engine to idle and check that the heater operates correctly and delivers warm air to the passenger compartment. If not, repeat the bleeding sequence.

6   Switch off the engine and let it cool down, then check the coolant level in the expansion tank and top it up if necessary.

5   Antifreeze mixture

1   The antifreeze mixture should be renewed every two years. This is

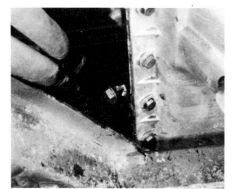

2.5A View of the cylinder block drain plug from beneath the car

2.5B Removing the cylinder block drain plug

4.2 Loosening the thermostat housing bleed screw

necessary not only to maintain the antifreeze properties, but also to prevent corrosion which would otherwise occur as the inhibitors become progressively less effective.

2 Always use an ethylene glycol based antifreeze/inhibitor for use in a mixed metal cooling system.

3 Before adding the mixture, the cooling system should be completely drained and flushed, and all hose connections checked for tightness.

4 The quantity of antifreeze required should be 35% to 40% of the cooling system capacity (see Specifications) for countries with temperate climates, and 50% for countries with cold climates. The mixture should be retained in the cooling system throughout the year.

5 Mix the antifreeze and water in the required proportions then pour it into the cooling system with reference to Section 1.

6 Attach a label to the radiator starting the date installed. Any subsequent topping-up should be made with the same type and concentration of antifreeze.

6 Radiator – removal, inspection, cleaning and refitting

1 The cooling system should first be drained as directed in Section 2. On automatic transmission models it will also be necessary to disconnect the oil cooler pipes from the radiator and plug them (Fig. 2.2) (photo).Disconnect the upper pipe first and allow the fluid to drain back into the transmission before disconnecting the lower pipe.

2 On models which are fitted with a fan guard housing, it will be necessary to raise the front of the vehicle sufficiently in order to gain enough clearance under the vehicle to lower the fan guard housing down through the engine compartment. To remove the fan guard housing, undo the retaining screws along the upper edge (Fig. 2.3), slide the guard housing first sideways then slightly upward, to disengage the lower guide tabs, then lower it down through the engine compartment (on USA models temporarily locate the guard over the fan blades).

3 Disconnect the upper and lower hose connections and the small bore hose from the expansion tank (photo).

4 On models equipped with air conditioning, disconnect the wiring from the switch located at the bottom of the radiator right-hand tank.

5 On 528i USA models disconnect the wiring from the temperature switch located in the radiator.

6 Unbolt the support bracket from the right-hand side of the radiator and carefully lift the radiator out of the rubber support mountings,

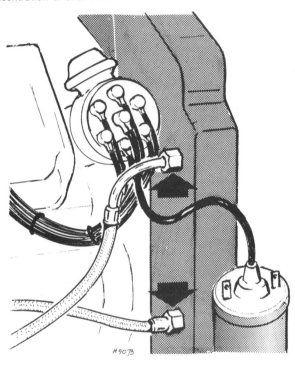

Fig. 2.2 Automatic transmission oil cooler pipe locations on the radiator – upper pipe is supply (Sec 6)

6.1 Removing the oil cooler pipes from the radiator on an automatic transmission model

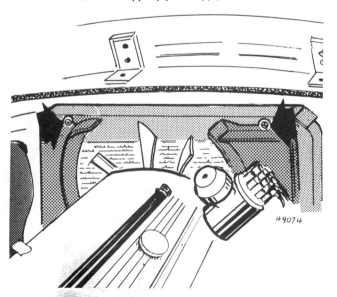

Fig. 2.3 Fan guard housing retaining screw locations (Sec 6)

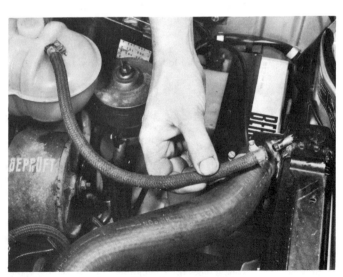

6.3 Disconnecting the overflow pipe from the radiator

taking care not to damage the radiator matrix on the fan blades (photo).

7   Carefully inspect the radiator for signs of damage and leakage. Clean away any debris from the matrix with a soft brush, or blow through it with an air line. The radiator should then be flushed out thoroughly as described in Section 3. On automatic transmission models the oil cooler can be flushed out with clean petrol but it is essential to stand the radiator up in such a way that all the residue runs out and no petrol is left inside the unit. Flushing the oil cooler in this way is generally only necessary if there has been gearbox damage.

8   Radiator repairs can be rather tricky, and are best entrusted to radiator repair specialists. Minor repairs may be tackled with a soldering iron, a good acid flux, and a low melting point solder. However, extreme care should be exercised, as, if too much heat is applied, the radiator joints may begin to separate. If the leak is very small, it may be possible to stop it by using one of the proprietary radiator sealants, which can only be added when the system is filled.

9   Examine all the hoses and clips, and renew any which show signs of deterioration. Check the radiator rubber mountings for wear, and renew them if necessary.

10 Refitting of the radiator is the reverse of the removal procedure. When refitting the side support bracket press the radiator down to ensure that it is seated properly. Finally refill the system as described in Section 4.

7   Thermostat – removal, testing and refitting

1   The thermostat is located in the cylinder head outlet branch housing at the front of the engine. If it fails to open at the correct temperature, the engine may overheat, and conversely, if it fails to shut, the engine will not warm up as quickly as it should, and the heater will not operate efficiently.

2   Before attempting to remove the thermostat, drain the cooling system as described in Section 2.

3   Remove the four bolts securing the thermostat cover housing (note the AIS check valve support bracket on certain USA models), pull the housing away and extract the thermostat (photos).

4   Test the operation of the thermostat by suspending it in a pan of water, heating it, and checking the temperature at which it commences to open with a thermometer. This reading should be as indicated in the Specifications Section.

5   If the thermostat is at all faulty, ie opens too late or too early, discard it and fit a new unit.

6   Clean all traces of the gasket and sealing ring from the branch housing and cover (photo). Apply jointing compound to each side of the new gasket and sealing ring and stick them to the branch housing.

7   Locate the thermostat in the branch housing, bellows first with the outer bracket vertical. Refit the cover and tighten the bolts evenly.

8   Refill the cooling system as described in Section 4.

6.6 Removing the radiator

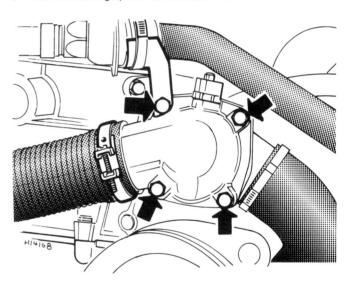

Fig. 2.4 Thermostat cover retaining bolt locations and bottom hose clip, showing AIS check valve support bracket fitted to certain USA models (Sec 7)

7.3A Removing the thermostat cover housing ...

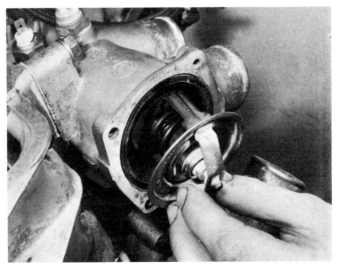

7.3B ... and thermostat

7.6 Removing the thermostat sealing ring

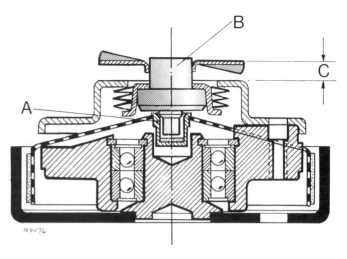

Fig. 2.5 Cross section diagram of the friction type fan coupling (Sec 8)

A   Spring cup   B   Thermo element   C   5 mm (0.197 in)

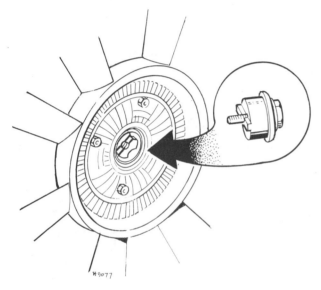

Fig. 2.6 Viscous type fan coupling showing central bolt and stepped spacer (Sec 8)

8.8A Unscrew the central retaining bolt ...

8.8B ... remove the stepped spacer ...

8.8C ... and withdraw the viscous fan unit

8 Fan blades and coupling – removal and refitting

1 One of two types of fan coupling may be fitted, these being either of the friction or viscous type. First remove the radiator as described in Section 6.
2 Remove the fan belt as described in Section 11.

Friction coupling

3 Flatten the lockplates, unscrew the four bolts, and withdraw the fanblades from the front of the water pump.
4 Separate the thermo element from the fanblades.
5 Remove the circular spring with the friction linings then unbolt the bearing and drum from the water pump hub.
6 Refitting is a reversal of removal but check that the dimension C in Fig. 2.5 is as specified and that the piston is correctly located in the thermo element. Note that should the coupling be faulty, it can be locked by fitting longer bolts to the front of the fanblades; two bolts are sufficient located opposite each other to prevent any imbalance. Do not forget to lock the bolts with the backplate.

Viscous coupling

7 The viscous coupling should be renewed if it has siezed (ie fanblades cannot be turned with engine stopped), if it has excessive play, or if there is loss of oil.
8 Remove the central retaining bolt together with the stepped spacer, then withdraw the coupling (photos).
9 Unbolt the fan blades from the coupling.
10 Refitting is a reversal of removal, but make sure that the stepped spacer is correctly located in the grooved flange. Refit the radiator and tension the fanbelt with reference to Sections 6 and 11 respectively.

9 Water pump – removal and refitting

1 Remove the fanblades and coupling as described in Section 8.
2 Remove the water pump pulley. Where a friction coupling is fitted simply ease the pulley from the hub, but where a viscous coupling is fitted unscrew the coupling drive flange bolts using an Allen key then remove the flange and pulley (photos). On some USA models the AIS air pump drivebelt and puller must also be removed at the same time.
3 Unbolt the front engine hanger from the timing cover and cylinder block (photo).
4 Loosen the clip and disconnect the inlet hose from the water pump.
5 Unscrew the retaining bolt in diagonal sequence, and withdraw

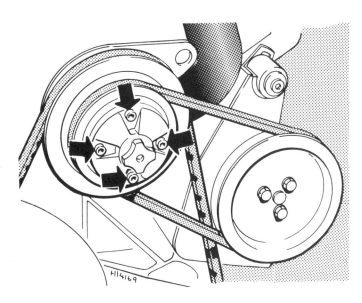

Fig. 2.7 Viscous type fan coupling drive flange to water pump hub bolt locations, showing AIS air pump and drive belt fitted to certain USA models (Sec 9)

9.2A Unscrew the Allen bolts ...

9.2B ... remove the flange ...

9.2C ... and water pump pulley

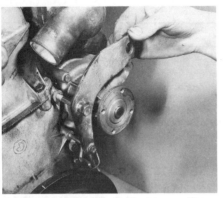

9.3 Removing the front engine hanger

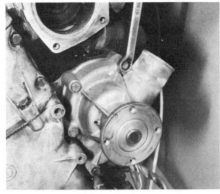

9.5A Unscrew the bolts ...

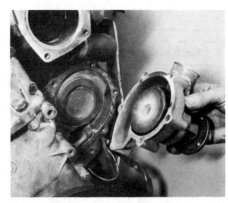

9.5B ... and remove the water pump

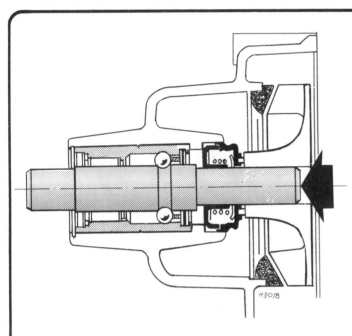

Fig. 2.8 Method of removing water pump shaft and bearing (Sec 10)

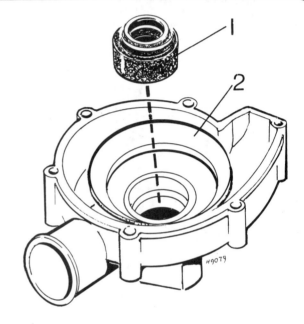

Fig. 2.9 Water pump gland seal (1) and cover ring (2) (Sec 10)

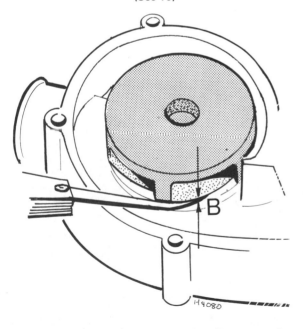

Fig. 2.10 Checking the water pump impeller to cover ring clearance (B) with a feeler blade (Sec 10)

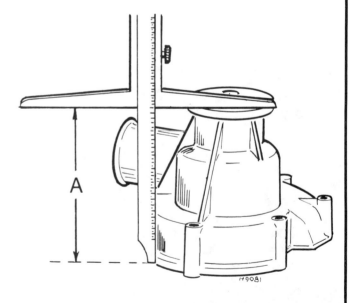

Fig. 2.11 The water pump hub to housing face dimension (A) must be 99.8 mm (3.929 in) (Sec 10)

the water pump from the cylinder block together with the gasket (photos). If it is stuck, tap the water pump housing with a soft faced mallet.
6   Scrape away all traces of the gasket from the water pump and cylinder block.
7   Refitting is a reversal of removal but use a new gasket and tighten the bolts evenly in diagonal sequence. Refer to Section 8 for the refitting of the fan blades and coupling.

10 Water pump – overhaul

1   Before starting work, check that spares are available. A two-legged puller and pressing facilities are also essential in order to overhaul the water pump.
2   Clean the exterior of the water pump with a suitable solvent.
3   Using the puller remove the hub from the water pump shaft. Note that the double stepped side faces the pump.
4   Extract the bearing retaining circlip, then support the pump housing with the impeller uppermost and press out the shaft and bearing. The impeller will be released at the same time and may be removed.
5   Using a drift, drive out the gland seal and remove the cover ring.
6   Clean the components and examine them for wear and deterioration. In particular check the gland seal, and the impeller for corrosion damage. Renew the components as necessary.
7   Reassembly is a reversal of dismantling but press the impeller onto the shaft to provide the specified clearance from the cover ring; the impeller hose should also be coated with a suitable liquid locking agent. Press the hub onto the shaft to provide the dimension shown in Fig. 2.11.

11 Fanbelt – renewal and adjustment

1   The fanbelt should be checked and re-tensioned every 10 000 miles (15 000 km) on UK models, or every 12 500 miles (20 000 km) on USA models). Examine the full length of the belt for cracks and deterioration and renew it if necessary.

Renewal
2   On models equipped with power steering, air conditioning, or AIS (USA models), remove the drivebelts from the power steering pump, air conditioning compressor and AIS air pump as described in Chapters 11, 12 and 3 respectively.
3   Loosen the alternator pivot and adjustment bolts, and swivel the alternator in toward the cylinder block.
4   Slip the fanbelt from the alternator, water pump, and crankshaft pulleys.
5   Fit the new fanbelt over the pulleys, then refit the power steering

pump, air conditioning compressor, and AIS air pump drivebelts as applicable with reference to Chapters 11, 12 and 3. Adjust the fanbelt tension as follows.

Adjustment
6   With the pivot and adjustment bolts loose, lever the alternator away from the cylinder block until the fanbelt tension is as given in the Specifications (photo). The alternator must only be levered at the drive end bracket.
7   Tighten the adjustment bolt then the pivot bolt.

12 Temperature gauge transmitter – removal and refitting

1   Drain one third of the coolant from the cooling system with reference to Section 2.
2   Disconnect the electrical lead then unscrew the transmitter and remove it from the cylinder head outlet branch.
3   Fit a new sealing ring to the transmitter then screw it into the outlet branch and tighten it to the specified torque. Refit the lead.
4   Refill the cooling system with reference to Section 4.

13 Electric fan temperature switch – removal, testing and refitting

1   Models equipped with air conditioning have an electric cooling fan in addition to the belt driven fan. The fan is controlled by a thermostatic switch located in the radiator right-hand tank.
2   To remove the switch first drain the cooling system as described in Section 2.
3   Disconnect the wires then unscrew and remove the switch from the radiator.
4   To test the switch connect it in series with a 12 volt testlamp. With the switch cold, the testlamp should not light up. Immerse the switch sensor in hot water and heat it 96°C (205°F) at which point the testlamp should light up. Now allow the temperature to drop, and the testlamp should go out at 92°C (197°F). Renew the switch if it is faulty. Note that the cut-in and cut-out temperatures are stamped on the switch hexagon.
5   Fit a new seal and tighten it to the specified torque. Reconnect the wires.
6   Refill the cooling system as described in Section 4.
7   Should the electrical supply to the temperature switch fail, check the auxiliary fan relay which is located next to the coil on UK models and next to the fusebox on USA models.

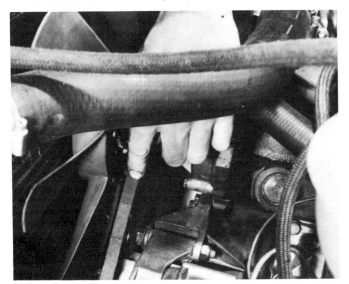

11.6 Checking the fanbelt tension

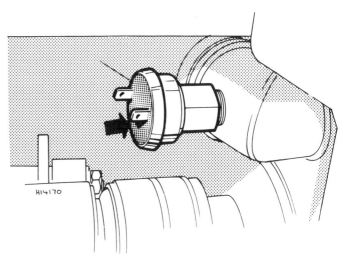

H14170

Fig. 2.12 Electric fan temperature switch location in the radiator on models equipped with air conditioning (Sec 13)

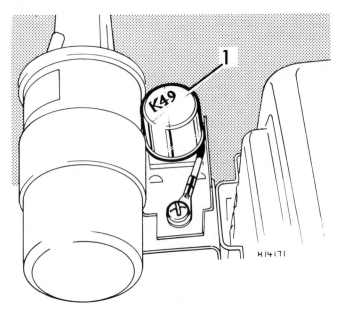

Fig. 2.13 Air conditioning electric fan temperature switch relay (1)
on UK models (Sec 13)

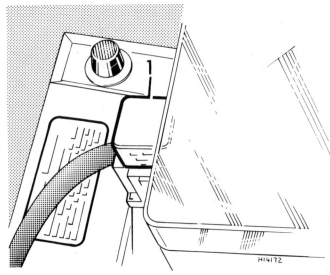

Fig. 2.14 Air conditioning electric fan temperature switch relay (1)
on USA models (Sec 13)

14 Fault diagnosis – cooling system

Symptom	Reason(s)
Overheating	Low coolant level
	Faulty expansion tank pressure cap
	Thermostat sticking shut
	Fanbelt slipping
	Open circuit temperature switch (where applicable)
	Faulty cooling fan motor (where applicable)
	Clogged radiator matrix
	Retarded ignition timing
Slow warm-up	Thermostat sticking open
	Faulty fan coupling
Coolant loss	Damaged or perished hoses
	Leaking water pump, cylinder head outlet branch gasket or thermostat cover gasket
	Blown cylinder head gasket
	Leaking radiator or cylinder block core plug

Chapter 3 Fuel, exhaust and emission control systems

For modifications, and information applicable to later models, see Supplement at end of manual

Contents

Specifications

Fuel pump (mechanical)
Make and type .... Pierburg diaphragm pump, driven by rod from camshaft eccentric
Pressure at 4000 rpm .... 3.0 to 4.0 lbf/in² (0.21 to 0.30 bar)

Fuel pump (electric)
Make and type .... Bosch, roller cell
Operating pressure .... 43.0 lbf/in² (3.0 bar)

to 0.30

Fuel tank capacity
UK models .... 15.5 Imp gal; 18.5 US gal; 70 litre
USA models (pre-1978) .... 15.5 Imp gal; 18.5 US gal; 70 litre
USA models (1978 on) .... 13.6 Imp gal; 16.4 US gal; 62 litre

Carburettor
Type:
Early 525 models .... Two Zenith 32/40 INAT 2-stage carburettors
Early 528 models .... Two Zenith 35/40 INAT 2-stage carburettors
Later 525 and 528 models .... Single Solex DVG 4A1 twin barrel 2-stage carburettor

Zenith carburettor

	Zenith 32/40	Zenith 35/40
Idle speed	850 to 950 rpm	850 to 950 rpm
CO% at idle speed:		
Without TM starter	1.5 to 2.0	3.0 to 4.0
With TM starter	0.5 to 1.5	0.5 to 1.5
Fast idle speed	1800 to 2000 rpm	1800 to 2000 rpm
Choke gap:		
Without TM starter	2.8 mm (0.110 in)	3.0 mm (0.118 in)
With TM starter	2.5 mm (0.098 in)	2.5 mm (0.098 in)
Stage 2 throttle gap	0.05 mm (0.002 in)	0.05 mm (0.002 in)
Float needle valve	2.0	2.0
Venturi diameter:		
Stage 1	24 mm (0.945 in)	24 mm (0.945 in)
Stage 2	30 mm (1.181 in)	30 mm (0.181 in)
Main jet:		
Stage 1	115	117.5 with TM
		115 without TM
Stage 2	140	145 with TM
		140 without TM

	Zenith 32/40	Zenith 35/40
Idle jet:		
Stage 1	42.5 with TM 47.5 without TM	42.5 with TM 45 without TM
Idle air jet:		
Stage 1	120	125
Air correction jet:		
Stage 1	80	100 with TM 80 without TM
Stage 2	120	120 with TM 100 without TM
Emulsion tube:		
Stage 1	4S	6S
Stage 2	11N	4N
Auxiliary fuel jet:		
Stage 1	40	40
Auxiliary fuel/air jet:		
Stage 1	80	80

Solex 4A1 carburettor

Idle speed	850 to 950 rpm
CO% at idle speed	0.5 to 1.5
Throttle idle stop gap	2.9 mm (0.114 in)
Choke gap (Stage 1)	3.2 to 4.2 mm (0.126 to 0.165 in)
Fuel level	7.0 mm (0.275 in)
Venturi diameter:	
Stage 1	20 mm (0.787 in)
Stage 2	54 mm (2.126 in)
Main jet:	
Stage 1	97.5
Stage 2	B5 (525 models) B7 (528 models)
Air correction jet:	
Stage 1	2.1 H7
Stage 2	3.7 H7
Float needle valve	3.0
Idle jet	42.5
Idle air jet	120 or 125 (525 models) 115 (528 models)

Electronic fuel injection system

Make and type	Bosch L-Jetronic
Idle speed:	
528 (UK)	850 to 950 rpm
528 (USA)	800 to 1000 rpm
530 (USA)	850 to 1050 rpm
CO% at idle speed:	
528 (UK)	0.5 to 2.0
528 (USA)	0.2 to 0.8
530 (USA)	1.5 to 3.0
Coolant temperature sensor resistance at 20°C (68°F)	2500 ohm
Temperature time switch switching point – except 528 (USA)	15°C (59°F)
528 USA	35°C (95°F)
Fuel injector pressure	28 to 43 lbf/in^2 (2 to 3 bar)

Torque wrench settings

	lbf ft	Nm
Exhaust manifold	22 to 24	30 to 33
Carburettor – Solex DVG	9	12
Zenith INAT	12	17
Idle cut-off valve – Solex DVG	3.6	5
Zenith INAT	2	3
Fuel pump (mechanical)	7 to 10	10 to 14
Coolant temperature sensor	6	8
Temperature time switch	15 to 18	20 to 24
Fuel injectors	6 to 8	9 to 11
Fuel tank	31 to 35	43 to 48

1 General description

The fuel system consists of a rear mounted fuel tank, mechanically operated fuel pump (carburettor models) or electric type fuel pump (fuel injection models), and carburettor or fuel injection equipment mounted in the engine compartment.

Cars destined for North America, are fitted with an exhaust emission control system, together with a fuel evaporative emission control system. Fuel supply pressure is regulated and excess fuel is returned to the fuel tank (photo).

2 Air cleaner – servicing, removal and refitting

1   Every 10 000 miles (15 000 km) on UK models, or 12 500 miles (20 000 km) on USA models the air cleaner element should be

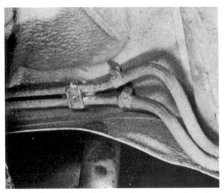

1.1 Fuel supply and return lines located on the underbody

2.2A Remove the air cleaner control nut ...

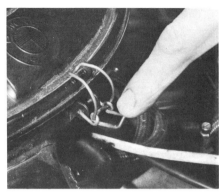

2.2B ... and spring clips ...

2.2C ... and withdraw the element

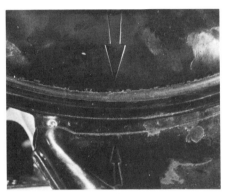

2.3 Air cleaner cover alignment arrows

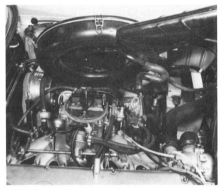

2.11 Removing the air cleaner body ...

renewed. In dusty operating conditions renew the element more frequently.

2   To remove the element on twin carburettor models lever open the spring clips, lift the cover and withdraw the elements. On single carburettor models remove the central nut and lever open the spring clips, then lift the cover and withdraw the element (photos). On fuel injection models lever open the spring clips, lift the cover, and withdraw the rectangular element.

3   Clean the air cleaner body and cover, then fit the new element using a reversal of the removal procedure. The side marked 'TOP – OBEN' should face upward on the fuel injection models, and on single carburettor models the arrow on the cover should align with the arrow on the body (photo).

4   If it is required to remove the complete air cleaner, proceed as follows.

Twin carburettor models

5   Remove the elements and lift the air cleaner body from the carburettors after removing the nuts. Disconnect the crankcase ventilation hoses and carburettor vent hose.

6   Where fitted disconnect the wires from the thermo switch.

7   Disconnect the intake hose and the warm air hose to the exhaust manifold, then withdraw the air cleaner body.

8   Remove the sealing rings from the carburettors.

9   To test the thermo switch (where fitted) switch cn the ignition. At an ambient temperature below 14°C (57°F) with both wires connected to the switch, only the green/white wire should be live. Above this temperature both wires should be live.

10   Refitting is a reversal of removal.

Single carburettor models

11   Remove the element then lift the air cleaner body from the carburettor (photo).

12   Disconnect the crankcase ventilation hose and carburettor vent hose.

13   Disconnect the intake hose and warm air hose to the exhaust

manifold, then withdraw the air cleaner body and remove the sealing ring (photo).

14   Refitting is a reversal of removal.

Fuel injection models

15   The air cleaner is removed together with the air flow sensor then disconnected from the sensor. First disconnect the multi-plug from the sensor.

16   Loosen the hose clip on the engine side of the air flow sensor.

17   Unscrew the air cleaner mounting nuts and withdraw the air cleaner and air flow sensor.

18   Loosen the hose clip and detach the air flow sensor, then remove the element as described in paragraph 2.

19   Refitting is a reversal of removal.

---

3   Air intake pre-heat valve – description and adjustment

1   The air intake pre-heat valve is located in the air cleaner entry tube assembly, and is actuated by a temperature sensitive element which operates a control flat (photo). With the flap in the horizontal position, air is drawn direct from the front of the car, but, should the air temperature fall below the predetermined level, the element will effectively raise the flap, and allow air to be drawn from the lower intake. This lower intake is connected to an exhaust manifold heat shield plate, and heated air is thus drawn into the air cleaner. Under operating conditions, the pre-heat valve will provide a mixture of hot and cold air whilst the flap is moving between the fully open and fully shut positions.

2   To check the pre-heat valve for operation, it will be necessary to remove the air cleaner complete as described in Section 2.

3   Immerse the pre-heat valve, whilst still fitted to the air cleaner, in a water bath held at a temperature of 15°C (59°F).

4   After a period of approximately five minutes, the control flap should just close the warm air aperture. If the control flap is not in the desired position, slacken the locknut and adjust the pre-heat valve until

2.13 ... and sealing ring

3.1 Air intake pre-heat control valve

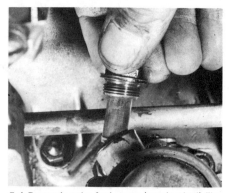

5.4 Removing the fuel pump (mechanical) filter on early models

5.5A Removing the fuel pump cover ...

5.5B ... showing the filter

5.5C Fuel pump cover alignment marks (arrowed)

the control flap is just closed. Tighten the locknut.

5   Now repeat the test procedure, and if the operation is correct, refit the air cleaner to the carburettor.

4   Fuel filter (in-line) – renewal

1   An in-line fuel filter is provided in the supply hose to the carburettor(s) or injectors. The carburettor version should be renewed every 20 000 miles (30 000 km) and the fuel injection version every 12 000 miles (20 000 km).

2   Slacken the hose clips either side of the filter and release the retaining clip(s) around the filter body.

3   Pull off the pipe connections and remove the filter assembly.

4   When fitting the new filter make sure that it is fitted the correct way round. The filter is usually marked 'EIN' (IN) and 'AUS' (OUT).

5   Fuel pump – description and routine maintenance

1   Carburettor engines are fitted with a mechanically operated fuel pump, which is mounted on the left-hand side of the cylinder head, and is actuated by means of a short pushrod from the camshaft. A diaphragm, incorporated in the fuel pump body, provides the necessary pressure variations required to pump the fuel from the fuel tank.

2   Engines with fuel injection have an electrically operated roller cell type fuel pump which is mounted together with a small expansion tank above the right-hand driveshaft of the rear axle, on the main body section. This type of pump starts to operate as soon as the ignition key is switched on and can be heard before the engine is started.

3   At the intervals specified in 'Routine Maintenance', clean the fine mesh filter of the mechanical type pump.

4   On twin carburettor models the filter is accessible after removal of the threaded plug in the lower centre section of the fuel pump. Using a 13 mm spanner undo the plug and remove the fine mesh filter. Clean the filter in petrol and refit it. The threaded plug can now be refitted, but check and, if necessary, renew the sealing washer (photo).

5   On single carburettor models use an angled screwdriver to remove the cover screw, then lift off the cover and seal and remove the filter. Clean the filter in petrol and refit it using a reversal of the removal procedure. Renew the seal if it is unserviceable. Note the alignment marks on the cover and body (photos).

6   Fuel pump (mechanical) – testing, removal, overhaul and refitting

Note: *The fuel pump fitted to later single carburettor models is of sealed construction and cannot be dismantled.*

1   Disconnect the outlet hose from the fuel pump.

2   Disconnect the distributor LT lead or the central HT lead from the coil to prevent the engine firing and then turn the ignition key to actuate the starter. Observing the outlet nozzle of the pump, well-defined spurts of fuel should be ejected. If this is not the case and the cover and inlet hose of the pump are secure, the pump must be removed and overhauled.

3   To remove the pump, disconnect both hoses from the pump and remove the securing nuts and fibre sleeves where fitted (photos).

4   Remove the thick insulator block and two thin gaskets and withdraw the operating pushrod (photo).

5   Scratch a line across the edges of the upper and lower pump flanges so that they can be reassembled in their original positions.

6   Remove the 13 mm plug in the side of the upper section and extract the fuel filter.

7   Remove the flange screws and separate the two halves of the pump.

8   To renew the diaphragm/rod assembly, remove the small cover plate (two screws) extract the operating arm pivot pin circlip and remove the pivot pin. Withdraw the arm and the diaphragm/spring assembly.

9   Renew any worn components. On this type of pump the valves in the pump upper body are renewable.

10   Reassembly is the reversal of dismantling. Tighten the pump flange screws only when the operating arm is held in the depressed

Fig. 3.1 Exploded view of the early mechanical type fuel pump (Sec 6)

1   Operating rod
2   Insulator
3   Lower body
4   Collar
5   Retainer
6   Spring
7   Upper body
8   Filter
9   Nut
10   Lockwasher
11   Insulating bush
12   Pivot
13   Circlip

6.3A Disconnecting the fuel pump inlet hose

6.3B Removing the fuel pump (late type)

6.3C Fuel pump fibre sleeves

6.3D Removing the fuel pump (early type)

6.4 Removing the fuel pump insulator block

(inward) position. Make sure the upper and lower body scratch marks are in alignment and the diaphragm is not twisted.

11 Refitting of the fuel pump is a reversal of removal but renew the thin gaskets which are located one each side of the flange insulator. On no account increase the overall thickness of these parts or the correct operation of the actuating rod and arm will be upset.

7 Fuel pump (electric) – testing, removal and refitting

1 The fuel pump is only energised when the starter motor is operating, or when signals from the airflow meter show that the engine is running.
2 Testing of the pump is described in Section 17.
3 If the pump relay operates but the pump does not, disconnect the wiring block connector from the pump and connect a 12 volt test lamp across the connector terminals. Proceed as if to run the pump: if the lamp lights, the fault is in the pump. If the lamp does not light, the fault is in the relay or the wiring.
4 If the fault lies with the pump then a new one must be fitted. BMW do not recommend that the fuel pump be stripped down, and in any case spare parts are not available.
5 Removal of the fuel pump is effected by first disconnecting the battery negative terminal for safety reasons.
6 Disconnect the wiring block connector at the fuel pump, if this has not already been done.
7 Disconnect the fuel pipes and plug the one that runs from the main fuel tank.
8 Remove the nuts securing the pump assembly to the chassis brackets and lift the pump and expansion tank assembly away together with the fuel filter where fitted.
9 Unbolt the pump securing clip and the interconnecting hose clip and separate the fuel pump from the expansion tank.
10 Refitting is a reversal of removal, but ensure that the union hose clips are all secure, and the wiring block connector is refitted the correct way round. Theoretically, it is impossible to reconnect the wiring block connector incorrectly due to the design of the two parts, but if undue force is used the connection can be made – so use caution.

8 Fuel tank – removal and refitting

1 Disconnect the battery negative lead.
2 Remove the fuel tank filler cap (photo).
3 Using a length of tubing syphon out all of the fuel.
4 From within the luggage compartment remove the floor covering and the tank unit cover (3 screws) (photo).
5 Note the location of the wires and hoses then disconnect them (photo). If crimped clips are fitted it will be necessary to obtain new screw type clips.
6 Jack-up the rear of the car and support it on axle stands. Chock the front wheels.
7 Where applicable remove the right-hand panel from the luggage compartment and disconnect the hoses from the expansion tank after noting their location. Remove the cover from the filler neck.
8 Unhook the rear and intermediate exhaust mounting rubbers then unbolt and remove the rear mounting bracket.
9 Unbolt the fuel tank at the luggage compartment floor (photo).Tilt the tank at its forward end when lifting it out. Unclip the hoses where necessary.
10 If the tank is to be cleaned of sediment it will usually be adequate to shake it vigorously using two or three changes of paraffin and finally washing it out with clean fuel. Before shaking the tank it will be advisable to remove the transmitter unit. To do this on UK models use two crossed screwdrivers engaged in the rim cut-outs to unscrew the unit then withdraw it together with the seal. On USA 530i models remove the screws and withdraw the unit and gasket. On USA 528i models remove the nuts and lift out the predelivery pump and gasket, then remove the screws and withdraw the unit and gasket.
11 If there is a leak in the tank, make only temporary repairs with fibreglass or similar materials. Any permanent repairs by soldering or welding must be left to professionals due to the risk of explosion if the tank is not purged of fumes by steam cleaning. On the end of the

intake tube is a fine mesh filter, which should be cleaned thoroughly before refitting the unit. The filter should be regularly cleaned every 20 000 miles (30 000 km).
12 Refitting of all components is the reverse of the removal procedure. In respect of the cord ring sealing the transmitter unit, always use a new one and coat the ring with petroleum jelly when fitting it. The ring swells when in contact with petrol and in this way forms a perfect seal. Before refitting the fuel tank, refit the rubber sealing ring in the filler neck orifice; this is far easier than trying to refit it after the tank has been fitted.

9 Carburettor – general description

The Zenith INAT carburettor is of 2-stage type incorporating an automatic choke, idle cut-off valve, and a TM starter unit. The Stage 1 throttle is operated mechanically by the throttle linkage, but when it is approximately two thirds open the Stage 2 throttle is released and is automatically operated by a vacuum box. Two INAT carburettors are fitted to each engine.

The Solex DVG 4A1 carburettor is of twin barrel 2-stage type and essentially incorporates the features of the two INAT carburettors in one complete carburettor (photo).

10 Carburettor – removal and refitting

1 Drain half of the cooling system with reference to Chapter 2.
2 Remove the air cleaner assembly as described in Section 2.
3 Disconnect all fuel, vacuum and coolant hoses.
4 Disconnect the wiring from the idle cut-off valves and automatic choke (photo).
5 Disconnect the throttle linkage at the balljoint (photo).
6 Unscrew the mounting nuts and withdraw the carburettor from the inlet manifold. Remove the gasket (photo).
7 Refitting is a reversal of removal, but always fit a new gasket – where applicable the graphite side of the gasket should contact the manifold. Adjust the idling speed as described in Section 11.

11 Carburettor(s) – slow running adjustment

Note: *Where tamperproof seals are fitted it may be a contravention of current emission legislation to remove them.*

INAT carburettors without mixture bypass system

1 With the engine at operating temperature, remove the air cleaner housing and disconnect the adjustable link rod at the rear carburettor by releasing the ball coupling.
2 To obtain an initial mixture setting point screw in fully both the mixture adjustment screws (photo) and then back them off equally by between $1\frac{1}{2}$ and 2 complete turns.
3 Depending on which type of carburettor balancing device (or air flow meter) is used, it may be necessary to remove the air cleaner housing securing studs from the carburettors in order to use the device.
4 It will now be necessary to make up an adaptor unit to join the rocker cover breather pipe to the small vent pipe which normally locates to the underside of the air cleaner.
5 Start the engine and adjust the idling speed screws until the engine idling speed is 900 rpm and the carburettors are synchronized as shown by the balancing device (photo).
6 Now adjust each of the carburettor mixture adjustment screws to obtain the fastest idling speed possible and then readjust the engine idling speed as described in paragraph 5.
7 Repeat the adjustments detailed until the mixture/idling speed and synchronization of the carburettors is correct. The final adjustment to the engine idling speed should always be made by means of the mixture adjustment screws.
8 When reconnecting the throttle link the idling speed should not be affected; if it is, the link can be adjusted by means of the knurled adjuster until it just fits.
9 After refitting the air cleaner housing it may be found necessary to make slight adjustments to the idling speed by turning the mixture

8.2 Fuel tank filler cap

8.4 Fuel tank sender unit location

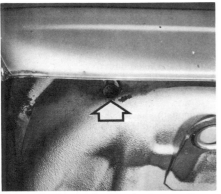

8.5 Fuel tank vent pipe location (arrowed)

8.9 A fuel tank mounting bolt

9.1 The Solex DVG 4A1 carburettor

10.4 Idle cut-off valve location (Solex DVG 4A1)

10.5 Disconnecting the throttle linkage

10.6 Removing the carburettor (Solex DVG 4A1)

11.2 Idle mixture screw location (Zenith INAT)

11.5 Idle speed screw location (Zenith INAT)

adjustment screws. Turn each screw an equal amount until the engine idles evenly at 900 rpm.

INAT carburettors with mixture bypass system

10 With the engine at operating temperature, remove the air cleaner housing and disconnect the adjustable link rod at the rear carburettor by releasing the ball coupling.

11 Make up a suitable adaptor and join together the rocker cover breather pipe and the small vent pipe which is normally joined to the lower side of the air cleaner housing.

12 Depending on which type of carburettor balancing device (airflow meter) is to be used it may now be necessary to remove the air cleaner housing securing studs from the carburettors in order to use the balancing tool.

13 Start the engine and adjust the engine idling speed to between 900 and 1000 rpm whilst balancing the air flow through the carburettors. Adjustments shoulds be made by turning the additional auxiliary mixture adjustment screws (Fig. 3.2).

14 In order to adjust the mixture correctly it will be necessary to remove the screw plugs from the exhaust manifolds and to insert special test probes (No 7062) which in turn can be coupled to an exhaust gas analyser.

15 With this unit installed repeat the adjustments detailed in paragraph 13 and then adjust the idle mixture regulating screws until a CO percentage within the specified limits is obtained. After adjusting the idle mixture it may be found necessary to readjust the idling speed as described in paragraph 13.

16 Finally, when the CO analysis and idling speed are both set, reconnect the throttle link rod. When reconnecting this link the idling speed should remain unchanged; if it alters, the rod should be adjusted by means of the knurled wheel until it just fits.

4A1 carburettor

17 With the engine at operating temperature remove the air cleaner then adjust the idling speed to 900 rpm. Stop the engine.

18 Note the setting of each mixture screw by counting the number of turns necessary to screw them fully in, then unscrew one to its original setting and unscrew the remaining one the same amount.

19 Start the engine again and let it idle.

20 For accurate mixture adjustment it will be necessary to use an exhaust gas analyser. Provision is made for inserting probes in the exhaust manifold by removing the special plugs. If this method is used, adjust each mixture screw by equal amounts until the specified CO percentage is obtained. The less accurate method is to adjust the mixture screws by equal amounts to give the highest engine speed.

21 If necessary readjust the idling speed.

22 Note that if the idle speed screw is altered, the choke pull down adjustment must be checked as described in Section 14.

12 Carburettor – overhaul

INAT carburettor

1 Remove the carburettor, as described in Section 10, and clean the external surfaces of the carburettor thoroughly with petrol or paraffin.

2 Before dismantling, lay a clean sheet of paper on the worktop so that each part of the carburettor can be laid out in the order of removal.

3 To remove the upper section of the carburettor, prise out the plastic plug from the side and release the locking screw securing the automatic choke control rod. Remove the upper section securing screws and the stud which secures the air cleaner housing. Lift the upper section away.

4 Unscrew the idling jet and remove the intermediate section retaining screws.

5 Lift the intermediate section away and invert it. From the lower side of the intermediate section remove the pump suction valve, pump pressure valve, intermediate jet and main jets.

6 The float assembly is retained by a U-shaped plate, which is in turn retained by a single screw. Remove the screw and lift the float assembly away.

7 Access can now be gained to the check valve, which can be removed using a socket or box spanner. Underneath the check valve is a special spacer/sealing washer, the thickness of which is critical to the float height.

8 From the other side of the intermediate section remove the air correction jets followed by the emulsion tubes.

9 Remove the screw securing the accelerator pump operating arm. Lift the arm away and extract the accelerator pump piston.

10 On carburettors with a mixture bypass system unscrew the fuel inlet union and extract the filter assembly.

11 To disconnect the second stage vacuum box remove the retaining screws and release the control rod from the linkage. This unit can be further dismantled by removing the cover screws and extracting the spring and diaphragm unit. When assembling this unit ensure that any components which are renewed are suited to the application. If maximum speed cannot be obtained it is likely that an incorrect spring has been fitted. If the diaphragm is damaged then it should be renewed. On installing a new diaphragm it is important to make sure that the overall length of the diaphragm and rod is 2.559 in (65 mm).

12 Mark the position of the choke bi-metallic spring housing in relation to the carburettor, and remove the securing screws.

13 Withdraw the housing and note the location of the choke operating lever.

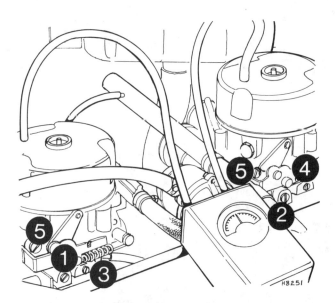

Fig. 3.2 Location of the auxiliary mixture adjustment screws (1 and 2) and idle mixture screws (3 and 4). The INAT carburettors are shown with a synchronizer device fitted. Do not alter screws (5) (Sec 11)

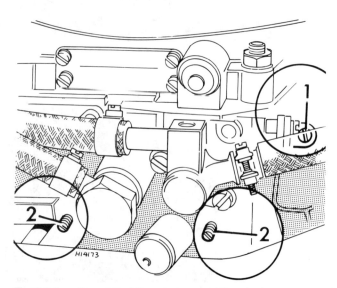

Fig. 3.3 Location of the idle speed screw (1) and mixture screws (2) on the Solex DVG 4A1 carburettor (Sec 11)

14 Unscrew and remove the idle and mixture regulating screws.

15 Remove the fuel shut-off valve.

16 Clean the carburettor body with petrol and then blow dry with compressed air. Blow the carburettor and float chamber air or fuel passages in the direction of flow.

17 Check that all the jets are as given in the Specifications Section for your particular model (a previous owner may have changed some).

18 Check that the throttle spindles are not worn by attempting to rock them from side to side in their housings. Undue wear of the spindles or carburettor housing will cause a weak mixture and erratic idling. Renew any worn parts as necessary.

19 Operate the float chamber check valve by hand and inspect the

valve and its seating. Renew the check valve if it is sticking or the seat is damaged.

20 Before reassembling the carburettor, test the heat sensitive starting valve (where applicable). Remove the cover screws and lift it away to expose the resistor and valve assembly. Ensure the carburettor is free of fuel, and then connect a feed wire from the battery positive (+) terminal to the input terminal of the starting valve.Connect another lead from the carburettor body to a convenient earthing point to complete the circuit. At an air temperature of 15°C (57°F), the valve must be just lifting away from its seat, but at temperatures below 15°C (57°F), the bi-metallic spring should raise the valve between 0.040 in and 0.078 in (1 and 2 mm) after the

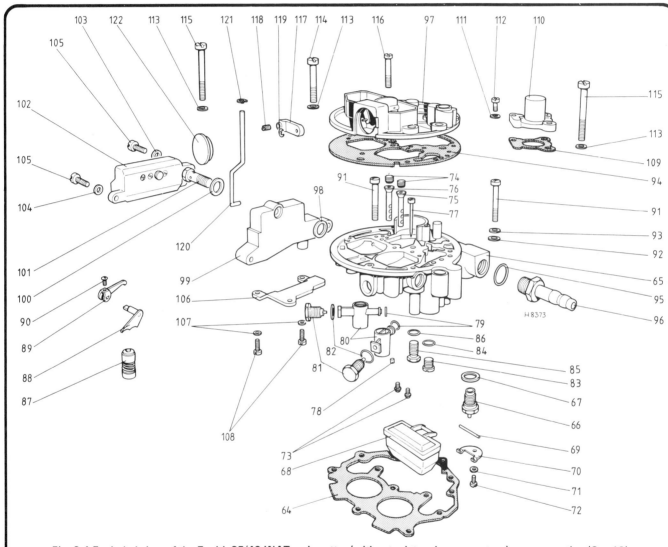

Fig. 3.4 Exploded view of the Zenith 35/40 INAT carburettor (without mixture bypass system) – upper section (Sec 12)

64 Gasket	80 Pre-atomizer	95 Sealing ring	109 Gasket
65 Bedplate	81 Contact pin screw	96 Stud pipe	110 Cover
66 Float needle	82 Sealing ring	97 Carburettor cover	111 Spring washer
67 Sealing ring	83 Pump suction valve	assembly	112 Screw
68 Float	84 Sealing ring	98 Sealing ring	113 Screw
69 Shaft	85 Pump pressure valve	99 Holder	114 Screw
70 Holder	86 Sealing ring	100 Sealing ring	115 Screw
71 Spring washer	87 Pump piston	101 Hollow screw	116 Screw
72 Screw	88 Pump lever	102 'Thermostart' valve	117 Pivot
73 Main jet	89 Pump lever	103 Spring washer	118 Setscrew
74 Air correction jet	90 Countersunk screw	104 Spring washer	119 Circlip
75 Mixing tube	91 Screw	105 Screw	120 Connecting rod
76 Mixing tube	92 Washer	106 Strap	121 Clamp ring
77 Idle jet	93 Sealing ring	107 Spring washer	122 End cap
78 Jet	94 Carburettor cover	108 Screw	
79 O-ring	gasket		

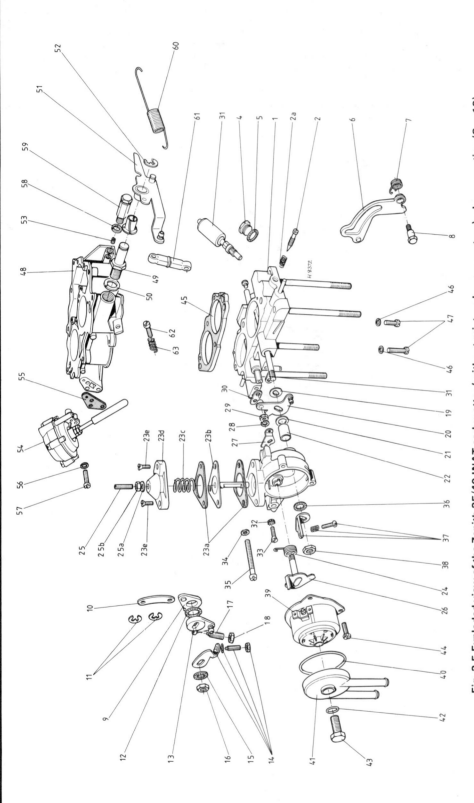

Fig. 3.5 Exploded view of the Zenith 35/40 INAT carburettor (without mixture bypass system) – lower section (Sec 12)

1	Throttle butterfly section
2	Idle mixture screw
2a	Coil spring
3	Shutoff valve
5	Washer
6	Gate lever
7	Torsion spring
8	Stud
9	Locking lever
10	Connecting lever
11	Circlip
12	Washer
13	Throttle lever
14	Stop lever
15	Fan washer
16	Nut
17	Threaded rod
18	Nut
19	Washer
20	Throttle lever
21	Fan washer
22	Spacing sleeve
23a	Gasket
23b	Diaphragm
23c	Coil spring
23d	Cover
23e	Domed head countersunk
24	Torsion spring
25	Adjusting screw
25a	Sealing ring
35b	Nut
26	Actuating lever
27	Transfer lever
28	Lockwasher
29	Nut
30	Gasket
31	Gasket
32	Toothed washer
33	Countersunk screw
34	Spring washer
35	Screw
36	Fan washer
37	Stop lever
38	Nut
39	Choke cover
40	O-ring
41	Water connecting pipes
42	Sealing ring
43	Screw
44	Screw
45	Insulating flange
47	Screw
48	Float housing
49	Pivot pin
50	Spring washer
51	Actuating lever
52	Lockwasher
53	Threaded rod
54	Vacuum cap
55	Gasket
56	Spring washer
57	Screw
58	Spring washer
59	Retaining pin
60	Tension spring
61	Connecting rod
62	Idle adjusting screw
63	Coil spring

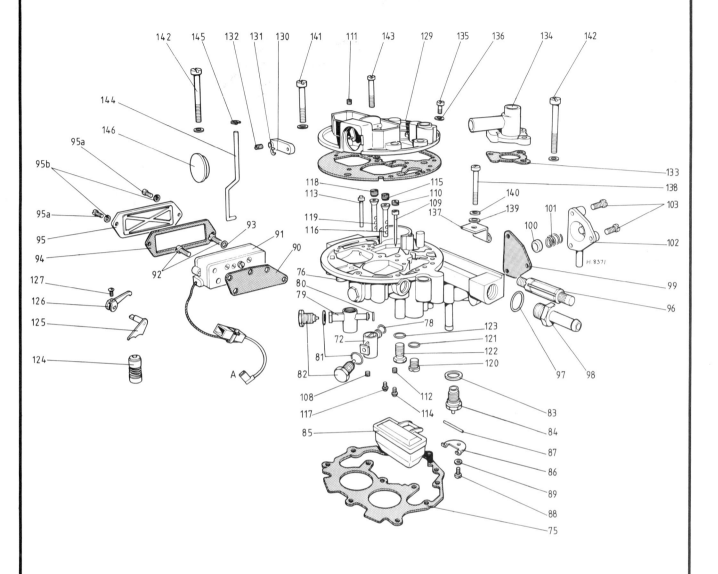

Fig. 3.6 Exploded view of the Zenith 35/40 INAT carburettor (with mixture bypass system) – upper section (Sec 12)

75 Gasket
76 Bedplate
77 Pre-atomizer, stage I
78 O-ring
79 Pre-atomizer, stage II
80 O-ring
81 Sealing ring
82 Contact screw
83 Sealing ring
84 Float needle valve
85 Float
86 Holder
87 Shaft
88 Screw
90 Gasket
91 'Thermostart' valve
92 Screw
93 Spring washer

94 Gasket
95 Cover plate
95a Screw
96 Fuel filter
97 Sealing ring
98 Threaded stub pipe
99 Diaphragm
100 Spring plate
101 Coil spring
102 Valve cup
103 Countersunk screw
108 Additional mixture
    screw
109 Idle jet
110 Idle air jet
111 Starting air jet
112 Starting fuel jet

113 Starting immersed tube
114 Main jet, stage I
115 Air correction jet,
    stage I
116 Mixing tube, stage I
117 Main jet, stage II
118 Air correction jet,
    stage II
119 Mixing tube, stage II
120 Pump section valve
121 Sealing ring
122 Pump pressure valve
123 Sealing ring
124 Pump piston
125 Pump lever
126 Pump lever
127 Countersunk screw

128 Gasket
129 Carburettor screw
130 Pivot
131 Lockwasher
132 Setscrew
133 Gasket
134 Cover
135 Screw
137 Clip
138 Screw
139 Washer
141 Screw
142 Screw
143 Screw
144 Connecting rod
145 Clamp ring
146 End cap

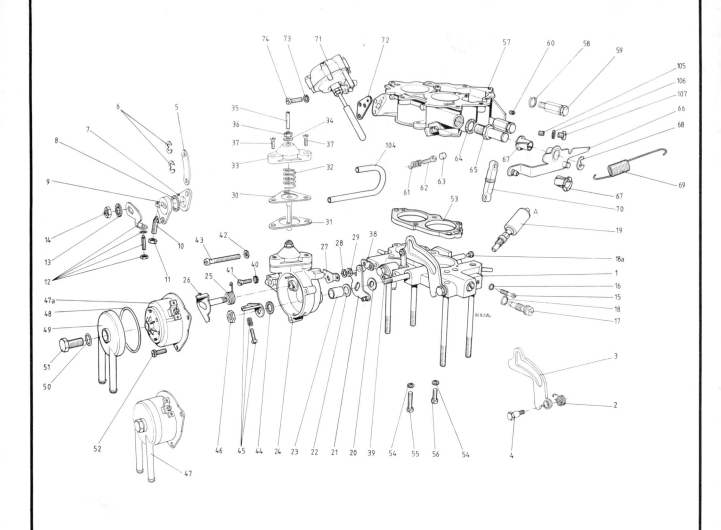

Fig. 3.7 Exploded view of the Zenith 35/40 INAT carburettor (with mixture bypass system) – lower section (Sec 12)

1 Throttle butterfly section	18a End plug screw	38 Gasket	58 Spring washer
2 Torsion spring	19 Shutoff valve	39 Gasket	59 Retaining pin
3 Gate lever	20 Spacing washer	40 Washer	60 Screw
4 Stud screw	21 Throttle lever, stage I	41 Countersunk screw	61 Coil spring
5 Connecting lever	22 Fan washer	43 Screw	62 Idle adjustment screw
6 Lockwasher	23 Spacing bushing	44 Fan washer	63 Cap
7 Lock lever	24 Choke unit	45 Stop lever	64 Lockwasher
8 Washer	25 Torsion spring	46 Nut	65 Pivot pin
9 Throttle lever, stage II	26 Actuating lever	47 Choke cover (complete)	66 Actuating lever
10 Setscrew	27 Transfer lever	47a Choke cover	67 Bearing bushing
11 Nut	28 Lockwasher	48 O-ring	68 Lockwasher
12 Stop lever	29 Nut	49 Connecting stub pipes	69 Tension spring
13 Fan washer	30 Diaphragm	50 Sealing ring	70 Connecting rod
14 Nut	31 Gasket	51 Screw	71 Vacuum cap
15 Mixture screw	32 Coil spring	52 Screw	72 Gasket
16 O-ring	33 Cover	53 Insulating gasket	74 Screw
17 Bypass mixture screw	34 Sealing ring	54 Spring washer	104 Connecting hose
18 O-ring	35 Setscrew	55 Screw	105 Additional fuel jet
	36 Nut	56 Screw	106 Sealing ring
	37 Countersunk screw	57 Float housing	107 Screw plug

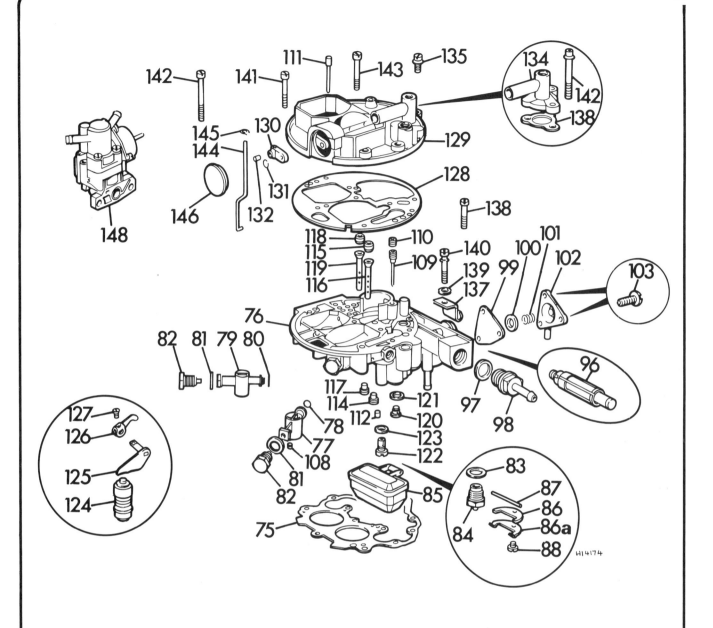

Fig. 3.8 Exploded view of the Zenith 35/40 INAT carburettor (with TM starter) – upper section (Sec 12)

75 Gasket	97 Seal	118 Air correction jet II	133 Gasket
76 Platinum block	98 Adaptor	119 Mixture tube stage II	134 Cover
77 Atomizer	99 Diaphragm spring	120 Pump suction valve	135 Cylinder head screw
78 O-ring	100 Spring retainer	121 Seal	138 Cylinder head screw
79 Atomizer	101 Spring	122 Pump pressure valve	139 Washer
80 O-ring	102 Valve cover	123 Seal	140 Cylinder head screw
81 Seal	103 Oval head screw	124 Pump piston	141 Cylinder head screw
82 Pressure bolt	108 Auxiliary mixture jet	125 Pump lever	142 Cylinder head screw
83 Seal 1.0	109 Idle jet	126 Pump lever	143 Cylinder head screw
84 Float needle valve	110 Idle air jet	127 Oval head screw	144 Connecting rod
85 Float	111 Starter air jet	128 Gasket	145 Clamping ring
86 Holder	112 Starter fuel jet	129 Carburettor cover	146 Cap
86a Holder	114 Main jet stage I	130 Pivot	147 Gasket
87 Shaft	115 Air correction jet I	131 Lockwasher	148 Thermo auxiliary
88 Cylinder head screw	116 Mixture tube stage I	132 Stud	choke
96 Filter screen	117 Main jet stage II		

current has been connected for approximately one minute. If this is not the case, the resistor is defective or the flat plug is not carrying the current. The valve seat is pre-set during manufacture and should never be re-adjusted.

21 Obtain a carburettor repair kit which will contain all the necessary gaskets, washers and O-rings.

22 Reassembly is basically a reversal of the dismantling procedure but observe the following points:

(a) Make sure that the bi-metallic spring engages with the end of the operating arm, and the alignment marks coincide, as the housing cover is being fitted.

(b) Check that the float needle valve seating washer is of the correct thickness or else the fuel level in the float chamber will be incorrect.

(c) Adjust the second stage butterfly so that there exists a gap of 0.002 in (0.05 mm) between the butterfly and the side of the

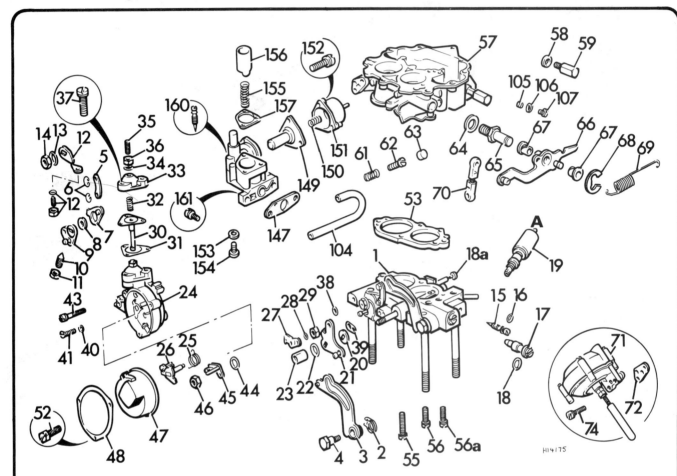

Fig. 3.9 Exploded view of the Zenith 35/40 INAT carburettor (with TM starter) – lower section (Sec 12)

1 Throttle housing assembly	20 Spacer	43 Cylinder head screw	70 Connecting rod
2 Spring	21 Throttle lever	44 Lockwasher	71 Vacuum box no. 04
3 Gate lever	22 Lockwasher	45 Stop lever	72 Gasket
4 Screw	23 Spacer	46 Hexagon nut	74 Cylinder head screw
5 Connection lever	24 Choke	48 Holder	104 Hose
6 Lockwasher	25 Spring	52 Hexagonal head screw	105 Auxiliary fuel jet
7 Locking lever	26 Operating lever	53 Insulator	106 Seal
8 Washer	27 Transmitting lever	55 Cylinder head screw	107 Plug
9 Throttle lever	28 Lockwasher	56 Cylinder head screw	149 Valve
10 Stud	29 Hexagon nut	56a Cylinder head screw	150 Diaphragm spring
11 Hexagon nut	30 Diaphragm spring no. 42	57 Float housing	151 Valve cover
12 Stop lever	31 Gasket	58 Lockwasher	152 Cylinder head screw
13 Lockwasher	32 Spring	59 Retaining pin	153 Seal
14 Hexagon nut	33 Cover no. 24	61 Spring	154 Hexagonal head screw
15 Mixture control screw	34 Seal	62 Idle adjusting screw	155 Spring
16 O-ring	35 Stud	63 Cap	156 Piston
17 Idle bypass control screw	36 Hexagon nut	64 Lockwasher	157 Gasket
18 O-ring	37 Cylinder head screw	65 Bearing pin	158 Connecting cover
18a Screw	38 Gasket	66 Operating lever	159 Cylinder head screw
19 Cut-off valve	39 Gasket	67 Bearing sleeve	160 Mixture control screw
	40 Lockwasher	68 Lockwasher	161 Cylinder head screw
	41 Screw	69 Spring	

carburettor housing between the two venturi. The carburettor will have to be inverted to carry out this adjustment. This adjustment is effected by slackening the locknut, and turning the adjusting screw located adjacent to the second stage vacuum box. If this gap is set to a smaller dimension the second stage butterfly will jam.

(d) The throttle butterfly must now be tensioned with the spring loaded stop pin. To carry out this adjustment slacken the locknut and turn the adjusting screw until the spring-loaded stop pin just touches the locking lever. Now turn the adjusting screw $\frac{1}{3}$ of a revolution more and tighten the locknut. If the throttle butterfly is given more than 0.012 in (0.3 mm) of tension by the spring-loaded stop pin the roller will probably jam in the slotted gate.

(e) With the carburettor fully assembled, check the accelerator pump injection volume by filling the float chamber with fuel through the air vent. Hold the carburettor above a jar, and move the throttle linkage fully in both directions ten times. It should average out that each stroke should inject 0.6 to 0.9 cc of fuel. If this is not the case, adjust the stroke on the

accelerator pump operating arm, to give the desired quantity.

23 Finally refit the carburettor as described in Section 10 and then carry out the various adjustments as described in Sections 11 and 14.

DVG 4A1 carburettor

24 Remove the carburettor as described in Section 10.
25 Clean the exterior of the carburettor with paraffin and clear a space for putting the components in order as they are removed.
26 Disconnect the choke link from the operating arm by extracting the clip (photo).
27 Remove the top cover screws, disconnect the vacuum hose, and lift off the cover. Remove the gasket (photos).
28 Lift out the spring clip and remove the float together with the needle valve, noting that the needle is attached to the arm by a clip entered from the float side (photos).
29 Note the position of the inlet union pipe, then unscrew the bolt and remove it together with the filter (photo).
30 Note the location of all the jets then unscrew and remove them.
31 Remove the central screw and withdraw the Stage 1 air correction

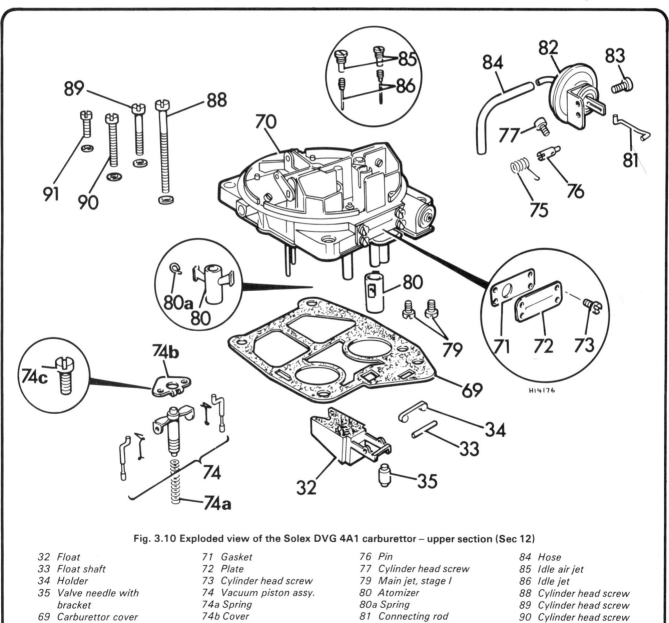

Fig. 3.10 Exploded view of the Solex DVG 4A1 carburettor – upper section (Sec 12)

32 Float	71 Gasket	76 Pin	84 Hose
33 Float shaft	72 Plate	77 Cylinder head screw	85 Idle air jet
34 Holder	73 Cylinder head screw	79 Main jet, stage I	86 Idle jet
35 Valve needle with bracket	74 Vacuum piston assy.	80 Atomizer	88 Cylinder head screw
69 Carburettor cover gasket	74a Spring	80a Spring	89 Cylinder head screw
	74b Cover	81 Connecting rod	90 Cylinder head screw
70 Carburettor cover	74c Cylinder head screw	82 Damper	91 Cylinder head screw
	75 Spring	83 Cylinder head screw	

jet needles with the holder, piston and spring.

32 Extract the clip and remove the pivot pin, lever, and Stage 2 air correction jet needles.

33 Disconnect the hose from the starter unit, then remove the screws and withdraw the unit and gasket.

34 Unscrew and remove the accelerator pump cover screws and remove the cover, diaphragm, spring, and cap (photo). Disconnect the pull rod from the lever.

35 If necessary dismantle the automatic choke with reference to Section 14.

36 Clean all the components and check them for wear. Use an air line to clear all the internal passages of sediment. Obtain a repair kit of gaskets.

37 Reassembly is a reversal of dismantling, but several adjustments must be made as described in the following paragraphs.

38 To test the starter unit run water at a temperature of 22°C (72°F) through the unit and check that the gap as shown in Fig. 3.12 is between 2.0 and 2.2 mm (0.079 and 0.087 in). If not, adjust the end screw as necessary.

39 Before fully assembling the Stage 2 air correction jet needles,

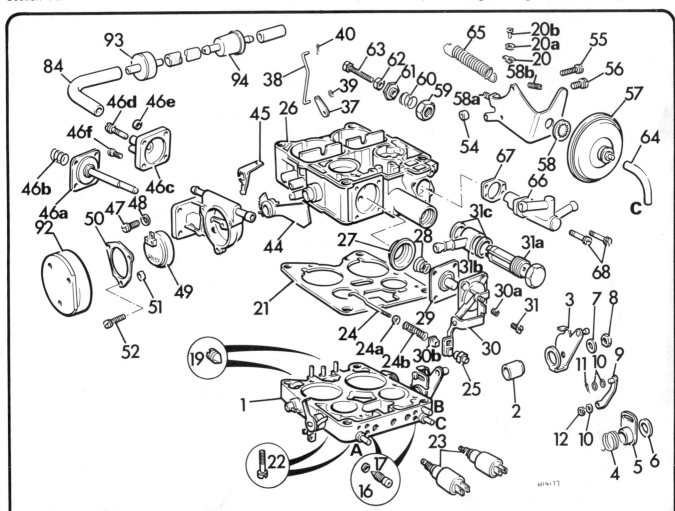

Fig. 3.11 Exploded view of the Solex DVG 4A1 carburettor – lower section (Sec 12)

1 Throttle housing	22 Cylinder head screw	40 Spring lock	57 Vacuum control
2 Bushing	23 Cut-off valve	44 Stepped disc	58 Lockwasher
3 Lever	24 Pump linkage assy	45 Lever	58a Holder
4 Spring	25 Nut	46a Diaphragm spring	58b Stud
5 Lever	26 Float housing	46b Spring	59 Hexagon nut
6 Washer	27 Cap	46c Valve cover	60 Spring
7 Lockwasher	28 Spring	46d Adjusting screw	61 Collared nut
8 Hexagon nut	29 Diaphragm spring assy.	46e O-ring	62 Hexagon nut
9 Connecting rod	30 Pump cover assy.	46f Cylinder head screw	63 Hexagonal head screw
10 Washer	30a Stud	47 Cylinder head screw	64 Hose
11 Spring lock	30b Guide sleeve	48 Washer	65 Spring
12 Lockwasher	31 Cylinder head screw	49 Choke cover no. 80	66 TM starter unit
16 Control screw	31a Fuel filter	50 Holder	67 Gasket
17 O-ring	31b Ring hose connector	51 Spacer	68 Cylinder head screw
19 Control screw	31c Seal	52 Hexagonal head screw	92 Guard
20 Flat male plug	37 Lever	54 Spacer	93 Pulldown delayer
20a Washer	38 Connecting rod	55 Cylinder head screw	94 Expansion tank
20b Cylinder head screw	39 Clamping ring	56 Cylinder head screw	
21 Insulating flange			

12.26 Disconnecting the choke link (Solex DVG 4A1)

12.27A Remove the cover screws ...

12.27B ... and lift off the cover ...

12.27C ... and gasket

12.27D View of the top cover lower face (Solex DVG 4A1)

12.28A Lift out the spring clip ...

12.28B ... and remove the float

12.29 Removing the inlet union and filter (Solex DVG 4A1)

12.34 Accelerator pump location on the Solex DVG 4A1

Fig. 3.12 Starter unit adjustment dimension (A) on the Solex DVG 4A1 carburettor (Sec 12)

1 Piston	3 Adjusting screw
2 Housing	

insert the needles only in their respective jets and measure the dimension A shown in Fig. 3.13. To this dimension add 3.2 mm (0.126 in) for 525 models, and 2.9 mm (0.114 in) for 528 models. After assembling the lever check that dimension B shown in Fig. 3.14 is of the revised amount. If not, bend the lever as necessary.

40 With the accelerator pump assembled, operate the throttle lever and check that fuel is ejected into both venturis. Adjust the throttle idle speed screw to provide a gap of 2.5 mm (0.098 in) then check that the accelerator pump lever is just making contact with the diaphragm piston. If necessary adjust the pull rod nuts to correct.

---

13 Fuel idle cut-off valve – testing, removal and refitting

1 The idle cut-off valve is located in the side of the carburettor, and its function is to stop the flow of fuel as soon as the ignition is switched off. Two are fitted to the DVG 4A1 carburettor (photo).

2 To test the valve operation disconnect the wiring connection, at the valve, with the engine running. If the valve is functioning correctly the engine will run slower or unevenly. On reconnecting the wire a single quiet 'clicking' sound should be heard.

3 To remove the valve, unscrew it from the carburettor body, after having disconnected the supply lead.

4 Before refitting the valve, make sure the tapered sealing face is in good condition, and then screw the valve into the carburettor body.

5 Tighten the valve to the specified torque wrench setting – be careful not to tighten it above this setting.

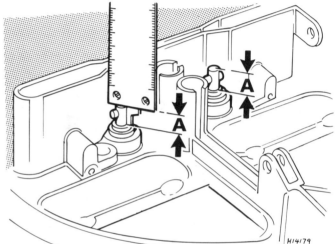

Fig. 3.13 Stage 2 air correction jet needle initial dimension (A) on the Solex DVG 4A1 carburettor (Sec 12)

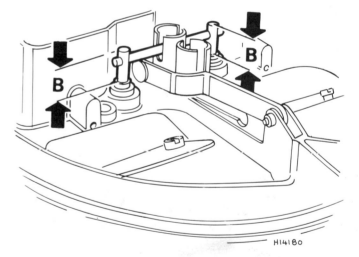

Fig. 3.14 Stage 2 air correction jet needle final dimension (B) on the Solex DVG 4A1 carburettor (Sec 12)

---

14 Automatic choke – adjustment and testing

INAT carburettor
Fast idle speed

1 Adjust the idling speed as described in Section 11.

2 With the air cleaner removed and the engine stopped disconnect

13.1 The fuel idle cut-off valves (Solex DVG 4A1)

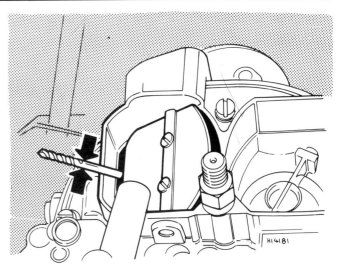

Fig. 3.15 Setting the choke valve during the fast idle adjustment on the INAT carburettor (Sec 14)

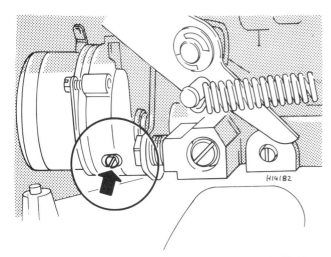

Fig. 3.16 Fast idle adjustment screw location on the INAT carburettor (Sec 14)

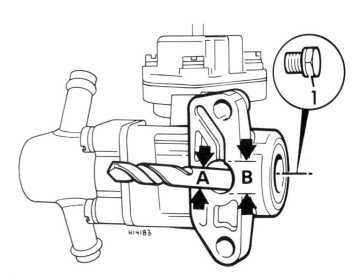

Fig. 3.17 TM starter circuit gap adjustment (Sec 14)

1   Endplug
A = 4.4 mm (0.173 in) if B = 9.0 mm (0.354 in)
A = 3.1 mm (0.122 in) if B = 6.4 mm (0.252 in)

the throttle linkage from both carburettors.

3   Open the throttle on one carburettor and then manually close the choke valve so that the lower edge of the valve is 3.0 mm (0.118 in) from the carburettor wall. Use a twist dwell to check the gap (Fig. 3.15). Release the throttle then the choke valve.

4   Start the engine and let it idle. The idle speed should be 1400 rpm. If not, stop the engine, open the throttle, and turn the adjustment screw at the bottom of the choke housing (Fig. 3.16) as necessary noting that one turn clockwise will increase the engine speed by approximately 300 rpm.

5   Finally open the throttle with the engine stopped to release the choke fast idle cam.

6   Repeat the procedure given in paragraphs 3 to 5 on the remaining carburettor then check the combined fast idle speed as follows. Connect the throttle linkage and open both throttles. Position both choke valves as described in paragraph 3 and release the throttle linkage then choke valves. Start the engine without touching the accelerator pedal and check that the fast idle speed is now as given in the Specifications.

Choke valve preload

7   The notch in the automatic choke cover should normally be aligned with the mark on the body. If, however, difficult starting from cold is experienced, the starting mixture can be enriched by progressively turning the covers in an anticlockwise direction to a maximum of 90° from the mark on the body. It will be necessary to loosen the clamp screws to do this.

TM starter unit

8   With the air cleaner removed, set the starter unit mixture by tightening the upper screw, then loosening it two and a half turns.

9   To adjust the cut-out point of the starter unit, remove it from the carburettor and take off the expander and housing. Remove the end plug, then heat the unit to 20°C (68°F) in water. Using a twist drill check the gap as shown in Fig. 3.17 and if necessary adjust it with the screw located in the piston.

Choke connecting rod

10   With the choke cover removed, turn the operating lever fully anti-clockwise so that the choke valve is completely shut. The distance A in Fig. 3.18 should be between 0.2 and 0.5 mm (0.008 and 0.020 in). If not, loosen the clamp screw on the top of the connecting rod (plug removed) and reposition the rod as necessary. Make sure that the spring clip contacts the clamp.

Choke opening

11   With the choke cover removed, press the vacuum opening rod fully upward. The bottom edge of the choke valve should now be 2.3 to 2.5 mm (0.091 to 0.098 in) from the carburettor wall. If not, loosen the locknut and adjust the stop screw in the top of the pull down unit.

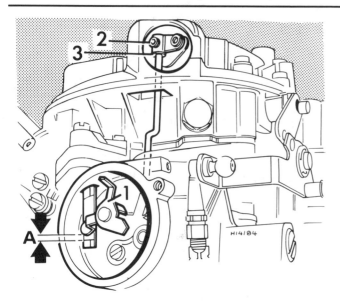

Fig. 3.18 Choke connecting rod adjustment A on the INAT carburettor (Sec 14)

1	Operating lever	3 Spring clip
2	Clamp screw	

Thermo switch (air)

12 This switch, located in the air cleaner body, controls the automatic choke heating elements. At an ambient temperature above 14°C (57°F) the switch must be on, but below this temperature it must be off.

DVG 4A1 carburettor

Thermo switch (coolant)

13 This switch, located on the underside of the inlet manifold, controls the automatic choke heating element (photo). It can be tested by immersing it in water – at temperatures above 17°C (63°F) the switch must be on.

Choke pull-down

14 Adjust the idling speed as described in Section 11.

15 With the engine stopped and the air cleaner removed, check that the choke valves can be moved freely without any indication of seizure.

16 Adjust the throttle positioner vacuum capsule bolt away from the throttle lever so that the lever contacts the idle adjustment screw (photo).

17 With the choke cover removed, hold the vacuum opening rod fully to the right, then turn the choke operating lever anti-clockwise. Using a twist drill check that the gap between the lower edge of the choke valves and the carburettor wall is 3.2 mm (0.126 in). If not, turn the adjustment screw located below the choke housing as necessary.

18 Open the throttle valves at least half way, and hold the vacuum opening rod fully to the left. Turn the choke operating lever anti-clockwise then use a twist drill to check that the gap between the lower edge of the choke valves and the carburettor wall is 4.2 mm (0.165 in). If not, turn the adjustment screw located in the end of the vacuum pull down housing as necessary (photo).

Throttle positioner

19 Unscrew the throttle positioner adjusting bolt until the gap between the throttle lever and idle adjusting screw is between 2.8 and 3.0 mm (0.110 and 0.118 in) then tighten the locknut (photo).

20 Check the length of the throttle positioner spring between the nuts – it should be 23 mm (0.905 in). If not, turn the large nut as necessary.

Pull-down delay valve

21 With the engine idling and air cleaner removed, disconnect the vacuum hose from the damper box (do not plug the hose) (photo).

22 Disconnect the hose at the pull-down unit and connect it to the

14.13 Thermo switch location on the inlet manifold

14.16 Throttle positioner (Solex DVG 4A1)

14.18 Choke vacuum pull-down housing (Solex DVG 4A1)

14.19 Showing throttle lever and throttle positioner adjustment bolt (Solex DVG 4A1)

14.21 Secondary choke damper box (Solex DVG 4A1)

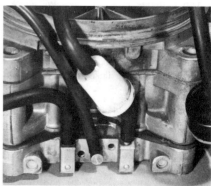

14.22 Choke pull down delay valve and vacuum hose (Solex DVG 4A1)

14.23 Automatic choke cover alignment mark location on the Solex DVG 4A1

damper box. The damper box plunger must move to the final stop and reach it within 14 seconds. If the hose is connected without the delay valve, the plunger must return immediately. When completed reconnect the hoses in their correct positions (photo).

Choke valve preload
23 The notch on the automatic choke cover must always be aligned with the mark on the body (photo).

15 Thermo valves (INAT carburettors) – general

1 A thermo valve is located to the rear of the thermostat housing and controls vacuum from the inlet manifold to the distributor vacuum advance capsule. At coolant temperatures up to 20°C (68°F) the valve is open and full vacuum is channelled to the vacuum advance capsule to supplement vacuum from the carburettor vacuum post under closed throttle conditions. Above 20°C (68°F) the valve is closed and vacuum advance is only channelled from the carburettor post.
2 The valve can be checked by removing it after partially draining the cooling system, and attempting to blow through it while heating it in water.
3 A thermo time valve is located on the carburettor and controls the vacuum to the throttle positioner and TM starter. It is operated by an electric heating coil energised when the ignition is switched on. At ambient temperatures above 20°C (68°F) the valve is open and channels vacuum from the inlet manifold to the throttle positioner and TM starter. Below 20°C (68°F) the valve will open approximately 15 seconds after the ignition has been switched on, during which time the engine will have been started.

16 L-Jetronic fuel injection system – general description

The Bosch L-Jetronic fuel injection system may be fitted to 528 models and is standard for 530 models. The essential features of the system are described below.

Fuel supply
An electric pump supplies fuel from the fuel tank to the injectors. A pressure regulator controlled by inlet manifold vacuum maintains the pressure of the fuel in constant relation to the inlet manifold vacuum so that the volume of fuel delivered by the injectors depends only on their period of opening.

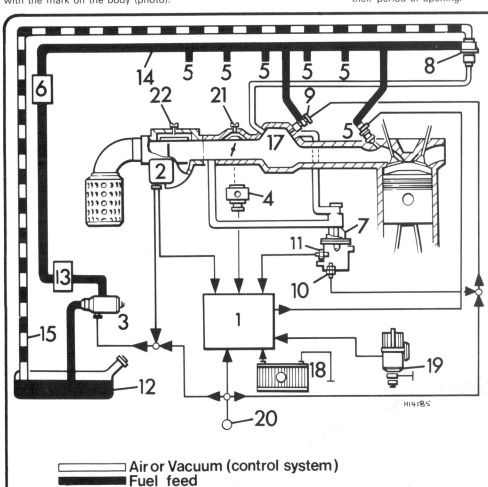

Air or Vacuum (control system)
Fuel feed
Fuel return

Fig. 3.19 Diagram of the L-Jetronic fuel injection system (Sec 16)

1 Control unit
2 Airflow meter
3 Electric fuel pump
4 Throttle butterfly switch
5 Injectors
6 Fuel filter
7 Additional air valve
8 Fuel pressure regulator
9 Cold-start valve
10 Heat-sensitive time switch
11 Coolant temperature sensor
12 Fuel tank
13 Expansion tank
14 Fuel distribution line
15 Fuel return line
16 Air cleaner
17 Air collector
18 Battery
19 Distributor (transistorized coil ignition)
20 Ignition/starter switch
21 Idle air screw
22 Recirculating air screw

Injector operating period

All the injectors are wired in parallel and operate once every crankshaft revolution, this being possible as the injectors are located in the inlet manifold. The injectors are controlled by an electronic control unit which is provided with an electrical impulse from an air flow meter and potentiometer located in the induction system.

Cold start

The control unit is provided with additional electrical information which it computes for cold start and warm-up conditions. Coolant temperature sensors, a heat sensitive time switch, and a throttle butterfly switch are utilised and the control unit also considers whether the starter motor is working. When additional fuel is being supplied to the engine, the extra air necessary for combustion is provided by an additional air slide valve.

17 System fuel pressure (L-Jetronic) – checking

1 Connect a suitable pressure gauge between the fuel rail and the cold start injector.
2 Disconnect the multi-plug at the air flow sensor.
3 Using a short length of wire, bridge connections 36 and 39 in the plug. (For connector identification, see Chapter 13, Fig. 13.14.)
4 Switch on the ignition; a soft click confirms that the fuel pump relay is in order, a soft humming indicates that the fuel pump is running.
5 If the pressure is low even though the pump is running, the fault may lie in the pump or in the fuel pressure regulator. A clogged fuel filter can also cause low pressure. Consult a BMW dealer or fuel injection specialist.

18 Air flow sensor (L-Jetronic) – testing, removal and refitting

1 The intake air flow sensor can only be tested by a BMW dealer equipped with special test apparatus.
2 To remove the air flow sensor first pull the multi-plug connector.
3 Loosen the hose clip and release the air cleaner quick-lock fasteners.
4 Lift away the air flow sensor and air cleaner assembly.
5 Remove the securing nuts and bolts and separate the air flow sensor from the air cleaner assembly.
6 The intake air temperature sensor is a permanent part of the air flow sensor unit and cannot be replaced separately.
7 Refitting is a reverse of the removal procedure.

19 Cold start valve, temperature time switch and cold start relay (L-Jetronic) – testing, removal and refitting

Cold start valve
1 Remove the nuts securing the cold start valve and lift the cold start valve away from the manifold.
2 Disconnect the multi-plug at the air flow sensor and connect terminals 36 and 39 together at the plug.
3 Carefully pull out the cold start relay plugs and connect a live feed to terminal 87.
4 Switch on the ignition; the cold start valve should eject fuel. If not, the relay wiring may be faulty.
5 Refit the components in the reverse order to removal.

Temperature time switch
6 Carefully pull out the cold start relay plugs and connect an ohmmeter between wire 46 and earth. The ohmmeter should read between 40 and 70 ohms.
7 Now connect the ohmmeter between terminal 85 or 86c as applicable (connection W on temperature time switch) and earth. Also connect a live feed to terminal 86 (connection G on temperature time switch).
8 The reading on the ohmmeter is proportional to the temperature above 15°C (59°F).
9 The reading must be zero for a certain time at temperatures below 15°C (59°F). This time varies from zero at 15°C (59°F) to 8 seconds at -20°C (-4°F).
10 If the above readings are not obtained then the temperature time switch must be renewed.

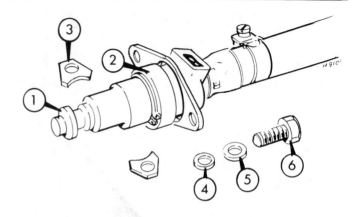

Fig. 3.20 Fuel injector components (Sec 20)

1	*Rubber ring*	*4*	*Insulator*
2	*Rubber ring*	*5*	*Washer*
3	*Shell flange*	*6*	*Retaining bolt*

11 Renewal of the temperature time switch entails draining of the cooling system.

Cold start relay
12 Carefully pull out the cold start relay and disconnect the wiring plugs.
13 Connect a live feed to the (central) terminal 30 and terminal 86C.
14 Connect terminal 85 to earth.
15 Using a test lamp, with one lead connected to a good earthing point, test if there is power at terminals 87 or 86. Failure of the test lamp bulb to illuminate will indicate a faulty cold start relay.

20 Injectors (L-Jetronic) – removal and refitting

1 Remove the intake manifold with reference to Section 24.
2 Disconnect the wiring plugs.
3 Remove the fuel distribution line by loosening the hose clips and unscrewing the union nuts.
4 Unscrew the mounting bolts and remove the injectors noting the location of the washers, insulators, and sealing rings.
5 Cut the crimped clip and pull the hose from the distribution line. If necessary burn off the hose using a soldering iron. Obtain a new screw-type clip.
6 Refitting is a reversal of removal, but renew the sealing rings if necessary and note that the collar on the ring faces the injector.

21 Control unit (L-Jetronic) – removal and refitting

1 Open the glovebox and push back the cover to expose the control unit.
2 Depress the spring clip tab, then extract the multi-plug.
3 Unbolt and remove the control unit.
4 Refitting is a reversal of removal, but when completed, adjust the engine idling speed as described in Section 23.

22 Throttle housing (L-Jetronic) – removal and refitting

1 Remove the air cleaner assembly as described in Section 2, and disconnect the bellows.
2 On the coil return spring version, disconnect the multi-plug, and disconnect all the hoses after identifying them for position. Unscrew the nuts and withdraw the throttle housing and gasket, however it will be necessary to either remove the lower stud or remove the engine valve cover.
3 On the torsion spring version remove the engine valve cover and disconnect the throttle linkage (and detent cable on automatic

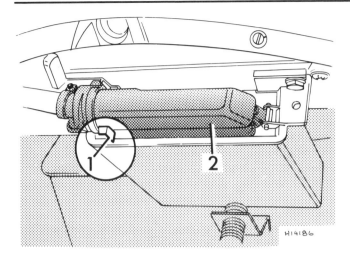

Fig. 3.21 L-Jetronic control unit (Sec 21)

1 *Clip*

2 *Multiplug*

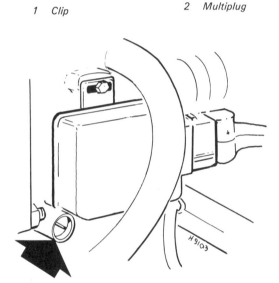

Fig. 3.22 Idling speed screw location on the L-Jetronic fuel injection system (Sec 23)

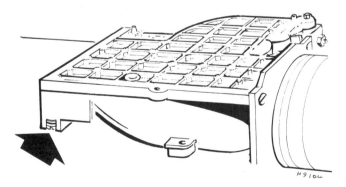

Fig. 3.23 Idle air control screw location on the air flow sensor (Sec 23)

transmission models). Disconnect all hoses after identifying them for position, and also disconnect the multi-plugs. Clamp the water hoses, then disconnect them from the throttle housing. Unscrew the nuts and withdraw the throttle housing and gasket.

4   Refitting is a reversal of removal, but when completed, adjust the engine idling speed as described in Section 23.

23 L-Jetronic fuel injection system – slow running adjustment

1   In order to carry out these adjustments accurately it is essential to have at your disposal an exhaust gas analyser (CO meter) and a tachometer.
2   First ensure that the ignition timing, contact breaker gap (where applicable), spark plugs, valve clearances and air cleaner element are either adjusted correctly or in good order. It is also essential that the engine has reached its normal operating temperature before commencing this operation.
3   Connect up the exhaust gas analyser and tachometer according to manufacturer's instructions.
4   On USA models disconnect the hose to the carbon filter, but do not plug it. Disconnect and plug the hose at the air pump.
5   Start the engine and adjust the idling speed screw to obtain the specified idling speed.
6   Having set the idle speed correctly, check the CO content which should be as specified. If the CO level is too low it could be due to one or a combination of the following faults:

> (a) *Leak in intake system (after the air flow sensor)*
> (b) *Defective auxiliary air valve*
> (c) *Fuel pressure regulator faulty*
> (d) *Fuel filter partially blocked*
> (e) *Incorrect fuel pump pressure*
> (f) *Faulty vacuum restriction valve*
> (g) *Defective control unit*
> (h) *Leak in EGR valve*
> (i) *Faulty vacuum control valve*

7   Should the CO level be too high it could be a fault with one or a combination of the following components:

> (a) *Oil dipstick seal in guide tube faulty*
> (b) *Too much engine oil in sump*
> (c) *Inlet or exhaust valves seating incorrectly*
> (d) *Defective air flow sensor*
> (e) *Cold starting device does not shut off*
> (f) *Fuel leakage from injection valves*

8   Having checked the above items and rectified any defect, the CO can be adjusted by turning the idle air control screw which is located under a plastic cap near the air flow sensor, or below the throttle housing.

24 Manifolds and exhaust system – general

1   Removal and refitting of the inlet and exhaust manifolds (photos) and the induction header assembly (fuel injection), is straightforward, but certain models will have coolant hose connections to the inlet manifold for the purpose of induction heating and car interior heating. Various electrical leads will need to be disconnected from their control switches and, in the case of carburettor engines, the complete air cleaner and carburettor(s) will have to be removed (photos).
2   Take particular note of the gaskets removed, as some of these should only be fitted a certain way round. They should always be fitted to clean dry surfaces (photos).
3   A sectional exhaust system is fitted, and incorporates a primary and secondary silencer (photos). It will be necessary to jack-up the car in order to remove either section of the exhaust system unless an inspection pit is available.
4   When fitting new components, use new flange gaskets and clamps. Do not tighten the clamps fully until the complete system is fitted and its suspended attitude checked for proximity to adjacent suspension and bodywork components (photo).
5   The exhaust suspension rubbers should be periodically checked for cuts and signs of perishing, and renewed if necessary (photos).
6   It is imperative that the exhaust mounting bracket at the rear of the transmission unit is assembled free of stresses, otherwise resonance can occur when the car is running. Assemble, the bracket with all bolts fingertight. Then with the exhaust system centralised, tighten the manifold flange connections followed by the transmission support bracket and the remaining clamps.

24.1A Removing a coolant hose from the inlet manifold

24.1B Removing the fuel return hose

24.1C Removing the inlet manifold

24.1D Remove the exhaust manifold heat shield bolt ...

24.1E ... and heat shield

24.1F Removing the exhaust manifold

24.2A Fitting a new inlet manifold gasket

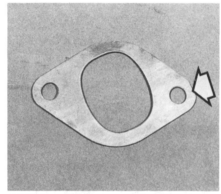

24.2B Note the flat (arrowed) on the exhaust manifold gasket

24.2C Fitting a new exhaust manifold gasket

24.3A Showing the exhaust pipe to manifold nuts

24.3B Exhaust pipe intermediate flanges

24.4 Using a special tool to crimp the vacuum hose to the inlet manifold

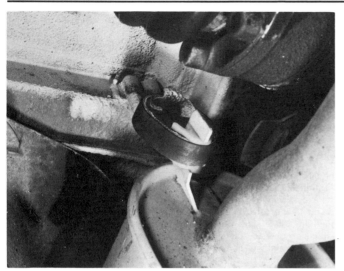

24.5A An intermediate exhaust mounting

24.5B Showing the rear exhaust mounting rubber O-rings

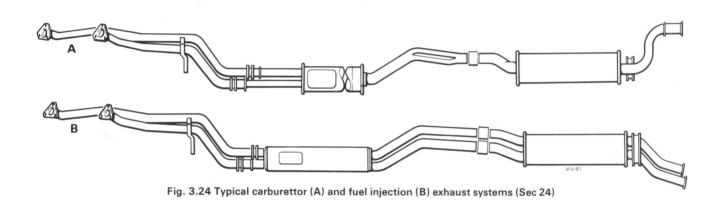

Fig. 3.24 Typical carburettor (A) and fuel injection (B) exhaust systems (Sec 24)

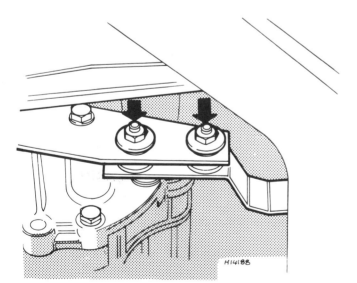

Fig. 3.25 Exhaust mounting bolts at the rear of the transmission
(Sec 24)

25 Emission control system – general

Both carburettor and fuel injection engines are fitted with one or more of the following emission control systems, the particular systems fitted depending on the regulations in force within the operating territory of the car.

   (a)   *Crankcase emission control system*
   (b)   *Exhaust emission control system with air pump*
   (c)   *Fuel evaporative emission control system*

Crankcase emission control system

1   A positive type system is installed whereby gases, which accumulate in the engine crankcase, are drawn out through the rocker cover and into the air cleaner. The gases are then drawn into the engine combustion chambers, where they are burned during the normal combustion cycle.

2   Maintenance consists only of checking the hoses for tightness and periodically removing them to clean out any residue which may have accumulated.

Exhaust emission control system

EGR (exhaust gas recirculation) system

3   This system recirculates a small quantity of exhaust gases into the combustion chamber during low engine loads; a larger amount is recirculated during high load and acceleration conditions. Circulation is rendered non-effective at wide throttle openings, at engine speeds over 3000 rpm and during idling. The reason for this is to ensure that maximum performance and smooth idling characteristics are maintained and at the same time the nitric oxide level in the exhaust gases is reduced.

EGR valve

4   The EGR valve in this system has two diaphragms and operates in two stages. When a vacuum is applied to the upper diaphragm it rises and in so doing partially lifts the valve disc which allows a small

quantity of exhaust gas to flow. A vacuum control valve which senses the absolute pressure in the inlet manifold controls the second stage of the EGR valve. When the second stage of the EGR valve is brought into action the valve disc is lifted fully away from its seating, thus allowing a completely unobstructed exhaust gas flow in the system.

Vacuum control valve

5   A vacuum control valve is incorporated in the system and senses the vacuum in the inlet manifold. When the inlet manifold vacuum is high the vacuum control valve shuts off the vacuum supply to the EGR valve. When the inlet manifold vacuum is low the control valve will open and allow the vacuum to operate the second stage of the EGR valve thus allowing full exhaust gas recirculation to take place.

Temperature and engine speed controlled vacuum solenoid

6   A temperature sensor, fitted into the water jacket of the inlet manifold, and an engine speed switch control a vacuum solenoid valve. When the engine coolant temperature is below 45°C (113°F), or if the engine speed is in excess of 3000 rpm, the solenoid valve will shut off the vacuum flow to the vacuum control valve and the EGR valve will not be permitted to operate. The reason for this arrangement is to maintain tractability of the car when the engine is cold and to maintain

the engine performance when the engine is running at speeds in excess of 3000 rpm.

Thermal reactor and air pump

7   Within the thermal reactor, conditions are created whereby the exhaust gases continue to burn, thus reducing the hydrocarbon and carbon monoxide content of the exhaust gases. An additional air supply to the reactor is necessary to create the burning and this is supplied by a belt-driven air pump. Some models additionally have a catalytic converter in the exhaust system.

Fuel evaporative emission control system

8   This system ensures that the fuel vapours from the fuel tank are initially collected in a liquid-vapour separator unit, and then passed through an activated charcoal canister. When the engine is running, the excess vapours are drawn from the activated charcoal canister via the air cleaner into the combustion chambers and burned in the normal manner. The liquid-vapour separator tank also allows for fuel expansion of a completely filled fuel tank.

9   The system is completely free from maintenance but it is recommended that periodically each individual component is examined and, if found to be defective, renewed.

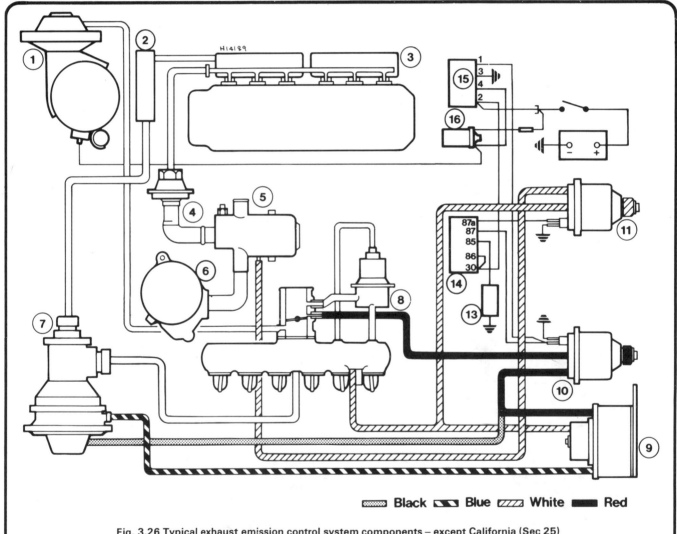

Black **Blue** **White** **Red**

Fig. 3.26 Typical exhaust emission control system components – except California (Sec 25)

1 Distributor	5 Blow-off valve	10-11 Electric control	14 Control relay
2 Cyclone exhaust gas	6 Air pump	valve	15 Speed switch
filter	7 EGR valve	13 Coolant temperature	16 Ignition coil
3 Reactor	8 Vacuum limiter	switch	
4 Check valve	9 Vacuum control valve		

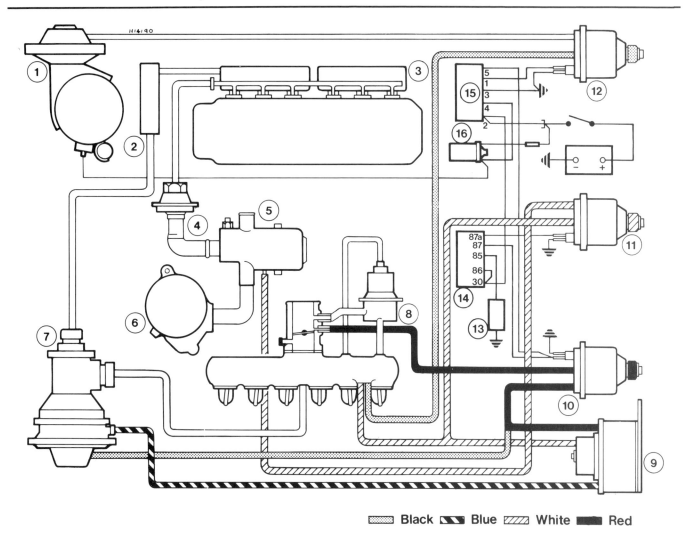

H14190

Black ▧ Blue ▨ White ▬ Red

Fig. 3.27 Typical exhaust emission control system components – California (Sec 25)

1   Distributor
2   Cyclone exhaust gas filter
3   Reactor
4   Check valve
5   Blow-off valve
6   Air pump
7   EGR valve
8   Vacuum limiter
9   Vacuum control valve
10-12 Electric control valve
13   Coolant temperature switch
14   Control relay
15   Speed switch
16   Ignition coil

26 Exhaust emission control system – testing

EGR system – leak test

1   Sprinkle water onto the various connections and joints between the EGR valve and the inlet manifold with the engine running. If a leak exists and water gets into the system the engine idle speed will drop. The second part of the system between the EGR valve and the thermal reactor should be visually checked. If a visual inspection does not reveal the leak then it is advisable to remove the section between the EGR valve and the reactor and pressure check it using a compressed air supply. Very small leaks in this section do not have any effect on the emissions or the engine performance.

EGR valve – first stage test

2   Using a length of hose connect the first stage of the EGR valve to an inlet manifold vacuum supply with the engine idling. When the valve is connected the engine idling speed should drop noticeably. If the engine speed does not decrease, examine the connections and then blow into the valve whilst blocking the second stage connection with your finger. A leakage will indicate that the metal casing of the valve is damaged. If this simple test still fails to indicate the source of leakage then it is best to renew the EGR valve.

EGR valve – second stage test

3   Disconnect the second stage vacuum hose at the control valve and connect it to a convenient vacuum supply point on the inlet manifold with the engine running. The effect of connecting the system in this way should cause the engine idling speed to drop causing rough running. If this does not occur then it will be necessary to check the valve for a vacuum leakage. If the valve is leaking renew it.

EGR line and filter

4   Should the EGR valve be working correctly but a fall in the engine speed does not occur, then it will be necessary to clean all the EGR system lines. If a great deal of foreign matter is found then the EGR filter is probably blocked and will need renewal.

Testing vacuum control valve

5   Start the engine and allow it to idle with all the hoses connected properly. Now pull off the red vacuum hose at the throttle housing and connect it to a convenient vacuum source in the inlet manifold. Pull off the hose from the first stage of the EGR valve and plug the end of this hose; the engine speed should not fall. Now remove the hose from the second stage of the valve and feel if there is a vacuum at the end of this hose. If a vacuum is present then it is an indication that the control valve is leaking and will therefore need renewing. Now reconnect the

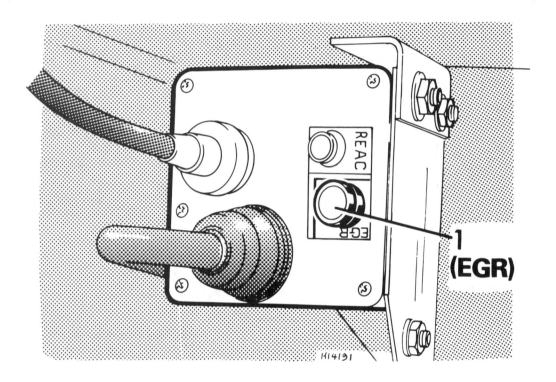

Fig. 3.28 Exhaust emission control system mileage interval switch showing the EGR
reset button (1) (Sec 27)

red vacuum hose to the throttle housing and with the engine still idling disconnect the vacuum hose from the second stage. Check that this hose is not blocked by blowing through by mouth and not compressed air. If the valve still fails to operate then it will have to be renewed.

Testing vacuum solenoid valve
6   Pull off the pipes to the valve; when de-activated it should be possible to blow through it. Now connect a 12 volt supply to the solenoid; the valve should close. Renew if faulty.

Testing coolant temperature switch
7   With the engine coolant temperature below 45°C (113°F) and the engine stopped, switch on the ignition. Pull off the wiring plug at the solenoid valve and connect a 12 volt test lamp. The test lamp bulb should illuminate. Start the engine and allow it to warm up until the coolant temperature is in excess of 45°C (113°F). Repeat the test above, this time the test lamp bulb will not illuminate. Failure of the test lamp to illuminate or not as described above will indicate either a faulty temperature switch or relay.

Testing speed switch
8   With the engine running and at normal operating temperature disconnect the wiring plug at the solenoid valve. Connect a 12 volt test lamp between the disconnected plug and a convenient earthing point. The test lamp should be illuminated at engine speeds in excess of 3000 rpm. If this is not so the speed switch is faulty and should be renewed.

27 Exhaust emission control system – maintenance

Thermal reactor
1   At 25 000 mile (40 000 km) intervals a dashboard warning light will illuminate thus indicating that the thermal reactor should be

removed and inspected for signs of cracks or other damage. After refitting or renewing the thermal reactor it will be necessary for the mileage interval switch to be reset.

EGR system
2   At intervals of 25 000 miles (40 000 km) an EGR service warning light will illuminate on the dashboard indicating that the cyclone filter of the EGR system is due for renewal. After renewing the filter the mileage interval switch will need to be reset.

Mileage interval resetting
3   This switch is connected to the speedometer drive assembly on the left-hand side of the engine compartment. Within the switch assembly are two contacts one marked 'Reac' and the other 'EGR'. Press the correct contact inwards with a pin to extinguish the warning lamp and to reset the mileage recorder.

Air pump drivebelt
4   Periodically inspect the air pump drivebelt; if there are any signs of the belt fabric splitting or deteriorating, renew the belt. It is also necessary to check the drivebelt tension at a point midway between the longest belt run. When correctly tensioned the drivebelt will deflect between 0.2 and 0.4 in (5 and 10 mm) under an applied pressure of 22 lbf (10 kgf).

Oxygen sensor (where applicable)
5   At intervals of 25 000 miles (40 000 km) a dashboard warning light will illuminate indicating that the oxygen sensor should be renewed. To do this, disconnect the wiring then unscrew and remove the sensor.
6   Apply copper paste to the threads of the new sensor then fit it using a reversal of the removal procedure. Depress the interval reset button to extinguish the warning light.

28 Fault diagnosis – fuel, exhaust and emission control systems

Symptom	Reason(s)
General	
Excessive fuel consumption	Air cleaner chokes
	Incorrectly adjusted fuel mixture
	Leakage from pump, tank or fuel lines
	Incorrect valve clearances
	Faulty or incorrectly adjusted ignition components
	Tyres under-inflated
	Binding brakes
Insufficient fuel delivery or weak mixture	Fuel tank vent pipe blocked
	Incorrectly adjusted fuel mixture
	Clogged fuel line filter
	Inlet manifold gaskets leaking
Carburettor models	
Excessive fuel consumption	Float chamber flooding (incorrect fuel level or badly seating needle valve or valve body loose in carburettor cover)
	Mixture too rich
	Automatic choke mechanism faulty or incorrectly adjusted
Weak mixture or insufficient fuel delivery	Incorrectly adjusted carburettor
	Fuel pump lid or pipe connections loose
	Fuel pump diaphragm split
	Faulty fuel pump valves
	Fuel inlet needle valve clogged or stuck
Difficult starting, uneven running, lack of power, cutting out	One or more jets blocked or restricted
	Fuel pump not delivering sufficient fuel
	Carburettors out of balance (where applicable)
Fuel injection models	
Engine will not start	Fuel tank empty
	Fuel pump or wiring defective
	Defective cold start relay, cold start valve or temperature time switch
	Defective pressure regulator
	Auxiliary air valve closed
Poor cold starting	Defective cold start relay, cold start valve, temperature time switch
	Auxiliary air valve closed
Engine starts but does not run properly	Air flow sensor multi-plug disconnected
	Defective pump contact
	Disconnected or split hoses
	CO exhaust content incorrect
	Coolant temperature sensor defective
Hot start difficulties	Vacuum line to pressure regulator, or pressure regulator itself defective
	Faulty cold start relay or temperature time switch
Knocking noise after cold start	Fuel line resonating (no fault)

Chapter 4 Ignition system

For modifications, and information applicable to later models, see Supplement at end of manual

Contents

Specifications

System type

Except 528i	12 volt battery, coil, and distributor with conventional contact breaker points
528i	12 volt battery, coil, and breakerless distributor with pulse sensor and transistorized control unit

Coil

Type	Bosch
Primary coil resistance:	
Except 528i	1.7 to 2.1 ohm
528i	0.4 ohm

Distributor

Except 528i

Type	Bosch
Rotor rotation	Clockwise
Rotor governor cut-off speed (UK)	6450 to 6750 engine rpm
Condenser capacity	0.18 to 0.22 mfd
Dwell angle	35° to 41°
Dwell percentage	58% to 68%
Contact breaker gap:	
Standard distributor	0.35 mm (0.014 in)
Distributor part no 169 007	0.4 mm (0.016 in)

528i

Type	Bosch
Rotor rotation	Clockwise
Rotor governor cut-off speed (UK)	6450 to 6750 engine rpm
Dwell angle (and percentage):	
UK:	
1500 rpm	47° (78%)
4500 rpm	50° (83%)
USA:	
1500 rpm	32° to 52° (53 to 87%)
4500 rpm	47° to 57° (78 to 95%)
Pulse transmitter rotor air gap	0.35 to 0.70 mm (0.014 to 0.028 in)

Spark plugs

UK

	Type	Gap
Pre-1977 models	Beru 175/14/3A	0.6 mm (0.024 in)
	Bosch W175T30	0.65 mm (0.025 in)
	Champion N10Y	0.6 mm (0.024 in)
1977-on models except 528i	Beru 145/14/3A	0.6 mm (0.024 in)
	Bosch W145T30	0.65 mm (0.025 in)
	Champion N10Y	0.6 mm (0.024 in)
1977-on 528i models	Beru 175/14/3A	0.6 mm (0.024 in)
	Bosch W175T30	0.65 mm (0.025 in)
	Champion N10Y	0.6 mm (0.024 in)

USA

	Type	Gap
528i models	Bosch W125T30	0.7 mm (0.027 in)
530i models	Bosch W145T30	0.65 mm (0.025 in)
	Champion N10Y	0.6 mm (0.024 in)

Firing order 1–5–3–6–2–4

Ignition timing

Static (reference only)

UK models	TDC
USA models (except California)	15° BTDC
Californian models	12° BTDC

Dynamic (with vacuum disconnected)

UK models:

Distributor no 0231309006 (ie engine with Solex 4A1 carburettor)	22° BTDC at 1500 rpm
All models with Zenith 1NAT carburettor	22° BTDC at 1700 rpm
528i models	22° BTDC at 1800 rpm

USA models:

528i models	22° BTDC at 2100 rpm
530i models (except California)	22° BTDC at 1700 rpm
530i models (California)	22° BTDC at 2700 rpm

Torque wrench settings

	lbf ft	Nm
Spark plugs	20	28

---

1 General description

A conventional ignition system is fitted to 525, 528 and 530i models, and a transistorized ignition system is fitted to 528i models. Both systems employ a battery, coil, and spark plugs, but on the conventional system the distributor incorporates contact breaker points whereas on the transistorized system it incorporates a pulse sensor and transmitter. The transistorized system also incorporates an electronic control unit mounted in the right-hand side of the engine compartment. The distributor is driven by a gearshaft on the front of the camshaft.

The ignition system is based on feeding low tension (LT) voltage to the coil where it is converted to high tension (HT) voltage by means of the reaction between the primary and secondary windings. The high tension voltage is fed to the distributor cap and then via the rotor to the individual spark plugs where it discharges in the form of an HT spark. The timing of the HT spark is important for the engine to run correctly since it must ignite the fuel/air mixture in the combustion chambers at the correct instant.

The system functions in the following manner. Low tension voltage is changed in the coil to high tension voltage when switching the low tension (or primary) circuit on and off. In the conventional ignition system this is accomplished by the contact breaker points in the distributor, but in the transistorized system the pulse sensor and transmitter in the distributor send a signal to the electronic control unit which then switches the low tension circuit. The high tension voltage is then fed via the distributor cap and rotor to the indivudual spark plugs according to the position of the rotor. It is important to note that the HT spark occurs at the instant the primary circuit is broken (ie when the contact points open on the conventional system). The ignition is advanced and retarded automatically to ensure that the spark occurs at just the right instant for the particular lead at the prevailing engine speed. The distributor incorporates a centrifugal weight mechanism for advancing the ignition in relation to the engine speed. A vacuum diaphragm capsule attached to the distributor also controls the ignition advance or retard in relation to throttle position and inlet manifold vacuum.

The ignition primary circuit incorporates a resistance which is in circuit when the engine is running normally. However during starting the resistance is bypassed to provide increased voltage at the spark plugs in order to improve engine starting. On the conventional ignition system the resistance is in the form of a resistive wire, but on the transistorized system two separate resistors are employed and only one is bypassed during starting.

Where transistorized ignition is fitted always ensure that the ignition is switched off before working on the system, since the HT voltages are very high.

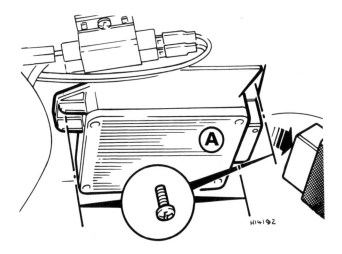

Fig. 4.1 The electronic control unit (A) for the transistorized ignition system – arrows indicate retaining screws (Sec 1)

---

2 Contact breaker points – checking and adjustment

1   Every 10 000 miles (15 000 km) on UK models, or 12 500 miles (20 000 km) on USA 530i models, the contact breaker points should be checked and adjusted. First release the two clips securing the distributor cap to the distributor body, and lift the cap away. Clean the cap inside and out with a dry cloth. It is unlikely that the six segments will be badly burned or scored, but if they are the cap will have to be renewed.

2   Inspect the carbon brush in the top of the distributor cap and press it into the recess to test the spring.

3   Check the condition of the rotor arm and renew it if the metal contacts are burned or if any cracks are evident.

4   Remove the contact breaker points protective cover (photo), and the movable point cover if fitted.

5   Prise the contact breaker points apart and examine the condition of their faces. If they are rough, pitted or dirty, it will be necessary to remove them for resurfacing, or for new points to be fitted.

6   Assuming that the points are satisfactory, or that they have been cleaned and refitted, measure the gap between the points by turning

2.4 Removing the contact breaker points protection cover

2.7A Slacken the contact plate securing screw ...

2.7B ... and adjust the gap using a screwdriver between the two 'pips'

3.3A Disconnecting the contact points low tension lead

3.3B Removing the contact breaker assembly

the engine crankshaft until the heel of the movable contact is on the high point of one of the cam lobes.

7   Using a feeler blade check that the gap between the two points is as given in the Specifications. If not, slacken the contact plate securing screw and insert the blade of a screwdriver between the two 'pips' on the contact set. Twist the screwdriver blade to either open or close the movable arm until the gap is correct. Tighten the securing screw (photos).

8   Although adjusting the contact points with a feeler gauge is reasonably accurate, it is recommended that the setting is always checked with a dwellmeter. This instrument measures the angle through which the distributor cam moves while the contact points are closed – the angle may also be expressed as a percentage of the total cam movement. Refer to the Specifications; if the dwell angle is too large the points gap should be increased, if it is too small reduce the gap.

9   Refit the distributor cap and protective covers as necessary, then check and if necessary adjust the ignition timing as described in Section 10. If the timing had previously been adjusted with correctly gapped points, no adjustment should be necessary now.

3   Contact breaker points – renewal

1   Prise away the clips, remove the distributor cap and place it to one side.
2   Remove the rotor arm, the protective cover, and where fitted the movable point cover.
3   Disconnect the low tension lead from the terminal inside the distributor body, then remove the retaining screw and withdraw the contact breaker assembly from th baseplate (photos).
4   Wipe clean the contact points baseplate and the cam, then apply one or two drops of clean engine oil to the felt pad in the cam recess and smear a little multi-purpose grease on the high points of the cam.
5   Before fitting the new points clean off the protective grease with

a fuel moistened cloth. Make sure that the movable contact moves freely on its pivot.
6   Fit the new contact points using a reversal of the removal procedure and adjust them as described in Section 2. Check and if necessary adjust the ignition timing as described in Section 10.

4   Condenser (conventional ignition) – testing, removal and refitting

1   The condenser (or capacitor) is fitted in parallel with the contact points and its purpose is to reduce arcing between the points and also to accelerate the collapse of the low tension coil winding magnetic field. A faulty condenser can cause the complete failure of the ignition system as the points will be prevented from interrupting the low tension circuit.
2   To test the condenser, remove the distributor cap, rotor arm, protective cover and where fitted the movable point cover, then rotate the engine until the points are closed. Switch on the ignition and, using an insulated screwdriver, separate the points. If this is accompanied by a strong blue flash, the condenser is faulty (a weak yellow spark is normal).
3   A further test can be made for short circuiting by removing the condenser and using a testlamp and leads connected in series with the condenser. If the testlamp lights, the condenser is faulty.
4   Probably the best test is to substitute a new unit and check whether the fault persists.
5   To remove the condenser, first remove the distributor cap, rotor arm, and protective cover.
6   Disconnect the contact points low tension lead from the terminal inside the distributor body and the main supply lead from the outer terminal.
7   Remove the condenser mounting screw, pull the connector grommet from the distributor body, and withdraw the condenser.
8   Refitting is a reversal of removal.

5 Pulse transmitter (transistorized ignition) – testing, removal and refitting

1 A voltmeter capable of accurately measuring 0.05 volt is necessary in order to test the pulse transmitter.
2 With the ignition switched off, disconnect the multi-plug located in the distributor to control unit wire loom.
3 Connect the voltmeter positive lead to terminal 7 in the multi-plug, and the negative lead to terminal 31d.
4 Operate the starter and check that a minimum of 0.05 volt registers on the voltmeter. If not, the pulse transmitter is faulty. Switch off the ignition.
5 To remove the pulse transmitter, first remove the distributor cap, rotor arm, and protective cover.
6 Remove the mounting screws, unhook the operating rod from the stator, and withdraw the vacuum control unit.
7 Remove the screw and pull the wire connector straight from the distributor.
8 Extract the circlip and expander ring, then lever off the rotor using two screwdrivers. The retaining dowel pin will come out at the same time. Remove the thrust washer.
9 Using an Allen key remove the three transmitter carrier plate retaining screws.
10 Extract the circlip. Remove the distributor cap retaining clips mounting screws, then lift out the carrier plate and pulse transmitter. Separate the transmitter from the carrier.
11 Refitting is a reversal of removal, but the transmitter terminals must be located as shown in Fig. 4.7, and the carrier must be turned fully anti-clockwise before reconnecting the vacuum control unit operating rod. Using a non-magnetic feeler blade check that the rotor to stator air gap is as given in the Specifications.

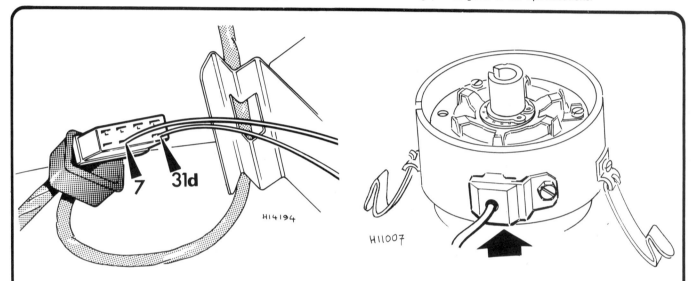

Fig. 4.2 Voltmeter connections for testing the pulse transmitter on the transistorized ignition (Sec 5)

Fig. 4.3 Wire connector location on the transistorized ignition distributor (Sec 5)

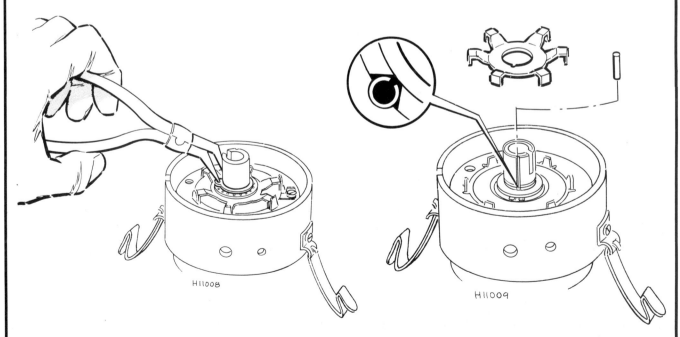

Fig. 4.4 Removing the circlip from the transistorized ignition distributor driveshaft (Sec 5)

Fig. 4.5 Showing rotor and retaining dowel pin on the transistorized ignition distributor (Sec 5)

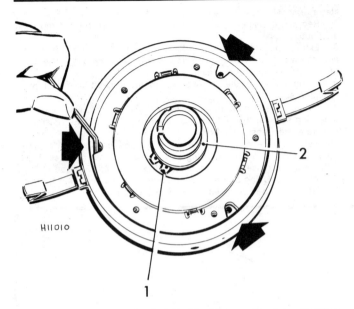

Fig. 4.6 Removing the transistorized ignition carrier plate retaining screws (arrowed) with an Allen key (Sec 5)

    1   Circlip   *2   Thrust washer*

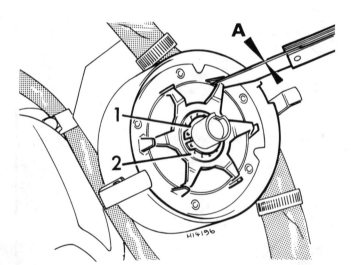

Fig. 4.8 Transistorized ignition rotor to stator air gap dimension A (Sec 5)

    1   Circlip   *2   Expander ring*

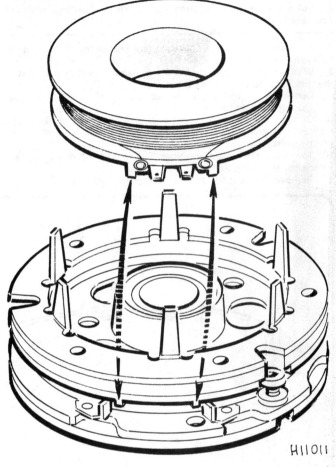

Fig. 4.7 Transistorized ignition transmitter and carrier plate alignment lugs – arrowed (Sec 5)

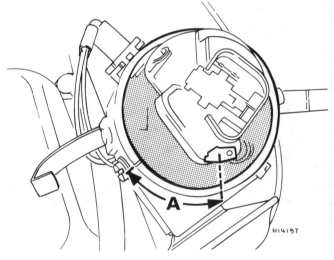

Fig. 4.9 Rotor arm movement A when removing the distributor (Sec 7)

6   Distributor cap and rotor arm (transistorized ignition) – checking

The procedue is described in Section 2, paragraphs 1 to 3, and it is recommended that it is carried out every 10 000 miles (15 000 km).

7   Distributor – removal and refitting

1   Disconnect the battery negative lead.
2   Remove the distributor cap, rotor arm, and protective cover, then refit the rotor arm. Removal of the cover will enable the notch in the distributor body to be seen.
3   Turn the engine in the normal running direction (clockwise from crankshaft pulley end) until the rotor arm approaches the notch in the distributor body rim, then continue turning the engine until the TDC (O/T) mark on the crankshaft pulley damper is in alignment with the timing lug on the front cover. The line on the rotor arm should now be aligned with the notch in the distributor body rim (photo). Use a spanner on the crankshaft pulley nut to turn the engine, or on manual transmission models engage top gear and pull the car forward.
4   Mark the distributor body in relation to the gear housing to ensure correct refitting.
5   Identify the vacuum hoses for position then disconnect them from the vacuum control unit (photos).

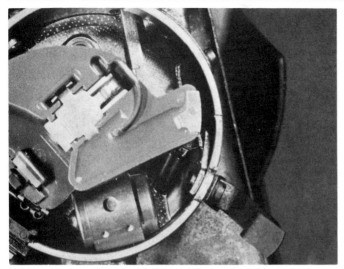

7.3 The rotor arm aligned with the notch in the distributor body rim

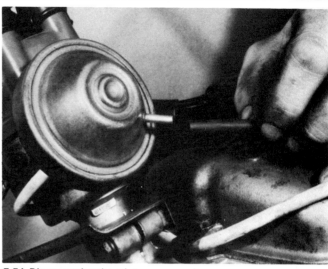

7.5A Disconnecting the advance vacuum hose

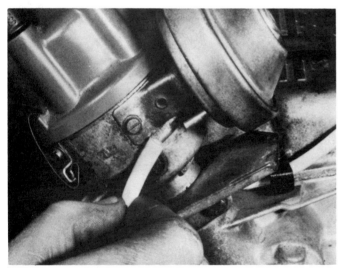

7.5B Disconnecting the retard vacuum hose

7.7A Removing the distributor

7.7B Removing the distributor clamp plate

6   Disconnect the wiring from the distributor (conventional ignition) or at the multi-plug (transistorized ignition).

7   Slacken the clamping bolt then pull the distributor straight out of its housing. As it is removed the rotor arm will turn anti-clockwise by approximately 35 mm (1.38 in). Remove the clamp plate if necessary (photos).

8   To refit the distributor, check that the rotor arm is in the position noted in paragraph 7 then, with the marks on the distributor body and gear housing aligned, push the distributor straight into position. As the drivegear engages, the rotor arm will turn clockwise, and when the distributor is fully entered, the line on the rotor will be aligned with the notch in the distributor body rim. If not, check that the TDC mark on the crankshaft pulley damper is still aligned with the lug on the front cover.

9   With all the marks aligned, tighten the clamping bolt.

10   Reconnect the wiring and vacuum hoses, refit the protective cover and distributor cap, and refit the battery negative lead.

11   Check and if necessary adjust the ignition timing as described in Section 10.

8   Distributor (conventional ignition) – overhaul

Note: *Always check that spares are available before starting work.*

Fig. 4.10 Levering the cam in order to extract the shaft jump ring (Sec 8)

Distributors are normally serviceable over very high mileages; when many of the components become excessively worn the complete distributor should be renewed.

1   Remove the contact breaker points and the condenser as described in Sections 3 and 4 respectively.

2   Extract the spring clip retaining the vacuum unit operating rod to the contact breaker base plate. Remove the screws and withdraw the vacuum unit from the distributor.

3   Remove the cap spring clips and retaining screws then withdraw the contact breaker base plate.

4   Leaving the felt pad in the cam recess, use two screwdrivers to lift the cam and force the jump ring out of its groove. If the pad is removed before this operation the jump ring may fly out. Do not fully remove the cam at this stage.

5   Grip the distributor drivegear and shoulder in a soft jawed vice and drill out the pin with a 3 mm (0.118 in) twist drill.

6   Remove the gear together with the thrust washer and insulator, then withdraw the shaft from the body also, together with the thrust washer and insulator.

7   Mark the cam in relation to the shaft, then disconnect the advance springs and separate the cam from the shaft together with the felt pad, circlip, and washer.

8   Extract the clips and remove the centrifugal weights.

9   Clean the components in a suitable solvent and examine them for wear and damage. In particular check that the holes in the centrifugal weights have not worn oval and also that the shaft bushes are not excessively worn. Renew the components as necessary and obtain a

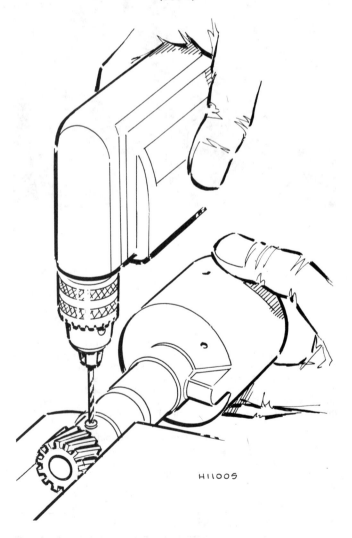

Fig. 4.11 Drilling out the distributor drivegear retaining pin (Sec 8)

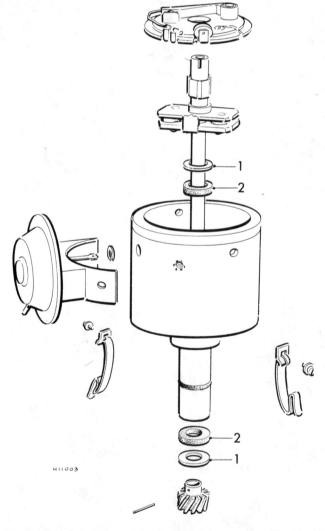

Fig. 4.12 Exploded view of the distributor (conventional ignition) (Sec 8)

1   Thrust washer   2   Insulator

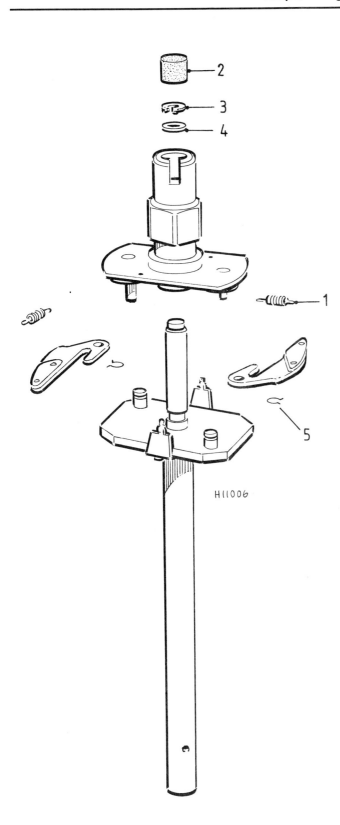

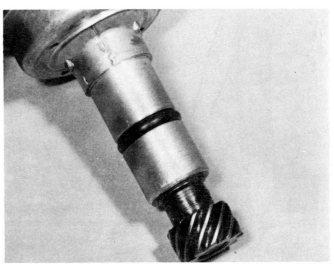

8.9 O-ring seal location on the distributor body

new pin for the drivegear. Note that if the springs or centrifugal weights are renewed it will be necessary to check the advance curve characteristics on a distributor test stand. Obtain a new rubber O-ring seal (photo).
10 Reassembly is a reversal of dismantling, but lubricate the centrifugal weight pivots and sliding surfaces with a little multi-purpose grease, and lubricate the cam bore and driveshaft with clean engine oil. Refer to Sections 3 and 4 as necessary.

9 Distributor (transistorized ignition) – overhaul

1   Refer to the preliminary note at the beginning of Section 8.
2   Remove the pulse transmitter as described in Section 5.
3   Remove the drivegear and shaft as described in Section 8.
4   Clean the distributor body, drivegear and shaft in a suitable solvent and examine them for damage. Renew the components as necessary.
5   Reassembly is a reversal of dismantling, but lubricate the driveshaft with clean engine oil. Refer to Section 5 for the refitting of the pulse transmitter.

10 Ignition timing – adjustment

Note: *There are two methods for timing the ignition, static and dynamic. The static method should be used for initial setting up in order to start the engine, but the dynamic method should always be used for final adjustment as it is the more accurate method. Some models are equipped with a TDC (top dead centre) sensor with a socket located at the front of the cylinder head, however the instrument for use with the system will not normally be available to the home mechanic. Where the contact breaker dwell angle is to be checked, always do this before adjusting the ignition timing.*

Static method
1   Remove the No 1 spark plug (nearest the radiator) and place the finger or palm of the hand over the aperture.
2   Turn the engine in the normal running direction (clockwise from the front) until pressure is felt in No 1 cylinder, indicating that the piston is commencing its compression stroke. Turn the engine with a spanner on the crankshaft pulley nut.
3   Continue to turn the engine until the TDC (O/T) mark on the crankshaft pulley damper is 29 mm (1.14 in) before the lug on the timing cover for engines with static timing of 15° BTDC, 23.2 mm (0.91 in) before the lug for engines with static timing of 12° BTDC, or aligned with the lug for engines with static timing of TDC.
4   Remove the distributor cap and check that the rotor arm is pointing in the direction of the No 1 terminal of the cap.
5   On models with conventional ignition remove the rotor arm and protective cover, then connect a 12 volt test lamp between the contact

Fig. 4.13 Exploded view of the distributor centrifugal mechanism (conventional ignition) (Sec 8)

1   Springs
2   Felt pad
3   Circlip
4   Washer
5   Clips

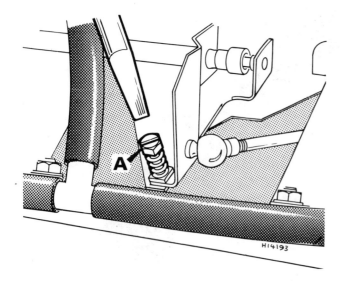

Fig. 4.14 Timing idle adjustment screw A (Sec 10)

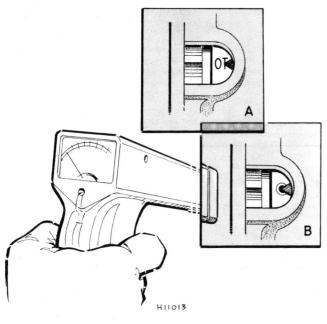

Fig. 4.15 Manual gearbox models flywheel timing marks (Sec 10)

A   TDC   B   Ball for ignition timing

point lead terminal and a suitable earthing point on the engine. Loosen the distributor clamp bolt and switch on the ignition. If the bulb is already lit turn the distributor body slightly clockwise until the bulb goes out. Now turn the distributor anti-clockwise until the bulb just lights up, indicating that the points have just opened. Tighten the clamp bolt, switch off the ignition, and remove the test lamp. Refit the cover and rotor arm.

6   On models with transistorized ignition remove the rotor arm and protective cover, and check that the rotor arms are aligned with the stator arms. If not, loosen the distributor clamp bolt, turn the distributor body as necessary, then tighten the bolt. Refit the cover and rotor arm.

7   On all models refit the distributor cap and No 1 spark plug and HT lead.

Dynamic method

8   Run the engine to operating temperature then stop the engine and connect a stroboscopic timing light and tachometer in accordance with the manufacturer's instructions.

9   Disconnect and plug the vacuum hose(s) at the distributor vacuum capsule.

10   At the left-hand rear of the engine there is an aperture in the transmission bellhousing (photo). A pointer will be seen in the aperture, wipe the pointer clean.

11   Start the engine and run it at the speed given in Specifications. On some models an independent adjusting screw is provided in the throttle linkage for this purpose, which does not disturb the idle setting screw.

12   Point the timing light at the aperture and check that the pointer is aligned with the centre of the ball in the flywheel (manual models), or with the long pin on the flywheel (automatic models), the short pin on automatic models indicates TDC (photo).

13   If adjustment is necessary, loosen the distributor clamp bolt and turn the body anti-clockwise to advance and clockwise to retard the ignition timing. Tighten the bolt when the setting is correct.

14   Return the engine to idling speed making sure that the adjusting screw (where fitted) is clear of the throttle linkage.

15   Gradually increase the engine speed while still pointing the timing light at the aperture – the flywheel and ball or pin (as applicable) will appear to move anti-clockwise, as viewed from the front of the engine, proving that the centrifugal weights are operating correctly.

16   Reconnect the vacuum hose(s) to the distributor vacuum capsule.

17   On models with a vacuum retard hose, temporarily increase the engine speed to 1000 rpm – the TDC mark must be visible in the timing aperture.

18   Switch off the engine and remove the timing light and tachometer.

11 Coil – description and testing

1   The coil is located on the right-hand side of the engine compartment (photo), and it should be periodically wiped down to prevent high tension (HT) voltage loss through possible arcing.

2   To ensure the correct HT polarity at the spark plugs, the LT coil leads must always be connected correctly. The LT lead from the distributor (conventional) or control unit (transistorized) should be connected to the negative terminal on the coil. The lead is black and

10.10 Ignition timing aperture (arrowed)

10.12 Long and short ignition timing pins on the flywheel of automatic transmission models

11.1 Ignition coil

Are your plugs trying to tell you something?

Normal.
Grey-brown deposits, lightly coated core nose. Plugs ideally suited to engine, and engine in good condition.

Heavy Deposits.
A build up of crusty deposits, light-grey sandy colour in appearance.
Fault: Often caused by worn valve guides, excessive use of upper cylinder lubricant, or idling for long periods.

Lead Glazing.
Plug insulator firing tip appears yellow or green/yellow and shiny in appearance.
Fault: Often caused by incorrect carburation, excessive idling followed by sharp acceleration. Also check ignition timing.

Carbon fouling.
Dry, black, sooty deposits.
Fault: over-rich fuel mixture. Check: carburettor mixture settings, float level, choke operation, air filter.

Oil fouling.
Wet, oily deposits. Fault: worn bores/piston rings or valve guides; sometimes occurs (temporarily) during running-in period.

Overheating.
Electrodes have glazed appearance, core nose very white – few deposits. Fault: plug overheating. Check: plug value, ignition timing, fuel octane rating (too low) and fuel mixture (too weak).

Electrode damage.
Electrodes burned away; core nose has burned, glazed appearance. Fault: pre-ignition. Check: for correct heat range and as for 'overheating'.

Split core nose.
(May appear initially as a crack). Fault: detonation or wrong gap-setting technique. Check: ignition timing, cooling system, fuel mixture (too weak).

WHY DOUBLE COPPER IS BETTER FOR YOUR ENGINE.

Unique Trapezoidal Copper Cored Earth Electrode — — 50% Larger Spark Area

— Copper Cored Centre Electrode

Champion Double Copper plugs are the first in the world to have copper core in both centre <u>and</u> earth electrode. This innovative design means that they run cooler by up to 100°C – giving greater efficiency and longer life. These double copper cores transfer heat away from the tip of the plug faster and more efficiently. Therefore, Double Copper runs at cooler temperatures than conventional plugs giving improved acceleration response and high speed performance with no fear of pre-ignition.

Champion Double Copper plugs also feature a unique trapezoidal earth electrode giving a 50% increase in spark area. This, together with the double copper cores, offers greatly reduced electrode wear, so the spark stays stronger for longer.

 FASTER COLD STARTING

 FOR UNLEADED OR LEADED FUEL

 ELECTRODES UP TO 100°C COOLER

 BETTER ACCELERATION RESPONSE

 LOWER EMISSIONS

 50% BIGGER SPARK AREA

THE LONGER LIFE PLUG

Plug Tips/Hot and Cold.
Spark plugs must operate within well-defined temperature limits to avoid cold fouling at one extreme and overheating at the other.
Champion and the car manufacturers work out the best plugs for an engine to give optimum performance under all conditions, from freezing cold starts to sustained high speed motorway cruising.
Plugs are often referred to as hot or cold. With Champion, the higher the number on its body, the hotter the plug, and the lower the number the cooler the plug. For the correct plug for your car refer to the specifications at the beginning of this chapter.

Plug Cleaning
Modern plug design and materials mean that Champion no longer recommends periodic plug cleaning. Certainly don't clean your plugs with a wire brush as this can cause metal conductive paths across the nose of the insulator so impairing its performance and resulting in loss of acceleration and reduced m.p.g.
However, if plugs are removed, always carefully clean the area where the plug seats in the cylinder head as grit and dirt can sometimes cause gas leakage.
Also wipe any traces of oil or grease from plug leads as this may lead to arcing.

the coil terminal marked 1. Incorrect connections can cause bad starting, misfiring, and short spark plug life.

3   Accurate testing of the coil requires special equipment, and for the home mechanic the easiest test is by substitution of a new unit.

12 Spark plugs and HT leads – general

1   The correct functioning of the spark plugs is vital for the correct running and efficiency of the engine. The spark plugs should be renewed every 10 000 miles (15 000 km) on UK models or every 12 500 miles (20 000 km) on USA models, however if misfiring or bad starting is experienced in the service period, they must be removed, cleaned, and regapped (photo).
2   The condition of the spark plugs will also tell much about the overall condition of the engine.
3   If the insulator nose of the spark plug is clean and white, with no deposits, this is indicative of a weak mixture, or too hot a plug. (A hot plug transfers heat away from the electrode slowly – a cold plug

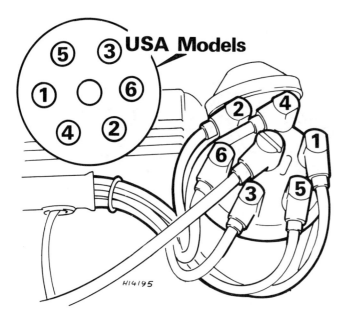

Fig. 4.16 HT lead connecting sequence on the distributor cap (Sec 12)

12.1 Removing a spark plug

transfers it away quickly).
4   If the tip and insulator nose is covered with hard black-looking deposits, then this is indicative that the mixture is too rich. Should the plug be black and oily, then it is likely that the engine is fairly worn, as well as the mixture being too rich.
5   If the insulator nose is covered with light tan to greyish brown deposits, then the mixture is correct and it is likely that the engine is in good condition.
6   If there are any traces of long brown tapering stains on the outside of the white portion of the plug, then the plug will have to be renewed, as this shows that there is a faulty joint between the plug body and the insulator, and compression is being lost.
7   Plugs should be cleaned by a sand blasting machine which will free them from carbon more thoroughly than cleaning by hand. The machine will also test the condition of the plugs under compression. Any plug that fails to spark at the recommended pressure should be renewed.
8   The spark plug gap is of considerable importance, as, if it is too large or too small, the size of the spark and its efficiency will be seriously impaired. The spark plug gap should be set to the figure given in the Specifications at the beginning of this Chapter.
9   To set it, measure the gap with a feeler gauge and then bend open, or close, the *outer* electrode until the correct gap is achieved. The centre electrode should *never* be bent as this may crack the insulation and cause plug failure, if nothing worse.
10 When refitting the plugs, remember to use new plug seating washers. The plug threads should be clean and dry. Tighten the plugs to the recommended torque wrench setting. Do not overtighten them; the cylinder head is made of aluminium alloy and the cylinder head threads can easily be stripped.
11 Periodically the spark plug leads should be wiped clean and checked for security to the spark plugs. Similarly check the coil HT lead.

13 Fault diagnosis – ignition system

By far the majority of breakdown and running troubles are caused by faults in the ignition system, either in the low tension or high tension circuit. There are two main symptoms indicating ignition faults. Either the engine will not start or fire, or the engine is difficult to start and misfires. If it is a regular misfire, ie the engine is only running on two or three cylinders, the fault is almost sure to be in the secondary, or high tension, circuit. If the misfiring is intermittent, the fault could be in either the high or low tension circuits. If the car stops suddenly, or will not start at all, it is likely that the fault is in the low tension circuit. Loss of power and overheating, apart from faulty carburation settings are normally due to faults in the distributor or incorrect ignition timing.

Engine fails to start
1   If the engine fails to start and the car was running normally when it was last used, first check there is fuel in the petrol tank. If the engine turns over normally on the starter motor and the battery is evidently well charged, then the fault may be in either the high or low tension circuits. First check the HT circuit. If the battery is known to be fully charged, the ignition light comes on, and the starter motor fails to turn the engine, check the tightness of the leads on the battery terminals and the security of the earth lead to its connection to the body. It is quite common for the leads to have worked loose, even if they look and feel secure. If one of the battery terminal posts gets very hot when trying to work the starter motor, this is a sure indication of a faulty connection to that terminal.
2   One of the most common reasons for bad starting is wet or damp spark plug leads and distributor. Remove the distributor cap. If condensation is visible internally dry the cap with a rag or wipe over the leads. Refit the cap.
3   If the engine still fails to start, check that current is reaching the plugs, by disconnecting each plug lead in turn at the spark plug end, and holding the end of the cable about $\frac{3}{16}$ in (5 mm) away from the cylinder block. Hold the HT leads with well insulated tongs to avoid electric shocks. Spin the engine on the starter motor.
4   Sparking between the end of the cable and the block should be fairly strong with a regular blue spark. If current is reaching the plugs, then remove them and clean and regap them. The engine should now start.

5 If there is no spark at the plug leads, take off the HT lead from the centre of the distributor cap and hold it to the block as before. Spin the engine on the starter once more. A rapid succession of blue sparks between the end of the lead and the block indicate that the coil is in order and that the distributor cap is cracked, the rotor arm faulty or the carbon brush in the top of the distributor cap is not making good contact with the rotor arm.

6 If there are no sparks from the end of the lead from the coil, check the connections at the coil end of the lead. If it is in order start checking the low tension circuit.

7 Use a 12 volt voltmeter or testlamp connected between the coil terminal 15 and a suitable earth. With the contact points open and the ignition switched on, approximately 12 volts should be registered or the testlamp should light up. No reading indicates a break in the supply from the ignition switch. Check the connections at the switch to see if any are loose. Refit them and the engine should run. A reading shows a faulty coil, faulty condenser (conventional ignition), or a broken LT lead.

8 On the conventional ignition system test the condenser as described in Section 4.

9 On the transistorized ignition system connect a voltmeter between the coil terminal 1 and earth. With the ignition switched on a maximum of 2 volts should be registered. If it is higher, the control unit is faulty.

10 If the engine starts when the starter motor is operated, but stops as soon as the ignition key is returned to the normal running position, the resistive wire (conventional) or primary resistor (transistorized) may have an open circuit. Connect a temporary lead between the coil terminal 15 (conventional) or resistor to starter terminal (transistorized) and the battery positive terminal. If the engine now runs correctly renew the resistive wire or resistor pack. Note that the resistor must not be permanently bypassed, otherwise the coil will overheat and be irreparably damaged.

Engine misfires

11 If the engine misfires regularly, run it at a fast idling speed. Pull off each of the plug caps in turn and listen to the note of the engine. Hold the plug cap in a dry cloth or with a rubber glove as additional protection against a shock from the HT supply.

12 No difference in engine running will be noticed when the lead from the defective circuit is removed. Removing the lead from one of the good cylinders will accentuate the misfire.

13 Remove the plug lead from the end of the defective plug and hold it about $\frac{3}{16}$ inch (5 mm) away from the block. Restart the engine. If the sparking is fairly strong and regular, the fault must lie in the spark plug.

14 The plug may be loose, the insulation may be cracked, or the point may have burnt away, giving too wide a gap for the spark to jump. Worse still, one of the points may have broken off. Either renew the plug, or clean it, reset the gap, and then test it.

15 If there is no spark at the end of the plug lead, or if it is weak and intermittent, check the ignition lead from the distributor to the plug. If the insulation is cracked or perished, renew the lead. Check the connections at the distributor cap.

16 If there is still no spark, examine the distributor cap carefully for tracking. This can be recognised by a very thin black line running between two or more electrodes, or between an electrode and some other part of the distributor. These lines are paths which now conduct electricity across the cap, thus letting it run to earth. The only answer in this case is a new distributor cap.

17 Apart from the ignition timing being incorrect, other causes of misfiring have already been dealt with under the section dealing with the failure of the engine to start.

18 If the ignition timing is too far retarded it should be noted that the engine will tend to overheat, and there will be a quite noticeable drop in power. If the engine is overheating and the power is down, and the ignition timing is correct, then the carburettor should be checked, as it is likely that this is where the fault lies.

Chapter 5 Clutch

For modifications, and information applicable to later models, see Supplement at end of manual

Contents

Specifications

Type .... Hydraulically operated, single dry plate, with diaphragm spring pressure plate

Driven plate
Outer diameter .... 240 mm (9.449 in)
Total thickness at lining (new) .... 10 to 10.9 mm (0.394 to 0.429 in)
Maximum run-out .... 0.6 mm (0.024 in) measured at radius of 119 mm (4.685 in)

Clutch release bearing .... Self-centering ball thrust bearing

Clutch pedal travel (measured at pedal)
Right-hand drive models .... 160 mm (6.299 in)
Left-hand drive models .... 155 mm (6.102 in)

Torque wrench settings

	lbf ft	Nm
Clutch to flywheel	16 to 17	22 to 24
Master cylinder	16 to 17	22 to 24
Slave cylinder	18 to 20	25 to 28
Master cylinder rod to pedal	23 to 26	32 to 36
Hydraulic unions	9.5 to 11.5	13 to 16

1 General description

The clutch is of single dry plate type with a diaphrgam spring, and actuation is by hydraulic master cylinder and slave cylinder. The pressure plate assembly is bolted to the flywheel and transmits drive to the driven plate which is splined to the gearbox input shaft. Friction linings are riveted to each side of the driven plate, and radial damper springs are incorporated in the driven plate hub in order to cushion rotational shocks. A further damper spring is fitted to the top of the clutch pedal on 528 and 530 models in order to provide smooth clutch engagement.

When the clutch pedal is depressed, the slave cylinder is actuated by hydraulic pressure and the release lever pushes the release bearing against the diaphragm spring fingers. Due to its pivoting action the diaphragm spring engages the pressure plate from the driven plate which then moves along the splined input shaft away from the flywheel. Drive then ceases to be transmitted to the gearbox.

When the clutch pedal is released, the diaphragm spring forces the pressure plate back into contact with the driven plate which then moves along the input shaft into engagement with the flywheel. Drive is then transmitted directly through the clutch to the gearbox.

Wear of the clutch driven plate linings is automatically compensated for, by the hydraulic system, however clutch wear should be checked at the interval given in Section 6.

2 Clutch pedal – removal and refitting

1 Remove the lower facia trim panel (6 screws), and where applicable on USA models, disconnect the wiring from the electric window automatic cut-out noting the location of the wires.
2 Where fitted disconnect the return spring from the clutch pedal.
3 On 528 and 530 modesl loosen the damper spring locknut and release the spring tension by unscrewing the end nut.
4 On all models disconnect the master cylinder pushrod from the pedal by removing the pivot bolt and nut. Remove the pivot bolt from the pushrod noting the location of the sleeves.
5 The clutch pedal pivot bolt also acts as a pivot for the brake pedal. Before removing it, obtain a short length of rod for inserting through the brake pedal.
6 On 528 and 530 models depress the pedal to release the damper spring from the bulkhead.
7 On all models unscrew the pivot bolt locknut and withdraw the pivot bolt, at the same time inserting the short length of rod through the brake pedal.
8 Remove the spacer and pedal from the pivot bolt together with the bushes.
9 Wash all the components in paraffin then examine them for wear and damage; renew them as necessary.
10 Refitting is a reversal of removal, but lubricate all bearing surfaces

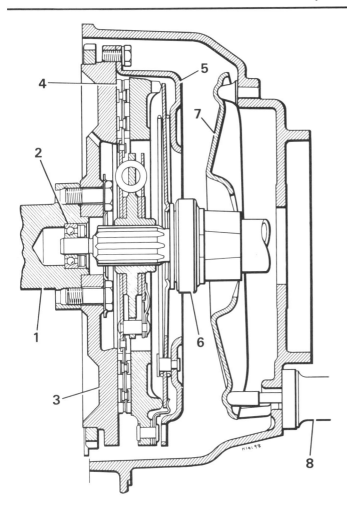

Fig. 5.1 Cross section diagram of the clutch (Sec 1)

1 Crankshaft	5 Pressure plate assembly
2 Spigot bearing (ball	6 Release bearing
or needle)	7 Release lever
3 Flywheel	8 Slave cylinder
4 Driven plate	

with multi-purpose grease. Ideally all self locking nuts should be renewed. Refer to Fig. 5.5 and 5.6 and adjust the clutch pedal position by loosening the pushrod locknut, adjusting its length, then tightening the locknut. Similarly on 528 and 530 models adjust the damper spring to the dimension shown in Fig. 5.6.

---

3 Master cylinder – removal, overhaul and refitting

1 Remove the lower facia trim panel (6 screws), and where applicable on USA models disconnect the wiring from the electric window automatic cut-out noting the location of the wires.
2 Unscrew and remove the master cylinder push-rod pivot bolt from the clutch pedal.
3 The clutch and brake fluid reservoir is a combined unit. The hydraulic fluid should be syphoned out until the level falls below the feed pipe to the clutch master cylinder.
4 Pull out the supply line from the master cylinder.
5 Carefully unscrew the outlet pipe, which connects the master cylinder to the slave cylinder, from beneath the master cylinder.
6 Remove the master cylinder securing bolts from the bulkhead and withdraw the master cylinder forward.
7 Be careful not to spill any fluid on the bodywork. It is preferable to wrap the master cylinder in a thick cloth before withdrawing it from the engine compartment.
8 Before dismantling, temporarily plug the inlet and outlet orifices

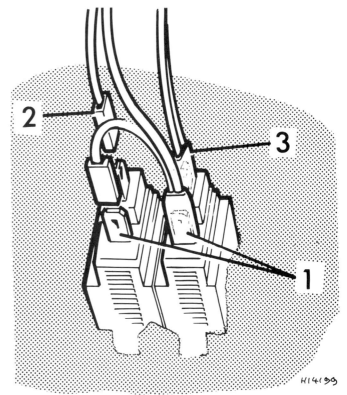

Fig. 5.2 Electric window automatic cut-out (Sec 2)

Wire colours
1 Green/red
2 Red
3 Red/white

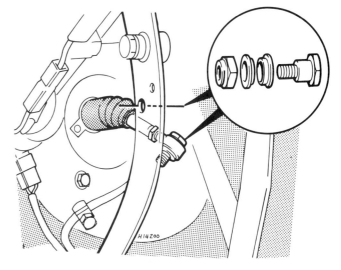

Fig. 5.3 Disconnecting the master cylinder pushrod from the clutch pedal (Sec 2)

Inset shows pivot bolt and sleeves

and then clean off all the dirt from the external surfaces. Remove the plugs.
9 Peel back the rubber boot from the rear end of the master cylinder and extract the circlip.
10 Withdraw the pushrod assembly, piston and spring.
11 Wash all the components in methylated sprit or clean hydraulic fluid – nothing else must be used. Examine the surfaces of the piston and cylinder bore and, if there are scratches, scoring or 'bright' wear

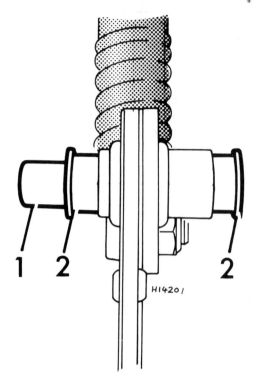

Fig. 5.4 Clutch pedal pivot spacer (1) and sleeves (2) (Sec 2)

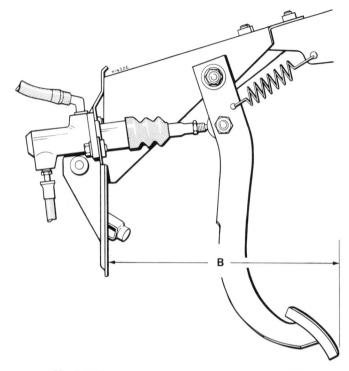

Fig. 5.5 Clutch pedal adjustment dimension on 525 models (Sec 2)

B = 247 mm (9.724 in) for LHD models or
256 mm (10.079 in) for RHD models

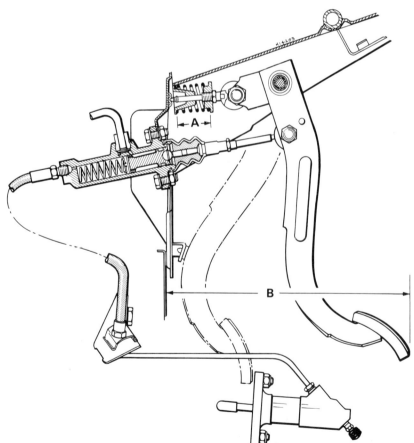

Fig. 5.6 Clutch pedal adjustment dimensions on 528 and 530 models (Sec 2)

A = 34 mm (1.338 in)
B = 247 mm (9.724 in) for LHD models or
256 mm (10.079 in) for RHD models

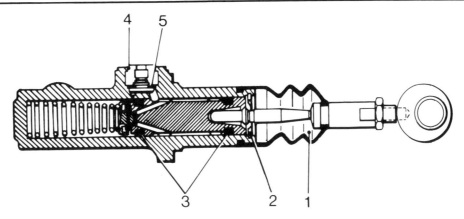

Fig. 5.7 Cross section diagram of the clutch master cylinder (Sec 3)

1	Boot	3	Seals	5	Washer
2	Circlip	4	Plug		

areas evident, then the master cylinder must be renewed as a complete unit.

12 If the components are in good condition, discard all the rubber seals and obtain the appropriate repair kit. Fit the seals using the fingers only to manipulate them into position, and then dip the components in clean hydraulic fluid before fitting them into the cylinder.

13 Refitting is a reversal of the removal procedure, but bleed the clutch hydraulic system as described in Section 5, and check the adjustment of the clutch pedal as described in Section 2.

4 Slave cylinder – removal, overhaul and refitting

1 The clutch slave cylinder is located on the left-hand side of the gearbox. First jack-up the front of the car and support it on axle stands. Apply the handbrake.

2 Syphon the hydraulic fluid from the combined clutch and brake fluid reservoir until the level falls below the feed pipe to the clutch master cylinder.

3 Where fitted unbolt the hydraulic pipe bracket from the clutch housing.

4 Unscrew the mounting nuts and withdraw the slave cylinder from the clutch housing.

5 Unscrew the union nut and disconnect the slave cylinder from the hydraulic pipe. Plug the pipe to prevent loss of fluid.

6 The overhaul procedure is similar to that described in Section 3 paragraphs 8 to 12.

7 Refitting is a reversal of removal, but lubricate the pushrod end cap with a molybdenum disulphide grease and make sure that the bleed nipple faces downward. Bleed the clutch hydraulic system as described in Section 5.

5 Clutch hydraulic system – bleeding

1 The need to bleed the hydraulic system arises when there is air present in the fluid, which may be the result of a faulty seal or pipe line connection, or the result of dismantling one of the system components. Bleeding is simply the process of venting the air out again.

2 Before proceeding to bleed the system it is possible to determine the slave cylinder pushrod travel. To do this insert a length of flat steel (filed to a pointed edge at one end) into the cut-out by the slave cylinder until it makes contact with the pushrod. Have an assistant fully depress the clutch pedal. When the slave cylinder is removed check the length of the mark made on the pushrod; if it is less than 20 mm (0.787 in) the hydraulic system is not functioning correctly and it is likely that there is air in the fluid. Refer also to Section 6 paragraph 1.

3 To bleed the system first make sure that the reservoir is filled and obtain a piece of $\frac{3}{16}$ inch (4.8 mm) bore diameter rubber tube about 2 to 3 feet (0.6 to 0.8 metres) long and a clean glass jar. A small quantity

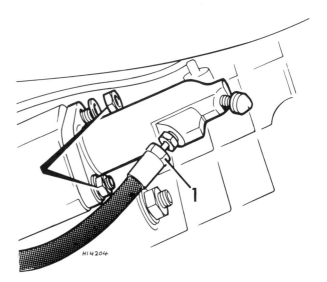

Fig. 5.8 Clutch slave cylinder mounting nuts (arrowed) and hydraulic pipe inlet union (1) (Sec 4)

of fresh, clean hydraulic fluid is also necessary.

4 Remove the bleed nipple dust cap (if fitted). Unscrew the nipple $\frac{1}{4}$ turn and fit the tube over it. Put about $\frac{1}{2}$ inch (12.7 mm) of fluid in the jar and put the other end of the tube in it. The jar can then be placed on the ground under the car.

5 The clutch pedal should now be depressed quickly and released slowly, by an assistant, until no more air bubbles can be seen emerging from the end of the bleed tube. Quick pedal action carries the air along rather than leaving it behind. During the bleeding operation it is essential to keep the fluid reservoir topped up.

6 When the air bubbles have stopped and only clear fluid is seen to be emerging from the end of the bleed nipple tube, tighten the bleed nipple at the end of a downward pedal stroke. Refit the bleed nipple dust cap.

7 Check the operation of the clutch and if necessary check the slave cylinder pushrod travel as described in paragraph 2. If it is difficult to obtain the correct travel, remove the slave cylinder without disconnecting the hydraulic hose and press the pushrod fully into the slave cylinder – this will disperse any residual air into the reservoir.

8 Always use clean hydraulic fluid which has been stored in an airtight container and has remained unshaken for the preceding 24 hours. Saving and reusing the fluid which has been bled out of the system is not recommended. Fluid which has already been used will contain impurities and will also have absorbed a small percentage of moisture.

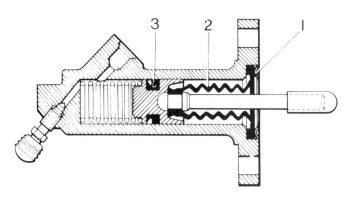

Fig. 5.9 Cross section diagram of the clutch slave cylinder (Sec 4)

1   Toothed ring   2   Boot   3   Seal

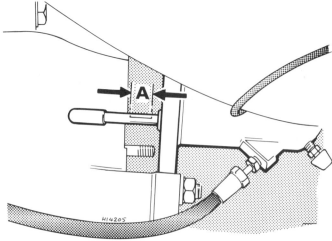

Fig. 5.10 Checking the clutch slave cylinder pushrod travel (Sec 5)

A   Mark indicating travel

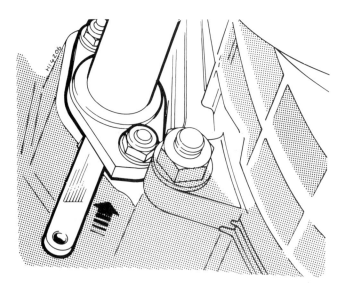

Fig. 5.11 Checking the clutch driven plate for wear (Sec 6)

6.5 Removing the clutch pressure plate and driven plate

6   Clutch – checking and removal

1   The clutch driven plate linings should be checked for wear every 20 000 miles (30 000 km) on UK models and every 25 000 miles (40 000 km) on USA models. The check can be made with the clutch and gearbox in situ by inserting a short length of flat steel of suitable thickness into the slave cylinder cut-out hole until it contacts the pushrod.

2   If, when the clutch pedal is depressed, the flat steel travels into the cut-out a further 5 mm (0.2 in), the driven plate is worn and should be renewed. This is because when the plate is worn, the end cap on the slave cylinder push rod moves back in line with the cut-out.

3   To remove the clutch first remove the gearbox as described in Chapter 6.

4   Mark the pressure plate cover in relation to the flywheel, then unscrew the bolts a turn at a time until the tension of the diaphragm spring is released. Hold the flywheel stationary by temporarily inserting one of the clutch housing bolts and engaging a wedged block of wood or length of steel with the flywheel ring gear.

5   Remove the bolts and withdraw the pressure plate assembly together with the driven plate (photo).

7   Clutch assembly – inspection

1   Examine the surfaces of the pressure plate and flywheel for signs of scoring. If this is only light the pressure plate may be reused, but if

very deep, it will have to be renewed. Should the flywheel be deeply scored, it should be removed and either machined or renewed. Providing it can be machined successfully, the overall balance of the engine unit should not be upset. Check also the spigot bearing in the rear of the crankshaft and if necessary renew it as described in Chapter 1.

2   The pressure plate unit riveted joints should also be checked, and if any are found to be loose or worn, the complete unit will have to be renewed.

3   The driven plate should be checked for signs of cracking and the thickness of the linings should be compared with the total new thickness. If wear of 2 mm (0.08 in) is evident the plate should be renewed.

4   Check that the driven plate damper springs are firmly seated, and that there is no oil contamination of the friction linings. Temporarily fit the plate to the gearbox input shaft and check that the maximum specified run out is not exceeded.

5   If the clutch components are contaminated with oil, the source of the leakage (ie crankshaft rear oil seal or gearbox input shaft oil seal) should be verified and corrected.

8   Release bearing – removal and refitting

1   The release bearing should be checked whenever the gearbox and

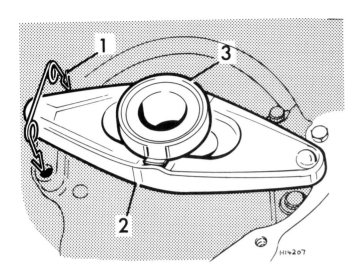

Fig. 5.12 Clutch release lever components (Sec 8)

1   Spring clip   2   Release lever   3   Release bearing

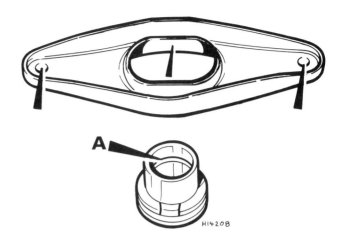

Fig. 5.13 Clutch release lever component lubricating points (Sec 8)

A   Release bearing interior groove

clutch housing is separated from the engine. Spin the bearing and check it for roughness, then attempt to move the outer race laterally against the inner one. If any excessive roughness or wear is evident, renew the bearing.

2   Mark the release lever in relation to the clutch housing.

3   Prise out the spring clip then withdraw the release bearing and lever from the front of the gearbox.

4   Clean the components and the inside of the clutch housing, but take care not to contaminate the bearing with solvent.

5   Lubricate the indentations on the lever with high melting point grease, then locate it over the guide and onto the pivot pin in the clutch housing. Refit the spring clip.

6   Pack the interior groove of the release bearing until with a molybdenum disulphide grease and smear a little high melting point grease on the flats which engage the lever.

7   Slide the release bearing over the gearbox input shaft onto the guide, and at the same time engage the flats with the release lever.

9   Clutch – refitting

1   Before refitting the clutch assembly to the flywheel, a guide tool for centralising the driven plate must be obtained. This can be an old input shaft from a dismantled gearbox, or a stepped mandrel made up to fit the centre spigot bearing in the flywheel and the inner diameter of the driven plate spline.

2   Locate the driven plate against the face of the flywheel, ensuring that the projecting side of the centre splined hub faces towards the gearbox.

3   Offer up the pressure plate assembly to the flywheel, aligning the marks prior to dismantling, and insert the retaining bolts finger tight. Where a new pressure plate assembly is being fitted, locate it to the flywheel in a similar relative position to the original, by reference to the index marking and dowel pin positions.

4   Insert the guide tool through the splined hub of the driven plate so

9.4 Centralising the driven plate with an old input shaft

that the end of the tool locates in the flywheel spigot bearing (photo).

5   Ensure the driven plate is centralised by rotating the guide tool. Remove and insert the guide tool several times to make sure. Now tighten the pressure plate securing bolts a turn at a time, in a diagonally opposite sequence, to the specified torque.

6   Remove the guide tool. Lightly lubricate the gearbox input shaft splines with high melting point grease.

7   Refit the gearbox with reference to Chapter 6.

see overleaf for 'Fault diagnosis – clutch'

10 Fault diagnosis – clutch

Symptom	Reason(s)
Clutch slip (engine speed increases with no increase in road speed)	Worn or oil contaminated driven plate Release bearing seizing on guide Pressure plate bolts loose
Clutch judder	Oil or grease contaminated driven plate linings Worn or loose engine or gearbox mountings Distorted pressure plate or driven plate Worn splines on gearbox input shaft or driven plate hub Worn spigot bearing in end of crankshaft Pressure plate bolts loose
Clutch drag (failure to disengage)	Driven plate striking on input shaft splines Seized spigot bearing in end of crankshaft Air in hydraulic system Faulty master or slave cylinder Pressure plate bolts loose
Noise when depressing clutch pedal	Worn, dry or damaged release bearing Worn or broken diaphragm spring fingers

Chapter 6 Manual gearbox and automatic transmission

For modifications, and information applicable to later models, see Supplement at end of manual

Contents

Specifications

Manual gearbox

Type .... Four forward speeds (five optional) with synchromesh, and reverse. Floor mounted gearshift

Model .... Getrag 262/8, 262/9, 265/6

Ratios

	4-speed	5-speed
1st	3.885 : 1	3.717 : 1
2nd	2.202 : 1	2.403 : 1
3rd	1.401 : 1	1.766 : 1
4th	1.000 : 1	1.263 : 1
5th	–	1.000 : 1
Reverse	4.300 : 1	4.230 : 1

Speedometer drive .... 2.5 : 1 (teeth 10/4)

Input shaft endplay .... 0 to 0.09 mm (0 to 0.0035 in)

Output shaft endplay .... 0 to 0.09 mm (0 to 0.0035 in)

Countershaft endplay .... 0.1 to 0.2 mm (0.004 to 0.008 in)

Synchro ring maximum wear limit .... 0.8 mm (0.031 in)

Lubricant capacity
4-speed .... 1.9 Imp pt; 1.2 US qt; 1.1 litre
5-speed .... 2.8 Imp pt; 1.7 US qt; 1.6 litre

Torque wrench settings

	lbf ft	Nm
Gearbox to clutch housing	52 to 58	72 to 80
Drain and filler plugs	29 to 43	40 to 60
Front cover	13 to 18	18 to 25
Output flange	72	100
Crossmember to body	16 to 17	22 to 24

Automatic transmission

Type .... Zahnradfabrik-Friedrichshafen (ZF) 3HP-20 or 3HP-22 or Borg-Warner 65

Ratios

	ZF 3HP-20	ZF 3HP-22	B-W 65
1st	2.50 : 1	2.478 : 1	2.39 : 1
2nd	1.50 or 1.52 : 1	1.478 : 1	1.45 : 1
3rd	1.00 : 1	1.00 : 1	1.00 : 1
Reverse	2.00 : 1	2.090 : 1	2.09 : 1
Speedometer	2.5 : 1	2.5 : 1	—

Torque converter diameter

525	260 mm (10.236 in)
528 and 530	280 mm (11.024 in)

Stall test rpm

525 (ZF 3HP-20)	1960 to 2060
525 (ZF 3HP-22)	2020 to 2120
528 (ZF 3HP-20)	1970 to 2070
528 (ZF 3HP-22/carburettor)	2120 to 2220
528 (ZF 3HP-22/injection)	2100 to 2200
528 (B-W 65)	2140 to 2240
530 (B-W 65)	1990 to 2090

Fluid capacity

Initial

525 (ZF 3HP-20)	10.2 Imp pt; 12.2 US pt; 5.8 litre
525 (ZF 3HP-22)	11.4 Imp pt; 6.9 US qt; 6.5 litre
528 (ZF 3HP-20)	11.2 Imp pt; 13.5 US pt; 6.4 litre
528 (ZF 3HP-22)	12.8 Imp pt; 7.7 US qt; 7.25 litre
528 (B-W 65)	13.6 Imp pt; 16.4 US pt; 7.76 litre
530 (B-W 65)	13.4 Imp pt; 8.0 US qt; 7.63 litre

Oil changing

525 (ZF 3HP-20)	3.2 Imp pt; 3.8 US pt; 1.8 litre
525 (ZF 3HP-22)	3.5 Imp pt; 4.2 US pt; 2.0 litre
528 (ZF 3HP-20)	3.2 Imp pt; 3.8 US pt; 1.8 litre
528 (ZF 3HP-22)	3.6 Imp pt; 4.2 US pt; 2.0 litre
528 (B-W 65)	3.3 Imp pt; 4.0 US pt; 1.9 litre
530 (B-W 65)	3.2 Imp pt; 1.9 US qt; 1.8 litre

Torque wrench settings

	lbf ft	Nm
Transmission to engine:		
M10	31 to 35	43 to 48
M8	16 to 17	22 to 24
Driveplate to converter	31 to 35	43 to 48
Drain plug (ZF)	25 to 28	35 to 39
Oil pan	6 to 6.5	8 to 9
Drain plug (B-W)	9 to 12	12 to 16
Oil cooler unions	20 to 22	27 to 30

1 Manual gearbox – general description

Both carburettor and fuel injection models are fitted with a Getrag gearbox incorporating a Borg-Warner type synchromesh on all forward speeds. The standard gearbox is 4-speed, but a 5-speed version is optional in the UK.

2 Manual gearbox – removal and refitting

1   Position the car over an inspection pit or on strong car ramps, to give plenty of working space beneath the gearbox. If the car is jacked up, take extra precautions to prevent the car from rocking when the gearbox is removed and refitted. Drain the gearbox oil (photo).
2   Disconnect the battery negative lead.
3   Remove the complete exhaust system as described in Chapter 3.
4   Remove the gear lever as described in Section 8.
5   Remove the propeller shaft as described in Chapter 7.
6   Support the gearbox with a trolley jack, then unscrew the crossmember to body nuts and remove the washers. Remove the front cover plate (photos).
7   Lower the gearbox so that the engine rests on the front suspension crossmember.
8   Disconnect the speedometer cable by removing the retaining bolt.
9   Remove the clutch slave cylinder as described in Chapter 5 but have the hydraulic line connected.

10   Disconnect the reversing light switch wires (photo).
11   The gearbox may either be removed complete with the bellhousing or alternatively removed leaving the bellhousing attached to the engine. With the latter method some difficulty may be experienced when refitting the gearbox as the clutch release thrust bearing must be accurately aligned with the gearbox front guide.
12   Unscrew and remove the bolts or nuts as applicable, then withdraw the gearbox to the rear. The help of an assistant is recommended as the gearbox is heavy and care must be taken to prevent damage to the input shaft and clutch.
13   Refitting is a reversal of removal with reference to Chapters 7 and 3, and Section 8 of this Chapter. Refill or top-up the gearbox with oil as necesasary.

3 Manual gearbox (4-speed) – overhaul

1   Drain the gearbox oil and remove the gearbox as described in Section 2.
2   Undo the nuts and bolts securing the gearchange linkage support plate (photo), the crossmember and the exhaust bracket to the rear of the gearbox. Remove these items.
3   Pull the selector shaft cover ring back, drive out the retaining pin, and pull the rod and knuckle off the end of the selector shaft (photo).
4   Undo the retaining nuts and draw off the flexible coupling.
5   From within the bellhousing disconnect the clutch release arm from the pivot post. Withdraw the arm and bearing.

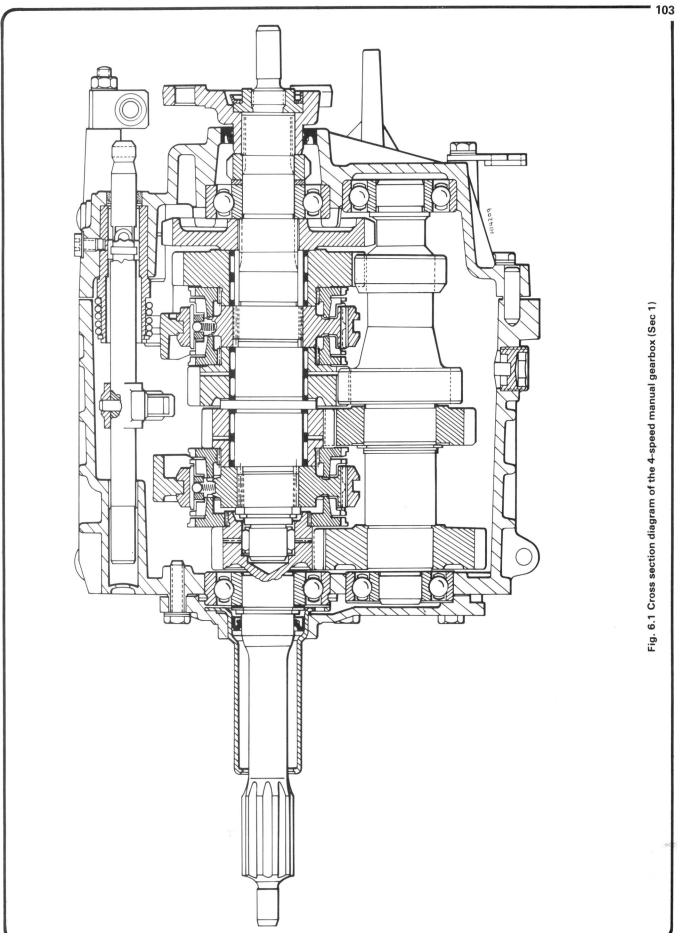

Fig. 6.1 Cross section diagram of the 4-speed manual gearbox (Sec 1)

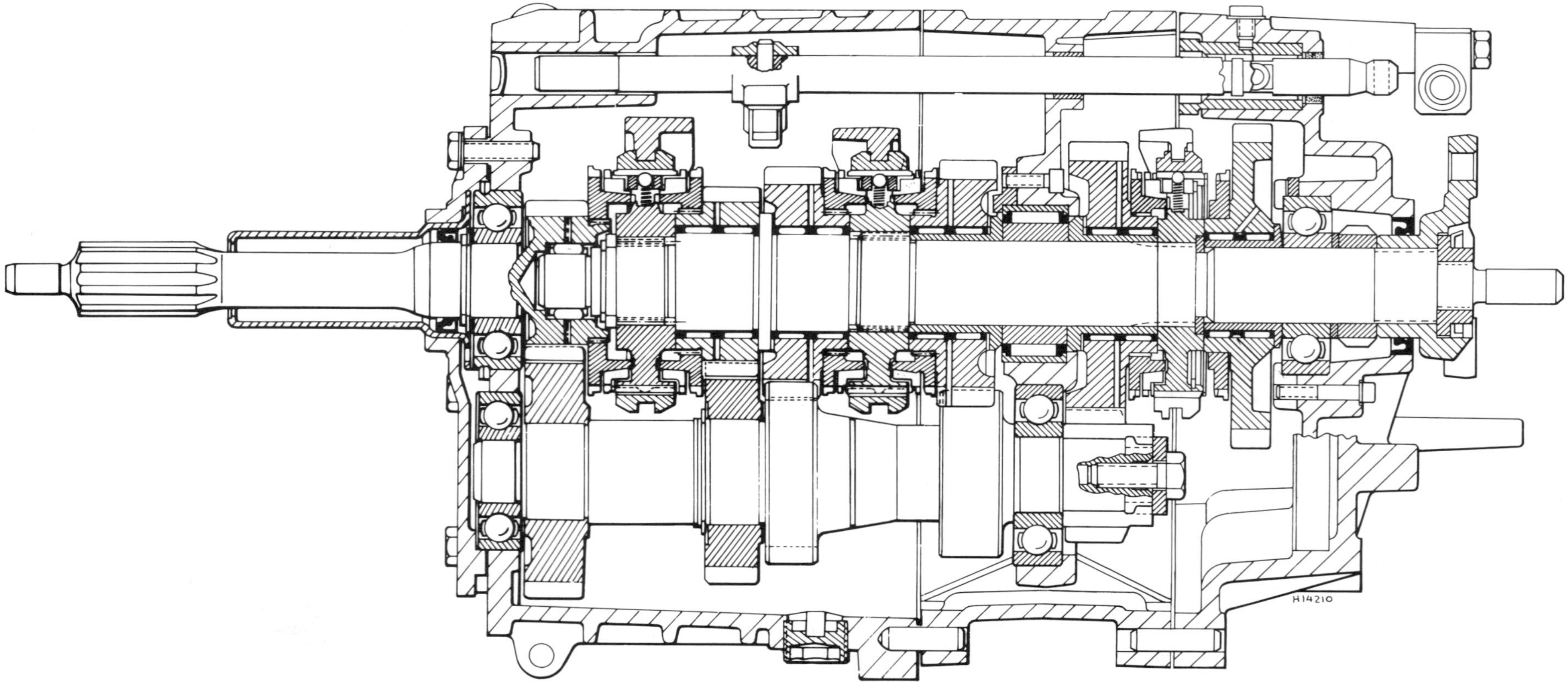

Fig. 6.2 Cross section diagram of the 5-speed manual gearbox (Sec 1)

H14210

2.1 Showing the gearbox drain and filler/level plugs

2.6A The gearbox crossmember

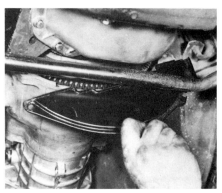

2.6B Removing the front cover plate

2.10 Reversing light switch and wires

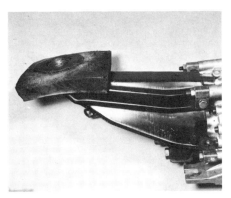

3.2 The gearchange linkage support plate

3.3 Removing the selector shaft knuckle

6 Undo the retaining nuts and pull off the bellhousing.

7 Tap back the crimped edge of the flange nut lockwasher (if fitted).

8 Hold the output flange quite still (using a length of flat steel bolted to two of the flange holes), and unscrew the flange nut using a suitable box spanner or socket.

9 Using a three-legged puller, withdraw the flange from its locating splines.

10 From the side of the gearbox, lever out the plug and extract the locking pin and spring.

11 Unscrew the reversing light switch from the side of the gearbox casing.

12 Remove the bolts from the release bearing guide sleeve housing and withdraw it. Note and retain the shims. Remove the gasket.

13 Using screwdrivers or a pair of external circlip pliers, remove the input shaft bearing external locking ring.

14 Undo the bolts and nuts securing the main and rear gearbox casings together.

15 Stand the gearbox on its rear end, pointing vertically upwards, and heat the gearbox casing in the region of the input and layshaft bearings. Heat the casing sufficiently to expand it thus enabling the main casing to be separated from the rear casing and the input and layshaft bearings. The alternative method to heating the casing is to draw off the bearings using BMW service tools 232060 and 232050.

16 Measure the distance between the outer edge of the reverse gear shift lever and the inside of the gearbox casing. *Note this dimension*, then unscrew the pivot bolt (Fig. 6.4) to release the shift lever.

17 Using a pin punch, drive out the roll pins securing the selector forks to the selector rods (Fig. 6.5). On some models there will be one long roll pin to each fork and in such instances it will be found necessary to hacksaw part of the roll pin off as it will foul on the gears before it can be driven out fully. Later models will have two roll pins per selector fork and extracting them is no problem. On models with the long single roll pin it is advisable to fit the later two roll pin set-up on reassembly.

18 Insert a rod through the hole in the end of the gearchange rod and turn the gearchange rod until the 3rd and 4th gear selector rod can be extracted. Note that a plunger and interlocking ball will drop out.

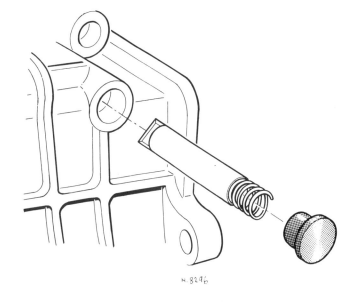

Fig. 6.3 Remove the plug, spring, and locking pin (Sec 3)

19 Withdraw the 1st and 2nd gear selector rod. Note that a plunger and interlocking balls will drop out.

20 Pull out the selector rod for reverse gear.

21 Remove the selector forks for 3rd/4th, 1st/2nd gears. It is advisable to slide them onto their respective selector rods to ease identification on refitting.

22 The selector shaft rod can now be extracted. Note the four rollers on its end (photo).

23 from the end casing remove the Allen screws which secure the supporting plate for the mainshaft end bearing (Fig. 6.6).

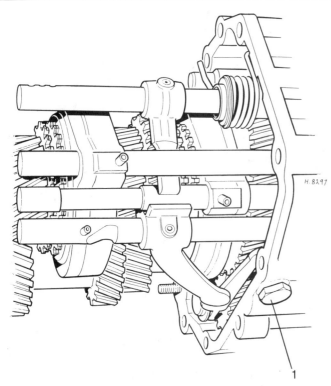

Fig. 6.4 Reverse gear support bolt (1) location (Sec 3)

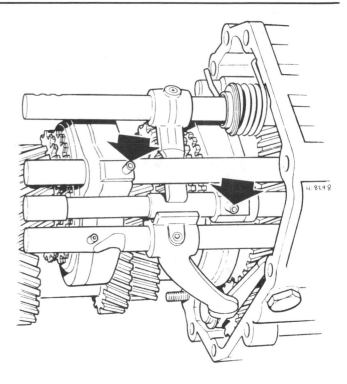

Fig. 6.5 Drive out the selector fork roll pins arrowed (Sec 3)

3.22 The selector shaft and rollers

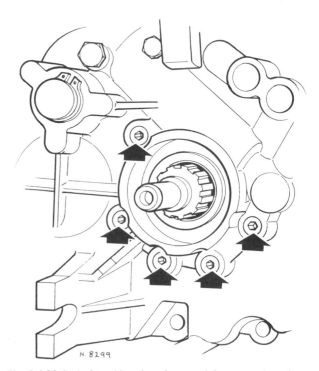

Fig. 6.6 Mainshaft end bearing plate retaining screw locations (Sec 3)

24 Heat the end casing in the area around the mainshaft bearing to approximately 80°C (176°F). The expansion of the casing will enable it to be lifted away from the gear clusters.

25 The gear clusters can now be dismantled. During the dismantling operation, lay the components out in a set fashion which will assist their identification and ease reassembly.

26 Commence dismantling by pulling off the input shaft together with its synchro ring. There is a needle roller cage bearing between the input and main shafts: this bearing may come away with the input shaft or remain in position on the mainshaft.

27 Extract the needle rolller cage bearing (photo).

28 From the end of the mainshaft extract the spring retainer ring and the spacer shim.

29 Carefully pull off the complete synchromesh hub unit for 3rd and 4th gears.

30 Extract the synchromesh ring for 3rd gear followed by the third gear and a needle roller bearing.

31 From the other end of the mainshaft pull off the speedometer drive gear and spacer ring (photo).

32 Using a suitable puller, draw off the mainshaft end bearing and extract the bearing end plate and shim.

33 From the mainshaft, remove reverse gear followed by 1st gear and its synchro ring. The 1st gear runs on a needle roller cage bearing at the rear of which is located a spacer ring.

34 Carefully pull off the 1st/2nd gear synchromesh unit followed by the 2nd gear and its synchro ring. Extract the 2nd gear needle roller bearing cage.

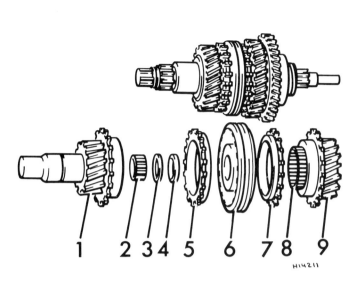

Fig. 6.7 Gear components (Sec 3)

1	Input shaft	4	Shim	7	3rd synchro ring
2	Needle bearing	5	4th synchro ring	8	Needle bearing
3	Retainer	6	3rd/4th synchro unit	9	3rd gear

3.27 Needle roller bearing located between the input and main shafts

35 The layshaft can be partially dismantled, if necessary, by pulling off the end bearing nearest the larger gear wheel. Pull off the larger gear which meshes with the gear machined on the input shaft, extract the circlip (photos) and withdraw the layshaft 3rd gear. The other gears on the layshaft are machined onto it and if damaged or worn the complete layshaft will have to be renewed.

36 Returning to the gearbox end casing, drill a small hole into each of the core plugs covering the ends of the selector rod holes. Insert a self-tapping screw, grip the screw firmly and pull out the core plugs. Extract the plunger springs and any remaining ball bearings.

37 With the gearbox now dismantled, examine all components for wear and renew as necessary. Renew all seals as a matter of routine. Pay particular attention to the synchromesh units, especially if there has been evidence of noisy gear changing. The teeth on the selector sleeves must have sharp edges and should not be chamfered with wear.

38 When dismantling the synchromesh units, do so carefully as there are three spring loaded balls projecting from the central hub unit (photo). Slide the hub unit out of the synchro sleeve and extract the

3.31 Removing the speedometer drive gear

3.35A The complete laygear

3.35B Circlip location on the layshaft

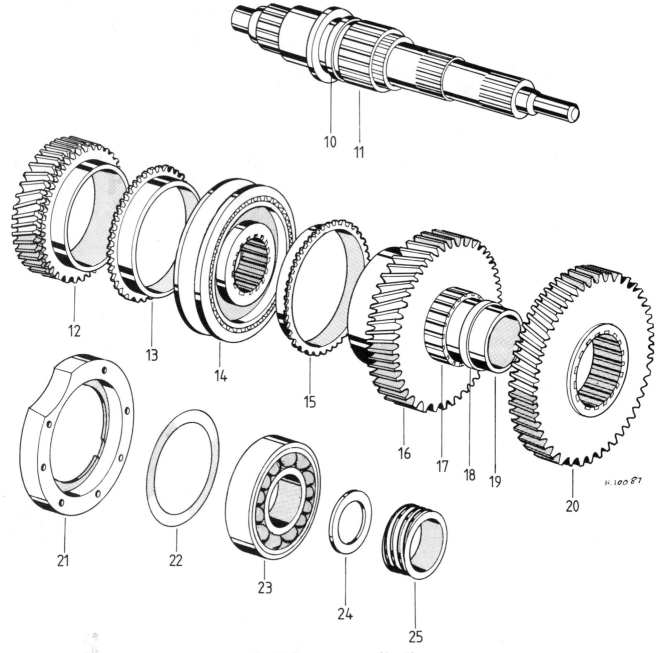

Fig. 6.8 Gear components (Sec 3)

10 Mainshaft
11 Needle bearing
12 2nd gear
13 2nd gear synchro ring
14 2nd/1st gear synchromesh
   unit

15 1st gear synchro ring
16 1st gear
17 Needle bearing
18 Spacer ring
19 Spacer sleeve
20 Reverse gear

21 Bearing support
22 Shim
23 Ball bearing
24 Spacer ring
25 Speedometer drivegear

three balls, springs and keys. When assembling the synchromesh unit it may be found helpful to assemble the hub and restrain the balls, springs and keys using a large hose clip, then the hub can be slid into the sleeve without the rear of the balls being ejected.

39 Examine the ball race and needle roller bearings for signs of scuffing, pitting or other wear indications. Renew them as found necessary. The ball race bearings can be drawn off the shafts using a suitable puller. Refitting is easily carried out using a length of pipe, the inner diameter of which should be just a little larger than the shaft diameter.

40 Take each synchro ring and place it on its respective gear, then measure the clearance between the synchro ring and the gear as shown in Fig. 6.10. If the gap is less than 0.0315 in (0.8 mm) then the

synchro ring must be renewed.

41 Examine the reverse sliding idler gear and its shaft. Obviously reverse gear is non-synchromesh and the leading edges of the gear teeth will be slightly marked and rounded. Renew the sliding gear only if excessive wear or damage is evident. The idler gear shaft if worn can be renewed after removing the locating circlip on the outside of the cover (photo) and driving the shaft out. It may be found beneficial to heat the casing up in order to prevent damage when driving out the shaft.

42 Examine the reverse gear plunger and spring housed in the front cover (photo). Press the plunger to ensure that it is free to move.

43 The gearbox is now ready for assembly. If a new mainshaft bearing is required then it will be necessary to calculate the thickness of shim

3.38 A synchromesh unit spring and key

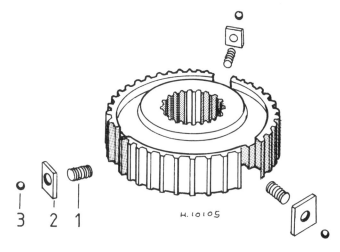

Fig. 6.9 Synchro unit hub components (Sec 3)

1   Spring   2   Key   3   Ball

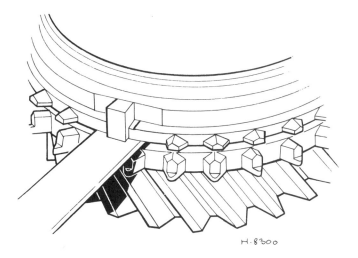

Fig. 6.10 Checking the synchro ring wear (Sec 3)

3.41 Reverse idler gear shaft retaining circlip

3.42 Reverse gear plunger and spring

required between the bearing and the bearing end plate.

44 The thickness of shim required is found by measuring the recess in the gearbox end cover in which the bearing sits using a depth gauge as shown in Fig. 6.11. We will assume that this dimension A is 0.5158 in (13.1 mm) for an example. Now measure the depth of the recess in the bearing endplate as shown in Fig. 6.12. We will assume that the dimension B is 0.2362 in (6.0 mm). If the overall width of the bearing is measured (C) (Fig. 6.13) which we will assume to be 0.7480 in (19.0 mm), it is now possible to calculate the thickness of shim D required as follows:

A	0.5158 in (13.1 mm)
+B	0.2362 in (6.0 mm)
	0.7520 in (19.1 mm)
-C	0.7480 in (19.0 mm)
D	0.0040 in (0.1 mm)

45 Commence assembly by rebuilding the mainshaft (photo). Slide on the third gear needle roller bearing.

46 Lubricate the needle roller bearing and slide on the 3rd gear and its synchro ring (photo).

47 Locate 3rd/4th gear synchromesh (photo) followed by the spacer

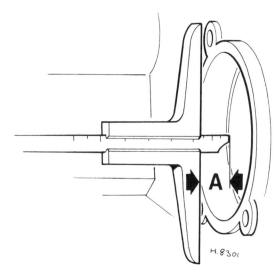

Fig. 6.11 Measuring the recess in the gearbox end cover (A) using a depth gauge (Sec 3)

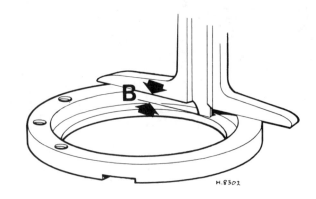

Fig. 6.12 Measuring the depth of the recess (B) in the bearing endplate (Sec 3)

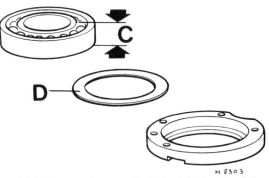

Fig. 6.13 Measure the overall width of the bearing (C) to calculate the thickness of the shim (D) (Sec 3)

shim ring and the spring retainer ring (photo). Ensure that the spring retainer ring is seated correctly in its locating groove on the shaft.

48 Working from the other end of the mainshaft, slide on the 2nd gear needle roller bearing.

49 Lubricate the needle roller bearing and slide on the 2nd gear together with its synchro ring (photo).

50 Slide onto the shaft the 1st/2nd gear synchromesh unit (photo).

51 Fit the spacer sleeve and needle roller bearing followed by the 1st gear synchro ring and 1st gear (photo). Remember to lubricate the needle roller bearing before fitting the 1st gear.

52 Fit the reverse gear (photo).

53 The bearing endplate can now be refitted (photo). If a new bearing is being fitted then it will be necessary to calculate the thickness of shim required between the bearing and the endplate as described in paragraph 44.

54 The bearing can be pressed on using a suitable length of pipe.

55 After fitting the bearing, fit the spacer ring and press on the speedometer drive gear in a similar manner.

56 Take the input shaft and fit the needle roller cage bearing into its end after lubricating the bearing. Locate on the input shaft the 4th gear synchro ring.

57 The input shaft (photo) and mainshaft can now be coupled together.

58 Assemble the layshaft as necessary and press on the bearings using a suitable length of pipe.

59 It will now be necessary to heat up the gearbox end casing in order to relocate the gear clusters and bearings. Before heating the casing stand it on suitable packing blocks. Make up some suitable length studs and screw them into the bearing end plate for location purposes (photo).

60 Heat the end casing to approximately 80°C (176°F) and insert the complete gear cluster and reverse idler gear together. This can be a little difficult but if you refer to the photograph you can see how it is done. Note that the reverse idler gear is balanced and lowered together with the gear clusters (photos).

61 Relocate the Allen screws and withdraw the guide studs. Note that there are special sealing washers under the heads of the Allen screws. Tighten the Allen screws.

62 Allow the end casing to cool down and then fit the output shaft and selector shaft oil seals as described in Section 4 and 5.

63 Slide in the selector shaft rod, taking care to prevent the rollers from dropping off (photo), and rest the selector forks in position on the synchromesh units as shown (photo).

64 The next operation is to refit the selector rods and the various balls and springs. When carrying out this operation it is helpful to refer to Fig. 6.14 which clearly shows the ball and spring layouts.

65 Begin by installing an interlocking spring and ball through the

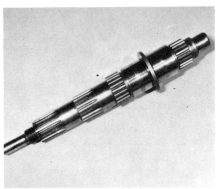

3.45 The mainshaft ready for rebuilding

3.46 Fit the 3rd gear and needle roller bearing

3.47A Installing 3rd/4th gear synchromesh unit

3.47B Installing 3rd gear spacer and spring retainer ring

3.49 Installing 2nd gear

3.50 Installing 1st/2nd gear synchromesh unit

3.51 Installing 1st gear

3.52 Installing reverse gear

3.53 Installing the mainshaft endplate and bearing

3.57 The input shaft

3.59 Screw in studs for location purposes

3.60A Mainshaft, input shaft, and laygear meshed together

3.60B Installing the gears into the end casing

3.63A Installing the selector shaft rod

3.63B Selector forks positioned on the synchro units

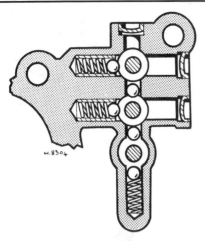

H.8304

Fig. 6.14 Cross section of detent and interlocking balls and springs (Sec 3)

upper access hole (photos). Depress the ball and spring and at the same time insert the reverse gear selector rod (photo). This can be difficult as the ball being round is not easy to depress. When the ball and spring are sufficiently depressed, the selector rod must be pressed down quickly or the ball will be ejected.

66 Having located the reverse gear rod, drop in through the upper access hole an interlock ball. Insert a detent spring and ball into the lower side access hole (photos). Depress the ball and spring and relocate the 1st/2nd gear selector rod.

67 Insert another interlock ball through the upper access hole and locate a detent spring and ball via the upper side access hole. Depress the detent ball and spring and insert the 3rd/4th gear selector rod (photo).

68 Line up the holes in the selector rods and forks then drive in the roll pins (2 to each fork) using a pin punch.

69 Apply jointing compound to the new core plugs and drive them

into the access holes until they are flush with the outer surface of the gearbox casing (photo).

70 Relocate the reverse gear operating arm (photo) and tighten the pivot bolt. This is easier said than done as the arm must not be topped and the pivot bolt must be tight. If you took the initial setting dimension of the arm (paragraph 6) you will have a set dimension to achieve. For those who did not, it is essential that the arm is upright and not bearing hard against the reverse idler gear.

71 Stand the gearbox upright so that it is resting on its rear casing. Heat the main gearbox casing in the region of the bearing holes to a temperature of approximately 80°C (176°F) then lower the main casing onto the gear clusters and rear casing (photo), having first located a new gasket.

72 Allow the casing to cool, but *do not* quench it with water to speed the cooling. When cool, the input shaft bearing locking ring can be fitted (photo) and the secure bolts tightened.

73 If a new bearing has been fitted to either the layshaft or input shaft then it will be necessary to calculate the shims which must be fitted to the ends of these shafts.

74 Using a depth gauge, measure the distance, A, from the outer face of the input shaft bearing to the gearbox face (Fig. 6.15). For an example we will call dimension A 0.2756 in (7.0 mm). Repeat this measurement, B, for the layshaft bearing. For our example we will call dimension B 0.1811 in (4.6 mm). Now stick the gasket to the input shaft housing cover after installing a new oil seal. Using the depth gauge measure the depth, C, of the recess provided for the input shaft bearing (Fig. 6.16). We will call dimension C 0.2952 in (7.5 mm). Similarly, measure the depth, D, of the recess provided for the layshaft bearing. For this example we will call dimension D 0.2086 in (5.3 mm). Carry out a calculation similar to that below in the example:

Shim on input shaft	Shim on layshaft
C 0.2952 in (7.5 mm)	D 0.2086 in (5.3 mm)
A 0.2756 in (7.0 mm)	B 0.1811 in (4.6 mm)
0.0196 in (0.5 mm)	0.0275 in (0.7 mm)

In our example the total value of shims which will be required on

3.65A Installing an interlock spring

3.65B Installing an interlock ball

3.65C Refit reverse gear selector rod

3.66A Inserting a detent spring

3.66B Inserting a detent ball

3.66C Relocating 1st/2nd gear selector rod

3.67 Relocating 3rd/4th gear selector rod

3.69 The core plugs after fitting

3.70 Refit the reverse gear operating arm

3.71 Installing the main gearbox casing

3.72 Fitting the main bearing locking ring

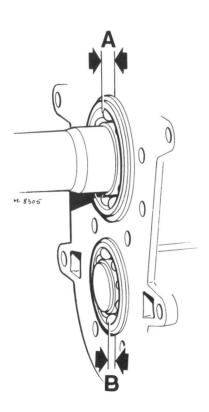

Fig. 6.15 Measuring the protrusion of the input shaft and layshaft bearings from the gearbox face (Sec 3)

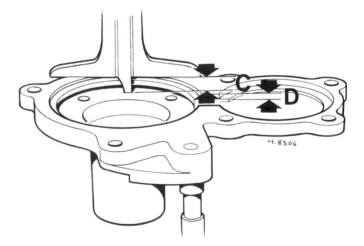

Fig. 6.16 Measuring the depth of the recesses in the front cover (Sec 3)

the input shaft will be 0.0196 in (0.5 mm) and the layshaft will need 0.0275 in (0.7 mm).

75 Apply jointing compound to the gasket and refit the input shaft housing (photo), having fitted the desired thickness of shims. Coat the threads of the bolts with sealing compound then insert them and tighten them to the specified torque in diagonal sequence.

76 Refit the bellhousing and fit the clutch release arm and bearing as described in Chapter 5.

77 Slide on the output drive flange and locking washer (if fitted) (photo).

78 Coat the threads on the mainshaft with a liquid locking agent then fit the nut and tighten it to the specified torque while holding the flange still. Where applicable drive the edge of the locking washer into

3.75 Refit the input shaft housing

3.77 Fitting the drive flange lock washer

3.83 Refitting the gearbox

the cut-out provided.

79 Refit the rubber drive coupling and tighten the nuts to the recommended torque setting.

80 Reconnect the selector shaft knuckle coupling, securing the pin and sliding the cover ring back to its original position.

81 Refit the reversing light switch and the locking pin, spring and plug. Ensure that the locking pin is fitted the correct way round.

82 Refit the gearchange linkage support plate, the exhaust bracket, and the crossmember.

83 The gearbox is now ready for refitting (photo) as described in Section 2.

4 Output flange oil seal (4 or 5-speed manual gearbox) – renewal

1 Drain the gearbox oil into a suitable container.

2 Remove the propeller shaft and flexible coupling as described in Chapter 7 and the exhaust system as described in Chapter 3.

3 Support the gearbox with a trolley jack and detach the mounting crossmember. Where applicable bend the locking washer from the output flange recess.

4 Hold the output flange quite still (using a length of flat steel bolted to two of the flange holes), and unscrew the flange nut with a suitable box spanner or socket.

5 Using a three-legged puller, withdraw the flange from its location splines.

6 Extract the oil seal with a suitable lever, taking care not to damage the oil seal housing or the output shaft splines.

7 Clean the oil seal locating surfaces of the housing, and carefully fit the new oil seal squarely into the housing (photo). An alloy tube of similar diameter to the oil seal is ideal for this operation.

8 Pack the cavity between the oil seal lips with grease, and refit the gearbox output flange, together with the locking washer (if applicable).

9 Coat the threads of the mainshaft with a liquid locking agent then fit the nut and tighten it to the specified torque while holding the flange still. Where applicable drive the edge of the locking washer into the cut-out provided.

10 Refit the flexible coupling, propeller shaft, and exhaust system with reference to Chapters 7 and 3, then fill the gearbox with the correct quantity of recommended oil.

5 Selector shaft oil seal (4 or 5-speed manual gearbox) – renewal

1 Remove the output flange as described in Section 4 paragraphs 1 to 5.

2 Select 1st gear then pull the selector shaft cover ring back, drive out the retaining pin and move the knuckle to one side.

3 Use a narrow, pointed, length of dowel rod, or a small screwdriver, to lever the selector shaft oil seal out of its location, and withdraw the oil seal off the shaft.

4 Before fitting the new seal, pack the cavity between the sealing lips with grease, and clean the locating groove in the housing.

5 Tap the oil seal in squarely with a suitable length of tube then refit the selector shaft knuckle.

6 Refit the output flange with reference to Section 4.

6 Speedometer drive seal (4 or 5-speed manual gearbox) – renewal

1 Jack up the front of the car and support it on axle stands. Apply the handbrake. Drain the gearbox oil into a suitable container.

2 Unscrew and remove the speedometer cable locating bolt from the gearbox housing, and withdraw the cable.

3 Using a length of stiff wire angled at 90° on the end, extract the speedometer drive bushing from the gearbox housing.

4 Slide the sealing ring off the bushing, and clean its locating surfaces.

5 Manipulate the new ring into position using the fingers only, and smear a thin film of gearbox oil on its periphery.

6 Carefully insert the drive bushing into the gearbox housing and press it fully onto the stop, making sure that the locating bolt recess is in alignment with the housing hole (photo).

7 Slide in the speedometer cable and secure the locating bolt.

8 Refill the gearbox with the correct amount of recommended oil, then lower the car to the ground.

7 Input shaft oil seal (4 or 5-speed manual gearbox) – renewal

1 Remove the gearbox as described in Section 2 after draining out the oil.

2 Separate the clutch release lever arm from the bellhousing as described in Chapter 5.

3 Unbolt and remove the bellhousing.

4 Unbolt the release bearing guide sleeve housing. Withdraw it over the input shaft, being careful to retain the adjustment shims (photo).

5 Extract the oil seal with a suitable screwdriver and clean the locating shoulder.

6 Insert the new oil seal into the guide sleeve, closed end first, and drive it firmly onto its seat with a tube of suitable diameter. Pack the cavity between the sealing lips with grease.

7 Refit the guide sleeve housing over the input shaft using a new gasket, making sure the shims are correctly positioned.

8 Tighten the securing bolts to the specified torque setting.

9 Refit the bellhousing.

10 Before refitting the release bearing, pack the inner groove with grease. Also apply a little grease to the bearing surfaces of the release arm, to prevent the mechanism seizing to the guide sleeve.

11 Refit the clutch release bearing and arm into the bellhousing, making sure that the retaining spring clip is fully entered.

12 Refit the gearbox and refill it with a suitable grade of oil.

8 Gear lever (4 or 5-speed manual gearbox) – removal and refitting

1 Jack up the front of the car and support it on axle stands. Apply the handbrake.

2 Working beneath the car disconnect the selector rod from the bottom of the gear lever (photo). To do this on early models unscrew

4.7 Fitting the output flange oil seal

6.6 Installing the speedometer drive bushing. Note the sealing ring

7.4 The input shaft oil seal (shown removed) together with the laygear bearing shim

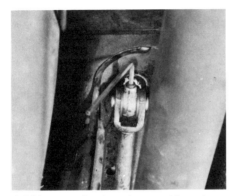

8.2 Disconnecting the selector rod from the bottom of the gear lever on early models

8.4 The gear lever components

the bolt with an Allen key and remove the pivot pin and washers. On later versions select reverse gear, remove the circlip and washer, and slide the rod from the gear lever.

3   Working inside the car pull the rubber gaiter from the central tunnel and move it up the gear lever.

4   Extract the circlip and withdraw the gear lever upward (photo).

5   Refitting is a reversal of removal, but lubricate the gear lever ball with grease, and when reconnecting the early type selector rod make sure that the recess in the pivot pin aligns with the bolt hole.

9   Manual gearbox (5-speed) – overhaul

1   Follow the procedure described in Section 3 paragraphs 1 to 13.

2   Unscrew the socket head bolts securing the front gearbox casing to the intermediate casing.

3   Stand the gearbox on its rear end and heat the front gearbox casing around the input and layshaft bearings sufficiently to expand the casing and enable it to be removed. The alternative method to heating the casing is to draw off the bearing using BMW service tools 232020 and 232050.

4   Select 3rd gear then drive out the selector fork roll pins from the 2nd/3rd and 4th/5th forks and shafts. Also drive the roll pin from the main selector shaft.

5   Remove the 4th/5th selector shaft, then lift the selector arm and remove the main selector shaft.

6   Remove the 2nd/3rd selector shaft. Take care not to lose the detent balls.

7   Unscrew the socket head bolts from the rear casing, and the bolts securing the rear casing to the intermediate casing.

8   Heat the end casing around the mainshaft bearing to approximately 80°C (176°F), then remove the rear casing from the intermediate casing. Take care not to lose the reverse idler spacer washer.

9   Withdraw the main selector shaft taking care not to lose the shaft rollers.

10 Remove the 2nd/3rd and 4th/5th selector forks after identifying them for position.

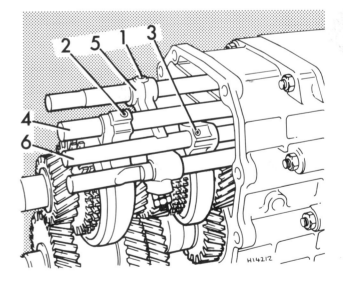

Fig. 6.17 5-speed gearbox with front casing removed (Sec 9)

1, 2, and 3 Roll pins	5 Main selector shaft arm
4 4th/5th selector shaft	6 2nd/3rd selector shaft

11 Using a puller located on the reverse gear, remove the speedometer drivegear, washer, ball bearing, support ring, and reverse gear from the mainshaft. Note the quantity of shims between the bearing and support ring.

12 Drive the roll pin from the dog on the 1st/reverse shaft.

13 Extract the split thrust washer then withdraw the synchro unit together with the 1st/reverse selector fork and shaft, at the same time removing the dog from the inner end of the shaft.

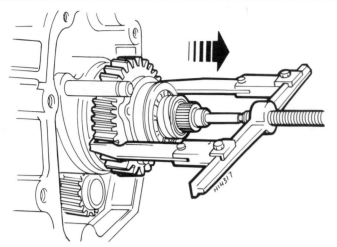

Fig. 6.18 Removing the speedometer drive gear, bearing and reverse gear (Sec 9)

14 Withdraw the 1st gear together with the synchro ring and needle bearings.

15 Using an Allen key remove the socket head bolts from the intermediate casing and remove the retainers from the inner side.

16 Heat the intermediate casing in the area around the mainshaft and layshaft bearings to approximately 80°C (176°F), then withdraw the mainshaft and laygear together from the intermediate casing using a wooden mallet to assist if necessary.

17 The gear clusters can now be dismantled. During the dismantling operation, lay the components out in order so that they can be reassembled correctly.

18 Commence dismantling by pulling off the input shaft together with its synchro ring.

19 Remove the needle bearing either from the mainshaft or the input shaft recess.

20 From the end of the mainshaft extract the circlip and spacer shim.

21 Pull off the synchro unit for 4th and 5th gears followed by the synchro ring, 4th gear, and the needle bearing.

22 From the other end of the mainshaft pull off the collared sleeve and bearing using a suitable puller. Note the spacer between the sleeve and bearing.

23 Using the puller remove the 2nd gear together with the needle bearing and collared sleeve.

24 Pull off the 3rd gear and 2nd/3rd synchro unit then separate the 3rd gear and remove both syncho rings.

25 Finally remove the needle bearing from the mainshaft.

26 The layshaft can be partially dismantled if necessary by removing the bolt and spacer. Prise off the 1st gear and remove the shim then use a puller to remove the ball bearing. Temporarily refit the bolt while removing the bearing to prevent damage to the threads in the layshaft.

27 Returning to the gearbox end casing, drill a small hole in each of the core plugs covering the ends of the selector rod holes. Insert a self tapping screw, grip the screw, and remove the core plug. Extract the plunger springs and any remaining detent balls.

28 Also from the end casing remove the reverse idler gear, the two needle bearings, and the spacer.

29 Follow paragraphs 37 to 40 of Section 3.

30 The gearbox is now ready for assembly. If new ball bearings or a new mainshaft roller bearing are to be fitted it will be necessary to calculate the thickness of shims. Otherwise refit the original shims.

31 Commence assembly by fitting the needle bearings and spacer to the end casing shaft followed by the reverse idler gear.

32 Press the ball bearing on the end of the layshaft with the groove on the outer track facing outward. Using a depth gauge determine dimension C Fig. 6.21. Now determine the width D of the layshaft 1st gear, and deduct D from C. The result is the thickness of shim.

33 Fit the shim and 1st gear having previously heated the gear to approximately 80°C (176°F).

34 Coat the threads of the retaining bolt with a liquid locking agent, then insert it with the layshaft together with the spacer and tighten it.

35 Locate the 3rd gear and needle bearing onto the rear of the mainshaft against the fixed spacer.

36 Fit the 3rd gear and 3rd synchro ring then drive on the 2nd/3rd synchro unit and locate the 2nd synchro ring in the synchro unit.

37 Locate the 2nd gear and needle bearing on the collared sleeve, then drive the sleeve onto the mainshaft next to the synchro unit.

38 Heat the roller bearing inner race to 80°C (176°F) and drive it fully onto the mainshaft.

39 Using a depth gauge determine dimension A Fig. 6.23. Position the 1st gear collared sleeve against the 1st/reverse synchro unit and determine dimension B Fig 6.24 using a micrometer. Deduct B from A and fit a shim of the resulting thickness next to the roller bearing inner race.

40 Fit the roller bearing outer race then tap on the 1st gear collared sleeve.

41 To the front of the mainshaft fit the needle bearing and 4th gear and locate the synchro ring on the gear. Drive on the 4th/5th synchro unit making sure that the keys engage the cut outs in the ring.

42 Fit a suitable spacer shim and insert the circlip.

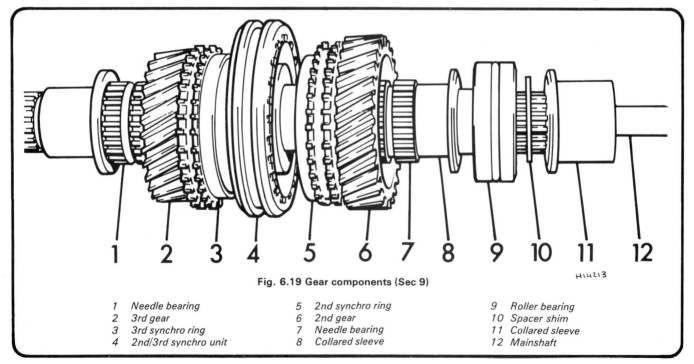

Fig. 6.19 Gear components (Sec 9)

1	Needle bearing	5	2nd synchro ring	9	Roller bearing
2	3rd gear	6	2nd gear	10	Spacer shim
3	3rd synchro ring	7	Needle bearing	11	Collared sleeve
4	2nd/3rd synchro unit	8	Collared sleeve	12	Mainshaft

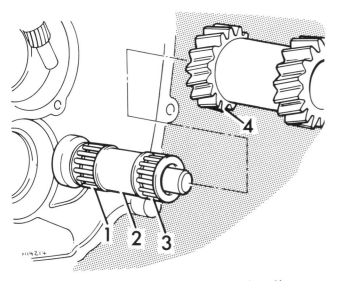

Fig. 6.20 Reverse idler gear components (Sec 9)

1 and 3 Needle bearing   2   Spacer   4   Reverse idler gear

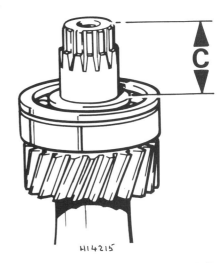

Fig. 6.21 Measuring dimension C on the layshaft (Sec 9)

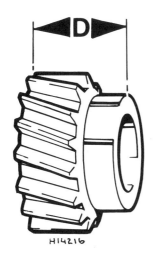

Fig. 6.22 Measuring width D of the layshaft 1st gear (Sec 9)

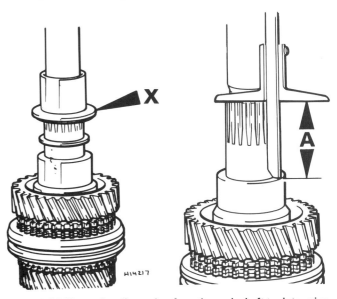

Fig. 6.23 Measuring dimension A on the mainshaft to determine thickness of shim X (Sec 9)

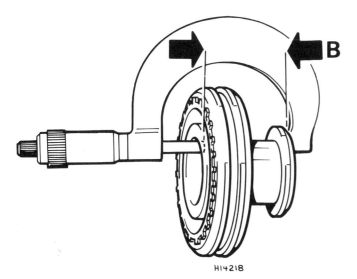

Fig. 6.24 Measuring dimension B on the 1st/reverse synchro unit (Sec 9)

43 Locate the needle bearing on the front of the mainshaft then fit the 5th synchro ring to the synchro unit and slide on the input shaft.
44 Mesh the laygear with the mainshaft then install the gears into the intermediate casing having previously heated the casing to approximately 80°C (176°F).
45 Locate the retainers behind the intermediate casing then insert and tighten the socket head bolts.
46 Fit the 1st gear needle bearing followed by the 1st gear and synchro ring.
47 Engage the 1st/reverse selector shaft and fork with the 1st/reverse synchro unit then insert the shaft in the intermediate casing and the synchro unit on the mainshaft and also slide the dog on the inner end of the shaft. Lock the dog by driving in the roll pin.
48 Fit the split thrust washer in the shaft groove.
49 Locate the reverse gear and needle bearing on the collared sleeve, then drive the sleeve onto the mainshaft having previously heated it to approximately 80°C (176°F).
50 Using a depth gauge determine dimension E Fig. 6.26, then position the bearing on the support ring and determine dimension F Fig. 6.27. Deduct F from E for the thickness of shim Y to be fitted between the bearing and support ring.
51 Locate a 0.5 mm (0.020 in) thick shim on the rear of the mainshaft followed by the support ring and shim.
52 Heat the bearing inner race and speedometer drive gear to

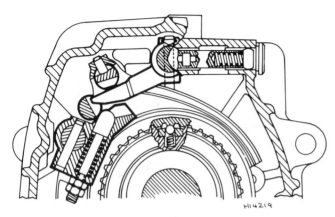

Fig. 6.25 Cross section of the selector shafts (Sec 9)

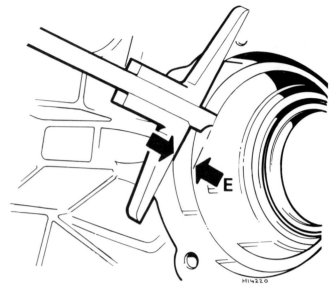

Fig. 6.26 Measuring dimension E in the rear end casing (Sec 9)

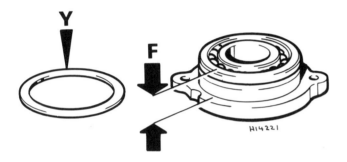

Fig. 6.27 Measuring dimension F on the rear bearing and support ring to determine thickness of shim Y (Sec 9)

approximately 80°C (176°F), then drive them onto the mainshaft with the washer located between them. The groove on the outer track must face outward.

53　Locate the 2nd/3rd and 4th/5th selector forks on their respective synchro units.

54　Insert the main selector shaft into the intermediate casing taking care not to lose the rollers. The shaft detent grooves should face the left-hand side of the casing.

55　Make up two long studs and screw them into the support ring for use as guides. Stick the reverse idler spacer washer over the hole in the intermediate casing. Locate a new gasket on the rear face of the casing. In the following procedure make sure that the opening and the support ring faces the bottom of the casing.

56　Heat the end casing to approximately 80°C (176°F) then fit it to the intermediate casing while inserting the guides. Do not displace the reverse idler spacer washer. As the 1st/reverse gear selector shaft enters the end casing, insert a spring and detent ball through the upper access hole then depress the ball and move the shaft over it.

57　Insert the rear casing to imtermediate casing bolts and tighten them evenly.

58　Insert the socket head bolts which secure the retaining ring and also remove the guide studs. Do not forget to fit the sealing washers on the bolts. Tighten the bolts evenly.

59　Insert the 2nd/3rd selector shaft through the fork and into the end casing. Insert the interlock ball through the upper access hole, and a spring and detent ball through the lower side access hole. Depress the ball and move the shaft over it.

60　Drive the roll pin through the 2nd/3rd selector fork and shaft.

61　Locate the selector arm on the main selector shaft and lower it into position.

62　Insert the 4th/5th selector shaft through the fork and into the end casing. Insert the interlock ball through the upper access hole, and a spring and detent ball through the upper side access hole. Depress the ball and move the shaft over it.

63　Drive the roll pins through the 4th/5th selector fork and shaft, and

the main selector arm and shaft.

64　Apply jointing compound to the new core plugs and drive them into the access holes until flush.

65　Stand the gearbox in its rear end then heat the front gearbox casing to approximately 80°C (176°F). Locate a new gasket on the intermediate casing then lower the front casing into position.

66　Insert the socket head bolts and tighten them evenly, then fit the locking ring to the input shaft bearing.

67　Follow the procedure given in Section 3 paragraphs 73 to 83.

10　Automatic transmission – general description

This type of transmission may be supplied as optional equipment on all models. There are two makes of automatic transmission fitted to the various models, ZF or Borg-Warner. Two model types of ZF automatic gearbox are to be found, these are the 3HP-20 and the 3HP-22.

Three forward speeds and one reverse speed are provided. There is a kickdown facility for rapid acceleration during overtaking when an immediate change to a lower speed range is required.

Due to the complexity of the automatic transmission unit and the need for special tools, if performance is not up to standard, or overhaul is necessary, it is imperative that this be left to your local BMW or automatic transmission specialist who will have the special equipment and knowledge for fault diagnosis and rectification. The contents of the following Sections are therefore confined to supplying general information and any service information and instruction that can be used by the owner.

11　Automatic transmission – routine maintenance

1　Every 10 000 miles (15 000 km) on UK models or 12 500 miles (20 000 km) on USA models the automatic transmission fluid level should be checked. To do this, run the car for a minimum of 5 miles (8 km), apply the handbrake and with the engine idling, move the speed selector lever to all positions, finally setting it in the P detent.

2　With the engine still idling, withdraw the dipstick, wipe clean, reinsert it and withdraw it again for a second time (photo). The fluid level should be between the 'low' and 'high' marks otherwise top it up to the correct level by pouring specified fluid down the combined filler/dipstick guide tube (photo).

3　Occasionally, check the security of all bolts on the transmission unit and keep the exterior clean and free from mud or oil to prevent overheating.

4　Every 20 000 miles (30 000 km) drain the transmission fluid (hot) and refill with fresh fluid. Renew the fluid filter screen at the same time (Chapter 13, Section 8).

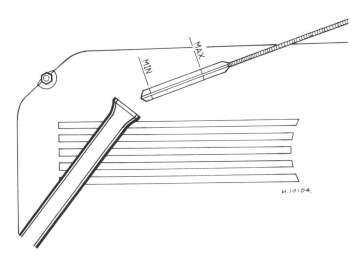

Fig. 6.28 Automatic transmission fluid level dipstick marks (Sec 11)

12 Automatic transmission (ZF type) – removal and refitting

1   This operation is within the scope of the home mechanic where a new or reconditioned unit is to be fitted or where a faulty unit must be removed for repair. It is emphasised however that the transmission should not be removed from the vehicle before the fault has been diagnosed under operation conditions by the repairing agent using special testing equipment.

2   Remove the lead from the battery negative terminal and the air cleaner complete.

3   Disconnect the downshift cable, and holder (as applicable) (photo).

4   Drain the transmission fluid by unscrewing the drain plug (photo).

5   Disconnect the oil filler tube support bracket and remove the tube from the transmission unit. Note the sealing O-ring and seal the opening with a piece of adhesive tape to prevent the entry of dirt.

6   Remove the complete exhaust system and the exhaust pipe support bracket from the rear end of the transmission.

7   Disconnect the oil cooler pipe line connections at the side of the transmission unit (photo). Plug the ends of the pipes.

8   Separate the multi-wiring plug connector at the side of the bellhousing (3HP-20 only).

9   Remove the bellhousing cover plate and vent plate (photos).

10   Turn the starter ring gear by inserting a screwdriver and undo the four bolts securing the torque converter to the driveplate (photo).

11   Detach the selector rod by removing the horseshoe clip or spring clip (photo).

12   Remove the propeller shaft as described in Chapter 7.

13   Undo the speedometer cable lock bolt and pull out the speedometer cable.

14   Support the transmission on a jack, preferably of the trolley type. Unbolt the rear mounting crossmember from the transmission and bodyframe.

15   Using a long socket bar and universal joint, remove the bolts securing the transmission to the engine.

16   Lower the jack carefully and withdraw the transmission to the rear. Use a strong screwdriver as a lever to keep the torque converter pressed into the converter housing during the withdrawal operation and expect some loss of fluid.

17   Refitting is a reversal of removal, however it is important that the torque converter is fully engaged with the oil pump. To check this place a straight-edge across the bellhousing. On the 3HP-20 the torque converter spigot must be below the straight-edge, and on the 3HP-22 the driveplate contact faces on the torque converter must be 12 mm (0.5 in) below the straight-edge. Refill the transmission with fluid and adjust the selector lever and downshift cable as described in Sections 14 and 15. Renew the oil filler tube O-ring to prevent the possibility of leakage. Likewise it will be found advantageous to renew the seals of the oil cooler connections.

11.2A Removing the automatic transmission fluid level dipstick

11.2B Topping-up the automatic transmission fluid level

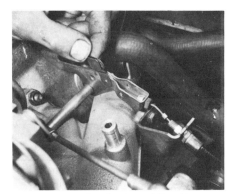

12.3 Disconnecting the downshift cable

12.4 Showing lower view of automatic transmission and drain plug (arrowed)

12.7 Disconnecting the oil cooler pipes

12.9A Remove the bellhousing cover plate ...

12.9B ... and vent plate

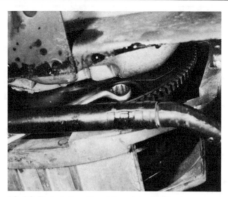

12.10 Removing the driveplate bolts

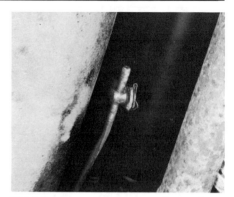

12.11 Selector rod to gear lever pivot and adjustment

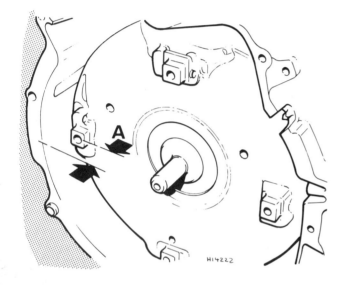

Fig. 6.29 With torque converter fully entered on ZF 3HP-22 type transmission, dimension A should be 12 mm (0.5 in) (Sec 12)

13 Automatic transmission (Borg-Warner type) – removal and refitting

1　This operation is within the scope of the home mechanic where a new or reconditioned unit is to be fitted or where a faulty unit must be removed for repair. It is emphasised however that the transmission should not be removed from the vehicle before the fault has been diagnosed under operational conditions by the repairing agent using special testing equipment.

2　Remove the lead from the battery negative terminal and separate the multi-wiring plug connector. Detach the cable bracket.

3　Remove the complete exhaust system and the exhaust pipe support bracket from the rear of the transmission.

4　Disconnect the downshift cable.

5　Remove the plug and drain out the transmission fluid.

6　Unscrew the oil filter tube mounting bolt and union nut, remove the tube and plug the hole to prevent the entry of dirt.

7　Note the location of the oil cooler flow and return pipes, unscrew the union nuts at the bracket, and also detach the bracket from the cylinder block.

8　Remove the bellhousing cover plate and the air grille.

9　Turn the starter ring gear by inserting a screwdriver and undo the four bolts securing the torque converter to the driveplate.

10　Detach the selector rod by removing the horseshoe clip.

11　Remove the propeller shaft as described in Chapter 7.

12　Support the transmission with a trolley jack and remove the crossmember.

13　Remove the lockbolt and pull out the speedometer cable.

14　Lower the jack until the oilpan rests on the front axle crossmember. Remove the bolts securing the transmission to the engine and detach the guard (where applicable).

15　Withdraw the transmission to the rear whilst lowering the jack. Use a strong screwdriver as a lever to keep the torque converter pressed into the converter housing during the withdrawal operation and expect some loss of fluid.

16　Refitting is a reversal of removal, however it is important that the torque converter is fully engaged with the oil pump. To check this place a straight-edge across the bellhousing – the driveplate contact faces on the torque converter must be below the straight-edge. Refill the transmission with fluid and adjust the selector lever and downshift cable as described in Sections 14 and 15.

14 Automatic transmission selector lever – adjustment

1　Jack up the front of the car and support it on axle stands. Apply the handbrake.

2　Engage neutral (position O) and check that the lever in the transmission is also in neutral. On ZF transmissions this is the third detent from the rear. On Borg-Wartner transmissions check that the selector arm pivot is 93.7 mm (3.689 in) behind the bellhousing to casing face.

3　Detach the long selector rod from the bottom of the selector lever.

4　With the selector lever inside the car and on the transmission in the neutral position (interior selector lever fully forward in O position), adjust the selector rod pivot so that it enters the bottom of the selector lever.

5　Now shorten the selector rod by turning the pivot the following number of turns:

ZF 3HP-30	3 complete turns
ZF 3HP-22	1 to 2 turns
B-W 65 (UK)	4 to 4½ turns
B-W 65 (USA)	2 to 2½ turns

6　Reconnect the long selector rod, then lower the car to the ground.

15 Automatic transmission downshift cable – adjustment

ZF 3HP-20 type

1　Remove the air filter housing (see Chapter 3), then check that the length of the vertical throttle linkage between centres is 275 mm (10.827 in). If not, disconnect one end and adjust the length as necessary.

2　Disconnect the horizontal throttle linkage and downshift cable from the relay lever. Turn the relay lever anti-clockwise to the full throttle position without expanding the tensioning element (ie not to the kick down position).

3　Pull out the downshift cable to the full throttle position and check that the pivot holes in the cable end and relay lever are exactly aligned. If not, adjust the cable end as necessary, then reconnect it to the relay lever.

4　Have an assistant fully depress the accelerator pedal to the kick down position. Turn the relay lever fully anti-clockwise to the kick

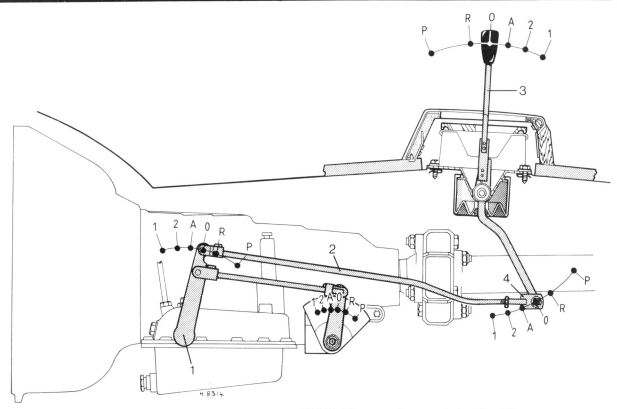

Fig. 6.30 Selector lever arrangement on ZF 3HP-20 automatic transmission (Sec 14)

1 Transmission selector lever
2 Selector rod
3 Interior selector lever
4 Adjustable pivot

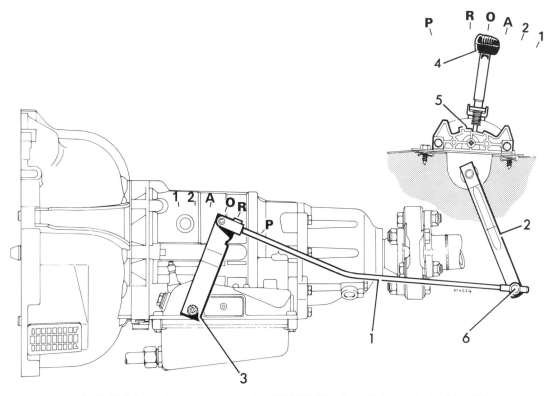

Fig. 6.31 Selector lever arrangement on ZF 3HP-22 automatic transmission (Sec 14)

1 Selector rod
2 Selector lever lower extension
3 Transmission selector lever
4 Interior selector lever
5 Selector stop plate
6 Adjustable pivot

Fig. 6.32 Selector lever arrangement on BW65 automatic transmission (Sec 14)

S   Selector rod   D   Adjustable pivot
B   Setting dimension

H.12259

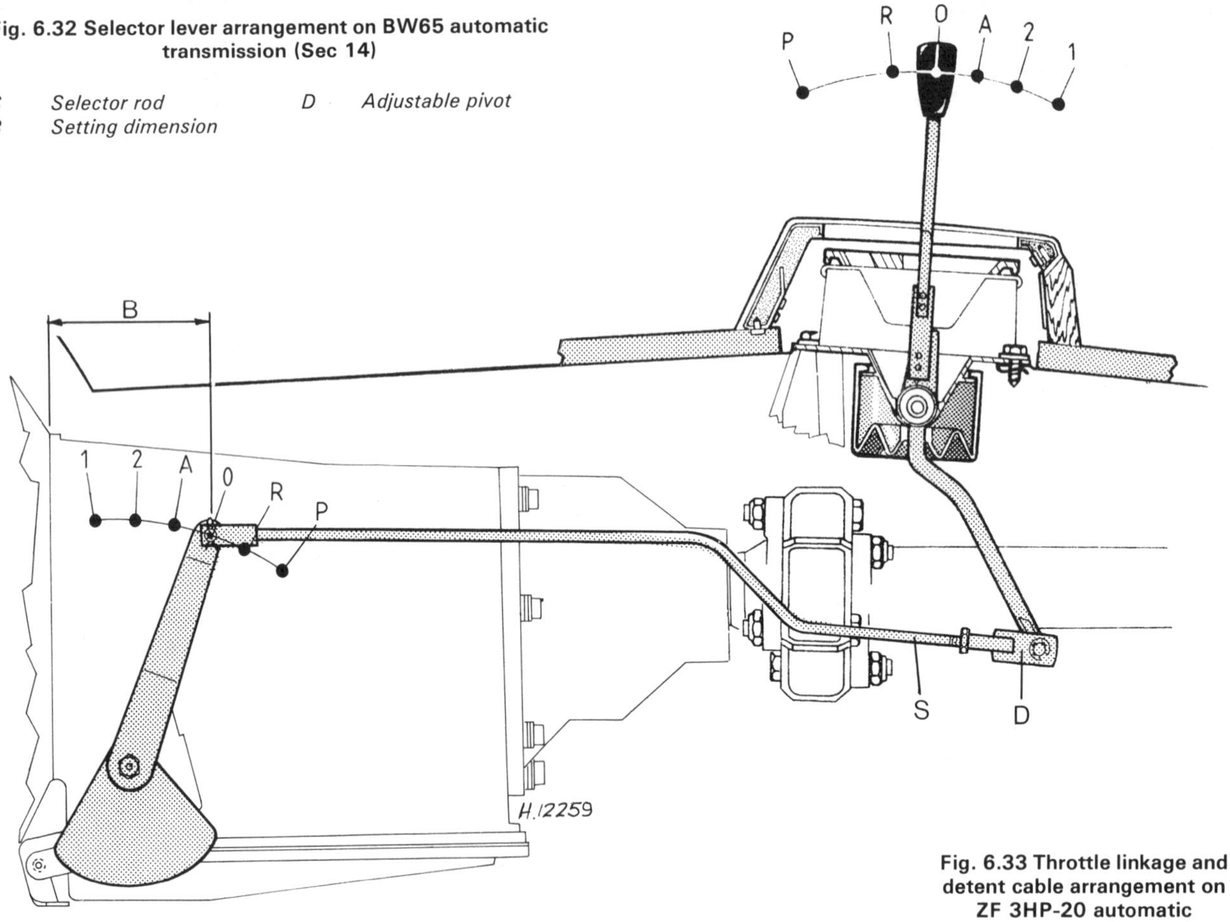

Fig. 6.33 Throttle linkage and detent cable arrangement on ZF 3HP-20 automatic transmission (Sec 15)

1   Tensioning element
2   Linkage
3   Detent cable end
4 and 5 Throttle valve
6   Relay lever
7   Adjustment
8   Accelerator pedal
9   Kick down stop
A   Setting dimension

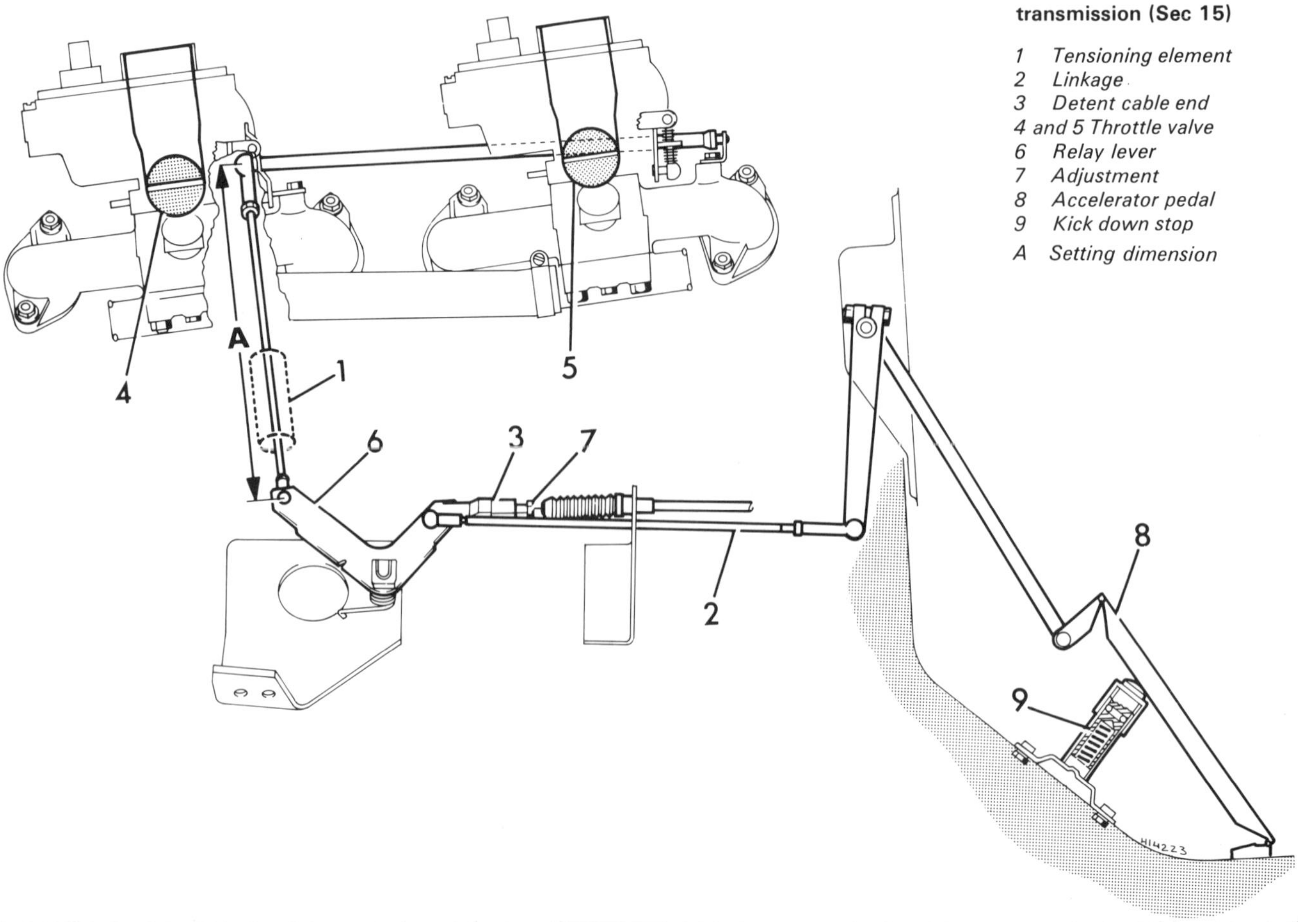

H14223

down position (ie with the tensioning element expanded) then adjust the length of the horizontal throttle linkage so that the ball end is aligned with the ball. Connect the ball end to the relay lever.
5   Refit the air filter housing (see Chapter 3).

ZF 3HP-22 type
6   Run the engine to normal operating temperature then switch it off.
7   Remove the air filter housing if necessary then check the length of the vertical throttle linkage between centres. On carburettor engines it should be 275 mm (10.827 in), on fuel injection engines 430 mm (16.929 in). Note that the tensioning element should be relaxed. If necessary, disconnect and adjust the linkage as necessary.
8   Start the engine and let it idle. The gap between the nipple on the downshift inner cable and the outer cable should be between 0.25 and 0.75 mm (0.010 and 0.030 in). If not, adjust the cable end as necessary. Switch off the engine.
9   On models with the early arrangement (Fig. 6.34), have an assistant fully depress the accelerator pedal to the kick down position. Check that the distance between the nipple on the downshift inner cable and the outer cable is between 44.0 and 51.0 mm (1.732 and 2.008 in). If not, adjust the length of the horizontal linkage as necessary.
10 On models with the later arrangement (Fig. 6.35), depress the accelerator pedal to the full throttle position (ie not the kick down position). If necessary adjust the kick down stop so that it just touches the accelerator pedal. Now have an assistant fully depress the accelerator pedal to the kick down position. Check that the distance between the nipple on the downshift inner cable and the outer cable is between 43.75 and 52.25 mm (1.722 and 2.057 in). If not, adjust the outer cable as necessary by repositioning the locknuts.

B-W 65 type
11 Adjust the engine idling speed as described in Chapter 3 with the vertical throttle linkage disconnected.
12 Turn the throttle linkage relay lever fully clockwise so that it contacts the stop and check that the vertical throttle linkage ball end is aligned with the ball on the relay lever. If not, adjust the length of the linkage as necessary then reconnect it.
13 Check that the gap between the nipple on the downshift inner cable and the outer cable is between 0.25 and 0.50 mm (0.010 and 0.020 in). If not, adjust the cable end as necessary.
14 With the engine stopped, have an assistant fully depress the accelerator pedal to the kick down position. Check that the distance between the nipple on the downshift inner cable and the outer cable is at least 43 mm (1.693 in). In the normal full throttle position (ie not kick down) the distance should be 37 mm (1.456 in). If necessary, adjust the length of the horizontal throttle linkage, but if this now increases the engine idling speed repeat the procedure from paragraph 10.

16 Automatic transmission rear oil seal – renewal

1   The rear oil seal can be renewed without removing the transmission. First remove the propeller shaft as described in Chapter 7.
2   For improved access support the transmission with a trolley jack, remove the rear mounting nuts, and lower the transmission. However this is not essential.
3   Prise the locking plate out of the output flange recess.

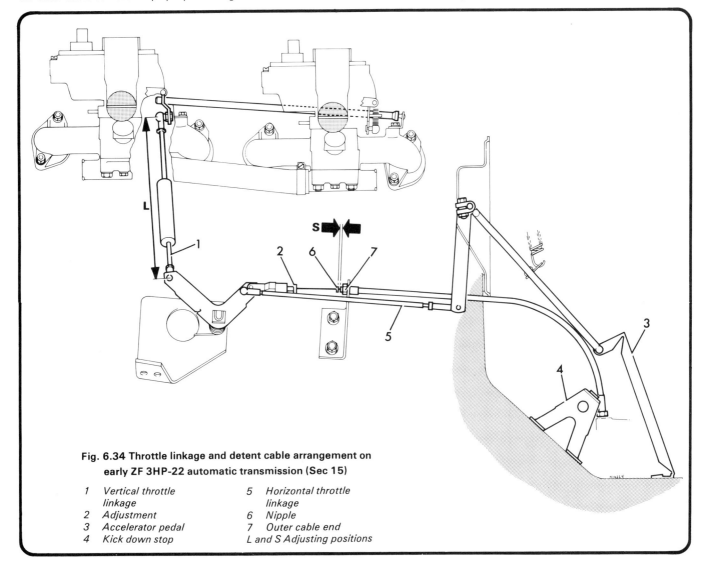

Fig. 6.34 Throttle linkage and detent cable arrangement on early ZF 3HP-22 automatic transmission (Sec 15)

1	Vertical throttle linkage	5	Horizontal throttle linkage
2	Adjustment	6	Nipple
3	Accelerator pedal	7	Outer cable end
4	Kick down stop	L and S	Adjusting positions

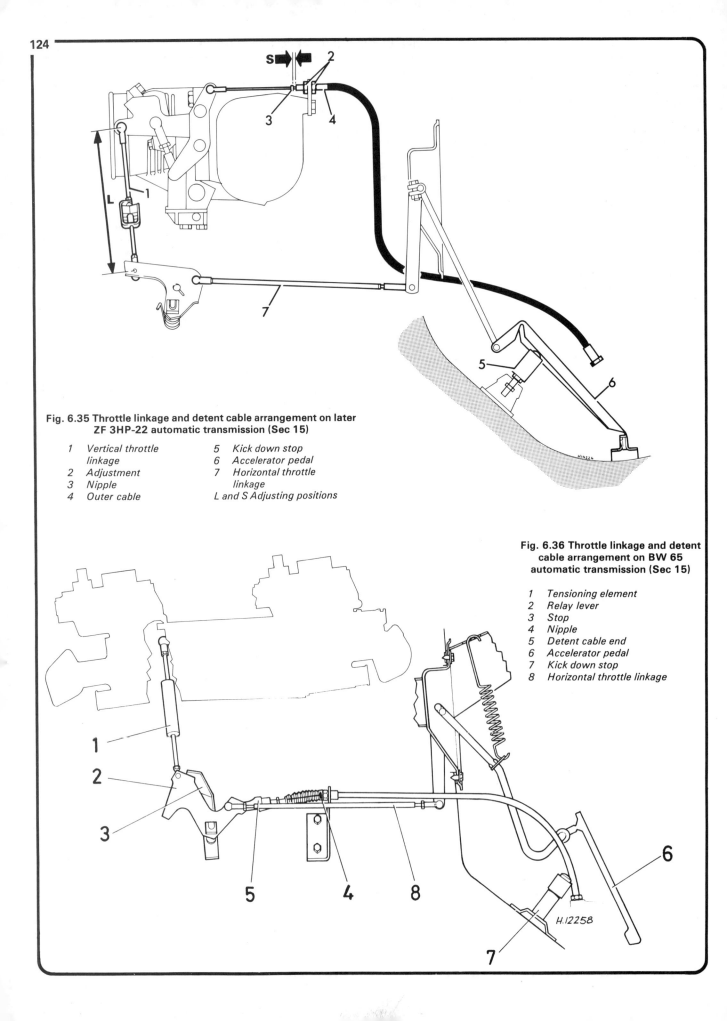

**Fig. 6.35 Throttle linkage and detent cable arrangement on later
ZF 3HP-22 automatic transmission (Sec 15)**

1	Vertical throttle linkage	5	Kick down stop
2	Adjustment	6	Accelerator pedal
3	Nipple	7	Horizontal throttle linkage
4	Outer cable		L and S Adjusting positions

**Fig. 6.36 Throttle linkage and detent
cable arrangement on BW 65
automatic transmission (Sec 15)**

1 Tensioning element
2 Relay lever
3 Stop
4 Nipple
5 Detent cable end
6 Accelerator pedal
7 Kick down stop
8 Horizontal throttle linkage

H.12258

4   Hold the output flange quite still (using a length of flat steel bolted to two of the flange holes), and unscrew the flange nut with a suitable box spanner or socket.

5   Pull off the output flange.

6   The rear oil seal is now exposed and it may be extracted by levering or using a two-legged puller, the pressure from the centre screw being applied to the end of the transmission output shaft.

7   Clean the oil seal locating surfaces and pack the cavity between the oil seal sealing lips with grease. Drive in the new seal using a piece of tubing as a drift. On ZF 3HP-20 transmissions the seal should be driven in to a depth of 0.118 in (3 mm) below the end face of housing.

8   Reassembly is a reversal of dismantling, but lock the output flange nut by tapping the locking plate into the special recess.

17.2 Removing the torque converter

17 Automatic transmission front oil seal – renewal

1   If loss of transmission fluid is evident at the base of the torque converter housing at the joint of the cover plate, then this is almost certainly due to a faulty front oil seal.

2   Access to this seal can only be gained if the engine or transmission is first withdrawn and the torque converter removed (photo).

3   The oil seal may then be prised out with a lever or using a two-legged extractor applying pressure from its centre screw to a suitable metal pad on the end of the transmission input shaft.

4   Drive in the new seal using a piece of tubing (photo).

5   Refitting is a reversal of removal and reassembly but make sure that the lugs of the torque converter are fully engaged with the primary oil pump (see Section 12 and 13).

18 Automatic transmission speedometer drive O-ring – renewal

1   Fluid leakage from this component can be rectified by unscrewing the lockbolt and withdrawing the pinion/gear assembly. Renew the O-ring seal.

2   If the internal seal is leaking (evident by fluid collecting in the lower loop of the speedometer cable) the pinion/gear assembly should be renewed.

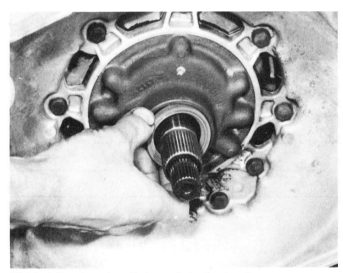

17.4 Installing the automatic transmission front seal

19 Automatic transmission selector lever – removal and refitting

ZF 3HP-20 and early B-W 65

1   Jack-up the front of the car and support it on axle stands. Apply the handbrake.

2   Disconnect the selector rod from the bottom of the lever by removing the circlip and washer.

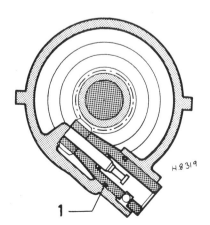

Fig. 6.37 Cross section showing speedometer drive (Sec 18)

1   Outer O-ring seal (renewable)

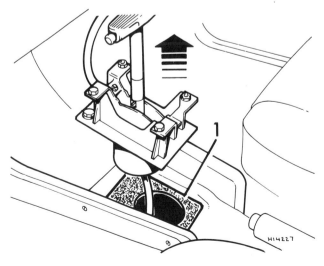

Fig. 6.38 Removing the automatic transmission selector lever assembly on a ZF 3HP-20 type (Sec 19)

1   Seal

19.10 Automatic transmission selector lever on a ZF 3 HP-22 type

3 Remove the crosshead screws from the sides of the centre console and withdraw the surround over the lever.
4 Unbolt and remove the selector lever assembly.
5 Refitting is a reversal of removal, but adjust the selector lever as described in Section 14.

ZF 3HP-22 and later B-W 65
6 Jackup the front of the car and support it on axle stands. Apply the handbrake.

7 Disconnect the selector rod from the bottom of the lever by extracting the spring retainer.
8 Remove the crosshead screws hidden beneath the brush material, and withdraw the centre console cover plate.
9 Remove the crosshead screws from the sides of the centre console and withdraw the surround over the lever.
10 Disconnect the wiring multi-plug then unbolt and remove the selector lever assembly (photo). Remove the sealing plate.
11 Refitting is a reversal of removal, but adjust the selector lever as described in Section 14.

20 Fault diagnosis – manual gearbox and automatic transmission

Symptom	Reason(s)
Manual gearbox	
Ineffective synchromesh	Worn synchro rings
Jumps out of gear	Weak or broken detent springs
	Worn selector forks
	Weak or broken synchro hub springs
Noisy operation (all gears)	Oil level low, or wrong grade of oil used
	Worn bearings
	Worn gears
Noisy operation (except top gear)	Worn input shaft to mainshaft needle roller bearing
Difficult engagement of gears	Worn selector components
	Clutch fault
	Worn synchro hubs
	Input shaft spigot bearing in flywheel seized
Automatic transmission	
Speed shifts too high or low	Downshift cable incorrectly adjusted
No kickdown	Downshift cable incorrectly adjusted
No forward or reverse drive	Low fluid level
Transmission slip	Low fluid level
	Downshift cable disconnected

Note: The faults listed are only those which are considered to be capable of rectification by the home mechanic.

Chapter 7 Propeller shaft

For modifications, and information applicable to later models, see Supplement at end of manual

Contents

Specifications

Type .... Two-section tubular shaft, centre bearing in flexible mounting supporting front of rear section, universal joints in the centre and rear, flexible coupling at the front

Centre bearing forward preload .... 2 mm (0.08 in)

Torque wrench settings

	lbf ft	Nm
Front flexible coupling	84 to 93	114 to 127
Propeller shaft to final drive	50 to 56	68 to 76
Heat shield to propeller shaft (USA models)	44 to 50	60 to 68
Centre bearing to body	16 to 17	22 to 24
Heat shield to centre bearing	9 to 10	12 to 14

1 General description

There are two types of propeller shaft available, one for the automatic transmission models, which incorporates a joint disc connection to the transmission output flange, and another type for manual transmission models which is slightly different and incorporates a 'Guibo' coupling to the gearbox output flange.

On both types, it is not possible to renew the universal joints, as they are staked in position, and the complete shaft is balanced to very fine limits when manufactured. When dismantling, always mark the positions of the components, so that they can be refitted in the same relative position.

2 Propeller shaft – removal and refitting

1   Jack-up the front and rear of the car and support it on axle stands. Release the handbrake.
2   Remove the complete exhaust system as described in Chapter 3.

3   Unscrew the locknuts retaining the front coupling to the gearbox/transmission rear flange, while holding the bolt heads stationary (photo). Remove the bolts noting that the heads face rearward. If they are difficult to remove tighten a large clip around the coupling or alternatively obtain the special BMW tool (see Fig. 7.2).
4   Mark the front and rear propeller shaft flanges in relation to the gearbox/transmission rear flange and final drive flange.
5   Unscrew the locknuts retaining the rear flange to the final drive flange, and remove the bolts noting that the heads face forward (photo).
6   On USA models unbolt and remove the heat shield.
7   On all models support the centre bearing then unscrew the centre bearing nuts (photo).
8   Loosen the gearbox/transmission rear mounting crossmember to body nuts and push the left-hand side of the crossmember forward.
9   Lower the centre bearing and detach the rear section from the final drive flange, then withdraw the complete propeller shaft rearward from the pin on the gearbox/transmission rear coupling. Note the location of any washers between the centre bearing and the body as these ensure the correct alignment of the propeller shaft.

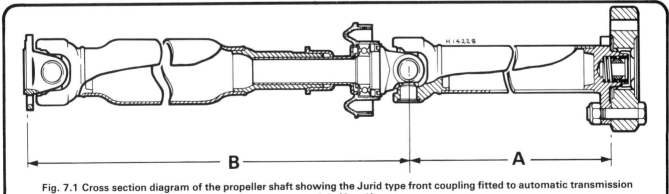

Fig. 7.1 Cross section diagram of the propeller shaft showing the Jurid type front coupling fitted to automatic transmission models (Sec 1)

Dimension 'a' and 'b' vary according to model

2.3 Propeller shaft front coupling

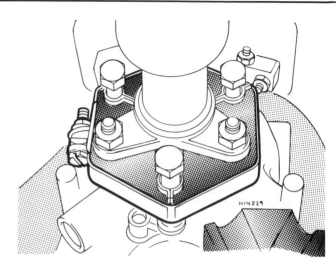

Fig. 7.2 The special tool for compressing the 'Guibo' front coupling (Sec 2)

2.5 Propeller shaft rear coupling and final drive flange

2.7 Centre bearing and mounting bracket

10 Refitting is a reversal of removal, but observe the following points:

   (a) *When refitting the front coupling, use new nuts, and avoid undue stress on the coupling by tightening the nuts only, keeping the bolt heads still*

   (b) *Use new locknuts on the rear flange bolts*

   (c) *Preload the centre bearing, by pushing the mounting towards the front of the car by 0.079 in (2 mm), before tightening the securing nuts*

11 The alignment of the two section propeller shaft can be checked by the use of a straight edge and small blocks. Any misalignment could cause vibration and drumming noises during operation. To correct vertical misalignment, place washers under the centre bearing mounting bracket. To correct lateral misalignment, move the centre bearing bracket to either side as necessary.

---

3 Flexible coupling and centring bush – checking and overhaul

1 The propeller shaft front coupling and centring bush should be checked for wear and damage every 10 000 miles (15 000 km) on UK models, or every 12 500 miles (20 000 km) on USA models. To do this, attempt to move the propeller shaft front section up and down; any excessive movement or play indicates that the coupling and/or

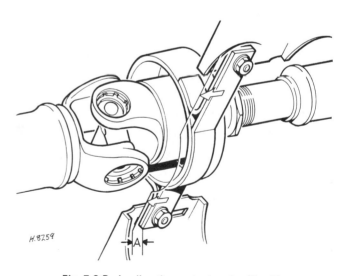

Fig. 7.3 Preloading the centre bearing (Sec 2)

A = 2.0 mm (0.079 in)

centring bush requires renewal.

2   To avoid unnecessary strain on the centre bearing first remove the complete propeller shaft as described in Section 2.

3   Unbolt the flexible coupling from the propeller shaft. On manual gearbox models tighten a large clip around the Guibo coupling to facilitate removal of the bolts, and note that the bolt heads face forward. On USA 528i models slide the coupling heat shield onto the propeller shaft front section.

4   Examine the flexible coupling for wear and damage and renew it if necessary.

5   Examine the gearbox/transmission rear flange centring pin and the centring bush components in the front of the propeller shaft. Excessive wear on the pin will necessitate the renewal of the gearbox/transmission mainshaft, however this is rarely necessary. If the centring bush is worn, renew it as follows.

6   Fill the space between the bush and flange with thick grease, then insert a 14 mm (0.551 in) diameter metal rod through the bush and drive it in with a hammer. The pressure will drive the bush from the flange.

7   Extract the circlip and withdraw the centring bush and spring.

8   Scoop the thick grease from the flange and wash all the components in a suitable solvent.

9   Reassembly is a reversal of dismantling, but lubricate the centring bush components with 6 grams of molybdenum grease, and drive the bush into the flange until it protrudes by the amount shown in Fig. 7.7.

10 When refitting the flexible coupling always use new locknuts. On automatic transmission models the arrows on the periphery of the coupling must point to a flange arm (ie not to a bolt head). If this precaution is not taken the coupling may be noisy and short lived.

11 Refit the propeller shaft with reference to Section 2.

---

4   Centre bearing and flexible mounting – removal and refitting

1   Remove the propeller shaft as described in Section 2.

2   Mark the propeller shaft front and rear sections in relation to each other.

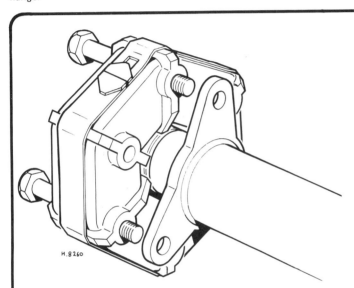

Fig. 7.4 The 'Guibo' coupling showing the clip fitted to new units which must be removed when the coupling is fully installed (Sec 3)

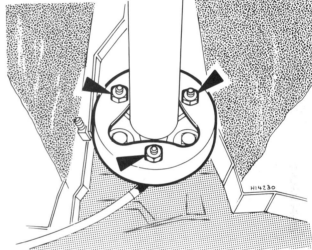

Fig. 7.5 Coupling bolts (arrowed) and heat shield fitted to USA 528i models (Sec 3)

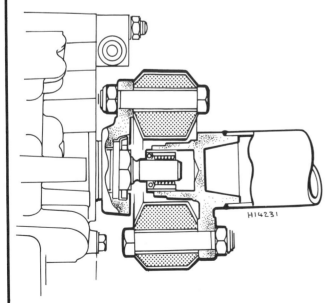

Fig. 7.6 Cross section of the 'Guibo' front coupling showing the centring pin and bush (Sec 3)

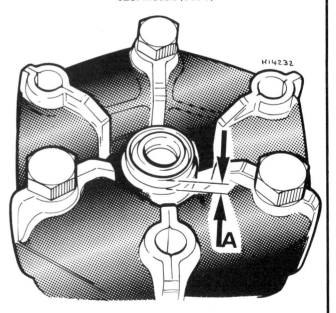

Fig. 7.7 Centring bush protrusion dimension (Sec 3)

A = 5 mm (0.197 in)

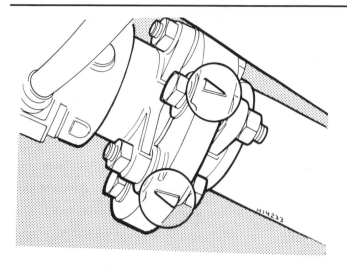

Fig. 7.8 Location arrows on the 'Jurid' front coupling fitted to
automatic transmission models (Sec 3)

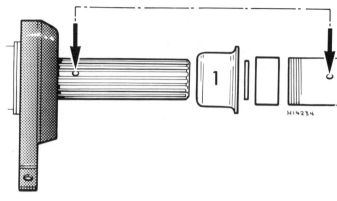

Fig. 7.9 Propeller shaft centre sliding joint showing alignment
marks (arrowed) and felt retaining collar (1) (Sec 4)

3   Unscrew the collar then slide the rear section from the front
section (photo).
4   Extract the circlip from the front section followed by the dust cover
noting which way round the cover is.
5   Using a two-legged puller pull the flexible mounting from the
bearing. Do not hook the puller legs over the front dust cover.

4.3 View of the centre bearing from the rear, showing felt retaining
collar

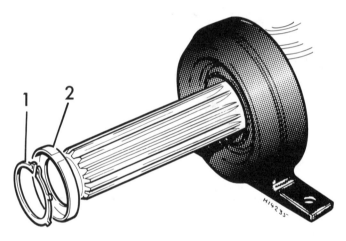

Fig. 7.10 Centre bearing retaining circlip (1) and dust cover (2)
(Sec 4)

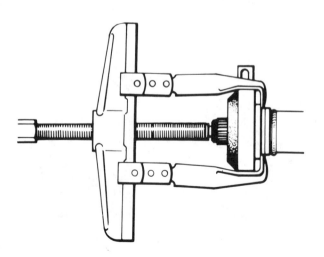

Fig. 7.11 Removing the centre bearing flexible mounting (Sec 4)

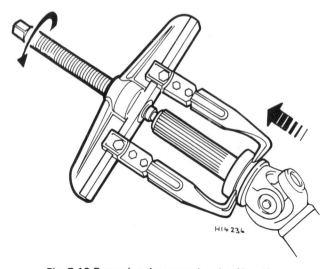

Fig. 7.12 Removing the centre bearing (Sec 4)

6 Spin the bearing outer race and check it for wear by attempting to move it laterally. If necessary remove the bearing from the splined shaft with a two-legged puller engaged in the outer race groove. Remove the front dust cover.

7 Clean all the components in a suitable solvent.

8 Locate the front dust cover on the splined shaft and drive on the centre bearing using a metal tube against the inner race.

9 Coat the inner bore of the flexible mounting with water then drive it onto the centre bearing using a suitable metal tube.

10 Refit the rear dust cover and circlip.

11 Coat the splines with molybdenum grease, then slide the rear section onto the front section making sure that the previously made marks are aligned.

12 Tighten the collar, then refit the propeller shaft with reference to Section 2.

5 Universal joints – testing for wear

1 The propeller shaft universal joints should be checked for wear every 10 000 miles (15 000 km) on UK models, or every 15 000 miles (20 000 km) on USA models. Wear is normally characterized by vibration, 'clonks' on taking up the drive, and in extreme cases metallic squeaking, grating, and shrieking sounds as the bearings break up.

2 To test the joints, jack-up the car and support it on axle stands. Attempt to turn the rear shaft section in alternate directions while holding the final drive flange stationary (for the rear joint) or the front shaft section stationary (for the centre joint).

3 Now attempt to move the shaft up and down by the joint.

4 If wear is evident in the universal joints, the complete propeller shaft must be renewed.

6 Fault diagnosis – propeller shaft

Symptom	Reason(s)
Vibration	Incorrect alignment
	Worn coupling centre bearing
	Worn shaft centre ball bearing
	Worn or tight universal joints
	Flexible coupling deteriorated
	Propeller shaft balance weight broken off
	Worn sliding splines
Knock or clunk when taking up drive	Worn universal joints
	Worn sliding splines
	Loose flange bolts
Whistling noise	Faulty centre bearing
Metallic grating noise consistent with road speed	Dry and worn universal joints

Chapter 8 Final drive unit and driveshafts

Contents

Specifications

Type .... Hypoid bevel final drive unit with open driveshafts incorporating double constant velocity joints. Limited slip differential optional

Ratios (stamped below filler plug)

		(No of teeth)
525 models	3.64 to 1	(40 : 11)
528 models	3.45 to 1	(38 : 11)
530 models to 1977	3.64 to 1	(40 : 11)
530 models 1977 on	3.45 to 1	(38 : 11)

Oil capacity (initial filling) .... 2.82 Imp pt; 1.7 US qt; 1.6 litre

Torque wrench settings

	lbf ft	Nm
Final drive to carrier	52 to 58	72 to 80
Final drive to mounting	52 to 58	72 to 80
Side cover	16 to 18	22 to 25
Vent cover	6.5 to 7	9 to 10
Filler and drain plugs	36 to 43	50 to 60
Pinion drive flange	108	150
Driveshaft bolts	43 to 48	60 to 67
Output flange bolt	65 to 72	90 to 100

1 General description

The final drive unit is of the hypoid gear type, and is mounted at its front end on the rear suspension subframe, and at its rear end to a single rubber mounting attached to the body underframe. Open driveshafts transmit the drive to the wheels through double constant velocity joints which are maintenance-free.

The optional limited slip differential counteracts the characteristic of a normal differential to transmit drive to a spinning roadwheel in preference to the roadwheel on firm ground. The limited slip differential is effectively locked by internal friction discs up to a predetermined torque limit, thus preventing wheelspin by an individual wheel. The torque limit varies according to the torque applied to the crownwheel, as the differential side gears directly influence the pressure on the friction discs.

Owing to the need for special tools and gauges, it is recommended that only the operations described in this Chapter are carried out. Where a compete overhaul of the final drive is necessary, this work should be entrusted to a BMW garage or alternatively a new or reconditioned unit fitted.

2 Final drive unit – removal and refitting

1   Jack up the rear of the car, and place it on suitable stands positioned on the side jacking points. Chock the front wheels, to prevent the car from moving. Alternatively, and preferably, use an inspection pit, with facilities for standing a trolley jack beneath the final drive unit.

2   Detach the propeller shaft from the final drive input flange as described in Chapter 7.

3   Mark the position of the driveshafts in relation to the drive flanges on the final drive unit. Unscrew the flange securing socket screws using a suitable size Allen key.

4   Tie each of the driveshafts up out of the way.

5   Support the final drive unit on a jack (preferably a trolley jack). Unscrew the bolts retaining the front of the final drive unit to the rear suspension subframe bracket (Fig. 8.2).

6   Remove the single bolt retaining the rear of the final drive to the rear rubber mounting (Fig. 8.3).

7   Lower the jack, and withdraw the final drive unit from under the car.

8   Refitting must be carried out in the following sequence, to avoid any tendency to drumming or vibration when the car is in operation:

   (a) Locate the final drive to the front support bracket. Insert the bolts, but only tighten them to finger tightness
   (b) Reconnect the propeller shaft
   (c) Fit the single rear supporting bolt and tighten it to the recommended torque wrench setting
   (d) Allow the final drive unit to take up its own alignment, within the limits of the four front support bracket bolt holes, and then tighten these bolts to the recommended torque wrench setting

9   Reconnect the driveshafts to their respective flanges, making sure that the location marks previously made coincide.

10 The rear support bracket rubber bushes are not supplied as spare parts, and if they are worn, the complete bracket should be renewed.

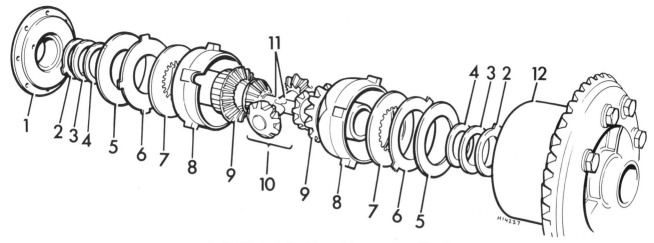

Fig. 8.1 Limited slip differential components (Sec 1)

1	Cover	4	Thrust washer	7	Inner plate
2	Tab disc	5	Spring plate	8	Pressure ring
3	Spring plate	6	Outer plate	9	Side gear

10	Differential gears
11	Shafts
12	Differential case

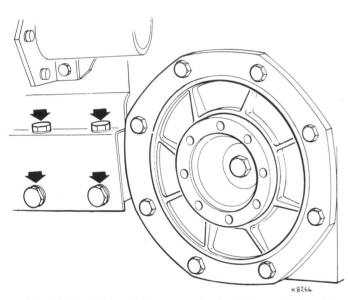

Fig. 8.2 Final drive unit front mounting bolts (arrowed) (Sec 2)

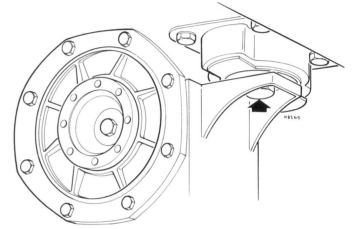

Fig. 8.3 Final drive unit rear mounting bolt (arrowed) (Sec 2)

3 Final drive output flange oil seals – renewal

1 Jack up the rear of the car and support it on axle stands. Chock the front wheels.
2 Mark the final drive flange and driveshaft in relation to each other, then unscrew the socket scerws with an Allen key and tie the driveshaft up out of the way.
3 The old type flange is retained with a single bolt. To remove this type, unscrew the bolt while holding the flange stationary with a length of flat steel bolted to it, or alternatively with a lever between two bolts fitted to the flange.
4 Place a container beneath the final drive unit in order to catch any spilled oil, then pull the flange from the differential using a suitable puller. The BMW tool recommended is shown in Fig. 8.4 and in fact pushes against the final drive housing. But if a normal puller is used the flange central bolt can be temporarily reinserted on a few threads.
5 The new type flange is retained with a snap ring. To remove this type either use two levers placed opposite each other, or obtain the BMW tool described in paragraph 4. First place a container beneath the final drive unit to catch any spilled oil.
6 With the flange removed use a screwdriver to prise the oil seal

from the cover. Wipe clean the seal seating in the cover.
7 Dip the new oil seal in gear oil, then drive it squarely into the cover until flush using a suitable length of tubing and making sure that the seal lip faces inward.
8 If the flange splines are excessively worn, the flange should be renewed, but where a little wear is evident clean the splines and apply a liquid locking agent.
9 Refit the flange using a reversal of the removal procedure. On the old type tighten the central bolt to the specified torque. On the new type make sure that the snap ring is fully entered in the groove in the cover, and when inserting the flange turn it slightly until the snap ring is heard to drop into the flange groove.
10 Refit the driveshaft noting the previously made alignment marks, and tighten the screws to the specified torque.
11 Lower the car to the ground and top-up the final drive oil level as necessary.

4 Pinion oil seal – renewal

1 Remove the final drive unit as described in Section 2.
2 Unscrew the drain and filler plugs using a 10 mm Allen key, and drain the oil into a suitable container (photos). Refit the drain plug.
3 Tap back the edge of the flange nut locking washer from the cut-out in the drive flange and extract the locking washer.
4 Mark the relative positions of the drive flange, pinion shaft and

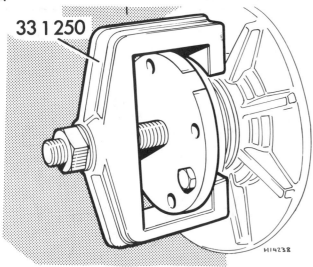

Fig. 8.4 BMW tool for removing the final drive output flange (Sec 3)

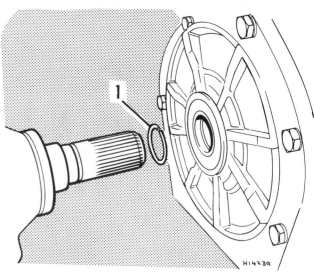

Fig. 8.5 New type output flange showing snap ring (1) (Sec 3)

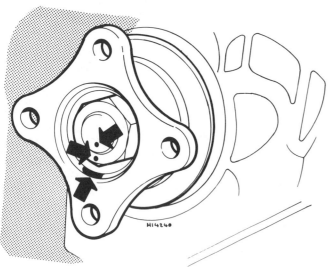

Fig. 8.6 Pinion and flange alignment marks (arrowed), also showing locking washer (Sec 4)

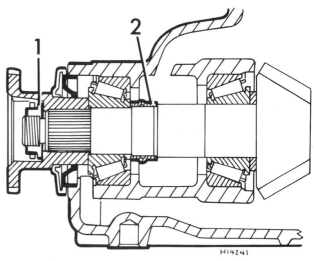

Fig. 8.7 Cross section diagram of the final drive pinion (Sec 4)

1	Collared nut		2	Collapsible spacer

4.2A Final drive drain plug location

4.2B Final drive filler plug location

securing nut in relation to one another, using a dot punch.

5 Using a length of cord wound round the pinion driving flange and a spring balance attached to the end of the cord, determine the turning torque required to start the pinion rotating. Record this figure.

6 Hold the driving flange still, as described in Section 3, and unscrew the drive flange securing nut.

7 Using a two or three legged puller, draw the drive flange off the pinion shaft.

8 Turn the legs of the puller around if possible so that it can be used to draw the oil seal out from the final drive casing. Alternatively use a screwdriver to prise the oil seal out. Wipe clean the oil seal seating.

9 Dip the new oil seal in gear oil, then drive it squarely into the casing until its outer face is flush with the casing. Use a length of metal tube initially then a block of wood around the pinion shaft, and make sure that the oil seal lip faces inward.

10 Refit the driving flange by pressing it into position. Remember to align the dot punch marks.

11 Tighten the flange nut until the dot punch marks are aligned and then check that the nut is tightened to at least the minimum specified torque.

12 Using the cord and spring balance check the turning torque of the pinion. This should be the figure recorded before dismantling plus 1.7 lbf in (0.2 Nm) to offset the drag of the new oil seal. When the correct preload is not reached, tighten the pinion nut to a fractionally higher torque wrench setting and recheck. Remember that if the preload of the bearings is set too high, it must not be reduced by backing off the nut. In this case the collapsible spacer sleeve between the pinion bearings will have to be renewed.

13 Refit the locking washer and tap the edge into the flange cut-out.

14 Fill the final drive unit with the correct amount of oil then refit the filler plug.

15 Refit the final drive unit with reference to Section 2.

5 Driveshafts – removal and refitting

1 Jack up the rear of the car and support it on axle stands. Chock the front wheels.

2 Mark the constant velocity joints in relation to the inner and outer drive flanges (photo).

3 Unscrew the socket screws with an Allen key and withdraw the driveshaft (photo).

4 During removal or refitting, support the shaft so that the joints are not strained beyond their maximum bending angles, otherwise they may be damaged or disconnected.

5 Refitting is a reversal of removal. Remember to refit the constant velocity joints in the same relationship to the inner and outer flanges.

6 Driveshaft bellows – renewal

1 The driveshaft bellows should be checked for splits and deterioration every 10 000 miles (15 000 km) on UK models or every 12 500 miles (20 000 km) on USA models.

2 To renew a bellows first remove the driveshaft as described in Section 5.

3 Prise the sealing cover from the end of the joint.

4 Using circlip pliers, extract the circlip from the end of the driveshaft.

5 Mark the constant velocity joint housing in relation to the driveshaft and also note the position of the bellows clip screws.

6 Loosen the clips, then support the constant velocity joint housing in a soft jawed vice and press out the driveshaft.

7 Slide the bellows from the driveshaft.

8 Clean the driveshaft, and the bellows contact surface of the constant velocity joint housing. Remove the old grease from the joint. Obtain a new bellows and repair kit.

9 Fit the new bellows together with the small clip over the end of the driveshaft. Locate the large clip onto the bellows.

10 Check that the driveshaft and joint splines are clean, then coat them with the liquid locking agent supplied with the repair kit. Press the driveshaft into the joint observing the previously made alignment marks, and fit the circlip.

11 Pack the joint and bellows with the 4.2 oz (120 g) of grease supplied with the repair kit.

12 Coat the bellows contact surface with the adhesive, correctly

5.2 View of the right-hand side driveshaft

5.3 Driveshaft constant velocity joint and socket screws

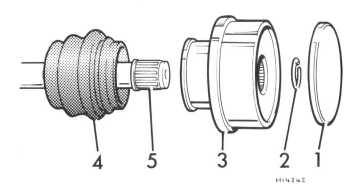

H14242

Fig. 8.8 Driveshaft components (Sec 6)

1	Sealing cover	4 Bellows
2	Circlip	5 Driveshaft
3	Constant velocity joint	

locate the bellows, and fit the clips.
13 Clean the sealing cover inner surface and apply the special sealer

supplied, then press the cover on the end of the joint.
14 Refit the driveshaft with reference to Section 5.

7 Fault diagnosis — final drive unit and driveshafts

Symptom	Reason(s)
Noise	Worn crownwheel and pinion
	Flange bolts loose
	Worn final drive mounting
	Lack of lubricant
	Incorrect crownwheel and pinion mesh
'Clonk' on acceleration and deceleration	Output flange splines worn
	Flange bolts loose
	Constant velocity joints worn
Oil leakage	Pinion oil seal worn
	Output flange oil seals worn
	Clogged vent
	Final drive cover seal broken
Vibration	Flange bolts loose
	Final drive bearings worn
	Constant velocity joints worn

Chapter 9 Braking system

For modifications, and information applicable to later models, see Supplement at end of manual

Contents

Specifications

System type

Four wheel hydraulic with discs front and rear, tandem master cylinder with 'H-I' type dual circuits with servo assistance. Cable operated handbrake to conventional shoes within rear disc/drum assemblies

Front brakes

Disc diameter:
525, 528, and 530 (1978-on) models .... 280 mm (11.024 in)
530 (pre-1978) models .... 272 mm (10.709 in)
Minimum disc thickness after refinishing:
525 and 530 (pre-1978) models .... 11.1 mm (0.437 in)
528 and 530 (1978-on) models .... 20.4 mm (0.803 in)
Maximum disc run-out (installed) .... 0.2 mm (0.008 in)
Minimum disc pad thickness (including backing plate) .... 7.0 mm (0.275 in)

Rear brakes

Disc diameter .... 272 mm (10.709 in)
Minimum disc thickness after refinishing .... 7.9 mm (0.311 in)
Maximum disc run-out (installed) .... 0.2 mm (0.008 in)
Minimum disc pad thickness (including backing plate) .... 7.0 mm (0.275 in)

Handbrake

Drum diameter .... 160 mm (6.299 in)
Maximum drum ovality .... 0.1 mm (0.004 in)
Minimum lining thickness .... 1.5 mm (0.06 in)

Master cylinder

Maximum clearance between piston and pushrod .... 0.5 mm (0.020 in)

Brake pedal

Pushrod maximum travel – left-hand drive models .... 36 mm (1.417 in)
– right-hand drive models .... 30 mm (1.181 in)
Stoplight switch adjustment .... 5 to 6 mm (0.197 to 0.236 in)

Torque wrench settings

	lbf ft	Nm
Caliper bleed nipple	2.5 to 3.5	3.5 to 5.0
Front caliper	58 to 68	80 to 95
Backing plate	6.5 to 7.0	9.0 to 10.0
Disc to hub (M6 bolt)	3.0 to 3.5	4.0 to 5.0
Disc to hub (M8 bolt)	22 to 24	30 to 33
Disc to hub (nut)	43 to 48	60 to 67
Rear caliper	43 to 48	60 to 67

lbf ft	Nm
12 to 18	16 to 25
11 to 13	15 to 18
7 to 10	10 to 14
9.5 to 11.5	13 to 16
16 to 17	22 to 24
18 to 19	25 to 27
9.0 to 9.5	12 to 13
11 to 14	15 to 20
4 to 5	6 to 7
20 to 23	28 to 31

Master cylinder to servo (left-hand drive models) ....
Brake line to front caliper ....
Brake line to rear caliper ....
Brake line couplings ....
Servo mounting ....
Pushrod to pedal ....
Pressure regulator ....
Handbrake lever ....
Handbrake cable locknut ....
Handbrake cable to trailing arm ....

1 General description

The braking system is hydraulic, and operates on all four wheels, disc brakes being fitted all round. The handbrake is of the usual drum/shoe type and the drum is formed in the centre of the rear brake disc. The rear shoes are operated mechanically by two cables connected to the handbrake lever inside the car. A tandem master cylinder is fitted with remote twin vacuum servo units on right-hand drive models or a single servo unit on left-hand drive models located between the brake pedal and master cylinder. The tandem master cylinder incorporates double acting pistons, which together with split braking circuits ensures that should one brake circuit fail, the front brakes will still operate.

The front disc calipers are of the four piston construction, whereas the rear disc calipers are of the two piston type. The disc brakes do not require adjustment as this is automatically compensated for by the caliper pistons. When the brake pads wear to a predetermined minimum thickness, a spreader spring in the disc brake caliper is brought into operation and increased pedal pressure is necessary. To protect the brake discs from scoring and damage, the pads should be renewed when this condition is reached.

The brake fluid reservoir is located in the engine compartment and is mounted independently of the master cylinder. The fluid in this reservoir also serves the clutch hydraulic system. The reservoir incorporates a low-level warning indicator, which shows up inside the car, and the reservoir is also transparent to enable a visual check to be made easily.

The braking system also incorporates a brake pressure regulator, which reduces the hydraulic fluid pressure to the rear brakes when a pre-determined pressure in the system is exceeded. This has the effect of improving the braking force available at the front wheels particularly during emergency conditions.

The vacuum servo unit utilises vacuum from the engine inlet manifold to assist the action of the footbrake pedal.

2 Routine maintenance

1 The brake fluid level should be checked every week and if necessary topped-up with the specified brake fluid to the maximum level mark. The reservoir is translucent and the check can be made without removing the filler cap.

2 Every 10 000 miles (15 000 km) on UK models or 12 500 miles (20 000 km) on USA models the front and rear disc pads should be checked for wear and renewed as necessary. At the same time the handbrake cable and shoes should be adjusted, and also the hydraulic pipes and unions should be checked for chafing, leakage, cracks and corrosion.

3 The manufacturers recommend that the brake fluid is renewed annually.

4 Every 40 000 miles (60 000 km) the handbrake shoes should be checked for wear and adjusted.

3 Handbrake — adjustment

1 Before adjusting the handbrake, drive the car a maximum of 400 m (450 yd) with the handbrake lever applied lightly; this will clean any corrosion from the rear drums.

2 Chock the front wheels, jack up the rear of the car, and support it on axle stands. Remove the rear roadwheels and fully release the handbrake.

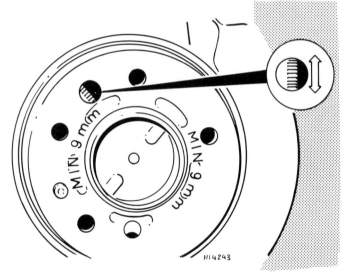

Fig. 9.1 Method of adjusting the handbrake shoes (Sec 3)

3 Turn the left-hand side drum/disc assembly until the large inspection hole is about 10° away from the vertical and toward the top and rear of the car.

4 Insert a flat bladed screwdriver through the inspection hole and locate it in the serrations of the adjuster wheel.

5 Using the screwdriver, turn the adjuster wheel until the brake shoes are in full contact with the drum/disc. Now back off the adjuster wheel by 4 to 6 notches so that the drum/disc is free to be rotated.

6 Adjust the right-hand side wheel in the same manner but turn the drum/disc assembly 10° toward the front of the car to locate the adjuster.

7 With both rear wheels adjusted apply the handbrake and count the number of notches. If the handbrake lever travels over more than 5 notches then the handbrake cables will require adjustment.

8 The handbrake cables are adjustable at their forward ends where they join the handbrake lever. First refit the roadwheels.

9 Pull off the rubber cap on the handbrake lever and loosen each of the cable locknuts, using a 10 mm open-ended spanner.

10 Pull on the handbrake by 4 notches and turn each of the cable adjustment nuts until the rear wheels are just locked.

11 Retighten the locknuts. Release the handbrake and reapply it one notch at a time, checking that both rear wheels lock up at the same time. Failure of this to occur indicates overadjustment of one cable.

12 Now fully release the handbrake lever and check that the rear brakes are not binding. Refit the rubber cap.

13 Lower the car to the ground.

4 Front disc pads — inspection and renewal

1 Jack up the front of the car and support it on axle stands. Apply the handbrake and remove the front roadwheels.

2 On USA 528i models pull the disc pad wear sensor from the inner disc pad if working on the left-hand side. Note that the wide side of the sensor faces the disc.

3 On all models drive out the two retaining pins and extract the spreader spring (photo).

4 Check the thickness of the disc pad linings. If worn below the specified minimum limit it will be necessary to renew the pads on both

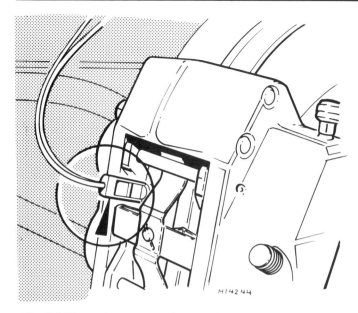

Fig. 9.2 Disc pad wear sensor (arrowed) being fitted to the left-hand side inner pad (Sec 4)

front brake discs.

5   Tap the disc pad backing plates outward to loosen them within the caliper, then withdraw them by gripping their ends with a pair of pliers (photo).

6   Clean the inside of the caliper with a small brush. Remember that the dust is harmful to inhale.

7   Check the level of the brake fluid in the reservoir and, if it is within 13 mm (0.5 in) of the top, syphon a little off. This is necessary because fluid is forced back into the reservoir, when the caliper pistons are

forced back into the caliper in order to accommodate the new thicker pads.

8   Use a flat piece of wood or metal to press the caliper pistons back into their bores, until they reach their stops. Avoid using excessive force as the disc can be damaged or distorted.

9   Insert the new pads into the caliper and make sure that the anti-squeak shims are located between the pads and the caliper pistons.

10 Fit the spreader spring and retaining pins, and on USA 528i models refit the disc pad wear sensor.

11 Apply the brake pedal several times to set the disc pads, then check and if necessary top-up the fluid level in the reservoir.

12 Repeat the procedure on the remaining front wheel then refit the roadwheels and lower the car to the ground.

13 The pads will need a little time to bed in and it is recommended that heavy braking is avoided during the first 375 miles (600 km).

5   Rear disc pads – inspection and renewal

1   Jack up the rear of the car and support it on axle stands. Chock the front wheels and remove the rear roadwheels.

2   Drive out the two retaining pins and extract the spreader spring (photos).

3   Where fitted on USA models pull the disc pad wear sensor from the inner disc pad if working on the right-hand side. Note that the wide side of the sensor faces the disc.

4   Check the thickness of the disc pad linings. If worn below the specified minimum limit it will be necessary to renew the pads on both rear brake discs.

5   Tap the disc pad backing plates outward to loosen them within the caliper, then withdraw them by gripping their ends with a pair of pliers (photo).

6   Clean the inside of the caliper with a small brush taking care to avoid inhaling the dust as it is harmful.

7   Check the level of the brake fluid in the reservoir, and if it is within 13 mm (0.5 in) of the top, syphon a little off to avoid it overflowing when the caliper pistons are subsequently pressed back.

4.3 Removing the front disc pad spreader spring

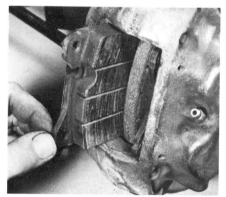

4.5 Removing a front disc pad

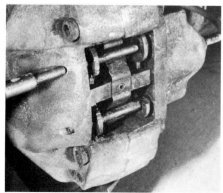

5.2A Using a punch to remove the rear disc pad retaining pins

5.2B Removing a rear disc pad spreader spring

5.5 Removing a rear disc pad

8 Using a flat piece of wood or metal, press the pistons back into their bores until they reach the stops. Avoid using excessive force as the disc can be damaged or distorted.

9 Check that the 20° cut-outs in the caliper pistons are positioned correctly as shown in Fig. 9.3 – a gauge can easily be made out of card. If necessary carefully turn the pistons to reposition the cut-outs.

10 Insert the new pads into the caliper and where fitted on USA models refit the disc pad wear sensor.

11 Fit the spreader spring and retaining pins.

12 Apply the brake pedal several times to set the disc pads, then check and if necessary top-up the fluid level in the reservoir.

13 Repeat the procedure on the remaining rear wheel, then refit the roadwheels and lower the car to the ground.

14 The pads will need a little time to bed in and it is recommended that heavy braking is avoided during the first 375 miles (600 km).

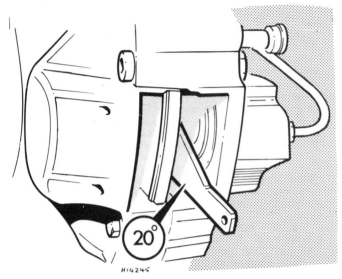

Fig. 9.3 Using a 20° gauge to check the rear caliper piston cut-out position (Sec 5)

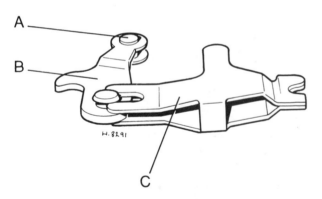

Fig. 9.4 Handbrake shoe expander unit (Sec 6)

A   Pin   B   Link   C   Strut

6   Handbrake shoes – inspection and renewal

1 Remove the rear brake disc as described in Section 10.

2 Check the thickness of the brake shoe linkage and if either is below the specified minimum, renew both shoes.

3 Note the position of the shoes and springs, then unhook and remove the lower spring using long nose pliers (photo).

4 Using an Allen key inserted through the hole in the hub flange, depress and turn the shoe retaining springs through 90° and remove them (photo).

5 Pull the shoes from the bottom expander mechanism, lift them over the hub flange, and disconnect them from the upper adjuster. Remove the upper return spring (photo).

6 Clean the backplate and hub with a small brush taking care not to inhale the dust as it is harmful. Check the adjuster and expander for wear and renew them if necessary – drive out the pin to remove the expander from the handbrake cable.

7 Check that the adjuster and expander are not seized, and lubricate them sparingly with a little high melting point grease.

8 Fit the shoes using a reversal of the removal procedure, but clean the drum/disc and check it for cracking and scoring. Adjust the handbrake as described in Section 3.

7   Disc caliper – removal and refitting

1 Remove the front or rear disc pads (as applicable) as described in Section 4 or 5.

2 To reduce the loss of brake fluid remove the reservoir filler cap then tighten it onto a piece of polythene sheeting.

3 Where fitted to USA models pull the disc pad wear sensor lead plug from the clips and disconnect the plug.

4 Unscrew the brake line union nut(s). Then remove and plug the brake line(s).

5 Unscrew the mounting bolts and withdraw the disc caliper (photos).

6 Refitting is a reversal of removal, but in addition bleed the brake hydraulic system as described in Section 16 – it may only be necessary to bleed the caliper which was removed, so check the brake pedal operation after doing this. Tighten the mounting bolts and union nuts to the specified torque.

8   Disc caliper (front) – overhaul

1 Remove the caliper as described in Section 7 and clean the exterior surfaces with a suitable solvent.

6.3 Handbrake shoes lower anchor

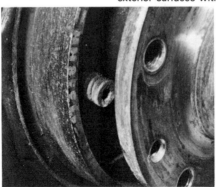

6.4 Handbrake shoe retaining spring location

6.5 Handbrake shoe upper adjuster and spring

7.5A Remove the disc caliper mounting bolts ...

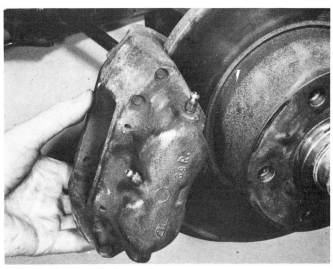
7.5B ... and remove the front caliper

7.5C Rear disc caliper

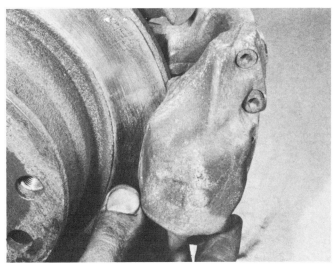
7.5D Removing the rear disc caliper

2   Lever the clamp ring and rubber cover from each piston.
3   Mark each piston in relation to the caliper. Using a narrow block of wood clamp one of the upper pistons in the caliper, then force the remaining upper piston out using air pressure in the upper fluid inlet.
4   Plug the empty caliper bore and remove the remaining upper piston with air pressure. Repeat the procedure to remove the bottom pistons.
5   Carefully prise out the sealing rings from the piston bores with a soft pointed object (eg a cocktail stick). Clean all the components with methylated spirits or brake fluid. Examine the bores and the pistons for scratches and score marks and, if there are any, renew the complete caliper.
6   Do not attempt to split the caliper into its separate halves, unless there is a leak between them. Under such circumstances, it will be necessary to renew the rubber O-ring seals and the special expansion bolts securing the two halves. After splitting the caliper, clean the mating surfaces with methylated spirits, fit the new oil seals and tighten the new expansion bolts in the correct order (Fig. 9.8).
7   Discard the old piston seals and obtain a repair kit.
8   Fit the new seals using the fingers only to manipulate them into position.
9   Coat the pistons with brake cylinder paste then insert them squarely into the caliper bores.
10 Coat the inside of the dust covers with brake cylinder paste then

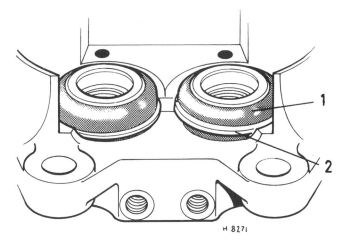
Fig. 9.5 Front disc caliper rubber cover (1) and clamp ring (2) (Sec 8)

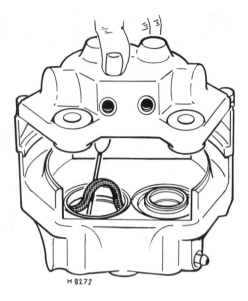

Fig. 9.6 Removing sealing rings from a front disc caliper (Sec 8)

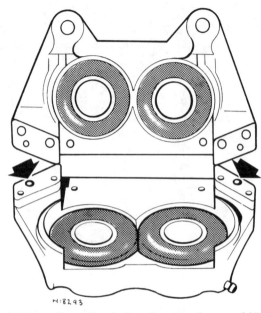

Fig. 9.7 Front disc caliper half sealing rings (arrowed) (Sec 8)

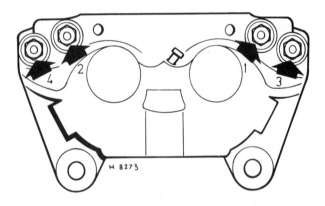

Fig. 9.8 Front disc caliper expansion bolt tightening sequence
(Sec 8)

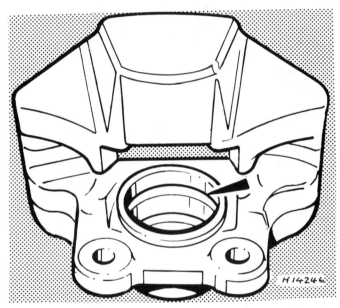

Fig. 9.9 Rear disc caliper sealing ring location (arrowed) (Sec 9)

locate them over the pistons and fit the clamp rings.
11 Refit the caliper as described in Section 7.

9 Disc caliper (rear) – overhaul

The procedure is virtually identical to that described in Section 8,
however the pistons must be positioned with the 20° cut-out facing
downward (ie against the forward rotation of the disc).

10 Brake disc – examination, removal and refitting

1 Remove the front or rear disc pads as described in Sections 4 or
5.
2 Examine the surface of the disc for deep scoring or grooving. Light
scoring is normal but anything more severe should be removed by
having the disc refaced, provided the thickness of the disc is not
reduced below the specified value. Otherwise a new disc will have to
be fitted (photo).

10.2 Checking a brake disc thickness with a micrometer

3 Check the disc for run-out. To do this, a dial gauge will be required although a reasonable check can be made using feeler blades between the face of the disc and a fixed point. Turn the disc slowly by hand, and if the run-out exceeds that stated in the Specifications, the disc must be renewed. Do not confuse wheel bearing play with disc run-out on the front disc.

Front brake disc

4 To remove the front brake disc, detach the hydraulic line bracket from the suspension strut, unbolt the caliper, and move it to one side. Tie the caliper to the coil spring to prevent straining the hydraulic hoses.

5 On models fitted with wheel bolts, use an Allen key to unscrew the single retaining screw, then withdraw the brake disc from the hub.

6 On models fitted with wheel nuts, remove the hub/disc assembly as described in Chapter 11. Mark the disc in relation to the hub, then unscrew the socket head bolts with an Allen key and separate the disc from the hub. The hub can be temporarily attached to a roadwheel during this operation to provide extra support.

7 Where ventilated brake discs are fitted take care not to displace any balance weights secured to the cooling vanes.

8 Refitting is a reversal of removal, but ensure that the disc to hub mating surfaces are clean. Tighten all retaining bolts to the specified torque. Refer to Section 4 when refitting the disc pads, and where applicable refer to Chapter 11 for refitting the hub and adjusting the wheel bearings.

Rear brake disc

9 To remove the rear brake disc, unbolt the caliper, release the brake pipe from the clip, and tie the caliper to one side (photo).

10 On models fitted with wheel bolts, use an Allen key to unscrew the single retaining screw, then withdraw the brake disc from the axle shaft flange (photos).

11 On models fitted with wheel nuts, withdraw the brake disc over the axle shaft flange studs.

12 If it is difficult to remove the disc on either type, back off the handbrake adjustment with reference to Section 3.

13 Refitting is a reversal of removal, but ensure that the disc to flange mating surfaces are clean and tighten all retaining bolts to the specified torque. On models fitted with wheel nuts make sure that the large hole in the disc/drum is aligned with the large hole in the axle shaft flange. Refer to Section 5 when refitting the disc pads, and finally adjust the handbrake as described in Section 3.

---

11 Footbrake pedal – removal and refitting

1 Working inside the car remove the crosshead screws and withdraw the lower facia panel from the bottom of the steering column. Where applicable on USA models disconnect the wires from the electric window automatic cut-out (see also Chapter 5).

2 On 528 and 530 models with a manual gearbox release the clutch pedal damper spring tension with reference to Chapter 5.

3 Unhook the brake pedal return spring.

4 Disconnect the pushrod from the brake pedal by extracting the clip and removing the pivot pin (photo).

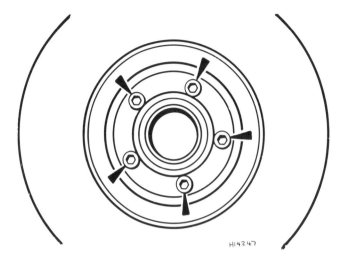

Fig. 9.10 Front brake disc retaining bolt locations (arrowed) on models with wheel nuts (Sec 10)

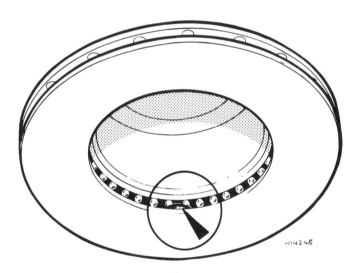

Fig. 9.11 Balance weight location (arrowed) on a ventilated brake disc (Sec 10)

10.9 Rear brake disc hydraulic pipe and clip located on the trailing arm

10.10A Removing the Allen screw ...

10.10B ... and rear brake disc

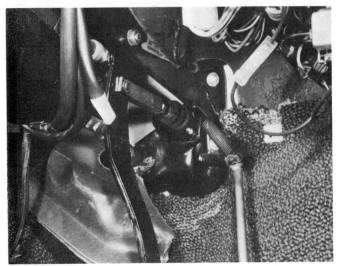

11.4 Showing footbrake pedal and pushrod

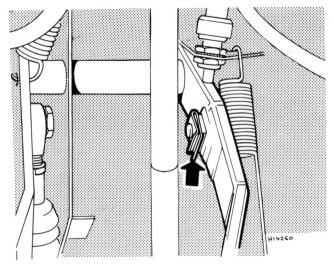

Fig. 9.12 Pushrod pivot clip (arrowed) on the footbrake pedal
(Sec 11)

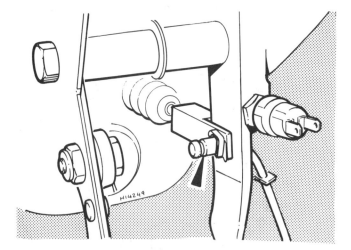

Fig. 9.13 Removing pushrod pivot pin (arrowed) from the
footbrake pedal (Sec 11)

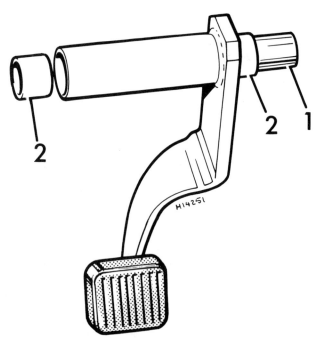

Fig. 9.14 Footbrake pedal spacer (1) and bushes (2) (Sec 11)

5   Unscrew the nut from the pedal pivot bolt, and withdraw the bolt until the footbrake pedal can be withdrawn downward. Do not fully remove the bolt on manual gearbox models as it also acts as a pivot for the clutch pedal.

6   Remove the spacer from the pedal bore, and drive out the bushes if necessary.

7   Wash all the components in paraffin then examine them for wear and damage; renew them as necessary.

8   Refitting is a reversal of removal, but lubricate all bearing surfaces with multi-purpose grease. Ideally the self locking nut should be renewed. Refer to Fig. 9.15 and first adjust the brake pedal position by loosening the pushrod locknut, turning the pushrod as necessary, then tightening the locknut. If necessary adjust the stoplight switch to pedal dimension to that shown in Fig. 9.15 (photo). On 528 and 530 models with a manual gearbox adjust the clutch pedal damper spring as described in Chapter 5.

12 Master cylinder (right-hand drive models) – removal and refitting

1   Unscrew the brake fluid reservoir filler cap and tighten it onto a piece of polythene sheeting. Alternatively use two tapered wooden dowel rods to plug the reservoir outlets (see Fig. 9.16).

2   Remove the crosshead screws and withdraw the lower facia panel

from around the foot pedals.

3   Unhook the brake pedal return spring.

4   Disconnect the master cylinder pushrod from the brake pedal by extracting the clip and removing the pivot pin.

5   Pull the fluid supply hoses from the master cylinder and plug them (photo).

6   Unscrew the union nuts and disconnect the hydraulic pipes.

7   Using an Allen key, unscrew the mounting bolts and withdraw the master cylinder from the front of the bulkhead – wrap it in cloth to prevent spilling fluid onto the body paintwork.

8   Refitting is a reversal of removal, but on completion bleed the hydraulic system as described in Section 16. Check the pedal adjustment as described in Section 11.

13 Master cylinder (left-hand drive models) – removal and refitting

1   Unscrew the brake fluid reservoir filler cap and tighten it onto a piece of polythene sheeting.

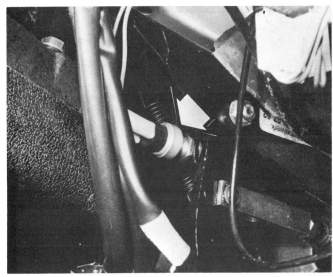

11.8 Stoplight switch location (arrowed)

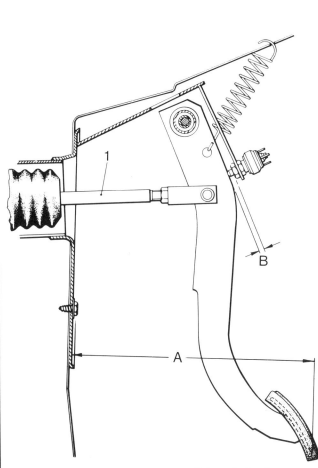

Fig. 9.15 Footbrake pedal and stoplight switch adjustment dimensions (Sec 11)

A   230 to 240 mm (9.055 to 9.449 in)
B   5 to 6 mm (0.197 to 0.236 in)
1   Pushrod

12.5 Master cylinder and fluid reservoir location on a RHD model

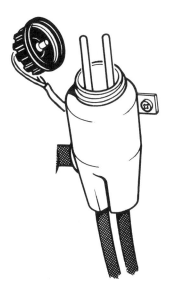

Fig. 9.16 Using two tapered wooden dowel rods to plug the brake fluid reservoir outlets (Sec 12)

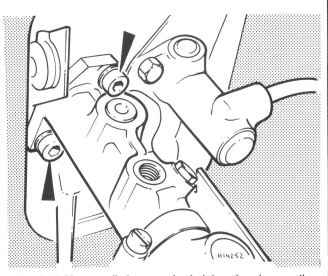

Fig. 9.17 Master cylinder mounting bolt locations (arrowed) on RHD models (Sec 12)

2   Where necessary to gain access on USA models, remove the relay and nuts, and place the holder to one side with the hoses and liner still attached.

3   On all models with a remote fluid reservoir, pull the supply hoses from the master cylinder and plug them. Take care not to damage the inlet elbows.

4   Unscrew the union nuts and disconnect the hydraulic pipes.

5   Unscrew the mounting nuts and withdraw the master cylinder from the front of the servo unit.

6   Refitting is a reversal of removal, but if necessary renew the rubber O-ring located between the master cylinder and the servo. Note that a faulty O-ring will prevent the correct vacuum build up. On completion bleed the hydraulic system as described in Section 16.

14   Master cylinder – overhaul

1   Obtain a repair kit which is specifically for the master cylinder which has been fitted to your car.

2   With the master cylinder removed from the car, brush and clean away all external dirt.

3   If the car is equipped with remote type servo units, withdraw the flexible bellows and pushrod from the rear end of the master cylinder.

4   Exert a little pressure on the end of the master cylinder piston and unscrew and remove the stop screw.

5   Extract the circlip from the end of the cylinder body and withdraw the primary piston and allied components.

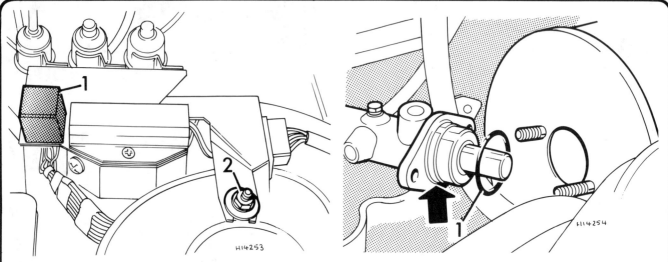

Fig. 9.18 Relay (1) and nut (2) locations on USA models (Sec 13)

Fig. 9.19 Rubber O-ring location (arrowed) between master cylinder and servo on LHD models (Sec 13)

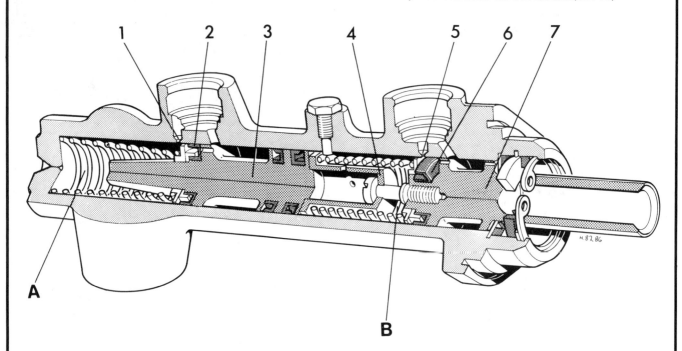

Fig. 9.20 Cut-away section of the master cylinder (Sec 14)

1 Compensation passage	3 Secondary piston	5 Compensation passage	7 Primary piston
2 Seal	4 Spring cap	6 Seal	

A   Chamber operating both front and rear wheel brakes
B   Chamber operating front wheel brakes only

6   Extract the secondary piston and spring by tapping the master cylinder on a block of wood.

7   Remove the screw from the primary piston and withdraw the retainer, spring, support, seal, and washer. From the front of the primary piston withdraw the stop washer, seal, intermediate ring, seal, and bearing ring.

8   Remove the spring from the rear of the secondary piston followed by the support ring, seal, and washer. Prise the two seals from the piston grooves.

9   Clean all the components in methylated spirit or hydraulic fluid and examine them for wear and damage. Examine the surfaces of the pistons and cylinder bore for scoring and bright wear areas, and if evident renew the complete master cylinder. If the components are in good condition discard the old seals and fit the items included in the repair kit.

10   Reassembly is a reversal of dismantling but dip the components in hydraulic fluid before inserting them in the cylinder. The primary piston seal lips must face into the cylinder, but the lips on the adjacent seals on the secondary piston unit face in opposite directions — refer to Fig. 9.23 if necessary. Manipulate the seals into position using the fingers only. Renew the stop screw copper washer if necessary.

---

15 Hydraulic brake lines and hoses – inspection, removal and refitting

1   At the intervals given in Section 2 check the hydraulic brake lines and hoses for chafing, leakage, cracks and corrosion, and renew them as necessary (photos).

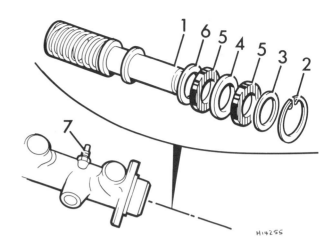

Fig. 9.21 Master cylinder primary piston outer components (Sec 14)

1	Primary piston	5	Seals
2	Circlip	6	Ring
3	Washer	7	Stop screw
4	Ring		

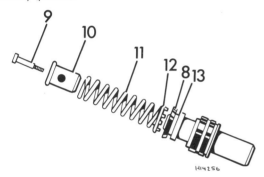

Fig. 9.22 Master cylinder primary piston inner components (Sec 14)

8	Seal	11	Spring
9	Screw	12	Support
10	Spring cap	13	Ring

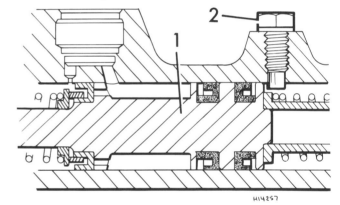

Fig. 9.23 Cross section of master cylinder showing intermediate seal positions (Sec 14)

1	Secondary piston	2 Stop screw

15.1A Front brake hydraulic line bracket and hoses

15.1B Rear brake hydraulic line connection

2   To renew a brake line or hose, first unscrew the brake fluid reservoir filler cap and tighten it onto a piece of polythene sheeting. Alternatively on right-hand drive models use two tapered wooden dowel rods to plug the reservoir outlets (see Fig. 9.16).

3   To remove a flexible brake hose, unscrew the rigid pipe union nuts at each end while holding the hose hexagons stationary. Remove the spring plates and withdraw the hose from the mounting brackets. Refitting is a reversal of removal, but make sure that the hose is not twisted and tighten the union nuts to the specified torque. On completion bleed the hydraulic system as described in Section 16.

4   To remove a rigid brake line, unscrew the union nuts at each end, then remove the retaining clips and withdraw the line from the car. Where the brake line connects to a flexible hose, hold the hose hexagon stationary while unscrewing the nut. Refitting is a reversal of removal, but tighten the union nuts to the specified torque. On completion bleed the hydraulic system as described in Section 16.

16 Hydraulic system – bleeding

1   The correct functioning of the brake hydraulic system is only possible after the removal of all air from the components and circuit; this is achieved by bleeding the system. Note that only clean unused brake fluid, which has remained unshaken for at least 24 hours, must be used.

2   If there is any possibility of incorrect fluid being used in the system the brake lines and components must be completely flushed with uncontaminated fluid and new seals fitted.

3   Never reuse brake fluid which has been bled from the system.

4   During the procedure, do not allow the level of the brake fluid to drop more than half way down the reservoir.

5   Before starting work check that all rigid pipes and flexible hoses are in good condition and that all hydraulic unions are tight. Take great care not to allow hydraulic fluid to come into contact with the car paintwork, otherwise the finish will be seriously damaged. Wash off any spilled fluid immediately with cold water.

6   There are a number of one-man, do-it-yourself, brake bleeding kits currently available from motor accessory shops. It is recommended that one of these kits should be used wherever possible as they greatly simplify the bleeding operation and also reduce the risk of expelled air and fluid being drawn back into the system. If one of these kits is not available then it will be necessary to gather a clean jar and a suitable length of clear plastic tubing which is a tight fit over the bleed screw, and also to engage the help of an assistant.

7   To bleed the system first remove the hydraulic fluid reservoir filler cap and top-up the level (photo). During the procedure check and top-up the fluid level after each two or three strokes of the footbrake pedal.

8   On right-hand drive cars clean the area around the bleed screw on one of the remote servo units, remove the rubber cap, and fit the bleed tube (photo). On left-hand drive cars connect the tube to one of the rear calipers.

9   If a one-man brake bleeding kit is being used, open the bleed screw half a turn and position the unit so that it can be viewed from the car. Depress the brake pedal to the floor and slowly release it, the one-way valve in the kit will prevent expelled air from returning to the system. Repeat the procedure then top-up the brake fluid level. Continue bleeding until clean hydraulic fluid free from air bubbles can be seen coming through the tube. Now tighten the bleed screw and remove the tube (photo).

10 If a one-man bleeding kit is not available, immerse the free end of the bleed tube in the jar and pour in sufficient brake fluid to keep the end of the tube submerged. Open the bleed screw half a turn and have your assistant depress the brake pedal to the floor and then slowly release it. Tighten the bleed screw at the end of the downstroke to prevent the expelled air and fluid from being drawn back into the system. Repeat the procedure then top-up the brake fluid level. Continue bleeding until clean hydraulic fluid free from air bubbles can be seen coming through the tube. Now tighten the bleed screw and remove the tube.

11 Repeat the procedure described in paragraphs 8 to 10 on the remaining remote servo unit (right-hand drive cars only) then the rear calipers followed by the front calipers. The front calipers should be bled in the sequence shown in Fig. 9.26.

12 When completed, recheck the fluid level in the reservoir, top-up if necessary and refit the cap. Check the 'feel' of the brake pedal which should be firm and free from any 'sponginess' which would indicate air still present in the system.

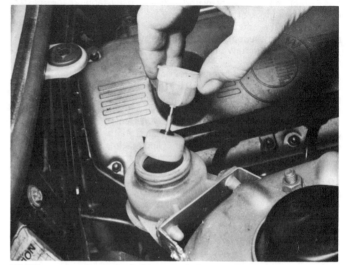

16.7 Removing the brake fluid reservoir filter and float

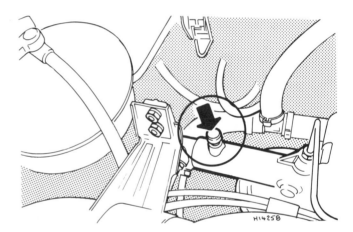

Fig. 9.24 Remote servo unit bleed screw location (arrowed) on RHD models (Sec 16)

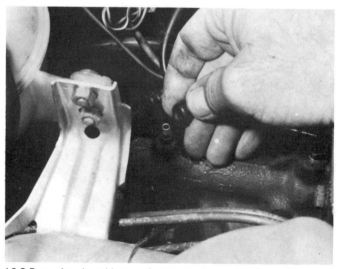

16.8 Removing the rubber cap from a remote servo unit bleed nipple

16.9 Bleeding a front brake caliper

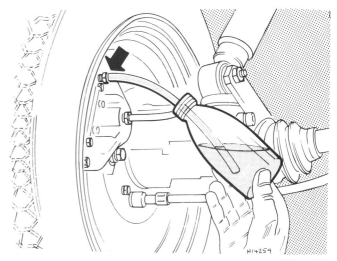

Fig. 9.25 Bleed tube connected to a rear caliper (arrowed) (Sec 16)

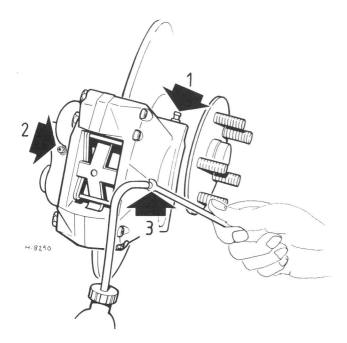

Fig. 9.26 Sequence for bleeding a front brake caliper (Sec 16)

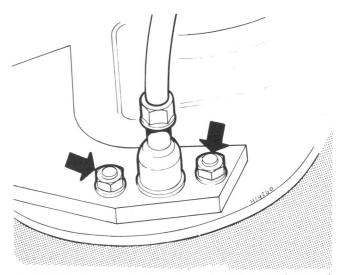

Fig. 9.27 Handbrake cable to rear brake backplate nuts (arrowed) (Sec 17)

17 Handbrake cable – removal and removal

1   Remove the handbrake shoes and expander as described in Section 6.

2   Working inside the car pull the rubber cover from the handbrake lever hose to expose the cable ends and adjusting nuts.

3   Unscrew and remove the locknut followed by the adjusting nut, and detach the cable end from the handbrake lever.

4   Unscrew the nuts securing the outer cable to the rear brake backplate, and remove the washers (photo).

5   Unhook the outer cable support clips from the suspension trailing arm (photo).

6   Withdraw the handbrake cable through the backplate, at the same time pulling the front inner cable through the support tube on the underbody transmission tunnel (photo).

7   Refitting is a reversal of removal, but make sure that the outer cable is correctly located in the support tube. Refer to Section 6 to refit the handbrake shoes and adjust the handbrake as described in Section 3.

17.4 Handbrake cable location on the backplate

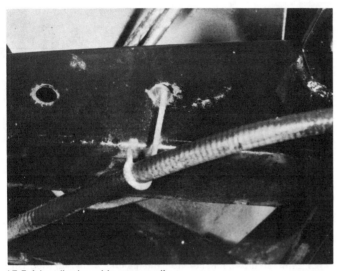

17.5 A handbrake cable support clip

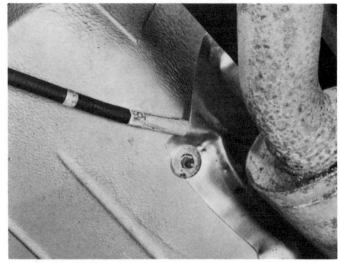

17.6 Handbrake cable location in the transmission tunnel

18 Handbrake lever – removal and refitting

1   Release the handbrake lever and chock the wheels.
2   Working inside the car pull the rubber cover from the handbrake lever hose to expose the cable ends and adjusting nuts.
3   Unscrew and remove the locknuts followed by the adjusting nuts, and detach the cable ends from the handbrake lever.
4   On early models extract the circlip and press out the lever pivot. On later models unscrew the nut and press out the bolt.
5   Ease the handbrake lever to the rear and withdraw it from the bracket.
6   Refitting is a reversal of removal, but adjust the handbrake as described in Section 3. Lubricate the pivot with a little multi purpose grease.

19 Brake pressure regulator – removal and refitting

1   Testing of the brake pressure regulator involves the use of special high pressure gauges, and is best left to your local BMW dealer. However, removal of the unit is quite within the scope of the owner, although it must be emphasised that the unit can only be tested in position on the car.
2   To remove the regulator first unscrew the brake fluid reservoir filler cap and tighten it onto a piece of polythene sheeting. Alternatively on right-hand drive models use two tapered wooden dowel rods to plug the reservoir outlets (see Fig. 9.16).
3   Note the location of the hydraulic pipes on the regulator then unscrew the union nuts and pull out the pipes (photo).
4   Unscrew the bolt and remove the brake pressure regulator from the bracket.
5   Refitting is a reversal of removal, but tighten the union nuts to the specified torque and bleed the hydraulic system as described in Section 16.

20 Handbrake and low fluid level indicator – description and testing

1   A switch is fitted to the rear of the handbrake lever to operate a warning light on the instrument panel when the handbrake is applied.
2   The warning light is also connected to the brake fluid level switch which is an integral part of the fluid reservoir filler cap. Should the fluid level drop below a predetermined minimum, the warning light will be switched on even with the handbrake lever released.
3   To test the fluid level switch first remove the fluid reservoir filler cap. With the ignition switched on and the switch pin in the centre of the cap released, the warning light should be illuminated with the handbrake lever released. Now depress the pin and the warning light should go out. Remove the filter and float from the reservoir and check that the float is not punctured, then refit the float, filter, and filler cap.

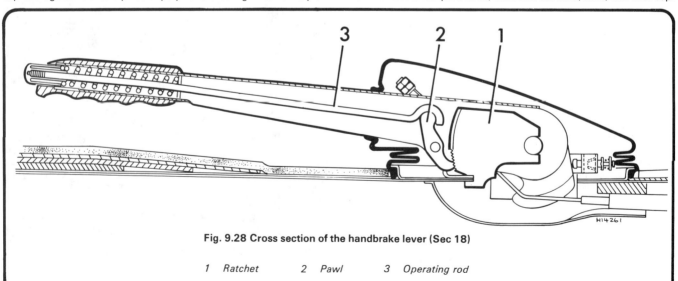

Fig. 9.28 Cross section of the handbrake lever (Sec 18)

1   Ratchet   2   Pawl   3   Operating rod

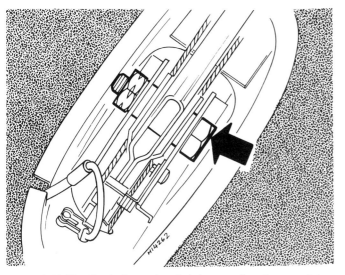

Fig. 9.29 Handbrake lever pivot bolt (arrowed) on later models (Sec 18)

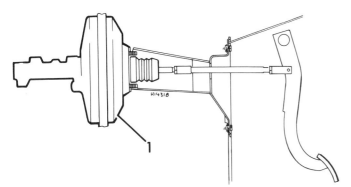

Fig. 9.30 Servo unit location (1) on a LHD model (Sec 21)

19.3 Brake pressure regulator location

21.1 Remote vacuum servo units as fitted to RHD models

21 Vacuum servo unit – description, removal and refitting

1   All models are fitted with vacuum servo assistance. However, on right-hand drive models two remote servo units are located on the left-hand side of the engine compartment and each unit serves a separate hydraulic circuit (photo). On left-hand drive models a single servo unit is located between the master cylinder and the bulkhead.

2   The servo unit operates by vacuum from the inlet manifold and it basically comprises a booster diaphragm and non-return valve.

3   With the brake pedal released, vacuum is channelled to both sides of the diaphragm, but when the pedal is depressed one side is opened to the atmosphere. The resultant unequal pressures are harnessed to provide assistance to the footbrake pedal movement.

4   Under normal operating conditions the vacuum servo unit is very reliable, and it is designed so that in the event of a failure the brake hydraulic system is still operative, although greater pedal pressure will be required. Besides cleaning the felt air filter, no other repairs are possible.

5   To test the servo unit, depress the footbrake pedal several times with the engine switched off in order to dissipate the vacuum, then keep the pedal depressed and start the engine. The pedal should move a small distance toward the floor as the engine vacuum operates the servo.

Right-hand drive models

6   To remove either servo unit on right-hand drive models it will be necessary to remove the air cleaner assembly on carburettor versions (see Chapter 3), and if the front servo is being removed it will be necessary to unbolt the cooling system expansion tank and move it to one side (see Chapter 2).

7   Unscrew the brake fluid reservoir filler cap and tighten it onto a piece of polythene sheeting. Alternatively use two tapered wooden dowel rods to plug the reservoir outlets (see Fig. 9.16).

8   Unscrew the hydraulic pipes union nut and bolt and disconnect the pipes.

9   Disconnect the vacuum hose from the front of the servo.

10 Unbolt and remove the servo unit from the engine compartment taking care not to spill hydraulic fluid on the bodywork.

Left-hand drive models

11 To remove the servo unit on left-hand drive models first remove the air cleaner assembly on carburettor versions (see Chapter 3).

12 Remove the master cylinder as described in Section 13.

13 Working inside the car remove the crosshead screws and withdraw the lower facia panel from the bottom of the steering column. Where applicable on USA models disconnect the wires from the electric window automatic cut-out (see also Chapter 5).

14 Disconnect the pushrod from the brake pedal by extracting the clip and removing the pivot pin.

15 Disconnect the vacuum hose from the front of the servo.

16 Unscrew the mounting nuts and withdraw the servo unit forward from the mounting bracket. Take care not to spill hydraulic fluid on the bodywork.

All models

17 Refitting is a reversal of removal, but bleed the hydraulic system

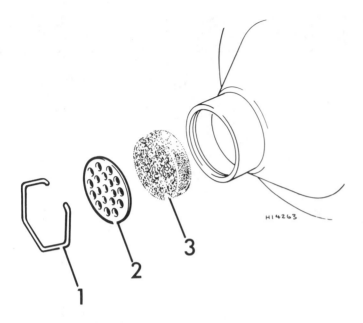

Fig. 9.31 Vacuum servo air filter components for RHD models (Sec 22)

1   Spring clip   3   Air filter
2   Holder

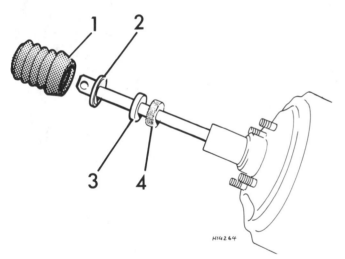

Fig. 9.32 Vacuum servo air filter components for LHD models (Sec 22)

1   Boot   3   Damper
2   Holder   4   Air filter

as described in Section 16. On left-hand drive models adjust the positions of the brake pedal and stoplight switch as described in Section 11.

22 Vacuum servo air filter – removal and refitting

1   The manufacturers do not recommend an interval for checking the vacuum servo air filter, but under average conditions this should be 30 000 miles (48 000 km).

Right-hand drive models

2   Prise the spring clip from the bottom of the servo unit and extract the perforated holder and the filter (photo).

22.2 Lower view of a remote vacuum servo unit showing air filter location

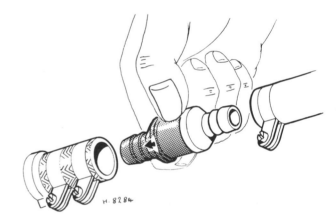

Fig. 9.33 Removing the vacuum servo non-return valve (Sec 23)
Arrow must face inlet manifold

Left-hand drive models

3   Remove the servo unit as described in Section 21.
4   Mark the two pushrod sections in relation to each other, loosen the locknut, then unscrew the outer section and locknut.
5   Pull off the rubber boot then extract the holder, damper, and filter from the rear of the servo unit.

All models

6   Clean all the components in fuel, but if the filter is deteriorated renew it.
7   Refitting is a reversal of removal, but on left-hand drive models refer to Section 21 as necessary.

23 Vacuum servo non-return valve – removal and refitting

1   Failure of the vacuum unit to maintain vacuum, may be due to a faulty non-return valve (assuming that the connecting hoses are tight, and not leaking).
2   The valve is located in the vacuum hose from the inlet manifold to the servo unit, and is removed by loosening the two clips, and releasing the unit from the hoses.
3   Make sure the unit is fitted the right way round; the arrow or the black end faces the inlet manifold.

24 Fault diagnosis – braking system

Symptom	Reason(s)
Excessive pedal travel	Brake fluid leak Air in hydraulic system Excessive disc run-out
Uneven braking and pulling to one side	Contaminated linings Seized or partially seized caliper piston Excessive disc pad or disc wear on one side Unequal tyre pressures Different lining material at each wheel
Brake judder	Excessive disc wear or run-out Wear in steering or suspension components
Brake pedal feels 'spongy'	Air in hydraulic system Faulty master cylinder seals
Excessive effort to stop car	Servo unit faulty Partially seized caliper pistons Incorrect lining material Contaminated linings Failure of one braking circuit New disc pads not yet bedded-in

Chapter 10 Electrical system

For modifications, and information applicable to later models, see Supplement at end of manual

Contents

Specifications

System type .... 12 volt, negative earth

Battery
Capacity (at 20 hr rate) .... 55 amp hr or 65 amp hr

Alternator
Type .... Bosch 14 volt
Maximum current .... 55 amp or 65 amp
Maximum power .... 770 watt or 910 watt
Charging begins at .... 1000 rpm or 1060 rpm
Minimum slip ring diameter .... 31.5 mm (1.240 in)

Voltage regulator
Type .... Bosch
Regulating voltage .... 13.7 to 14.5 volt

Starter motor
Type .... Bosch pre-engaged
Armature endplay .... 0.01 to 0.3 mm (0.0004 to 0.0118 in)
Minimum brush length .... 13.0 mm (0.512 in)

Fuses
Fusebox .... 11 x 8 amp; 4 x 16 amp; 2 x 25 amp
Spare fuses .... 2 x 8 amp; 1 x 16 amp; 1 x 25 amp

Bulbs
	Wattage
Headlamps	55 (HI Quartz Halogen)
Side/parking lights (front)	4
Front and rear indicator	21
Side/parking lights (rear)	10
Rear fog light	21
Stop light	21

	Wattage
Reversing light	21
Number plate light	5
Interior light	10
Luggage compartment light	10
Instrument panel warning lights	1.2
Battery charge indicator light	3
Automatic transmission selector illumination	1.2
Push button switch, control lighting, ashtray, and clock	1.2
Glovebox	4

Torque wrench settings

	lbf ft	Nm
Alternator pulley	25 to 32	35 to 45
Starter	34	47
Oil pressure switch	36	50
Stop light switch	3	4
Reversing light switch	4 to 7	6 to 10

1 General description

The electrical system is of 12 volt negative earth type. The battery is charged by a belt-driven alternator with a voltage regulator which is integral except on early 525 models. The starter motor is of pre-engaged type incorporating four brushes; when the ignition key is turned to the starting position a solenoid (integral with the starter motor) moves the drive pinion into engagement before the starter motor is energised.

Although repair procedures are given in this Chapter, it may well be more economical to renew worn components as complete units.

2 Battery – removal and refitting

1 The battery is located at the front left-hand side of the engine compartment, and is held in position by a clamp which is controlled by an extending handle (photo).

2 To remove the battery, first disconnect the negative (earth) lead, and bend it away from the battery, then disconnect the positive lead and bend it out of the way (photo).

3 Unscrew the clamp and carefully lift the battery out of its location. Keep it level to avoid spilling electrolyte, and if there is any corrosion prevent this from coming into contact with your skin or clothing. Should you spill any electrolyte on your skin or clothing, wash the affected area immediately with plenty of clean running water to neutralise the acid effect.

4 Refitting is a reversal of removal but clean the terminals and clamp before securing them, and then smear a little petroleum jelly over the terminals to protect them from corrosion.

3 Battery – maintenance

1 Normal weekly battery maintenance consists of checking the electrolyte level of each cell to ensure that the separators are covered with electrolyte. Lift off the cover and unscrew the caps. If the electrolyte level has dropped, add distilled or de-ionized water to each cell so that the level is 5.0 mm (0.197 in) above the separators.

2 At the same time wipe the top of the battery with a dry cloth to prevent the accumulation of dust and dampness which may cause the battery to become partially discharged over a period.

3 Every 12 months disconnect and clean the battery terminals and leads. After refitting them smear the exposed metal with petroleum jelly.

4 At the same time, inspect the battery clamp and tray for corrosion. If evident, remove the battery and clean the deposits away, then treat the affected metal with a proprietary anti-rust liquid and paint with the original colour.

5 When the battery is removed for whatever reason, it is worthwhile checking it for cracks and leakage. Cracks can be caused by topping-up the cells with distilled water in winter after instead of before a run. This gives the water no chance to mix with the electrolyte, so the former freezes and splits the battery case. If the battery case is fractured, it may be possible to repair it with a proprietary compound, but this depends on the material used for the case. If electrolyte has been lost from a cell, refer to Section 4 for details of adding a fresh solution.

6 If topping-up the battery becomes excessive and the case is not fractured, the battery is being over-charged and the voltage regulator will have to be checked.

7 If the car covers a very small annual mileage, it is worthwhile checking the specific gravity of the electrolyte every 3 months to

2.1 Removing the battery clamp

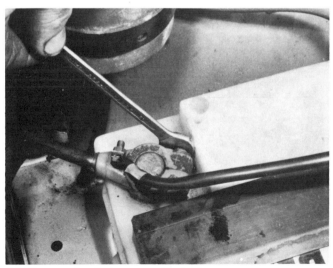

2.2 Disconnecting the battery positive lead

determine the state of charge of the battery. Use a hydrometer to make the check and compare the results with the following table.

	Ambient temperature above 25°C (77°F)	Ambient temperature below 25°C (77°F)
Fully charged	1.210 to 1.230	1.270 to 1.290
70% charged	1.170 to 1.190	1.230 to 1.250
Fully discharged	1.050 to 1.070	1.110 to 1.130

The specific gravity readings assume an electrolyte temperature of 15°C (60°F); for every 10°C (18°F) below 15°C (60°F) subtract 0.007, or above add 0.007.

8   If the battery condition is suspect, first check the specific gravity of electrolyte in each cell. A variation of 0.040 or more between any cells indicates loss of electrolyte or deterioration of the internal plates.

9   A further test can be made using a battery heavy discharge meter. The battery should be discharged for a maximum of 15 seconds at a load of three times the ampere-hour capacity (at the 20 hour discharge rate). Alternatively connect a voltmeter across the battery terminals and spin the engine on the starter with the coil HT lead earthed and the headlamps, heater, and heated rear window switched on.

10 If the voltmeter reading remains above 9.6 volts, the battery condition is satisfactory. If the reading is below 9.6 volts and the battery has already been charged as described in Section 5, it is faulty and should be renewed.

4 Battery – electrolyte replenishment

1   If after fully charging the battery, one of the cells maintains a specific gravity, which is 0.040 or more lower then the others, but the battery also maintains 9.6 volts during the heavy discharge test (Section 3), it is likely that electrolyte has been lost.

2   If a significant quantity of electrolyte has been lost through spillage, it will not suffice merely to refill the cell with distilled water. Instead top-up the electrolyte with a mixture of 2 parts sulphuric acid to 5 parts distilled water.

3   When mixing the electrolyte, *never add water to sulphuric acid*, always pour the acid slowly onto the water in a glass container. *If water is added to sulphuric acid, it will explode!*

4   After topping-up the cell with fresh electrolyte, recharge the battery, and check the hydrometer readings again.

5 Battery – charging

Note: *If the battery is to remain in the car whilst being charged always disconnect the terminals.*

1   In winter time when heavy demand is placed upon the battery, such as when starting from cold, and much electrical equipment is continually in use, it is a good idea to occasionally have the battery fully charged from an external source at the rate of 3.5 or 4 amps.

2   Continue to charge the battery at this rate until no further rise in specific gravity is noted over a four hour period.

3   Alternatively, a trickler charge charging at the rate of 1.5 amps can safely be used overnight.

4   Special rapid 'boost' charges, which are claimed to restore the power of the battery within 1 to 2 hours, can be most dangerous

unless they are thermostatically controlled, as overheating will buckle the battery plates and thus shorten the battery's useful life.

5   While charging the battery note that the electrolyte temperature should never exceed 100°F (37.8°C).

6 Alternator – maintenance and special precautions

1   Periodically wipe away any dirt which has accumulated on the outside of the unit, and also check that the wiring is firmly connected to the terminals. At the same time, check the tension of the drivebelt and adjust it if necessary as described in Chapter 2.

2   Take extreme care when making electrical circuit connections on the car, otherwise damage may occur to the alternator or other electrical components employing semi-conductors. Always make sure that the battery leads are connected to the correct terminals. Before using electric-arc welding equipment to repair any part of the car, disconnect the battery leads and alternator wiring. Disconnect the battery leads before using a mains charger. Never run the alternator with the battery leads or alternator wiring disconnected.

7 Alternator – removal and refitting

1   Disconnect the battery negative lead.

2   On USA models remove the fuel evaporative emission carbon filter with reference to Chapter 3.

3   On all models loosen the adjustment and pivot bolts, swivel the alternator toward the engine, and slip the fanbelt from the pulley (photos).

4   Remove the adjustment and pivot bolts, withdraw the alternator from the engine, and disconnect the wiring from the back of the alternator (photo).

5   Refitting is a reversal of removal, but adjust the tension of the fanbelt as described in Chapter 2.

8 Alternator and regulator – testing

Note: *This test can only be made on early 525 models with a voltage regulator mounted separate from the alternator.*

1   Should the warning light stay on when the engine is running, a quick check can be carried out to ascertain if the fault lies within the alternator or regulator. That is assuming that the drivebelt is not slack or missing.

2   With the engine stopped, pull off the multi-plug connector from the regulator. Using a suitable length of wire, bridge together the two lower flat connectors of the plug [blue lead (D/+61) and black lead (DF)]. This measure effectively cuts the regulator out of the charging circuit.

3   Start the engine and increase the engine speed to approximately 1000 rpm. If the generator warning light goes out completely then the regulator is faulty. If the generator warning light still glows or continues to burn brightly, then the fault is within the alternator.

4   A faulty regulator should be renewed. The alternator should only be overhauled to a limit of fitting new brushes, otherwise it should be repaired by your BMW agent or a new or reconditioned unit obtained.

7.3A loosening the alternator adjustment bolt

7.3B Removing the alternator pivot bolt

7.4 Rear view of the alternator with main cable disconnected

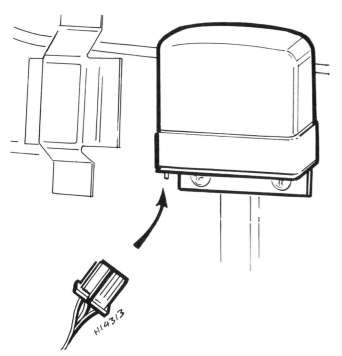

Fig. 10.1 Removing the multiplug from the remote mounted voltage regulator (Sec 8)

This arrangement is recommended due to the need for special tools and equipment and the fragile nature of the diodes incorporated in the alternator.

9 Alternator brushes – renewal

1   Remove the alternator as described in Section 7.
2   Remove the two screws and withdraw the brush holder and brushes from the back of the alternator. On models with an integral regulator the brush holder incorporates the regulator (photos).
3   Using a medium size electric soldering iron, heat up the connecting terminals just enough to release the brush leads, then withdraw the worn brushes.
4   Insert the new brushes and solder the connecting terminals in position. Do not let solder flow down the braided copper wire but solder only the tip of the lead and restrict the heat of the soldering iron as much as possible.
5   Clean the slip rings with a fuel moistened cloth and reassemble the alternator, reversing the dismantling procedure (photo).

10 Starter motor – description and testing

1   The starter motor assembly is of the pre-engaged type. A solenoid is mounted on the starter endplate, and operates a lever which slides the starter pinion into engagement with the flywheel ring gear.
2   The operation of the starter begins when the ignition key is turned to the starting position. Current then flows through the solenoid windings, and causes the armature to pull the pinion operating lever. The drive pinion is thus brought into engagement with the flywheel ring gear which, at this stage, is stationary. When the drive pinion reaches the end of its travel, an internal contact allows the full starter motor current to flow through the starter windings, and the pinion then drives the flywheel ring gear and the engine is rotated. As soon as the engine fires, the drive pinion is released from the starter driveshaft by means of a roller freewheel, and this prevents the starter from being driven by the engine, which would otherwise lead to the failure of the starter bearings. When the engine has started and the ignition key is returned to its ignition position, the current ceases to flow through the solenoid windings and the holding lever is released under spring pressure. The drive pinion is brought out of engagement with the flywheel ring gear, and the internal contacts separate, thus cutting-off the main starter current.
3   Should the starter not operate when the ignition key is turned to

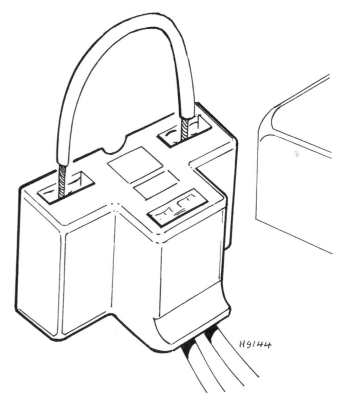

Fig. 10.2 Bridging the regulator multiplug when testing the alternator (Sec 8)

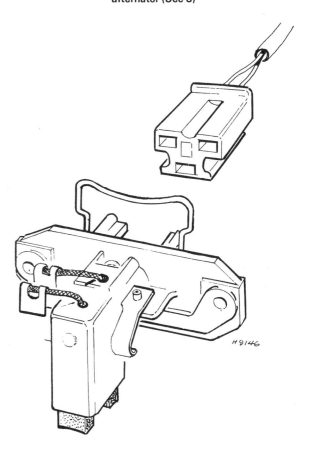

Fig. 10.3 Alternator brush holder on models with a remote regulator (Sec 9)

9.2A Remove the regulator screws ...

9.2B ... and withdraw the regulator from the alternator

9.2C Integral type alternator regulator incorporating brushes

9.5 Showing the alternator slip rings (regulator removed)

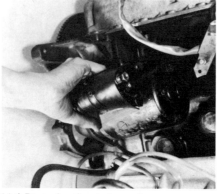
11.4 Removing the starter motor

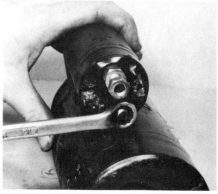
12.1 Disconnecting the starter motor feed wire

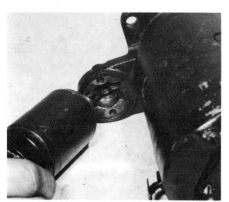
12.2 Removing the solenoid from the starter motor

12.3A Removing the starter motor dust cap ...

12.3B ... lockwasher ...

12.3C ... and shims

12.4A Removing the starter motor tie bolts ...

12.4B ... and end cover

the starting position, first check that the battery is in good condition by switching the headlights on. If they do not come on, check that the battery terminals are clean and tight, and that the battery is fully charged. If the starter is still inoperative, check that the solenoid terminal 50 (spade terminal) is receiving current, by connecting it, with a voltmeter or 12 volt test lamp, to an earthing point on the body or the battery negative terminal. Do this check with the ignition key in the starting position, and if current is available at terminal 50, but the starter is still inoperative, check that current is reaching terminal 30 (heavy cable from battery). Should current not be reaching either terminal 50 or terminal 30, the wiring circuits will have to be traced back to the ignition switch and battery respectively, and the fault rectified. With current available at both terminals, ascertain whether the solenoid is working by turning the ignition key to the starting position, when there should be an audible click as the solenoid armature operates, and the starter pinion is brought into engagement with the flywheel ring gear. If no noise is heard the solenoid unit must be removed, and the continuity of its windings tested. If the solenoid is working, the starter motor will have to be removed for testing and overhaul.

11 Starter motor – removal and refitting

1   Disconnect the battery negative lead.
2   Note the location of the wires on the starter solenoid then disconnect them.
3   On automatic transmission models remove the accelerator linkage bracket for better access, and on fuel injection models it is recommended that the intake pipe to No 6 cylinder is removed.
4   Unscrew the mounting bolts and withdraw the starter motor from the engine (photo).
5   Refitting is a reversal of removal, but tighten the mounting bolts to the specified torque and where applicable fit a new gasket to No 6 intake pipe by cutting a complete gasket.

12 Starter motor – overhaul

1   Disconnect the motor field winding lead from the solenoid terminal (photo).
2   Remove the screws which secure the solenoid to the drive end cover and withdraw the solenoid at the same time unhooking it from the drive engagement lever (photo).
3   Remove the dust cap from the end of the starter motor and extract the lockwasher, shims and gasket (photos).
4   Unscrew the tie bolts and withdraw the motor end cover (photos).
5   Extract the carbon brushes from their holders and remove the brush mounting plates (photo).
6   Withdraw the yoke from the drive end cover and then unscrew the engagement lever pivot bolt. Remove the blanking plate (photos).
7   Withdraw the armature complete with the engagement lever (photo).
8   Using a piece of suitable tubing, drive the stop ring back up the armature shaft to expose the jump ring. Extract the jump ring and pull off the starter drive components.
9   Measure the overall length of the four brushes and where they are worn below the minimum recommended (see Specifications) renew them. Using a medium electric soldering iron, heat up the terminals just enough to melt the solder and release the leads. Clean the brush holders and check that the brushes move freely in them.
10 Solder the new brush leads to the terminals, and test the joints for strength by lightly pulling on the brush leads.
11 Normally, the commutator may be cleaned by holding a piece of non-fluffy rag moistened with fuel against it as it is rotated by hand. If, on inspection, the mica separators are level with the copper segments then they must be undercut by 0.0197 in (0.5 mm). Undercut the mica separators of the commutator using an old hacksaw blade ground to suit. The commutator may be polished with a piece of very fine glass paper – never use emery cloth as the carborundum particles will become embedded in the copper surfaces.

12.5 Removing the brushes

12.6A Removing the starter motor yoke ...

12.6B ... blanking plate ...

12.6C ... and engagement lever pivot bolt

12.7 Removing the starter motor armature and engagement lever

12 Should the surface of the commutator be worn down in ridges then it will be essential to have the commutator surface skimmed on a lathe but it should be remembered that the minimum permissible diameter of the commutator is 1.3 in (33 mm).

13 The starter drive gear should be cleaned in paraffin, and checked for signs of wear, and components renewed as necessary.

14 Reassembly of the starter motor is a reversal of removal. When refitting the brushes to the brush holders use a bent piece of stiff wire to lift the brush springs. It is recommended that a smear of silicone grease is applied to the armature spiral and the engagement ring before assembling these components (photo).

15 The endfloat of the armature must be as specified. This can be adjusted by varying the amount of shims located under the starter motor dust cap.

13 Fuses – general

1 The fuses are located on the left-hand side of the engine compartment together with the relays. The transparent cover on the fusebox is marked with a list of the fuses and their ratings (photo).

2 The fuses and circuits protected are as follows:

Fuse number	Rating (amp)	Circuit
1	16	Electric fuel pump or automatic choke
2	8	RH headlamp, low beam
3	8	LH headlamp, low beam
4	16	Cigar lighter, electric aerial
5	8	Hazard lights, glovebox, luggage compartment, clock, headlamp (if fitted), central locking
6	8	Instrument panel warning lamps, fuel and temperature gauges, tachometer, reversing lights
7	8	RH headlamp, high beam
8	8	LH headlamp, high beam
9	8	RH parking/side lights, number plate, instrument panel illumination, rear fog lamp, engine compartment
10	8	LH parking/side lights
11	16	Direction indicators, wipe/wash system, horn, headlamp cleaners, electric mirror
12	8	Stop lights, radio
13	16	Heated rear window
13 (alternative)	25	Heated rear window, electric sliding roof
14	25	Heater, air conditioner fan
15	8	RH fog light
16	8	LH fog light
17	25	Spare terminal

3 Always renew a fuse with one of identical rating, and never renew it more than once without finding the source of the trouble.

14 Relays – general

1 Four relays are fitted as standard in the fusebox and their purpose is to protect the circuits for the headlamp high beam, headlamp low beam, horn, and general overload. An optional relay is fitted on models with front fog lights.

2 If any of the circuits given in paragraph 1 are faulty, first check for loose or broken leads, then check that an audible click is heard when the circuit is switched on. If the relay is being energised but fails to switch on the main current, it is faulty and should be renewed by pulling it directly from the fusebox (photo).

15 Bulbs – renewal

1 Always renew a bulb with one of the same rating.

Headlamps and side/parking lamps (UK models)

2 Pull the plastic cover from the rear of the headlamps in the engine compartment (photo).

3 Disconnect the wiring plug then turn the sealing cap anti-clockwise to release it (photos).

4 To remove the headlamp bulb, release the clip then withdraw the bulb and disconnect the wire from the terminal (photos).

5 To remove the side/parking lamp bulb from the outer headlamp, pull out the holder then push and twist the bulb to remove it (photo).

6 When refitting the headlamp bulbs note that the raised portion locates in the headlamp cut-out.

Sealed beam headlamp units (USA models)

7 Follow the procedure described in Section 16.

Front indicator lamps (UK models)

8 Remove the lens from below the front bumper (3 screws) (photos).

9 Push and twist the bulb to remove it (photo).

Front indicator/parking lamps (USA models)

10 Remove the lens (2 screws).

11 Push and twist the bulb to remove it.

Side marker lamps (USA models)

12 Remove the lens (2 screws).

13 Push and twist the bulb to remove it.

14 When refitting the lens, make sure that the water drain hole faces downward.

Rear light cluster

15 On early models, open the boot lid and then remove the rear light lens by unscrewing the knobs or mounting nuts.

16 On later models open the boot lid and remove the rear trim which is retained either by screws or retaining caps and clips. Unscrew the knurled nuts and withdraw the bulb holder (photos).

17 Push and twist the relevant bulb to remove it (photo).

12.14 The starter motor components

13.1 The fusebox and cover

14.2 Removing a relay

15.2 Removing the headlamp rear cover

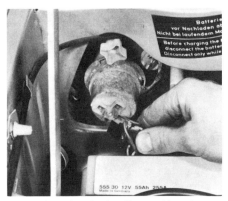

15.3A Removing the headlamp wiring plug

15.3B ... and sealing cap

15.4A Release the clip ...

15.4B ... and remove the headlamp bulb

15.5 Removing the side/parking light bulb (UK model)

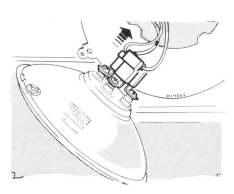

Fig. 10.4 Removing the multiplug from a sealed beam headlamp unit (Sec 15)

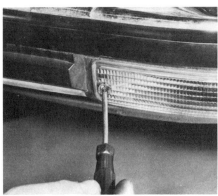

15.8A Remove the screws ...

15.8B ... and front indicator lamp lens (UK models)

15.9 Removing the front indicator lamp bulb (UK models)

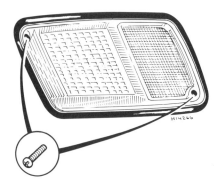

Fig. 10.5 Side marker lamp lens retaining screws (Sec 15)

15.16A Removing the rear trim retaining caps ...

15.16B ... and clips

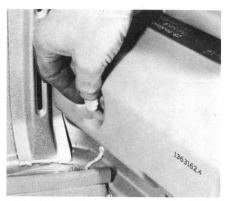
15.16C Removing the rear light bulbholder knurled nuts

15.17 Removing a rear light bulb

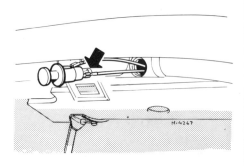
Fig. 10.6 Glovebox light bulb location (Sec 15)

15.23A Remove the screws ...

15.23B ... and withdraw the number plate light

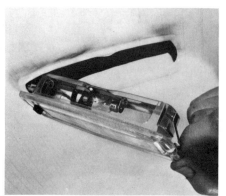
15.26 Removing the interior light

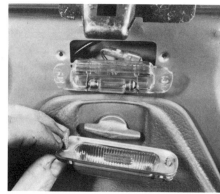
15.29 Removing the luggage compartment light

15.33 Removing an instrument panel warning light

16.2A Remove the headlamp retainer ring screws ...

16.2B ... and lift off the ring

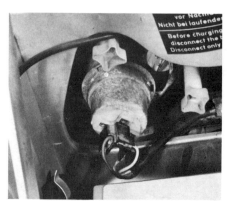
17.9 Showing location of the headlamp adjustment knobs

Engine compartment light

18 Open the bonnet and remove the lens (2 screws).
19 Remove the festoon type bulb.
20 Make sure that the contacts are tensioned sufficiently to hold the new bulb firmly.

Glovebox light

21 Disconnect the battery negative lead then open the glovebox and pull out the light.
22 Push and twist the bulb to remove it.

Number plate light

23 Remove the two screws and withdraw the glass lens and rubber seal from the rear body panel (photos).
24 Remove the festoon type bulb from the spring contacts.
25 When fitting the new bulb make sure that the spring contacts are tensioned sufficiently to hold the bulb firmly.

Interior light

26 Carefully unclip the light from the headlining (photo).
27 Remove the festoon type bulb from the spring contacts.
28 Make sure that the spring contacts are tensioned sufficiently to hold the new bulb firmly.

Luggage compartment light

29 Remove the two screws and withdraw the plastic lens (photo).
30 Remove the festoon type bulb from the spring contacts.
31 Make sure that the spring contacts are tensioned sufficiently to hold the new bulb firmly.

Instrument panel lights

32 Remove the instrument panel as described in Section 31.
33 Turn the bulb holders through 90° and withdraw them, then pull out the wedge type bulbs (photo).

16 Headlamps – removal and refitting

1 Remove the relevant side radiator grille with reference to Chapter 12.
2 Remove the screws holding the headlamp retainer ring, remove the ring, and withdraw the headlamp sufficient to disconnect the wiring plug (photos).
3 Withdraw the headlamp.
4 Refitting is a reversal of removal, but adjust the headlamp alignment as described in Section 17.

17 Headlamps – alignment

1 As headlamp beam alignment regulations are quite stringent in most countries, it is recommended that the headlamp beam adjustment is entrusted to a suitably equipped garage, where it can be checked with an optical alignment device.
2 In an amergency the light pattern may be altered by opening the bonnet lid, and adjusting the plastic screws at the rear of the headlamp units as shown in Fig. 10.7.
3 The car should first be positioned 16 ft 6 in (5 metres) from a flat vertical surface (eg a light coloured wall). Load the back seat with a 155 lb (70 kg) weight or get someone to sit in the middle of the rear seat.
4 Measure the height of the headlight centres from the ground, and mark a line (h-h) on the flat vertical surface at the same height.
5 Now mark on the flat vertical surface a vertical line (V-V) which coincides with the car's centre-line.
6 Mark on the flat vertical surface the distance of each inner headlight centre from the car's centre-line $\frac{e}{2}$ and mark vertical lines 'a' and 'b'.

To adjust the inner headlamps (main beam)

7 Cover up the outer headlamps and switch on the headlamps to the main beam position. The circle of maximum light intensity should be equally divided between the horizontal line (h-h) and vertical lines 'a' and 'b'. If adjustments are necessary turn the knurled adjustment screws.

To adjust the outer headlamps (dipped beam)

8 Now mark on the flat vertical surface distance $\frac{e^1}{2}$ which represents the distance of each outer headlamp centre from the centre-line of the car, and draw vertical lines (a') and (b') to intersect with the horizontal line. A further line (c) should now be drawn in 2 in (5 cm) below the horizontal line (h-h).
9 Uncover the outer headlamps and switch on the headlamps to the dipped beam position. Set the height of the outer headlamps, by turning the upper beam knurled adjustment screw, if necessary (photo). Now check the horizontal beam setting by turning the other knurled adjustment screw until the junction between the horizontal part of the beam's upper boundary and the part inclined upwards at 15° coincides with vertical line (a') and (b'). Note that the illustration is for right-hand drive cars, and that for left-hand drive models the lights will dip to the other side.
10 It must be emphasised that this method of adjustment should only be used in a real emergency, and arrangements should be made to have an optical check made at the earliest opportunity.

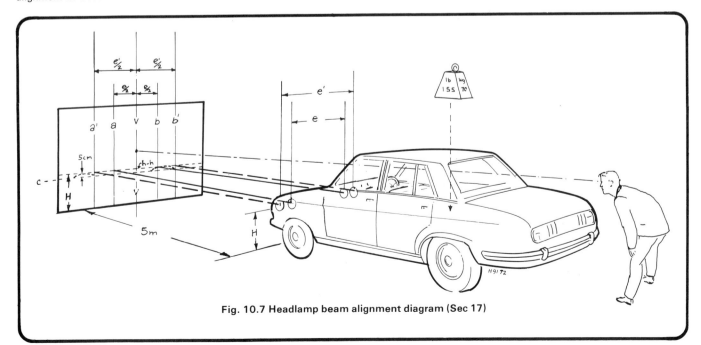

Fig. 10.7 Headlamp beam alignment diagram (Sec 17)

18 Direction indicator/hazard warning unit – removal and refitting

1 Disconnect the battery negative lead.
2 Remove the crosshead screws and withdraw the lower facia panel from the bottom of the steering column. Where applicable on USA models disconnect the wires from the electric window automatic cut-out (see also Chapter 5).
3 Push the unit upward and unclip it from the bulkhead (photos).
4 Separate the unit from the multi-plug.
5 Refitting is a reversal of removal.

19 Direction indicator/headlamp dipswitch – removal and refitting

1 Remove the steering wheel as described in Chapter 11.
2 Disconnect the battery negative lead.
3 Remove the crosshead screws and withdraw the lower facia panel from the bottom of the steering column. Where applicable on USA models disconnect the wires from the electric window automatic cut-out (see also Chapter 5).
4 Unscrew the steering column lower shroud screws, disconnect the wire and withdraw the lower shroud.
5 Remove the crosshead screws and withdraw the switch from the column (photo).
6 Disconnect the cable multi-plug and single wire connector, release the cable straps, and remove the switch from the car.
7 Refitting is a reversal of removal, but where applicable the cancelling cam gap must be adjusted to 3 mm (0.118 in) as described in Chapter 11.

20 Ignition switch – removal and refitting

1 Disconnect the battery negative lead.
2 Remove the crosshead screws and withdraw the lower facia panel from the bottom of the steering column. Where applicable on USA models disconnect the wires from the electric window automatic cut-out (see also Chapter 5).
3 Unscrew the steering column lower shroud screws, disconnect the wire and withdraw the lower shroud.
4 Remove the grub screw and withdraw the ignition switch from the column.
5 Release the cable straps then disconnect the cable multi-plug and single wire connector. Remove the ignition switch from the car.
6 Refitting is a reversal of removal but turn the ignition key to position 'O' first.

21 Windscreen wiper switch – removal and refitting

The procedure is identical to that for the direction indicator/headlamp dipswitch described in Section 19, however there is no single wire connector.

22 Light switch – removal and refitting

1 Disconnect the battery negative lead.
2 Remove the crosshead screws and withdraw the lower facia panel from the bottom of the steering column. Where applicable on USA models disconnect the wires from the electric window automatic cut-out (see also Chapter 5).
3 Pull out the switch knob, then unscrew the knob while holding the shaft stationary with a length of dowel rod inserted in the hole provided.
4 Unscrew the retaining nut, preferably using a slotted screwdriver.
5 Withdraw the light switch from the facia and disconnect the multi-plugs (photo).
6 Refitting is a reversal of removal.

23 Heated rear window switch – removal and refitting

1 Disconnect the battery negative lead.
2 Unscrew the knob followed by the retaining nut, preferably using a slotted screwdriver.
3 Withdraw the switch from the centre panel and disconnect the wires. On some models it may be necessary to remove the radio or the radio blanking plate.
4 Refitting is a reversal of removal.

24 Hazard light switch – removal and refitting

1 Disconnect the battery negative lead.
2 Remove the crosshead screws and withdraw the lower facia panel from the bottom of the steering column. Where applicable on USA models disconnect the wires from the electric window automatic cut-out (see also Chapter 5).
3 Pull the multi-plug from the rear of the switch then press the switch from the facia (photo).
4 Refitting is a reversal of removal.

25 Handbrake lever switch – removal and refitting

1 Pull the rubber gaiter from the handbrake lever base.
2 Disconnect the wire, then remove the adjustment screw and withdraw the switch.
3 Refitting is a reversal of removal, but adjust the switch position so that the warning light comes on when the handbrake lever reaches the first ratchet notch.

26 Central locking impact switch – removal and refitting

1 This switch is located beneath the passenger's side of the facia panel on models fitted with a central door locking system. In the event of a collision the switch automatically unlocks all the doors; the switch may be reset by opening the glovebox and depressing the safety button and the driver's door lock button.

18.3A Location of the direction indicator/hazard warning unit (arrowed) ...

18.3B ... showing the mounting clip

19.5 Location of the direction indicator/headlamp dip switch mounting screws (arrowed)

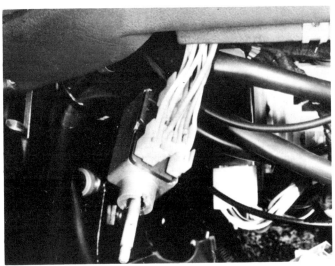
22.5 Removing the light switch

24.3 Removing the hazard light switch

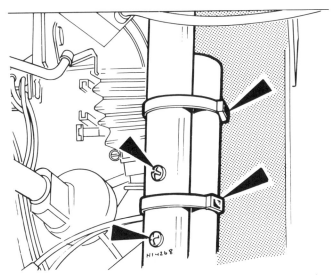
Fig. 10.8 Central locking impact switch retaining straps and screws (Sec 26)

27.4 Removing a courtesy light switch

2   To remove the switch, open the glovebox and disconnect the stays. Pull off the cover and unhook the springs, then remove the screws and withdraw the instrument panel control trim.
3   Disconnect the battery negative lead.
4   Disconnect the wiring from the switch. Remove the straps and screws and withdraw the impact switch.
5   Refitting is a reversal of removal.

27 Glovebox and courtesy light switches – removal and refitting

1   Disconnect the battery negative lead.

Glovebox light switch

2   Open the glovebox and prise the switch from the facia.
3   Disconnect the wiring and withdraw the switch.

Courtesy light switch

4   With the door open remove the screw and withdraw the switch (photo).
5   Disconnect the wiring from the switch, but make sure that the wiring does not drop back into the door pillar.
6   Refitting is a reversal of removal.

28 Wiper/washer intermittent action control unit – removal and refitting

The procedure is identical to that for the direction indicator/hazard warning unit described in Section 18.

29 Starter locking and electric window relays – removal and refitting

1   These relays are fitted to USA models. To remove either, first disconnect the battery negative lead.
2   Remove the crosshead screws and withdraw the lower facia panel from the bottom of the steering column. Where applicable disconnect the wires from the electric window automatic cut-out (see also Chapter 5).
3   Pull the relay from the holder.
4   Refitting is a reversal of removal.

30 Seat belt timer relay – removal and refitting

1   This relay is fitted to USA models. To remove it, first remove the

rear seat cushion as described in Chapter 12.
2   Disconnect the battery negative lead.
3   Remove the relay mounting screw, disconnect the wiring, and withdraw the relay.
4   Refitting is a reversal of removal.

31 Instrument panel – removal and refitting

1   Disconnect the battery negative lead.
2   Remove the crosshead screws and withdraw the lower facia panel from the bottom of the steering column. Where applicable disconnect the wires from the electric window automatic cut-out (see also Chapter 5).
3   Unscrew the speedometer cable upper connection. On left-hand drive models this is located at the bottom of the steering column, but on right-hand drive models it is located behind the air distribution vent in the centre of the facia (photo).
4   The instrument panel is retained by a cable and knurled nut located in a metal channel (photos). Remove the knurled nut from beneath the instrument panel.
5   Either unscrew the steering column retaining bolts and lower the steering column or remove the steering wheel with reference to Chapter 11.
6   Withdraw the instrument panel sufficiently to disconnect the wiring and multi-plugs after noting their locations. Also disconnect the speedometer cable (photos).
7   Refitting is a reversal of removal, but make sure that the felt ring is correctly located in the speedometer cable upper connection (photo).

32 Speedometer cable – removal and refitting

Upper cable
1   Remove the instrument panel as described in Section 31.
2   Withdraw the upper cable from behind the facia.
3   Refitting is a reversal of removal.

31.3 Speedometer cable upper connection (RHD models)

31.4A Showing the instrument panel retaining cable ...

31.4B ... and metal channel (arrowed)

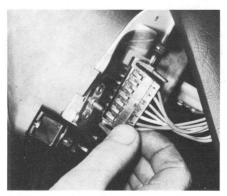
31.6A Removing an instrument panel multiplug

31.6B Wiring connections on the rear of the instrument panel

31.6C Speedometer cable to instrument panel connection

31.7 View of the instrument panel installed

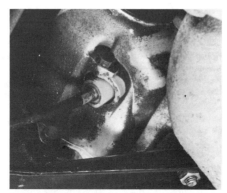
32.6 Speedometer cable location in the automatic transmission

32.8 Speedometer cable and retaining clips

Lower cable(s)

4   On left-hand drive models remove the lower facia panel from the bottom of the steering column. On right-hand drive models remove the air distribution vent from the centre of the facia. Unscrew the connection.
5   Jack-up the front of the car and support it on axle stands.
6   Disconnect the cable from the transmission by unscrewing the retaining bolt (photo).
7   Where applicable on USA models unscrew the cable(s) from the service interval switch.
8   Withdraw the cable(s) from the clips (photo).
9   Refitting is a reversal of removal. Refill the manual gearbox with oil where applicable.

33 Instrument panel instruments and gauges – removal and refitting

Tachometer

1   Remove the instrument panel as described in Section 31.
2   Remove the mounting plate screws and withdraw the tachometer. On automatic transmission models, disconnect the resistor.
3   Refitting is a reversal of removal.

Speedometer head

4   Remove the tachometer as described in paragraphs 1 to 3.
5   Remove the remaining mounting plate screws and withdraw the speedometer head.
6   Refitting is a reversal of removal.

Temperature gauge

7   Remove the tachometer as described in paragraphs 1 to 3.
8   Remove the battery charge and main beam warning lamp bulb holders.
9   Remove the screw and withdraw the temperature gauge and mounting plate.
10 Refitting is a reversal of removal.

Fuel gauge

11 Remove the speedometer head as described in paragraphs 4 to 6.
12 Remove the direction indicator and handbrake warning lamp bulb holders.
13 Remove the screw and withdraw the fuel gauge and mounting plate.
14 Refitting is a reversal of removal.

34 Temperature and fuel gauges – testing

Temperature gauge

1   With the temperature gauge removed from the instrument panel connect a lead between the positive terminal of the battery, and the temperature gauge positive terminal.
2   Connect a further lead from the negative terminal of the battery to the negative terminal of the temperature gauge.
3   The temperature gauge needle should move over to the red zone, but if this does not occur, the gauge is faulty and must be renewed.

Fuel gauge

4   With the fuel gauge removed from the instrument panel, connect a lead between the positive terminal of the battery, and the fuel gauge positive terminal.
5   Connect a further lead from the negative terminal of the battery, to the negative terminal of the fuel gauge.
6   The gauge needle should swing over to the 'full' reading, but if this does not occur, the gauge is faulty, and will have to be renewed.

35 Clock – removal and refitting

1   Remove the heater controls with reference to Chapter 12.

UK models

2   Unscrew the retaining knobs.

3   Unclip the wiring harness, withdraw the clock, and disconnect the wiring from the clock terminals.

USA models

4   Remove the screw and move the relay to one side leaving the wires attached.
5   Note the location of the wires on the rotary switch and clock, then disconnect them.
6   Unscrew the retaining knobs and withdraw the clock.

All models

7   Refitting is a reversal of removal.

36 Windscreen wiper motor and linkage – removal and refitting

1   Working in the engine compartment unbolt and remove the bulkhead cover. Note the upper screws.

Motor

2   Prise the linkage from the motor crank, then unscrew the nut retaining the crank (photo). Mark the crank and shaft in relation to each other, and remove the crank.
3   Unscrew the mounting plate bolts and withdraw the motor so that the multi-plug can be disconnected.
4   Refitting is a reversal of removal.

Linkage

5   Remove the wiper arms as described in Section 37.
6   Prise the linkage from the motor crank and pivots and remove the linkage.
7   Remove the pivot caps, nuts, and washers and remove the pivots from the bulkhead cross panel.
8   Refitting is a reversal of removal, but lubricate the linkage and pivots with a molybdenum disulphide based grease.

37 Windscreen wiper blades and arms – removal and refitting

1   The wiper blades should be renewed when they no longer clean the windscreen effectively or when they become perished or broken.
2   To remove a wiper blade, pivot the arm from the windscreen then raise the spring catch and pull out the blade (photo).
3   To remove a wiper arm, lift the cap at the pivot end and unscrew the nut (photo). The arm can then be removed from the splined pivot.
4   Refitting is a reversal of removal, but when fitting the wiper arm to the pivot first ensure that the wiper motor is in its parked position then fit the arm so that the wiper blade is parallel to the lower edge of the windscreen.

36.2 Windscreen wiper motor location in the bulkhead

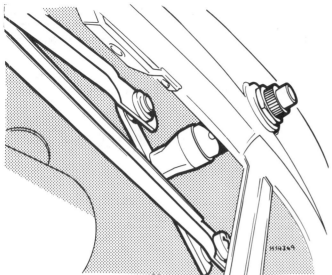

Fig. 10.9 Windscreen wiper linkage and pivot (Sec 36)

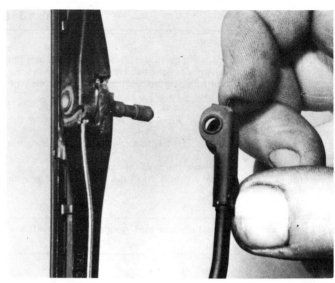

37.2 Removing a wiper blade

37.3 Removing a wiper arm

38.3 View of the horn from the front of the car

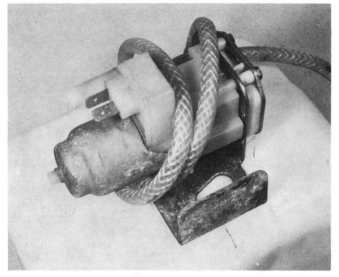

39.1 The windscreen washer motor

39.2 Removing a windscreen washer jet

38 Horn – removal and refitting

1 Disconnect the battery negative lead.
2 Remove the radiator grille side section as described in Chapter 12.
3 Disconnect the wiring and unbolt the horn from its mounting (photo).
4 Refitting is a reversal of removal.

39 Windscreen washer system – general

1 The windscreen washer reservoir is located on the right-hand side of the engine compartment and incorporates an electric pump (photo). A plastic tube is connected between the pump and the washer jets located on the bonnet.
2 The washer jets can be removed by disconnecting the tube and removing the crosshead screws (photo).
3 The washer jets should direct water in the middle of the wiper arms, approximately 650 mm (25.6 in) from the jets. If necessary bend the jets.

40 Radio – removal and refitting

1 The radio fitted as original equipment is located in the central console. To remove it first prise off the knobs and bezels.
2 On 1977-on models remove the centre tray with reference to Chapter 12.
3 Unscrew the nuts and remove the front cover.
4 Remove the front brackets as applicable.
5 Where the centre tray has ben removed, remove the rear bracket. If the tray is still in position, pull the radio from the clip.
6 Disconnect the battery negative lead then disconnect all the wiring and aerial from the radio. Remove the radio.
7 Refitting is a reversal of removal.

41 Radios and tape players – installation

This Section describes the fitting of in-car entertainment (ICE) equipment which was not fitted as standard or as an option by the car manufacturer during production of the car.

A radio or tape player is an expensive item to buy, and will only give its best performance if fitted properly. It is useless to expect concert hall performance from a unit that is suspended from the dashpanel by string with its speaker resting on the back seat or parcel shelf! If you do not wish to do the installation yourself, there are many in-car entertainment specialists who can do the fitting for you.

Make sure the unit purchased is of the same polarity as the vehicle. Ensure that units with adjustable polarity are correctly set before commencing installation.

It is difficult to give specific information with regard to fitting, as final positioning of the radio/tape player, speakers and aerial is entirely a matter of personal preference. However, the following paragraphs give guidelines to follow which are relevant to all installations.

Radios

Most radios are a standardised size of 7 in wide by 2 in deep – this ensures that they will fit into the radio aperture provided in most cars. If your car does not have such an aperture, then the radio must be fitted in a suitable position either in or beneath the dashpanel. Alternatively, a special console can be purchased which will fit between the dashpanel and the floor or on the transmission tunnel. These consoles can also be used for additional switches and instrumentation if required. Where no radio aperture is provided, the following points should be borne in mind before deciding exactly where to fit the unit:

(a) The unit must be within easy reach of the driver wearing a seat belt
(b) The unit must not be mounted in close proximity to an electronic tachometer, the ignition switch and its wiring, or the flasher unit and associated wiring
(c) The unit must be mounted within reach of the aerial lead, and in such a place that the aerial lead will not have to be routed

near the components detailed in the preceding paragraph 'b'
(d) The unit should not be positioned in a place where it might cause injury to the car occupants in an accident; for instance under the dashpanel above the driver's or passenger's legs
(e) The unit must be fitted really securely

Some radios will have mounting brackets provided, together with instructions; others will need to be fitted using drilled and slotted metal strips, bent to form mounting brackets. These strips are available from most accessory shops. The unit must be properly earthed by fitting a separate earthing lead between the casing of the radio and the vehicle frame.

Use the radio manufacturers' instructions when wiring the radio into the vehicle's electrical system. If no instructions are available, refer to the relevant wiring diagram to find the location of the radio 'feed' connection in the vehicle's wiring circuit. A 1 to 2 amp 'in-line' fuse must be fitted in the radio's 'feed' wire – a choke may also be necessary (see next Section).

The type of aerial used and its fitted position, is a matter of personal preference. In general the taller the aerial, the better the reception. It is best to fit a fully retractable aerial – especially, if a mechanical car-wash is used or if you live in an area where cars tend to be vandalised. In this respect electric aerials which are raised and lowered automatically when switching the radio on or off are convenient, but are more likely to give trouble than the manual type.

When choosing a position for the aerial, the following points should be considered:

(a) The aerial lead should be as short as possible; this means that the aerial should be mounted at the front of the vehicle
(b) The aerial must be mounted as far away from the distributor and HT leads as possible
(c) The part of the aerial which protrudes beneath the mounting point must not foul the roadwheels, or anything else
(d) If possible, the aerial should be positioned so that the coaxial lead does not have to be routed through the engine compartment
(e) The plane of the panel on which the aerial is mounted should not be so steeply angled that the aerial cannot be mounted vertically (in relation to the 'end-on' aspect of the vehicle). Most aerials have a small amount of adjustment available

Having decided on a mounting position, a relatively large hole will have to be made in the panel. The exact size of the hole will depend upon the specific aerial being fitted, although generally, the hole required is of $\frac{3}{4}$ inch diameter. On metal bodied cars, a 'tank-cutter' of the relevant diameter is the best tool to use for making the hole. This tool needs a small diameter pilot hole drilled through the panel, through which the tool clamping bolt is inserted. On GRP bodied cars, a hole-saw is the best tool to use. Again, this tool will require the drilling of a small pilot hole. When the hole has been made the raw edges should be de-burred with a file and then painted to prevent corrosion.

Fit the aerial according to the manufacturer's instructions. If the aerial is very tall, or if it protrudes beneath the mounting panel for a considerable distance, it is a good idea to fit a stay beneath the aerial and the vehicle frame. This stay can be manufactured from the slotted and drilled metal strips previously mentioned. The stay should be securely screwed or bolted in place. For best reception, it is advisable to fit an earth lead between the aerial and the vehicle frame; this is essential for GRP bodied cars.

It will probably be necessary to drill one or two holes through bodywork panels in order to feed the aerial lead into the interior of the car. Where this is the case, ensure that the holes are fitted with rubber grommets to protect the cable and to stop possible entry of water.

Positioning and fitting of the speaker depends mainly on its type. Generally, the speaker is designed to fit directly into the aperture already provided in the car (usually in the shelf behind the rear seats, or in the top of the dashpanel). Where this is the case, fitting the speaker is just a matter of removing the protective grille from the aperture and screwing or bolting the speaker in place. Take great care not to damage the speaker diaphragm whilst doing this. It is a good idea to fit a gasket beneath the speaker frame and the mounting panel in order to prevent vibration – some speakers will already have such a gasket fitted.

If a 'pod' type speaker was supplied with the radio, the best acoustic result will normally be obtained by mounting it on the shelf behind the rear seat. The pod can be secured to the mounting panel with self-tapping screws.

When connecting a rear mounted speaker to the radio, the wires should be routed through the vehicle beneath the carpets or floor mats – preferably along the side of the floorpan where they will not be trodden on by passengers. Make the relevant connections as directed by the radio manufacturer.

By now you will have several yards of additional wiring in the car; use PVC tape to secure this wiring out of harm's way. Do **NOT** leave electrical leads dangling. Ensure that all new electrical connections are properly made (wires twisted together will not do) and completely secure.

The radio should now be working, but before you pack away your tools it will be necessary to 'trim' the radio to the aerial. Follow the radio manufacturer's instructions regarding this adjustment.

Tape players

Fitting instructions for both cartridge and cassette stereo tape players are the same, and in general the same rules apply as when fitting a radio. Tape players are not usually prone to electrical interference like radios – although it can occur – so positioning is not so critical. If possible, the player should be mounted on an even-keel. Also it must be possible for a driver wearing a seatbelt to reach the unit in order to change or turn over tapes.

For the best results from speakers designed to be recessed into a panel, mount them so that the back of the speaker protrudes into an enclosed chamber within the car (eg door interiors or the boot cavity).

To fit recessed type speakers in the front doors, first check that there is sufficient room to mount the speaker in each door without it fouling the latch or window winding mechanism. Hold the speaker against the skin of the door and draw a line around the periphery of the speaker. With the speaker removed, draw a second cutting line within the first to allow enough room for the entry of the speaker back, but at the same time providing a broad seat for the speaker flange. When you are sure that the cutting-line is correct, drill a series of holes around its periphery. Pass a hacksaw blade through one of the holes and then cut through the metal between the holes until the centre section of the panel falls out.

De-burr the edges of the hole and then paint the raw metal to prevent corrosion. Cut a corresponding hole in the door trim panel, ensuring that it will be completely covered by the speaker grille. Now drill a hole in the door edge and a corresponding hole in the door surround. These holes are to feed the speaker leads through, so fit grommets. Pass the speaker leads through the door trim, door skin and out through the holes in the side of the door and door surround. Refit the door trim panel and then secure the speaker to the door using self-tapping screws. **Note:** *If the speaker is fitted with a shield to prevent water dripping on it, ensure that this shield is at the top.*

'Pod' type speakers can be fastened to the shelf behind the rear seat, or anywhere else offering a corresponding mounting point on each side of the car. If the 'pod' speakers are mounted on each side of the shelf behind the rear seat, it is a good idea to drill several large diameter holes through to the trunk cavity, beneath each speaker – this will improve the sound reproduction. 'Pod' speakers sometimes offer a better reproduction quality if they face the rear window – which then acts as a reflector – so it is worthwhile experimenting before finally fixing the speakers.

---

42 Radios and tape players – suppression of interference (general)

To eliminate buzzes, and other unwanted noises, costs very little and is not as difficult as sometimes thought. With a modicum of common sense and patience, and following the instructions in the following paragraphs, interference can be virtually eliminated.

The first cause for concern is the generator. The noise this makes over the radio is like an electric mixer and the noise speeds up when you rev up the engine (if you wish to prove the point, you can remove the fanbelt and try it). The remedy for this is simple; connect a 1.0 to 3.0 mf capacitor between earth (probably the bolt that holds down the generator base) and the large terminal on the generator. This is most important for if it is connected to the small terminal, the generator will probably be damaged permanently.

A second common cause of electrical interference is the ignition system. Here a 1.0 mf capacitor must be connected between earth and the SW or + terminal on the coil. This may stop the tick-tick sound that comes over the speaker. Next comes the spark itself.

There are several ways of curing interference from the ignition HT system. One is to use carbon film HT leads and the more successful method is to use resistive spark plug caps of about 10 000 to 15 000 ohm resistance. If due to lack of room these cannot be used, an alternative is to use in-line suppressors. If the interference is not too bad, it may be possible to get away with only one suppressor in the coil to distributor line. If the interference does continue (a clacking noise), then doctor all HT leads.

At this stage it is advisable to check that the radio is well earthed, also the aerial and to see that the aerial plug is pushed well into the set and that the radio is properly trimmed (see preceding Section). In addition, check that the wire which supplies the power to the set is as short as possible. At this stage it is a good idea to check that the fuse is of the correct rating. For most sets this will be about 1 to 2 amps.

At this point, the more usual causes of interference have been suppressed. If the problem still exists, a look at the cause of interference may help to pinpoint the component generating the stray electrical discharges. The radio picks up electromagnetic waves in the air; now some are made by regular broadcasters and some, which we do not want, are made by the car itself. The home made signals are produced by stray electrical discharges floating around in the car. Common producers of these signals are electrical motors, ie the windscreen wipers, electric screenwashers, electric window winders, heater fan or an electric aerial if fitted. Other sources of interference are electric fuel pumps, flashing turn signals and instruments. The remedy for these cases is shown for an electric motor whose interference is not too bad and for instrument suppression. Turn signals are not normally suppressed. In recent years, radio manufacturers have included in the live line of the radio, in addition to the fuse, an in-line choke.

All the foregoing components are available from radio stores or accessory stores. If you have an electric clock fitted, this should be suppressed by connecting a 0.5 mf capacitor directly across it as shown.

If after all this you are still experiencing radio interference, first assess how bad it is, for the human ear can filter out unobtrusive unwanted noises quite easily, but if you are still adamant about eradicating the noise, then continue.

As a first step, a few experts seem to favour a screen between the radio and the engine. This is OK as far as it goes, literally! The whole set is screened anyway and if interference can get past that then a small piece of aluminium is not going to stop it.

A more sensible way of screening is to discover if interference is coming down the wires. First, take the live lead; interference can get between the set and the choke (hence the reason for keeping the wires short). One remedy here is to screen the wire and this is done by buying screened wire and fitting that. The loudspeaker lead could be screened also to prevent pick-up getting back to the radio – although this is unlikely.

Without doubt, the worst source of radio interference comes from the ignition HT leads, even if they have been suppressed. The ideal way of suppressing these is to slide screening tubes over the leads themselves. As this is impractical, we can place an aluminium shield over the majority of the lead areas. In a vee or twin-cam engine this is relatively easy but for a straight engine, the results are not particularly good.

Now for the really difficult cases, here are a few tips to try out. Where metal comes into contact with metal, an electrical disturbance is caused which is why good clean connections are essential. To remove interference due to overlapping or butting panels, you must bridge the join with a wide braided earth strap (like that from the frame to the engine/transmission). The most common moving parts that could create noise and should be strapped are, in order of importance:

(a) *Silencer to frame*
(b) *Exhaust pipe to engine block and frame*
(c) *Air cleaner to frame*
(d) *Front and rear bumpers to frame*
(e) *Steering column to frame*
(f) *Bonnet and boot lids to frame*

These faults are most pronounced when (1) the engine is idling,

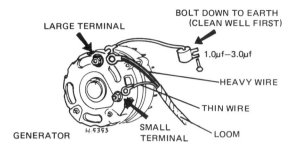

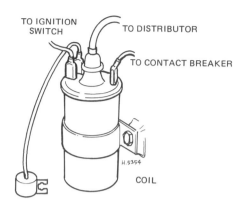

Fig. 10.10 The correct way to connect a capacitor to the generator (Sec 32)

Fig.10.11 The capacitor must be connected to the ignition switch side of the coil (Sec 32)

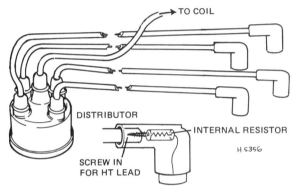

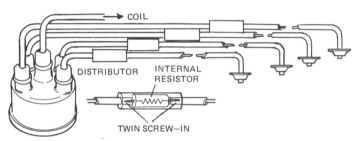

Fig. 10.12 Ignition HT lead suppressors (Sec 32)

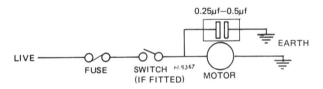

Fig 10.13 Correct method of suppressing electric motors (Sec 32)

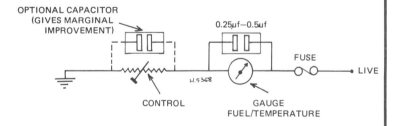

Fig. 10.14 Method of suppressing gauges and their control units (Sec 32)

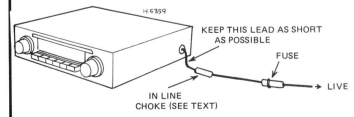

Fig. 10.15 An in-line choke should be fitted into the live supply lead as close to the unit as possible (Sec 32)

(2) labouring under load. Although the moving parts are already connected with nuts, bolts, etc, these do tend to rust and corrode, this creating a high resistance interference source.

If you have a 'ragged' sounding pulse when mobile, this could be wheel or tyre static. This can be cured by buying some anti-static powder and sprinkling inside the tyres.

If the interference takes the shape of a high pitched screeching noise that changes its note when the car is in motion and only comes now and then, this could be related to the aerial, especially if it is of the telescopic or whip type. This source can be cured quite simply by pushing a small rubber ball on top of the aerial as this breaks the electric field before it can form; but it would be much better to buy yourself a new aerial of a reputable brand. If, on the other hand, you are getting a loud rushing sound every time you brake, then this is brake static. This effect is more prominent on hot dry days and is cured only by fitting a special kit, which is quite expensive.

In conclusion, it is pointed out that it is relatively easy and therefore cheap, to eliminate 95 per cent of all noise, but to eliminate the final 5 per cent is time and money consuming. It is up to the individual to decide if it is worth it. Please remember also, that you cannot get a concert hall performance out of a cheap radio.

Finally, tape players and eight track players are not usually affected by car noise but in a very bad case, the best remedies are the first three suggestions plus using a 3–5 amp choke in the 'live' line and in incurable cases screen the live and speaker wires.

Note: If your car is fitted with electronic ignition, then it is not recommended that either the spark plug resistors or the ignition coil capacitor be fitted as these may damage the system. Most electronic ignition units have built-in suppression and should, therefore, not cause interference.

43 Fault diagnosis – electrical system

Symptom	Reason(s)
Starter fails to turn engine	Battery discharged or defective
	Battery terminal and/or earth leads loose
	Starter motor connections loose
	Starter solenoid faulty
	Starter brushes worn or sticking
	Starter commutator dirty or worn
	Starter field coils earthed
Starter turns engine very slowly	Battery discharged
	Starter motor connections loose
	Starter brushes worn or sticking
Starter noisy	Pinion or flywheel ring gear teeth badly worn
	Mounting bolts loose
Battery will not hold charge for more than a few days	Battery defective internally
	Electrolyte level too low
	Fanbelt slipping
	Alternator or regulator faulty
	Short circuit
Ignition light stays on	Alternator faulty
	Fanbelt broken
Ignition light fails to come on	Warning bulb blown
	Warning bulb open circuit
	Alternator faulty
Instrument readings increase with engine speed	Voltage stabilizer faulty
Fuel or temperature gauge gives no reading	Wiring open circuit
	Sender unit faulty
	Gauge faulty
Fuel or temperature gauge gives maximum reading all the time	Wiring short circuit
	Gauge faulty
Lights inoperative	Bulb blown
	Fuse blown
	Battery discharged
	Switch faulty
	Wiring open circuit
	Bad connection due to corrosion
Failure of component motor	Commutator dirty or burnt
	Armature faulty
	Brushes sticking or worn
	Armature bearings dry or misaligned
	Field coils faulty
	Fuse blown
	Wiring loose or broken
Failure of an individual component	Wiring loose or broken
	Fuse blown
	Bad circuit connection
	Switch faulty
	Component faulty

Key to wiring diagram (Fig. 10.16)

1 Front right indicator
2 Right dipped headlight; parking light
3 Right main beam headlight
4 Earth point
5 Right foglight (optional)
6 Right-hand horn
7 Left-hand horn
8 Left foglight optional
9 Earth point
10 Left main beam headlight
11 Left dipped headlight; parking light
12 Front left indicator
13 Engine compartment light
14 Engine compartment light switch
15 Engine compartment light plug
16 Washer pump
17 Battery
18 Foglight plug
19 Junction box with fuses
   (a) Main beam relay
   (b) Dipped beam relay
   (c) Horn relay
   (d) Load shedding relay
   (e) Fog light relay (optional)
   (f) Engine plug
   (g) Diagnosis tester socket
   (h) Washer pump socket
20 Ignition coil
21 Distributor
22 Diagnosis unit connection with lead and tester
23 Alternator
24 Starter motor
25 Oil pressure switch
26 Coolant thermometer sensor
27 Brake fluid level indicator switch
28 Reverse light switch plug
29 Transmission switch (automatics)
30 Starter relay (automatics)
31 Transmission switch plug (automatics)
32 Reverse light switch
33 Heater blower motor
34 Wiper motor
35 Solder point 58b
36 Centre console plug
37 Connection for electric windows, aerial, and sliding roof
38 Heated rear window switch
39 Heater control light
40 Heater control light
41 Heater controls
   (a) with clock
   (b) with clock light
42 Inspection lamp (optional)
43 Glove compartment light
44 Cigar lighter
45 Radio
46 Earth point
47 Plug II
48 Intermittent wash/wipe control unit
49 Hazard warning flasher unit
50 Wiper switch plug
51 Wiper switch
52 Hazard warning switch
53 Ignition/starter switch plug
54 Ignition/starter switch
55 Horn contact
56 Rear foglight switch
57 Ignition switch plug 50
58 Ignition/starter switch P
59 Foglight switch
60 Indicator/dipper beam switch plug

61 Indicator/dipped beam switch
62 Main light switch
63 3-pole connector
64 Plug 1
65 Fuel pump connection
66 Solder point 58b
67 Solder point 31
68 Earth point
69 Selector gate light I
70 Selector gate light II
71 Clock connection
72 Combined instrument
   (a) Oil pressure warning light
   (b) Coolant temperature indicator
   (c) Plug connector
   (d) Main beam indicator (blue)
   (e) Battery charge indicator (red)
   (f) Tachometer
   (g) Range indicator (automatics)
      P – white
      R – red
      O – white
      A – green
      2 – green
      1 – green
   (h) Speedometer
   (i) Fuel level warning light
   (k) Fuel gauge
   (l) Brake system warning light
   (m) Indicator warning light
   (n) Plug connector
   (0) Series resistor
   (p) Series resistor
73 Parking brake contact
74 Stop light switch
75 Front right door switch
76 Front left door switch
77 Rear right door switch
78 Rear left door switch
79 Rear window demister
80 Interior light
81 Boot light switch
82 Boot light
83 Boot light plug
84 Fuel tank transmitter
85 Earth point
86 Right number plate light
87 Left number plate light
88 Left tail light
   (a) Indicator
   (b) Rear light
   (c) Reverse light
   (d) Stop light
   (e) Rear foglight
89 Right tail light
   (a) Indicator
   (b) Rear light
   (c) Reverse light
   (d) Stop light
90 Front carburettor choke
91 Rear carburettor choke
92 Body earth point
93 Engine earth point
94 Rear window demister plug
95 Earth point
96 Connection point
97 Temperature switch
98 Connection for US carburettors
100 Rear carburettor choke
101 Voltage regulator

Wiring colour codes

BL	Blue	GN	Green	VI	Violet
BR	Brown	RD	Red	WH	White
YW	Yellow	BK	Black	TR	Transparent
GR	Grey				

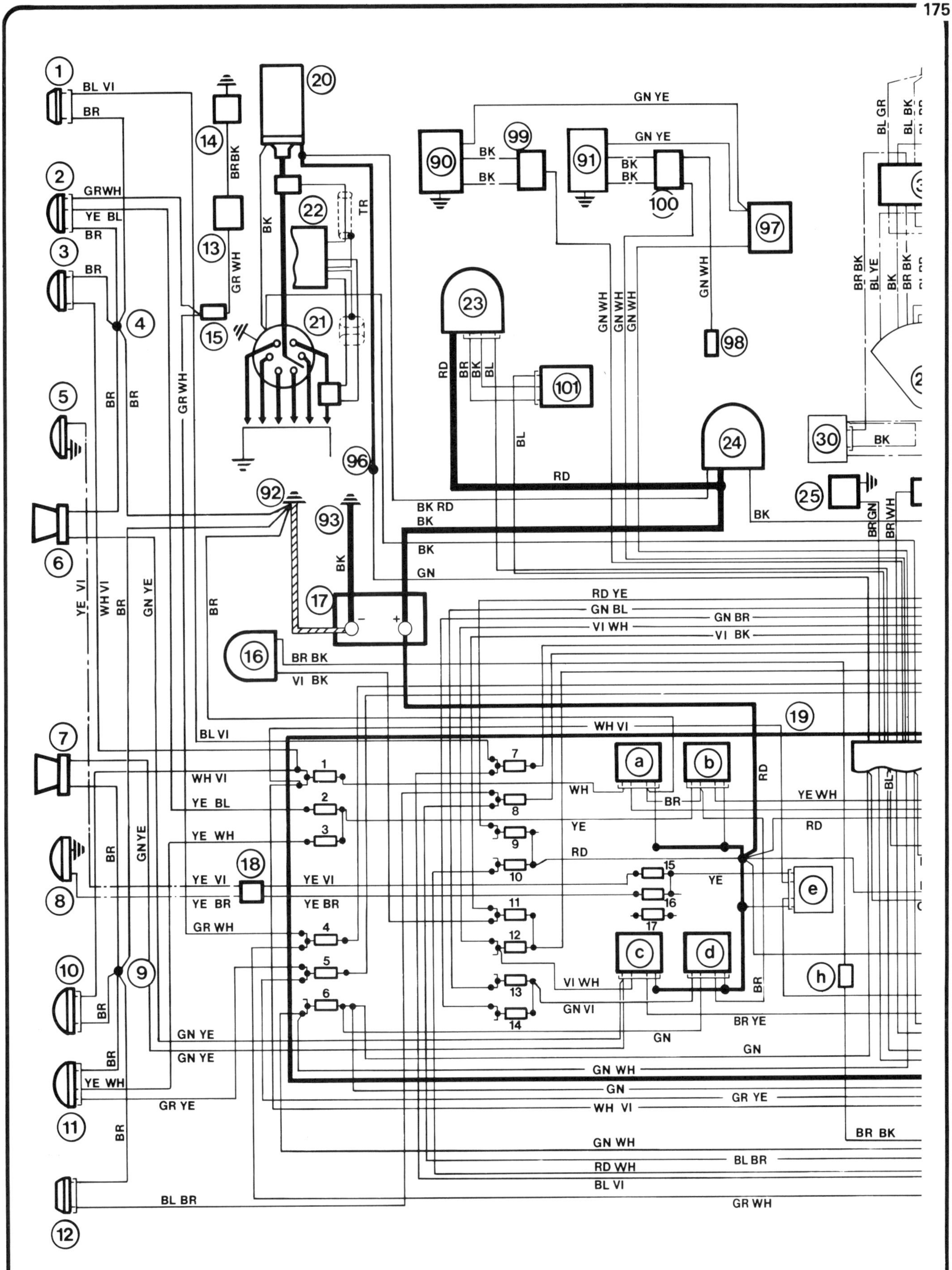

Fig. 10.16 Wiring diagram for early 525 models

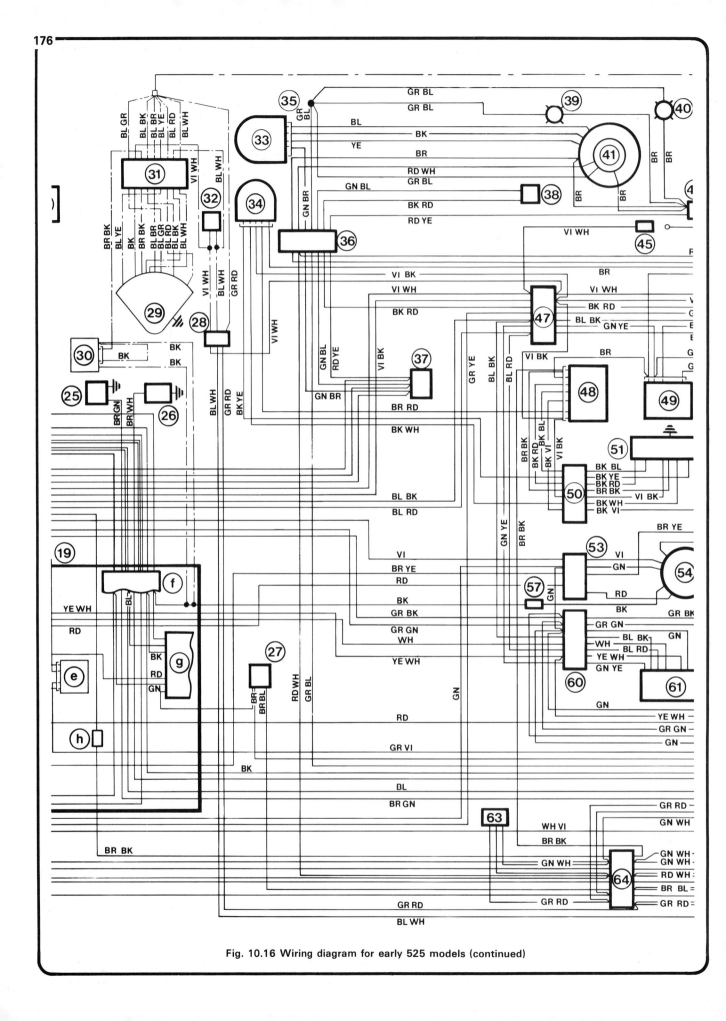

Fig. 10.16 Wiring diagram for early 525 models (continued)

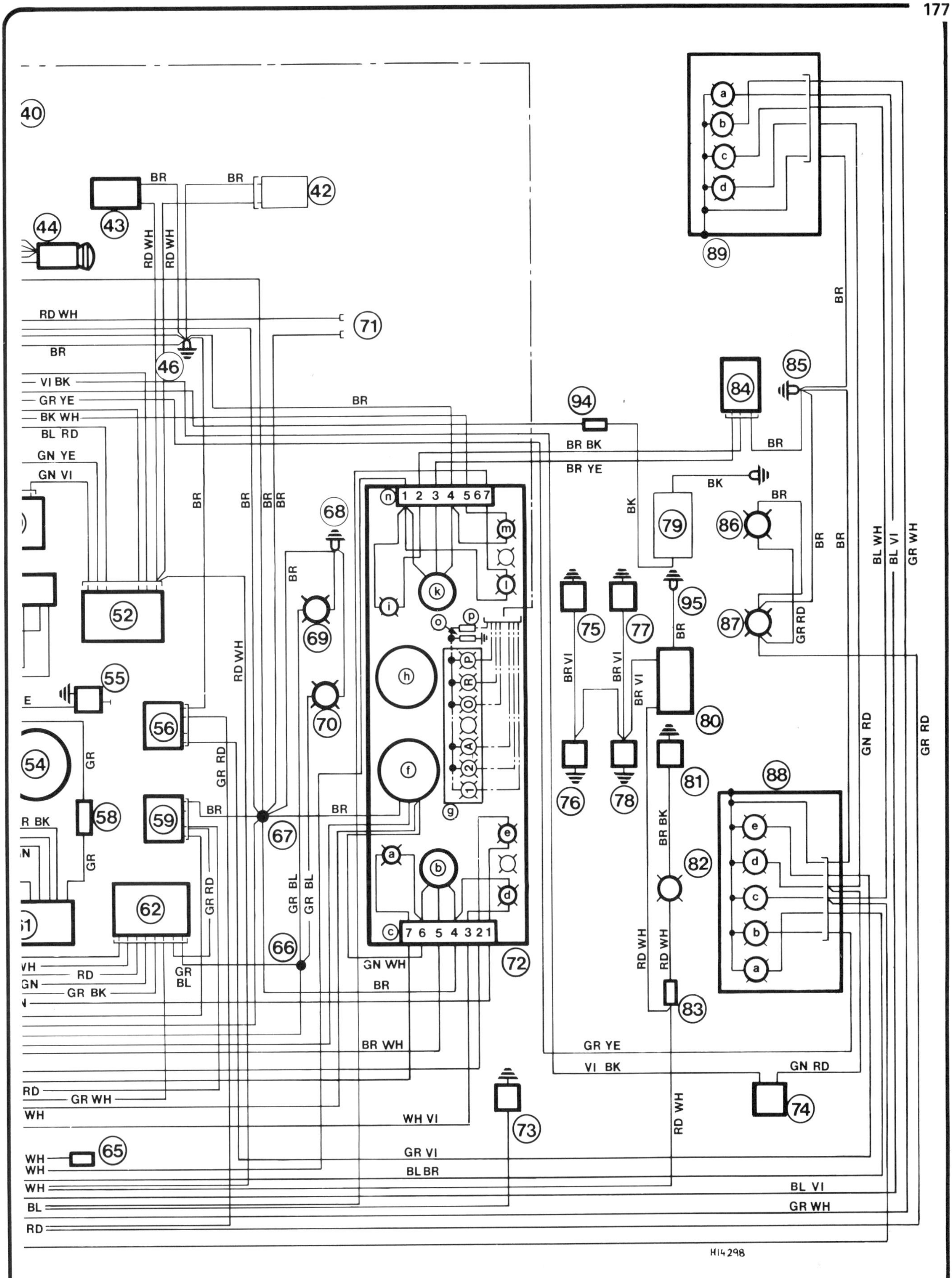

Fig. 10.16 Wiring diagram for early 525 models (continued)

H14298

Key to wiring diagram (Fig. 10.17)

1 Front right indicator
2 Right dipped headlight; parking light
3 Right main beam headlight
4 Earth point
5 Right foglight (optional)
6 Right-hand horn
7 Left-hand horn
8 Left foglight (optional)
9 Earth point
10 Left main beam headlight
11 Left dipped headlight; parking light
12 Front left indicator
13 Engine compartment light
14 Engine compartment light switch
15 Engine compartment light plug
16 Washer pump
17 Battery
18 Foglight plug
19 Current distributor with fuses
    (a) Main beam relay
    (b) Dipped beam relay
    (c) Two-tone horn relay
    (d) load shielding relay
    (e) Foglight relay (optional)
    (f) Engine socket
    (g) Diagnosis tester socket
    (h) Washer pump socket
20 Ignition coil
21 Distributor
22 Earth
23 Alternator with regulator
24 Starter motor
25 Oil pressure switch
26 Temperature sensor
27 Brake fluid level switch
28 Reverse light switch plug
29 Transmission switch (automatics)
30 Starter relay (automatics)
31 Transmission switch plug (automatics)
32 Reverse light switch
33 Heater blower motor
34 Wiper motor
35 Solder point 58b
36 Central console plug
37 Connection for electric windows, aerial,
    sliding roof exterior mirror
38 Rear window demister switch
39 Heater control light
40 Heater control light
41 Heater controls
    (a) with clock (optional)
    (b) with clock light (optional)
42 Handlamp
43 Glove compartment light
44 Cigar lighter
45 Radio
46 Earth point
47 Plug II
48 Intermittent wash/wipe control unit
49 Flasher
50 Wiper switch plug
51 Wiper switch
52 Hazard light switch
53 Ignition switch plug
54 Ignition switch
55 Horn contact
56 Rear foglight switch
57 Ignition lock plug 50
58 Ignition switch plug P
59 Foglight switch
60 Indicator/dipped beam switch plug

61 Indicator/dipped beam switch
62 Main light switch
63 Earth point
64 Plug I
65 Fuel pump plug
66 Fuel pump
67 Solder point 31
68 Earth point
69 Gate light I
70 Gate light II
71 Clock connection
72 Combination instrument
    (a) Oil pressure indicator
    (b) Coolant temperature indicator
    (c) Plug
    (d) Main beam indicator – blue
    (e) Battery charge indicator – red
    (f) Tachometer (optional; otherwise clock)
    (g) Range indicator (automatics)
        P – white
        R – red
        O – white
        A – green
        2 – green
        I – green
    (h) Speedometer
    (i) Foglight indicator
    (k) Fuel level indicator
    (l) Fuel level gauge
    (m) Brake fluid and parking brake indicator
    (n) Indicator warning light
    (o) Plug
    (p) Resistor
    (r) Resistor
73 Parking brake contact
74 Stop-light switch
75 Front right door contact
76 Front left door contact
77 Rear right door contact
78 Rear left door contact
79 Rear window demister
80 Interior light
81 Boot light switch
82 Boot light
83 Boot light plug
84 Fuel level transmitter
85 Earth point
86 Right number plate light
87 Left number plate light
88 Left tail light
    (a) Indicator
    (b) Tail light
    (c) Reverse light
    (d) Stop light
89 Right tail light
    (a) Indicator
    (b) Tail light
    (c) Reverse light
    (d) Stop light
90 Front carburettor
91 Rear carburettor
92 Body earth point
93 Engine earth point
94 Rear window demister plug
95 Earth point
96 Air temperature switch
97 Thermo time valve
98 Connector
99 Earth
100 Connector 15
101 Connector 15

Wiring colour codes

BL Blue	YW Yellow	GN Green	BK Black	WH White
BR Brown	GR Grey	RD Red	VI Violet	TR Transparent

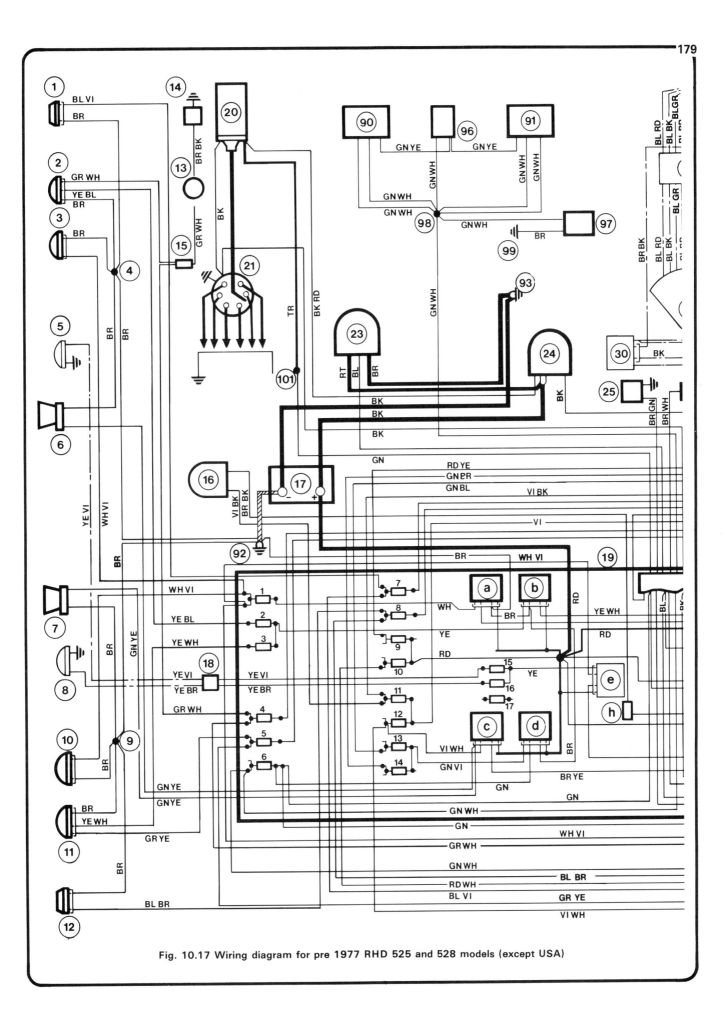

Fig. 10.17 Wiring diagram for pre 1977 RHD 525 and 528 models (except USA)

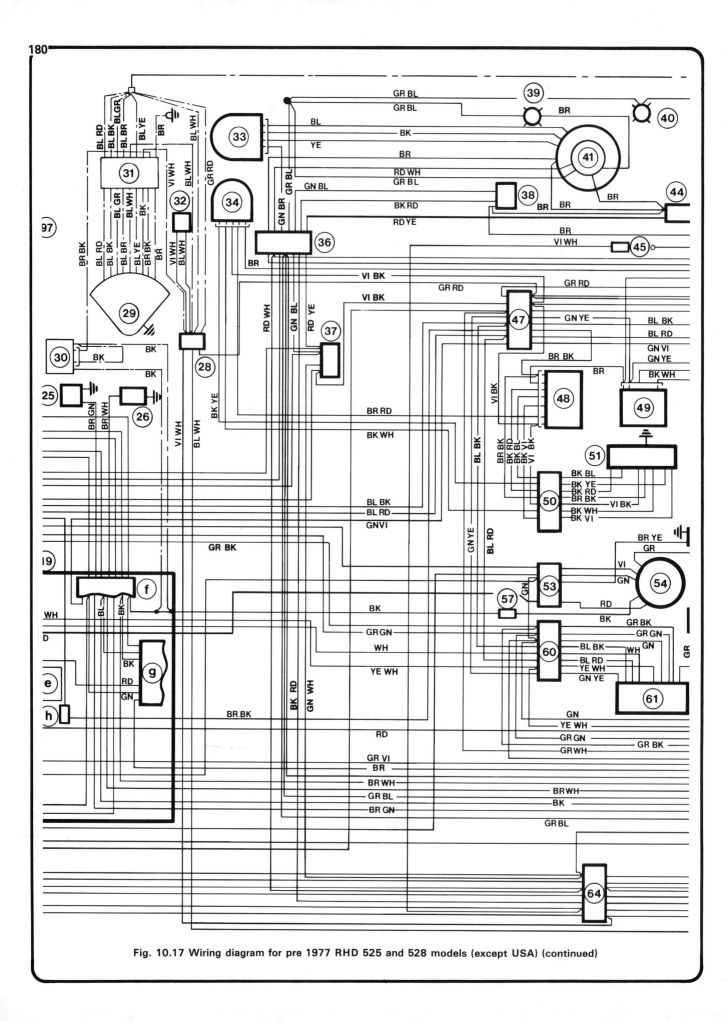

Fig. 10.17 Wiring diagram for pre 1977 RHD 525 and 528 models (except USA) (continued)

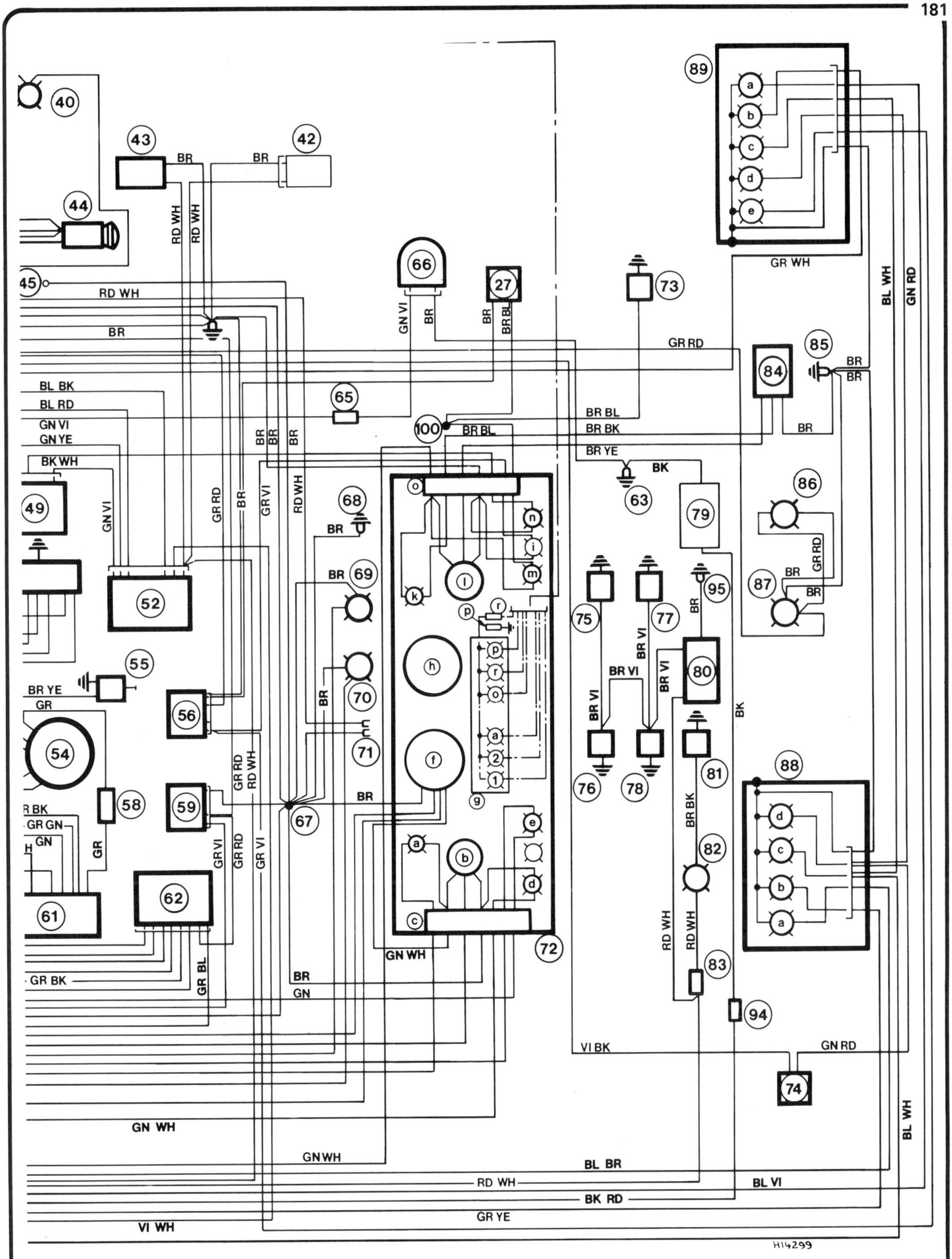

Fig. 10.17 Wiring diagram for pre 1977 RHD 525 and 528 models (except USA) (continued)

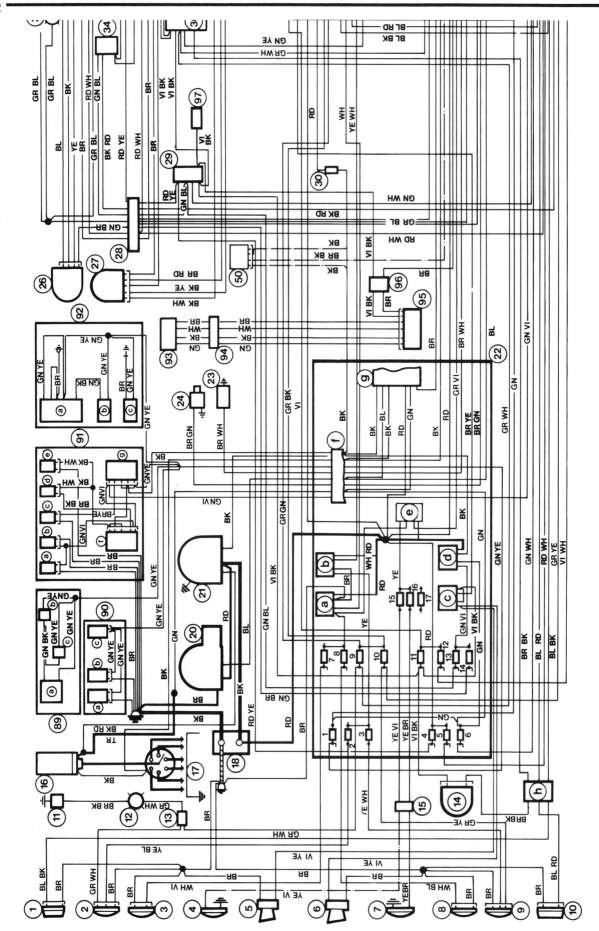

Fig. 10.18 Wiring diagram for 1977 on RHD 525 and 528 models (except USA)

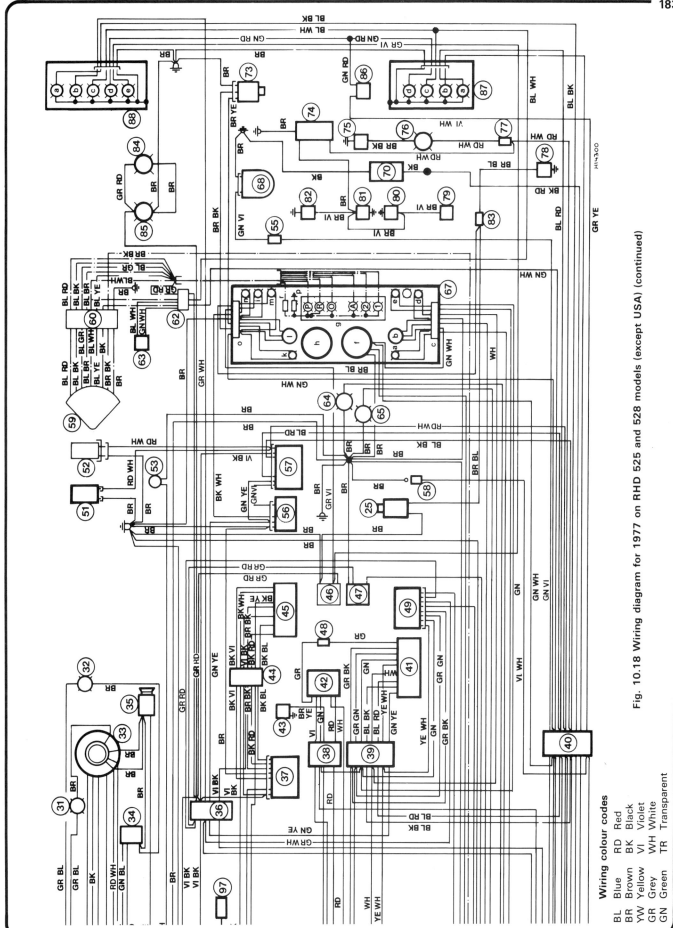

Fig. 10.18 Wiring diagram for 1977 on RHD 525 and 528 models (except USA) (continued)

Wiring colour codes

BL	Blue	RD Red
BR	Brown	BK Black
YW	Yellow	VI Violet
GR	Grey	WH White
GN	Green	TR Transparent

Key to wiring diagram (Fig. 10.18)

1   Front right indicator
2   Right dipped headlight; parking light
3   Right main beam headlight
4   Foglight (special equipment)
5   Right-hand horn
6   Left-hand horn
7   Foglight (special equipment)
8   Left main beam headlight
9   Left dipped headlight; parking light
10 Front left indicator
11 Engine compartment light switch
12 Engine compartment light
13 Engine compartment light plug
14 Washer pump
15 Foglight plug
16 Ignition coil
17 Distributor
18 Battery
20 Alternator with regulator
21 Starter motor
22 Power board and fuses
   (a)   Main beam relay
   (b)   Dipped beam relay
   (c)   Horn relay
   (d)   Releasing relay
   (e)   Foglight relay (special equipment)
   (f)   Engine plug
   (g)   Diagnosis tester socket
   (h)   5-pin plug
23 Temperature transmitter
24 Oil pressure switch
25 Brake fluid level switch
26 Heater blower motor
27 Windscreen wiper motor
28 Centre console plug
29 Connections for electric windows, aerial, sliding roof, exterior mirror
30 Ignition lock plug 50
31 Heater control light I
32 Heater control light II
33 Heater controls with clock
34 Rear window demister switch
35 Cigar lighter
36 Plug II
37 Intermittent wash/wipe control
38 Plug for ignition switch
39 Plug for indicator/dip beam switch
40 Plug I
41 Indicator/dip beam switch
42 Ignition switch
43 Horn contact
44 Wiper switch plug
45 Wiper switch
46 Rear foglight switch
47 Foglight switch
48 Plug for ignition switch
49 Light switch
50 Start relay (automatics)
51 Glove box light
52 Handlamp (special equipment)
53 Clock connections
55 Fuel pump connections
56 Hazard light flasher
57 Hazard light switch
58 Radio
59 Transmission switch (automatics)
60 Plug for transmission switch (automatics)
62 Plug for reverse light switch
63 Reverse light switch
64 Gate light I
65 Gate light II
67 Instrument cluster
   (a)   Oil pressure indicator light

   (b)   Coolant temperature gauge
   (c)   Plug
   (d)   Main beam indicator (blue)
   (e)   Battery charge indicator light (red)
   (f)   Tachometer
   (g)   Range indicator (automatics)
      P – white
      R – red
      O – white
      A – green
      2 – green
      1 – green
   (h)   Speedometer
   (i)   Foglight warning light
   (k)   Fuel level warning light
   (l)   Fuel level gauge
   (m)   Brake fluid and parking brake warning light
   (n)   Indicator warning light
   (o)   Plug
   (p)   Resistor
   (r)   Resistor
68 Fuel pump
70 Rear window demister
73 Fuel level transmitter
74 Inside light
75 Boot light switch
76 Boot light
77 Boot light plug
78 Parking brake contact
79 Front right door contact
80 Front left door contact
81 Rear left door contact
82 Rear right door contact
84 Right number plate light
85 Left number plate light
87 Right tail lights
   (a)   Indicator
   (b)   Tail light
   (c)   Reverse light
   (d)   Stop light
88 Left tail lights
   (a)   Indicator
   (b)   Tail light
   (c)   Reverse light
   (d)   Stop light
   (e)   Rear foglight
89 Models 525/528 only*
   (a)   Carburettor
   (b)   45°C switch
   (c)   17°C switch
90 Models 525/528 only*
   (a)   Choke heater
   (b)   Choke heater
   (c)   Solenoid valve
91 Fuel injection control unit*
   (a)   Resistor
   (b)   Resistor
   (c)   Inertia switch
   (d)   Thermotime switch
   (e)   Cold start valve
   (f)   Cold start relay
   (g)   Fuel pump relay
92 Models 525/528 only*
   (a)   Carburettor
   (b)   Coolant temperature switch
   (c)   Thermo time valve
93 Motor for electric exterior mirror
94 Exterior mirror connections
95 Mirror switch (525/528 models)
96 Door connections
97 1-pin plug
*Alternatives

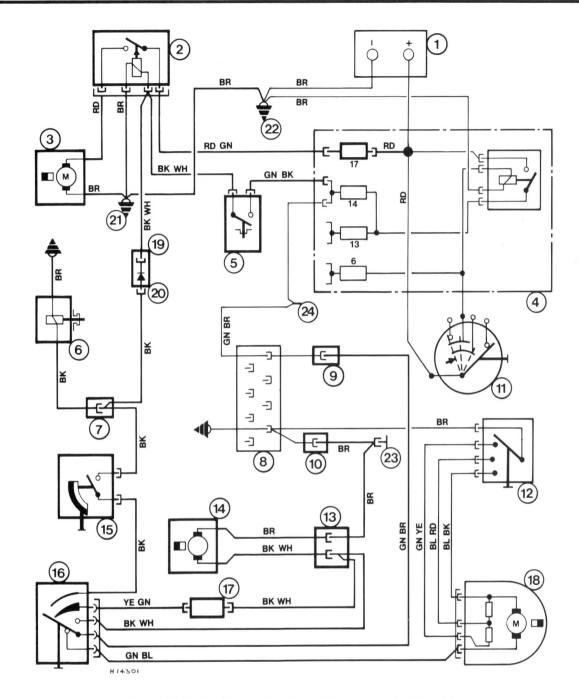

Fig. 10.19 Wiring diagram for air conditioner on pre 1977 models

Key to wiring diagram (Fig. 10.19)

1	Battery	7	Solenoid clutch connection	13	2-pin plug	19	Air conditioner/fan connection
2	Fan relay			14	Air conditioner blower motor	20	Diode
3	Fan motor	8	8-pin plug for heater controls			21	Fan earth point
4	Power distributor with releasing relay	9	1-pin plug	15	Temperature range switch	22	Earth connection
		10	1-pin plug	16	Air conditioner blower switch	23	Cigar lighter switch
5	Temperature switch	11	Ignition switch	17	Resistor	24	Connection for window controls
6	Compressor solenoid coupling	12	Blower switch	18	Heater blower motor		

Wiring colour codes

BL	Blue	YW	Yellow	GN	Green	BK	Black	WH	White
BR	Brown	GR	Grey	RD	Red	VI	Violet	TR	Transparent

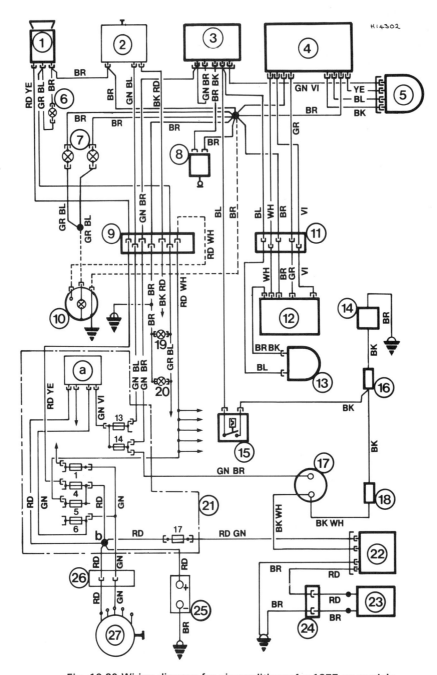

H14302

Fig. 10.20 Wiring diagram for air conditioner for 1977 on models

Key to wiring diagram (Fig. 10.20)

1 Cigar lighter and lamp	8 Micro switch	15 Temperature switch for	(a) Releasing relay
2 Rear window demister	9 Central console plug	compressor	(b) Power rail
switch	10 Clock	16 Compressor connection	22 Fan relay
3 Relay	11 Line connection for air	17 Fan temperature switch	23 Fan motor
4 Blower switch	conditioner blower	18 Diode	24 Fan motor connection
5 Heater blower motor	12 Evaporator	19 Gate light II	25 Battery
6 Ashtray light	13 Evaporator blower	20 Gate light I	26 Ignition switch plug
7 Heater light	14 Compressor	21 Power board	27 Ignition switch

Wiring colour codes

BL	Blue	YW	Yellow	GN	Green	BK	Black	WH	White
BR	Brown	GR	Grey	RD	Red	VI	Violet	TR	Transparent

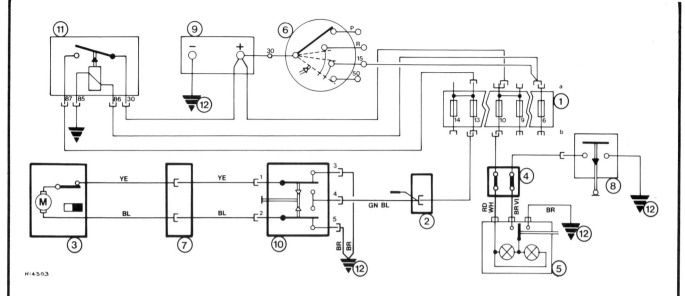

Fig. 10.21 Wiring diagram for sliding roof on early models

Key to wiring diagram (Fig. 10.21)

1	Fuse box	3	Sunroof motor	7	Plug	10	Sunroof switch
	(a) Inlet	4	Connector	8	Door contact switch	11	Relief relay
	(b) Outlet	5	Interior lamp	9	Battery	12	Earth points
2	Three-pin plug	6	Ignition switch				

Wiring colour codes

BL	Blue	YW	Yellow	GN	Green	BK	Black	WH	White
BR	Brown	GR	Grey	RD	Red	VI	Violet	TR	Transparent

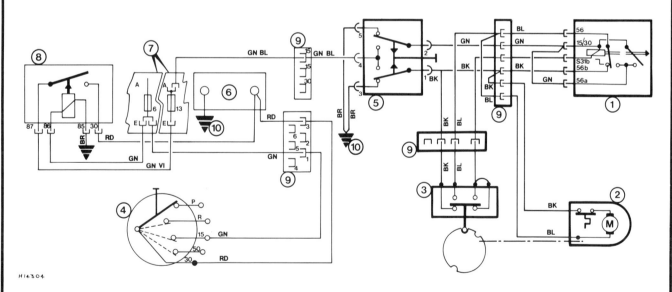

Fig. 10.22 Wiring diagram for sliding roof on later models

Key to wiring diagram (Fig. 10.22)

1	Step relay	4	Ignition switch	7	Fuse box	9	Plugs
2	Electric motor	5	Switch for sunroof	8	Relief relay	10	Earth connections
3	Microswitch	6	Battery				

Wiring colour codes

BL	Blue	YW	Yellow	GN	Green	BK	Black	WH	White
BR	Brown	GR	Grey	RD	Red	VI	Violet	TR	Transparent

Key to wiring diagram (Fig. 10.23)

1 Front right indicator; parking light
2 Front right sealed beam II
3 Front right sealed beam I
4 Earth point
5 Front right foglight (optional)
6 Right two-tone horn
7 Left two-tone horn
8 Front left foglight (optional)
9 Earth point
10 Front left sealed beam I
11 Front left sealed beam II
12 Front left indicator; parking light
13 Engine compartment light
14 Engine compartment light switch
15 Engine compartment light plug
16 Washer pump
17 Battery
18 Foglight plug
19 Power distributor and fuses
  (a) Main beam relay
  (b) Dipped beam relay
  (c) Horn relay
  (d) Power sharing relay
  (e) Foglight relay
  (f) Engine socket
  (g) Diagnosis tester socket
  (h) 5-pin plug
  (i) Diode
20 Ignition coil
21 Distributor
22 Diagnosis tester socket, cord and sensor
23 Alternator
24 Starter motor
25 Oil pressure switch
26 Temperature transmitter
27 Brake fluid level indicator switch
28 Reverse light and G.A.G. plug
29 Transmission switch (automatic)
30 Start relay
31 Transmission switch plug (automatics)
32 Reverse light switch
33 Heater blower motor
34 Windscreen wiper motor
35 Solder point 58b
36 Centre console socket
37 Connection for electric windows, automatic aerial and sun roof
38 Rear window defogger switch
39 Heater control light
40 Heater control light
41 Heater control and clock
42 Headlamp (optional)
43 Glove box light
44 Cigar lighter
45 Radio connection
46 Earth point
47 Plug
48 Intermittent wash/wipe control
49 Hazard light/indicator flasher
50 Wiper switch plug
51 Wiper switch with washer contact
52 Hazard light switch
53 Ignition switch plug
54 Ignition switch
55 Horn contact
57 Ignition lock plug 50
59 Front foglight switch
60 Indicator/dimmer switch plug
61 Indicator/dimmer switch
62 Light switch
64 Plug 1
65 Fuel pump plug
66 Solder point 58b
67 Solder point 31
68 Earth point
69 Gate light
70 Gate light
71 Fuel pump
72 Instrument cluster
  (a) Oil pressure indicator (orange)
  (b) Coolant temperature gauge
  (c) Plug
  (d) Main beam indicator (blue)
  (e) Battery charge indicator (red)
  (f) Tachometer
  (g) Range indicator (automatics)
    P - white
    R - red
    O - white
    A - green

    2 - green
    1 - green
  (h) Speedometer
  (i) Fuel level indicator (white)
  (k) Fuel gauge
  (l) Stop light indicator (red)
  (m) Indicator warning light (green)
  (n) Plug
  (o) Resistor
  (p) Resistor
  (r) Diode
73 Parking brake contact
74 Stop light switch
75 Front right door contact
76 Front left door contact
77 Rear right door contact
78 Rear left door contact
79 Rear window demister
80 Interior lamp
81 Boot light switch
82 Boot light
83 Boot light plug
84 Fuel level transmitter
85 Earth point
86 Right number plate light
87 Left number plate light
88 Left tail light
  (a) Indicator
  (b) Tail light
  (c) Reverse light
  (d) Stop light
89 Right tail light
  (a) Indicator
  (b) Tail light
  (c) Reverse light
  (d) Stop light
90 Double relay
91 Resistor
92 Body earth point
93 Engine earth point
94 Rear window demister plug
95 Earth point
96 Connection point
97 Valves
98 Temperature sensor
99 Solder point 31
100 Control unit
101 Cold start relay
102 Throttle switch
103 Thermo line switch
104 Air flow sensor
105 Cold start relay
106 Right indicator plug
107 Left indicator plug
108 Solder point 31
109 Service interval switch
110 Connection point
111 Solder point
112 Buzzer contact
113 Buzzer
114 Buzzer plug
115 Belt indicator
116 Belt/start control unit
117 Left belt switch plug
118 Left seat switch plug
119 Right belt switch plug
120 Right seat switch plug
121 Left belt switch
122 Left seat switch
123 Right belt switch
124 Right seat switch
125 Left side marker light plug
126 Left side marker light
127 Right side marker light plug
128 Right side marker light
129 Change-over relay
130 Ignition control solenoid
131 EGR solenoid
132 Diverter valve solenoid
133 Speed switch
134 Additional fan (automatics)
135 Additional fan motor plug (automatics)
136 Additional fan relay (automatics)
137 Temperature switch (automatics)
138 Air conditioner connection (automatics)
139 Solder point 31
140 Temperature switch
141 Tachometer plug

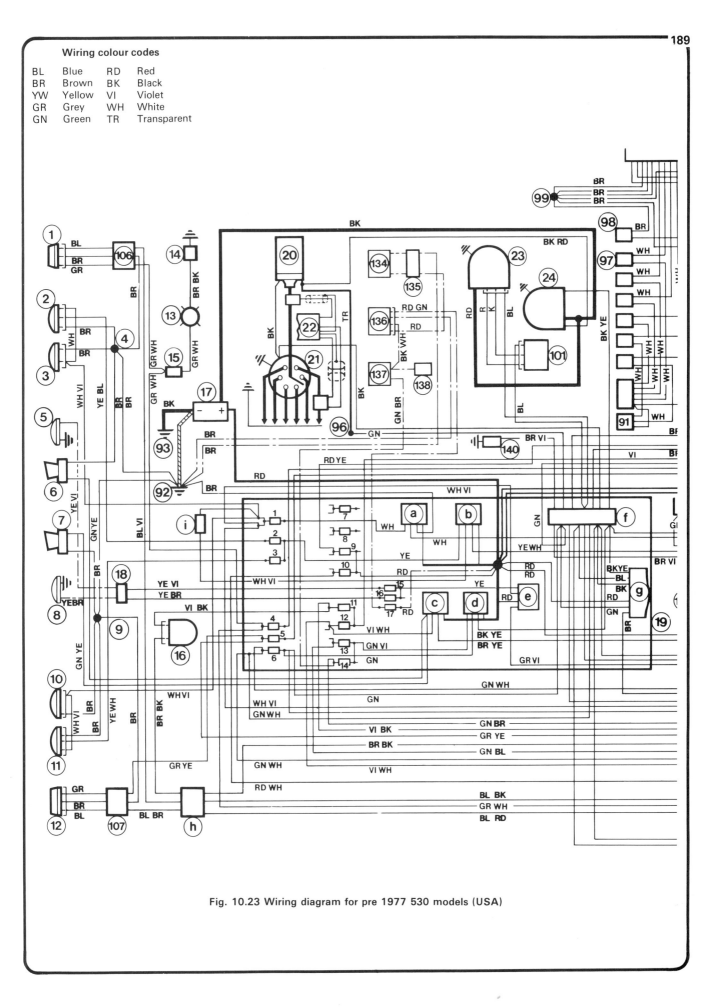

Fig. 10.23 Wiring diagram for pre 1977 530 models (USA)

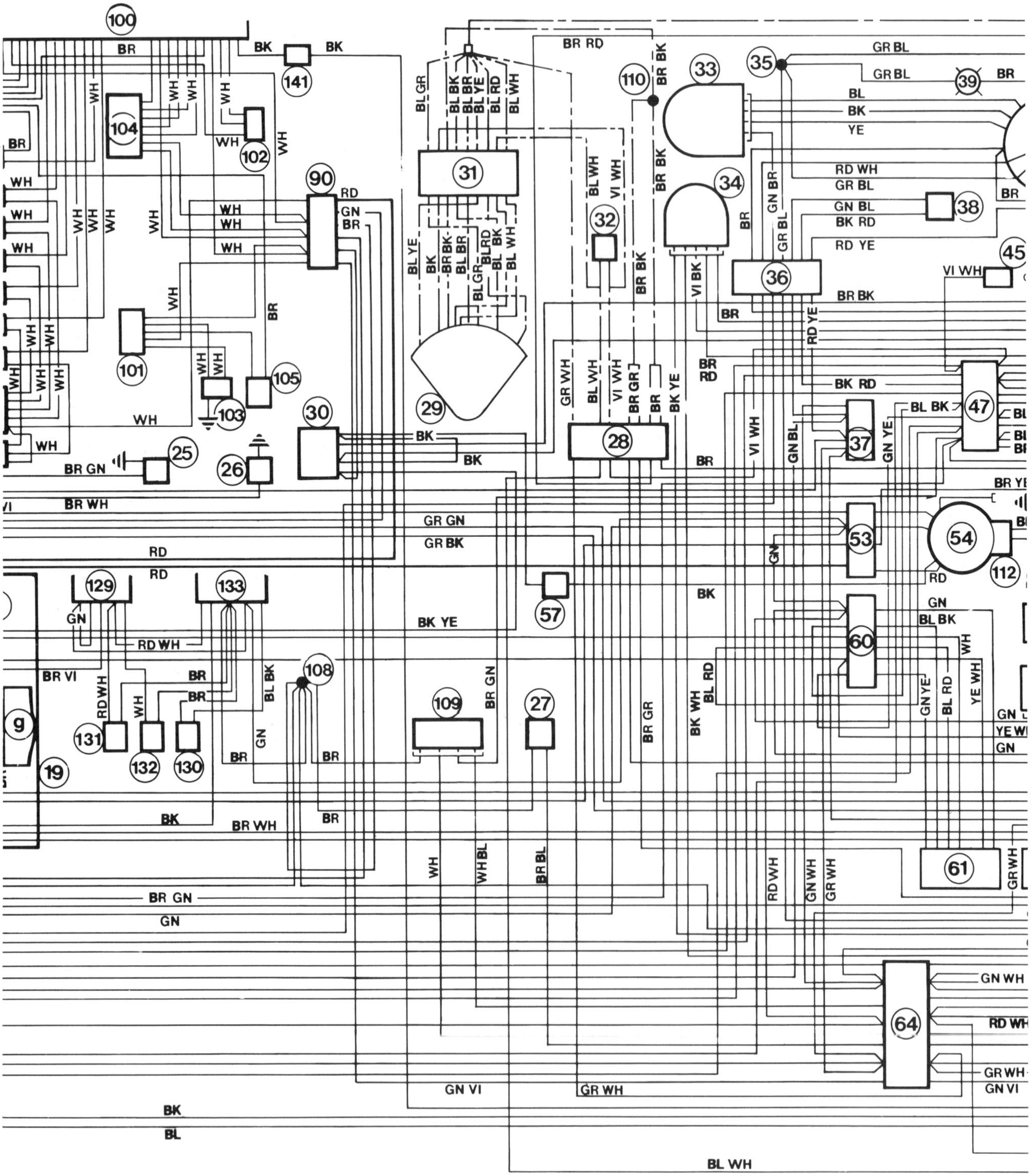

Fig. 10.23 Wiring diagram for pre 1977 530 models (USA) (continued)

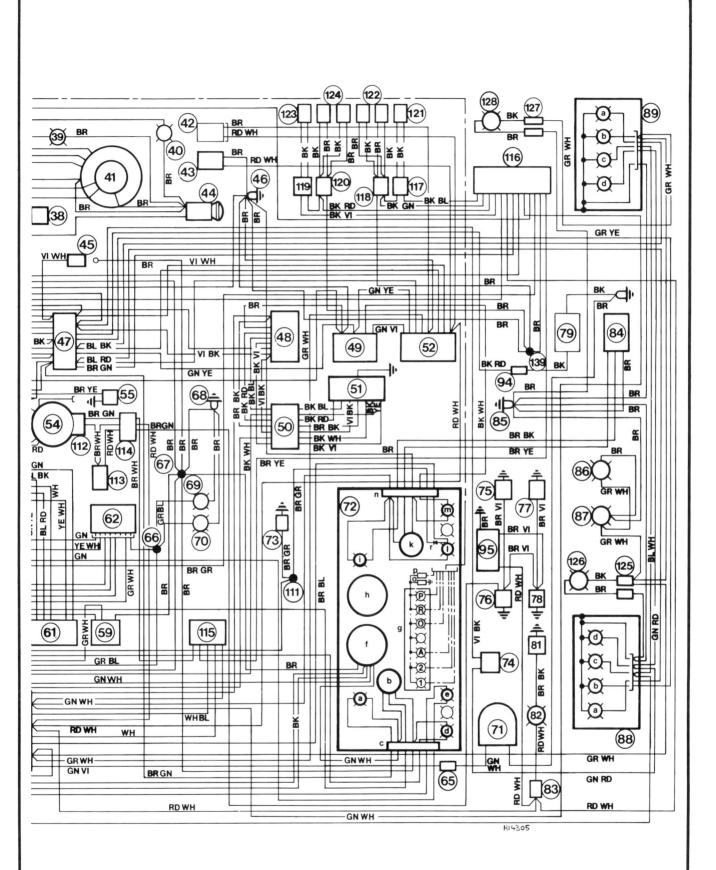

Wiring diagram for pre 1977 530 models (USA) (continued)

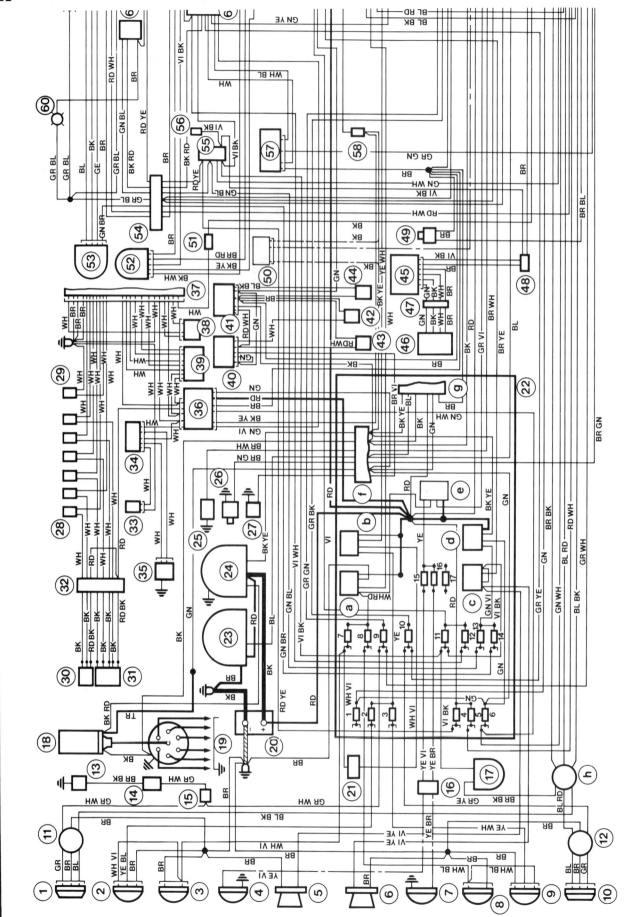

Fig. 10.24 Wiring diagram for 1977 530 models (USA)

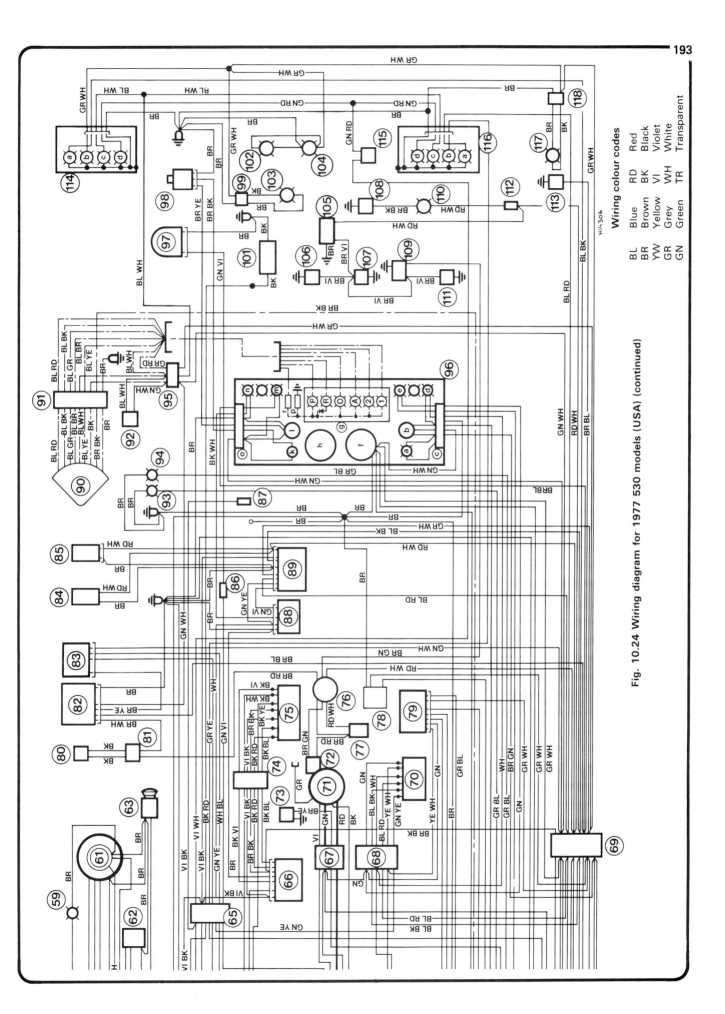

Fig. 10.24 Wiring diagram for 1977 530 models (USA) (continued)

Wiring colour codes

RD	Red		
BK	Black		
VI	Violet		
WH	White		
TR	Transparent		

BL	Blue
BR	Brown
YW	Yellow
GR	Grey
GN	Green

Key to wiring diagram (Fig. 10.24)

1 Front right indicator; parking light	71 Ignition switch
2 Front right sealed beam II	72 Buzzer contact
3 Front right sealed beam I	73 Horn contact
4 Right front foglight (optional)	74 Wiper switch plug
5 Right two-tone horn	75 Wiper switch
6 Left two-tone horn	76 Buzzer plug
7 Left front foglight (optional)	77 Buzzer
8 Front left sealed beam I	78 Foglight switch (optional)
9 Front left sealed beam II	79 Light switch
10 Front left indicator; parking light	80 Left belt switch
11 Front right indicator plug	81 Left belt switch plug
12 Front left indicator plug	82 Belt time relay
13 Engine compartment light switch	83 Fasten seat belts
14 Engine compartment light	84 Glove box light
15 Engine compartment light plug	85 Headlamp (optional)
16 Foglight plug	86 Fuel pump connection
17 Washer pump	87 Radio
18 Ignition coil	88 Hazard light flasher
19 Distributor	89 Hazard light switch
20 Battery	90 Transmission switch (automatics)
21 Diode	91 Transmission switch plug (automatics)
22 Power distributor and fuses	92 Reverse light switch
(a) Main beam relay	93 Gate light II
(b) Dipped beam relay	94 Gate light I
(c) Two-tone horn relay	95 Reverse light switch plug
(d) Power sharing relay	96 Instrument cluster
(e) Foglight relay (optional)	(a) Oil pressure indicator
(f) Engine socket	(b) Coolant temperature gauge
(g) Diagnosis tester connection	(c) Plug
(h) 5-pin plug	(d) Main beam indicator (blue)
23 Alternator and regulator	(e) Charge indicator (red)
24 Starter motor	(f) Tachometer
25 Temperature transmitter	(g) Range indicator (automatics)
26 Oil pressure switch	P - white
27 45°C switch	R - red
28 Fuel injectors	O - white
29 Coolant temperature sensor	A - green
30 Resistors	2 - green
31 Resistors	1 - green
32 Plug for resistors	(h) Speedometer
33 Cold start valve	(k) Fuel level indicator
34 Cold start relay	(l) Fuel level gauge
35 Temperature time switch	(m) Brake fluid and parking brake indicator
36 Double relay for fuel injection	(n) Indicator warning light
37 Fuel injection control unit	(o) Plug
38 Throttle switch	(p) Resistor
39 Air flow sensor	(r) Resistor
40 Change-over relay	97 Fuel pump
41 Speed switch	98 Fuel level transmitter
42 Diverter valve solenoid	99 Right side marker light
43 EGR solenoid	101 Rear window demister
44 Ignition control solenoid	102 Right number plate light
45 Mirror switch	103 Right side marker light
46 Exterior mirror motor	104 Left number plate light
47 Exterior mirror connection	105 Interior light
48 Door plug	106 Right rear door contact
49 Brake fluid level control switch	107 Left rear door contact
50 Start relay (automatics)	108 Boot light switch
51 Tap wire harness terminal 1	109 Front left door contact
52 Windscreen wiper motor	110 Boot lid
53 Heater blower motor	111 Front right door contact
54 Centre console plug	112 Boot light plug
55 Connection for electric window, mirror, aerial, sun roof	113 Parking brake contact
56 1-pin plug	114 Right tail light
57 Service interval switch	(a) Indicator
58 Ignition lock plug 50	(b) Tail light
59 Heater control light 1	(c) Reverse light
60 Heater control light II	(d) Stop light
61 Heater controls	115 Stop light switch
62 Rear window demister switch	116 Left tail light
63 Cigar lighter	(a) Indicator
65 Plug II	(b) Tail light
66 Intermittent wash/wiper control unit	(c) Reverse light
67 Ignition switch plug	(d) Stop light
68 Indicator/dimmer switch plug	117 Left side marker light
69 Plug 1	118 Left side marker light plug
70 Indicator/dimmer switch	

Key to wiring diagram (Fig. 10.25)

1 Front right indicator; parking light
2 Front right indicator plug
3 Front right sealed beam II
4 Front right sealed beam I
5 Right foglight (optional)
6 Right two-tone horn
7 Left two-tone horn
8 Left foglight (optional)
9 Foglight plug
10 Front left sealed beam I
11 Front left sealed beam II
12 Front left indicator; parking light
13 Front left indicator plug
14 Engine compartment light switch (optional)
15 Engine compartment light (optional)
16 Engine compartment light plug
17 Additional fan motor
18 Compressor temperature switch
19 Washer pump
20 Additional fan motor connection
21 Compressor
22 Compressor connection
23 Additional fan temperature switch
24 Diode
25 Additional fan relay
26 Power distributor
  (a) Main beam relay
  (b) Dipped beam relay
  (c) Engine socket
  (d) Diagnosis socket
  (e) Two-tone horn relay
  (f) Power sharing relay
  (g) Foglight relay (optional)
  (h) Power bar 30
  (i) Plug
27 Diode
28 Battery
29 Distributor
30 Ignition coil
31 Resistor
32 Resistor
33 Plug for resistors
34 Fuel injectors
35 Coolant temperature sensor
36 Temperature line switch
37 Cold start valve
38 Cold start valve relay
39 Alternator with regulator
40 Starter motor
41 Double relay for fuel injection
42 Air flow sensor
43 Throttle switch
44 Fuel injection control unit
45 45°C switch
46 Oil pressure switch
47 Temperature transmitter
48 EGR solenoid
49 Ignition control solenoid
50 Tap wire harness terminal I
51 Diverter valve solenoid
52 Change-over relay
53 Heater blower motor
54 Blower switch
55 Relay
56 Rear window demister switch
57 Altitude control
58 Speed switch
59 Clock
60 Mirror switch
61 Ashtray light
62 Air conditioning blower line plug
63 Evaporation blower
64 Heater light
65 Evaporator
66 Centre console plug
67 Cigar lighter with light
68 Special equipment conection
69 Exterior mirror plug*
70 Mirror switch*
71 Exterior mirror motor*
72 Windscreen wiper motor
73 Plug II
74 Exterior mirror connection
75 Ignition switch plug 50
76 Start relay (automatics)

77 Service interval switch
78 Brake fluid level control switch
79 Intermittent wash/wipe control unit
80 Wiper switch plug
81 Central lock connection
82 Wiper switch
83 Ignition switch plug
84 Ignition switch
85 Horn contact
86 Indicator/dimmer switch plug
87 Indicator/dimmer switch
88 Light switch
89 Plug I
90 Foglight switch (optional)
91 Buzzer
92 Buzzer contact
93 Buzzer plug
94 Hazard light flasher
95 Hazard light switch
96 Glove box light
97 Handlamp (optional)
98 Transmission switch (automatics)
99 Transmission switch plug (automatics)
100 Fuel pump connection
101 Instrument cluster
  (a) Oil pressure indicator
  (b) Coolant temperature indicator
  (c) Plug
  (d) Main beam indicator (blue)
  (e) Charge indicator (red)
  (f) Tachometer
  (g) Range indicator (automatics)
    P - white
    R - red
    N - white
    D - green
    2 - green
    1 - green
  (h) Speedometer
  (k) Fuel level indicator
  (l) Fuel level gauge
  (m) Brake fluid and parking brake indicator
  (n) Indicator warning light
  (o) Plug
102 Radio connection
103 Belt control connection
104 Belt time relay
105 Instrument light I
106 Instrument light II
107 Reverse light switch plug
108 Reverse light switch
109 Rear window demister
110 Fuel pump
111 Fuel level transmitter
112 Right tail light
  (a) Indicator
  (b) Tail light
  (c) Reverse light
  (d) Stop light
113 Rear right door contact
114 Right side marker light
115 Right side marker light plug
116 Interior light
117 Right number plate light
118 Rear left door contact
119 Boot light switch
120 Left number plate light
121 Front left door contact
122 Front right door contact
123 Boot light
124 Stop light switch
125 Left tail light
  (a) Indicator
  (b) Tail light
  (c) Reverse light
  (d) Stop light
126 Belt switch
127 Boot light plug
128 Left belt switch plug
129 Parking brake contact
130 Left side marker light
131 Left side marker light plug
  *Applicable to special versions without electric window controls. For standard versions see diagram applicable to electric window controls and exterior mirror.

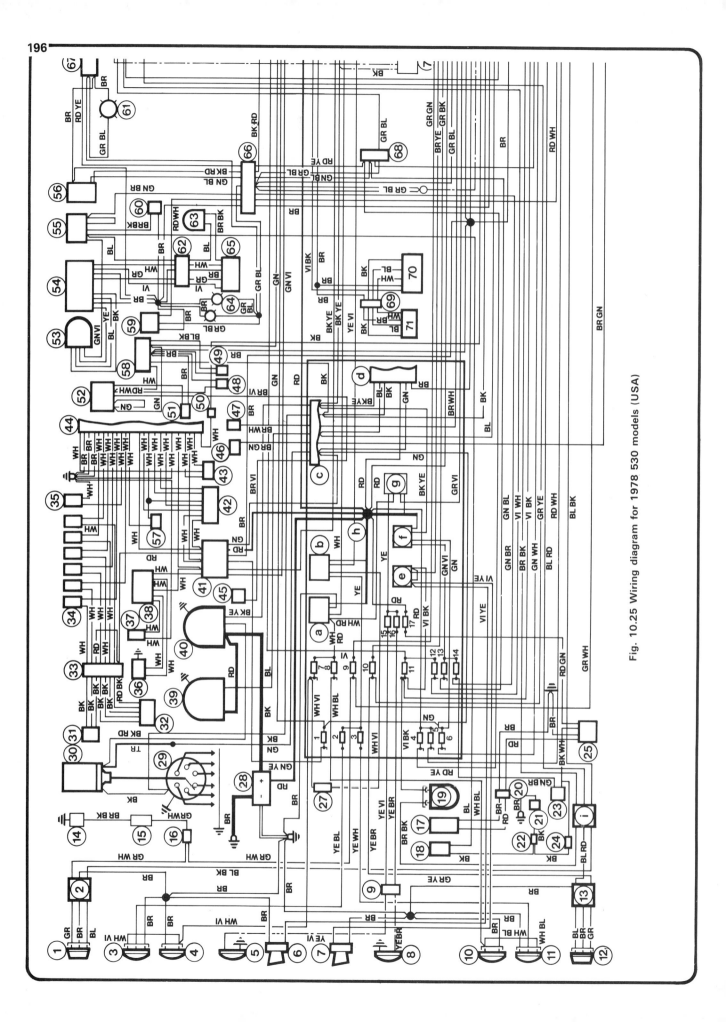

Fig. 10.25 Wiring diagram for 1978 530 models (USA)

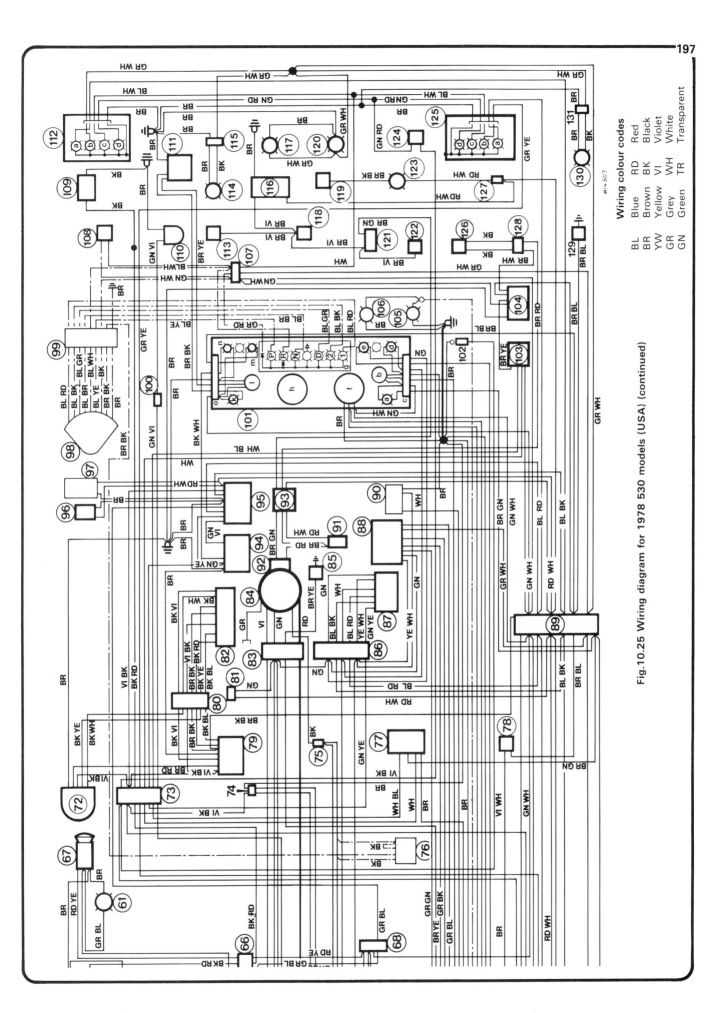

Fig. 10.25 Wiring diagram for 1978 530 models (USA) (continued)

Wiring colour codes

BL	Blue	RD	Red
BR	Brown	BK	Black
YW	Yellow	VI	Violet
GR	Grey	WH	White
GN	Green	TR	Transparent

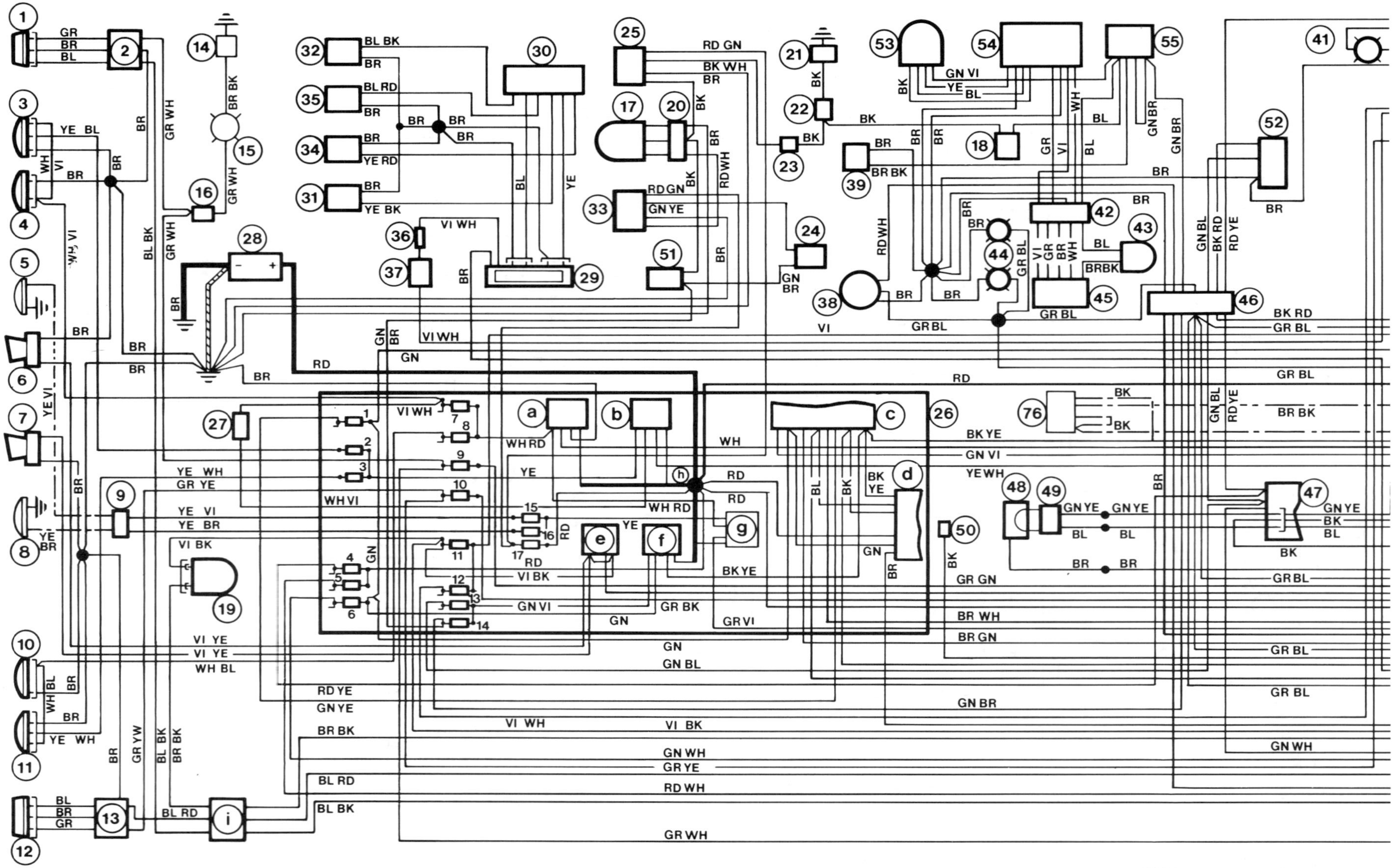

Fig. 10.26 Wiring diagram for 528 models (USA)

Wiring colour codes

BL	Blue	RD	Red
BR	Brown	BK	Black
YW	Yellow	VI	Violet
GR	Grey	WH	White
GN	Green	TR	Transparent

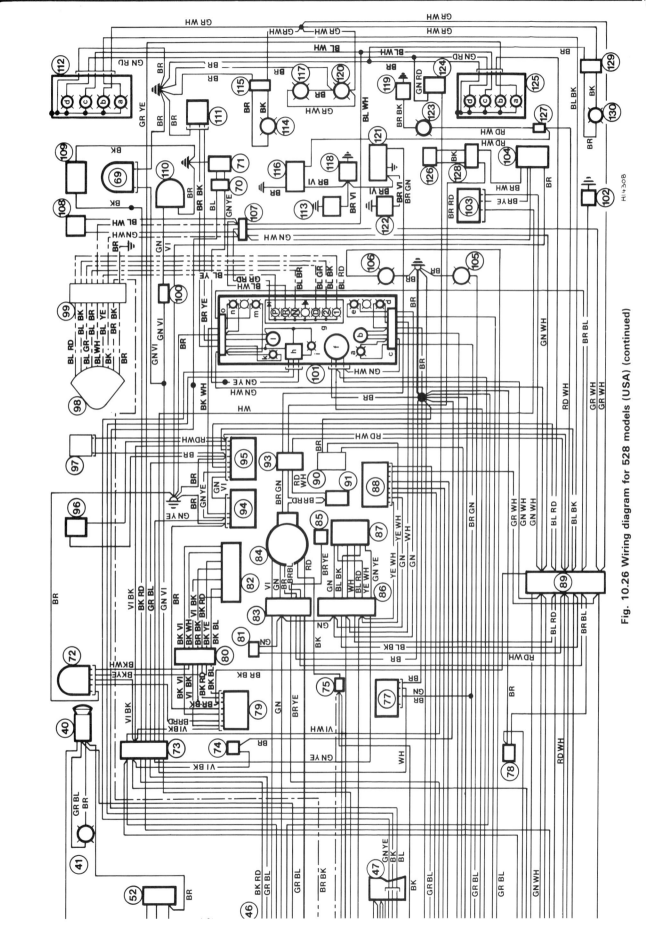

Fig. 10.26 Wiring diagram for 528 models (USA) (continued)

Key to wiring diagram (Fig. 10.26)

1 Front right indicator; parking light
2 Front right indicator plug
3 Front right sealed beam II
4 Front right sealed beam I
5 Right foglight (optional)
6 Right two-tone horn
7 Left two-tone horn
8 Left foglight (optional)
9 Foglight plug
10 Front left sealed beam I
11 Front left sealed beam II
12 Front left indicator; parking light
13 Front left indicator plug
14 Engine compartment light switch (optional)
15 Engine compartment light (optional)
16 Engine compartment light plug
17 Additional fan motor
18 Compressor temperature switch
19 Washer pump
20 Additional fan motor connector
21 Compressor
22 Compressor connector
23 Plug
24 Temperature switch 99°C
25 Relay stage I
26 Power distributor
  (a) Main beam relay
  (b) Dipped beam relay
  (c) Engine socket
  (d) Diagnosis socket
  (e) Two-tone horn relay
  (f) Power sharing relay
  (g) Foglight relay
  (h) Power bar 30
  (i) Plug
27 Diode
28 Battery
29 Radio
30 Loudspeaker balance
31 Left rear loudspeaker
32 Right rear loudspeaker
33 Relay stage II
34 Front left loudspeaker
35 Front right loudspeaker
36 Fuse
37 Radio
38 Clock
39 Microswitch
40 Cigar lighter and light
41 Ashtray light

42 Air conditioner blower line plug
43 Evaporator blower
44 Heater light
45 Evaporator
46 Centre console plug
47 Special equipment connection
48 Front left brake pad
49 Plug for front left brake pad
50 Electronic fuel injection connection
51 Temperature switch 91°C
52 Rear window demister switch
53 Heater blower motor
54 Blower switch
55 Change-over relay
69 Pre-delivery pump
70 Plug for rear brake pad
71 Rear brake pad
72 Windscreen wiper motor
73 Plug II
74 Exterior mirror connection
75 Ignition switch plug 50
76 Starter relay (automatics)
77 Service interval switch
78 Brake fluid level contact switch
79 Intermittent wash/wipe control unit
80 Wiper switch plug
81 Central lock connection
82 Wiper switch
83 Ignition switch plug
84 Ignition switch with buzzer contact
85 Horn contact
86 Indicator/dimmer switch plug
87 Indicator/dimmer switch
88 Light switch
89 Plug I
90 Foglight switch (optional)
91 Buzzer
93 Buzzer plug
94 Hazard light flasher
95 Hazard light switch
96 Glovebox light
97 Handlamp (optional)
98 Transmission switch (automatic)
99 Transmission switch plug (automatic)
100 Fuel pump plug
101 Instrument cluster
  (a) Oil pressure indicator
  (b) Coolant temperature gauge

(c) Plug
(d) Main beam indicator
(e) Change indicator
(f) Tachometer
(g) Range indicator (automatics)
  P – white
  R – red
  N – white
  D – green
  2 – green
  1 – green
(h) Brake pad indicator
(i) Brake pad indicator lamp
(k) Fuel level indicator
(l) Fuel level gauge
(m) Brake fluid and parking brake indicator
(n) Indicator warning light
(o) Plug
102 Parking brake contact
102 Fasten Seat Belts
104 Belt time relay
105 Instrument light I
106 Instrument light II
107 Reverse light switch plug
108 Reverse light switch
109 Rear window demister
110 Fuel pump
111 Fuel level transmitter
112 Right tail light
  (a) Indicator
  (b) Tail light
  (c) Reverse light
  (d) Stop light
113 Rear right door contact
114 Right side marker light
115 Right side marker light plug
116 Interior light
117 Right number plate light
118 Rear left door contact
119 Boot light switch
120 Left number plate light
121 Front left door contact
122 Front right door contact
123 Boot light
124 Stop light switch
125 Left tail light
  (a) Indicator
  (b) Tail light
  (c) Reverse light
  (d) Stop light
126 Left belt switch
127 Boot light plug
128 Left belt switch plug
129 Left side marker light plug
130 Left side marker light

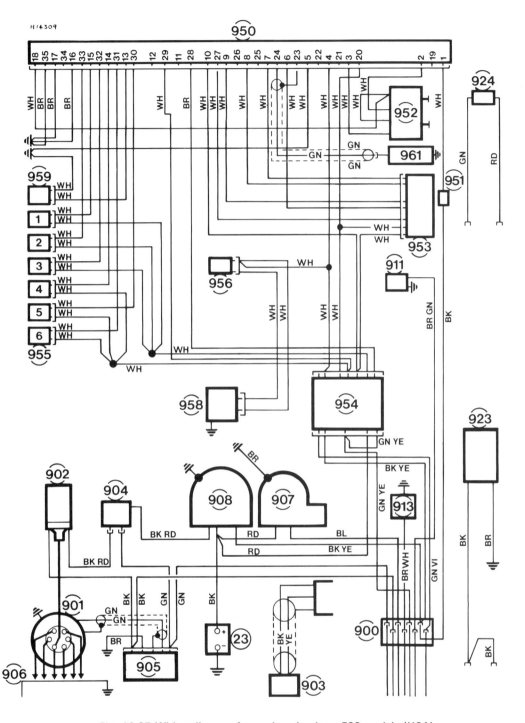

Fig. 10.27 Wiring diagram for engine circuit on 528 models (USA)

Key to wiring diagram (Fig. 10.27)

23 Battery	906 Spark plugs
900 Engine socket	907 Alternator
901 Distributor	908 Starter motor
902 Ignition coil	911 Oil pressure switch
903 Position transmitter	913 Temperature
904 Resistor	transmitter
905 Ignition control	923 Auxiliary air valve
switch	924 Thermo-sensor

950 Fuel injection control	relay
unit	955 Fuel injectors
951 Fuel injection control	956 Cold start valve
unit connection	958 Thermo line switch
952 Throttle switch	959 Coolant temperature
953 Air flow sensor	sensor
954 Fuel injection double	961 Lambda sensor

Wiring colour codes

BL	Blue	YW	Yellow	GN	Green	BK	Black	WH	White
BR	Brown	GR	Grey	RD	Red	VI	Violet	TR	Transparent

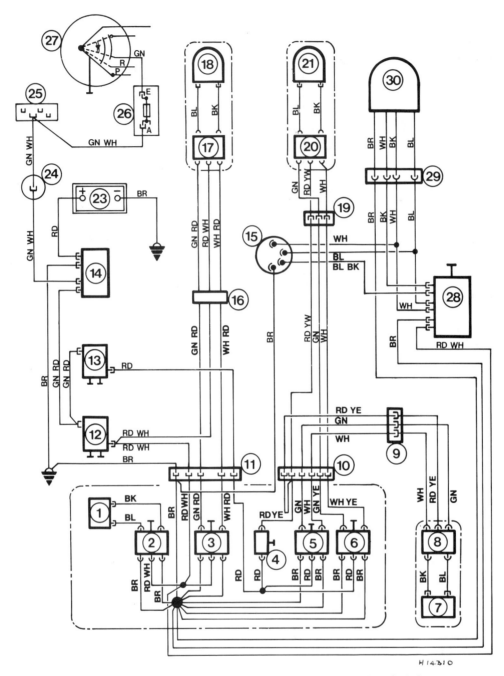

Fig. 10.28 Wiring diagram for electric windows and mirror (USA)

Key to wiring diagram (Fig. 10.28)

1	Electric window control motor	8	Switch		mirror connection	24	Special equipment connection
2	Driver door switch	9	Driver side rear door plug	16	Passenger door plug	25	Plug 1
3	Passenger door switch	10	Plug 2	17	Switch	26	Power distributor
4	Child safety switch	11	Plug 1	18	Electric window control motor	27	Ignition switch
5	Driver side rear door switch	12	Front door automatic cut-out	19	Passenger side rear door plug	28	Mirror switch
6	Passenger side rear door switch	13	Rear door automatic cut-out	20	Switch	29	Electric mirror connection
7	Electric window control motor	14	Relay 1	21	Window control motor	30	Exterior electric mirror
		15	Additional electric	23	Battery		

Wiring colour codes

BL	Blue	YW	Yellow	GN	Green	BL	Black	WH	White
BR	Brown	GR	Grey	RD	Red	VI	Violet	TR	Transparent

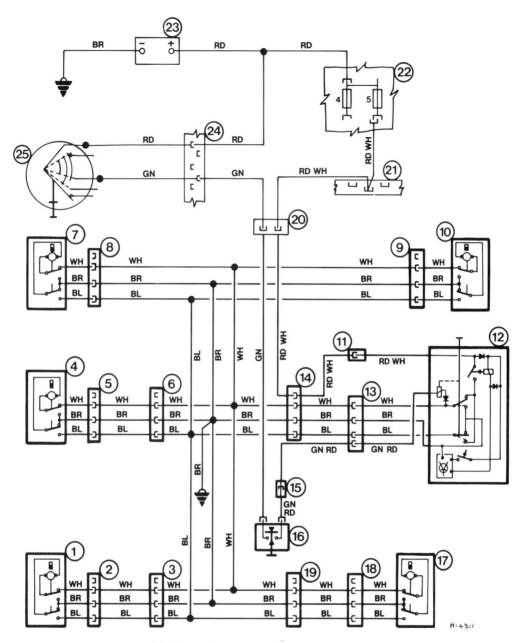

Fig. 10.29 Wiring diagram for central locking system (USA)

Key to wiring diagram (Fig. 10.29)

1	Passenger side rear door drive	6	Driver side rear door plug	13	Driver door contact plug	19	Passenger door drive plug
2	Passenger side rear door drive plug	7	Trunk lid drive	14	Driver door plug	20	Wiring harness connection
3	Passenger side rear door plug	8	Trunk lid drive plug	15	Impact switch connection	21	Plug 1
4	Driver side rear door drive	9	Tank flap drive plug	16	Impact switch	22	Power distributor
5	Driver side rear door drive plug	10	Tank flap drive	17	Passenger door drive	23	Battery
		11	Driver door contact plug	18	Passenger door drive plug	24	Ignition switch plug
		12	Driver door contact			25	Ignition switch

Wiring colour codes

BL	Blue	RD	Red
BR	Brown	BK	Black
YW	Yellow	VI	Violet
GR	Grey	WH	White
GN	Green	TR	Transparent

Chapter 11 Suspension and steering

For modifications, and information applicable to later models, see Supplement at end of manual

Contents

Specifications

Front suspension

Type .... Independent, coil springs and struts incorporating shock absorbers, control arms and radius links, stabiliser bar
Control arm balljoint maximum wear .... 1.4 mm (0.055 in)
Wheel bearing endplay .... 0 to 0.05 mm (0 to 0.002 in)
Strut oil capacity .... 50 cc (3.05 cu in)
Coil spring free length:
   UK models – standard .... 338 mm (13.307 in)
    – heavy duty pre-1977 except 528i .... 352 mm (13.858 in)
    – heavy duty 1977-on .... 373 mm (14.685 in)
   USA models (with air conditioning) – 530i pre-1977 .... 352 mm (13.858 in)
    – 530i 1977-on .... 368 mm (14.488 in)
    – 528i .... 373 mm (14.685 in)
   USA models (without air conditioning) – 528i .... 338 mm (13.307 in)
    – 530i .... 373 mm (14.685 in)

Rear suspension

Type .... Independent, coil springs and struts incorporating shock absorbers, semi-trailing arms, stabiliser bar
Wheel bearing endplay .... 0.05 to 0.10 mm (0.002 to 0.004 in)
Coil spring free length:
   UK models (standard) – 525/528 pre-1977 .... 334.8 mm (13.575 in)
    – 525/528 1977-on .... 343 mm (13.504 in)
    528i .... 343 mm (13.504 in)
   UK models (heavy duty) .... 341 mm (13.425 in)
   USA models – 530i pre-1977 .... 334.8 mm (13.181 in)
    – 530i 1977 on .... 341 mm (13.425 in)
    – 528i .... 341 mm (13.425 in)

Front wheel alignment and suspension angles

Toe-in (laden) .... 2.0 ± 0.6 mm (0.079 ± 0.024 in)
Camber .... 0° ± 30'
King pin inclination .... 8° ± 30'
Caster .... 7°40' ± 30'
Maximum caster difference between wheels .... 0°30'

Rear wheel alignment

Toe-in (laden) .... 1.2 to 2.8 mm (0.047 to 0.110 in)
Camber .... 2° ± 30' negative

Steering
Type:
Non power-assisted models	ZF Gemmer cam and roller with idler arm and three-piece track rod
Power-assisted models	ZF ball and nut with idler arm and three-piece track rod. Hydraulic pump belt driven from crankshaft pulley

Ratio:
Non-power assisted models	19.1 to 1
Power assisted models	14.5 to 1
Power steering pump drivebelt tension	5 to 10 mm (0.197 to 0.394 in)

Wheels
Type	Pressed steel or light alloy
Size (pressed steel) – 525	$5\frac{1}{2}$J X 14 H2-B
528/530	6J X 14 H2-B
Size (light alloy)	6J X 14 H2-B

Tyres
Size – 525	175 HR 14 (with steel wheels)
	175 SR 14 or 195/70 HR 14 (with alloy wheels)
– 528 (carburettor)	195/70 HR 14 (with steel wheels)
	195/70 VR 14 (with alloy wheels)
– 528i (UK)	195/70 VR 14
– 528i and 530i (USA)	195/70 HR 14

Pressures in bar (lbf/in^2) cold:

	Front	Rear
UK models		
525 (up to 4 persons)	2.1 (30)	2.1 (30)
525 (more than 4 persons)	2.2 (31)	2.5 (35)
528 (up to 4 persons)	2.1 (30)	2.1 (30)
528 (more than 4 persons)	2.2 (31)	2.4 (34)
USA models		
528 (up to 4 persons)	2.3 (33)	2.3 (33)
528 (more than 4 persons)	2.4 (34)	2.5 (35)
530 (up to 4 persons)	2.0 (28)	1.8 (26)
530 (more than 4 persons)	2.1 (30)	2.3 (33)

Torque wrench settings

	lbf ft	Nm
Front suspension		
Crossmember	53 to 59	73 to 81
Control arm to crossmember	59 to 65	81 to 90
Strut to control arm	51 to 65	70 to 90
Shock absorber ring	87 to 101	120 to 140
Strut to upper bearing	52 to 58	72 to 80
Strut bearing to body	16 to 18	22 to 25
Stabiliser to control arm	16 to 17	22 to 24
Stabiliser mountings	32 to 35	43 to 48
Rear suspension		
Trailing arm to crossmember	48 to 54	67 to 75
Strut to body	16 to 17	22 to 24
Shock absorber top mounting	18 to 20	25 to 28
Shock absorber bottom mounting	87 to 94	120 to 130
Shock absorber top plates	18 to 22	25 to 30
Stabiliser to trailing arm	16 to 17	22 to 24
Stabiliser mountings	16 to 17	22 to 24
Drive flange to rear axleshaft	289 to 325	400 to 450
Steering		
Steering gear	31 to 35	43 to 48
Worm end cover – Gemmer	16 to 17	22 to 24
– Power steering	25	34
Sector shaft end cover – Gemmer	16 to 17	22 to 24
– Power steering	22	31
Adjusting locknut – Gemmer	18 to 22	25 to 30
– Power steering	22	30
Steering drop arm to gear	101	140
Control arm to crossmember	60 to 66	81 to 90
Tie-rod castle nut	25 to 29	35 to 40
Tie-rod to control arm	43 to 50	60 to 70
Steering wheel	62 to 69	85 to 95
Power steering hose	33 to 36	45 to 50
Wheels		
Roadwheel nuts	60 to 66	81 to 90
Roadwheel bolts	66 to 81	90 to 110

1 General description

The front suspension is of the independent type, and consists of a lower track control arm, mounted on the front crossmember frame, and a suspension strut, which is bolted to the front wheel arch at its upper end, and to the track control arm at its lower end. Further location of the strut is provided by a trailing link arm mounted to the chassis frame at its forward end and to the track control arm at its rear. Additional stability is provided by a stabiliser bar which is fitted across the main crossmember frame. Both ends of the stabiliser bar are located to the track control arms by short link arms. The suspension struts incorporate double-acting hydraulic shock absorbers, and coil springs.

The rear suspension is also of the independent type, and consists of semi-trailing arms which are pivoted on the rear crossmember frame at two points. The suspension strut, which is connected to the semi-trailing arm and the rear wheel-arch, incorporates a double-acting hydraulic shock absorber, and coil spring.

The steering gear on non power-assisted models is of the ZF Gemmer worm and roller type. The steering motion is transmitted to the struts via the steering box drop arm, relay rod, idler arm and trackrods. On models with power-assisted steering a ZF ball and nut steering box is used. Hydraulic power assistance is provided by an engine belt-driven pump.

Radial ply tyres are fitted as standard equipment. The size varies according to the model and the particular type and width of road wheel fitted.

2 Routine maintenance

1   Every 10 000 miles (15 000 km) on UK models or every 12 500 miles (20 000 km) on USA models the steering gear oil level should be checked and if necessary topped-up. On power steering models check the oil level in the reservoir and top it up if necessary.

2   At the same interval check all steering and suspension nuts and bolts for security, and balljoints, bushes, and rubber dust covers for wear and deterioration.

3   Check the steering for excessive play and adjust the steering gear if necessary. On power steering models check the pump drivebelt tension and adjust it if necessary.

4   Every 40 000 miles (64 000 km) on UK models or 37 500 miles (60 000 km) on USA models check and adjust the front wheel bearing endplay.

5   At the same interval on power steering models the pump should be tested for correct function. However as this involves the use of special equipment and pressure gauges it is best entrusted to a BMW garage.

6   On power steering models renew the reservoir filter at the same interval.

3 Front wheel bearings – adjustment

1   Jack-up the front of the car and support it on axle stands. Apply the handbrake.

2   Prise the centre motif from the wheel, then tap or twist off the dust cap from the hub (photo). If difficulty is experienced remove the roadwheel.

3   Extract the split pin from the castellated adjusting nut (photo).

4   Using a torque wrench and socket, tighten the adjusting nut to 22 to 24 lbf ft (30 to 33 Nm) while turning the hub continuously (photo).

5   Fully unscrew the adjusting nut then tighten it to 2 lbf ft (3 Nm); if a suitable torque wrench is not available tighten the nut using fingers and thumb.

6   Turn the hub several times then check that it is just possible to move the tab washer (next to the nut) in each direction with a screwdriver.

7   Fit a new split pin and bend the ends over the nut. Refit the dust cap, roadwheel and motif as applicable and lower the car to the ground.

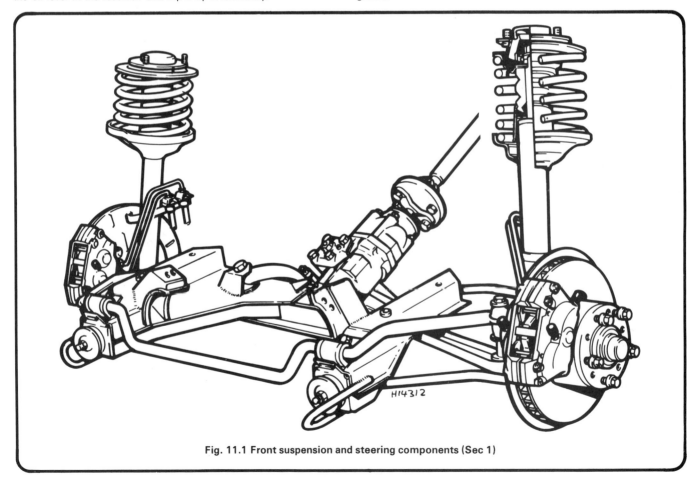

Fig. 11.1 Front suspension and steering components (Sec 1)

4 Front hub and wheel bearings – removal and refitting

1   Jack-up the front of the car and support it on axle stands. Apply the handbrake and remove the roadwheel.

2   Remove the disc pads as described in Chapter 9.

3   Detach the hydraulic line bracket from the suspension strut, unbolt the brake caliper, and move it to one side. Tie the caliper to the coil spring to prevent straining the hydraulic hoses.

4   Tap or twist off the dust cap, remove the split-pin and castellated nut.

5   Extract the thrust washer and then pull the hub assembly carefully from the stub axle. Catch the outer taper bearings (photos).

6   Using a suitable drift or lever (photo) remove the oil seal and extract the inner taper roller bearing.

7   If new bearings are to be installed, drive out the bearing tracks using a bearing puller or drift.

8   Clean the interior of the hub and dust cap and then install the new bearing tracks, the inner taper roller bearing and tap in a new oil seal.

9   Pack wheel bearing grease into the inside of the hub so that it fills the deeper recess but is no thicker than the bearing tracks. Press some grease into the bearing rollers and then reassemble by reversing the dismantling process.

10   Adjust the bearings, as described in Section 3 and refit the dust cap. Do not fill the cap more than $\frac{1}{3}$rd full with grease.

11   Refit the roadwheel and lower the jack.

5 Front suspension assembly – removal and refitting

1   Jack-up the front of the car and support it under the side bodyframe members just to the rear of the front crossmember.

2   Remove the roadwheels.

3   Remove the disc pads as described in Chapter 9.

4   Undo the nut and bolt locating the angle support bracket which

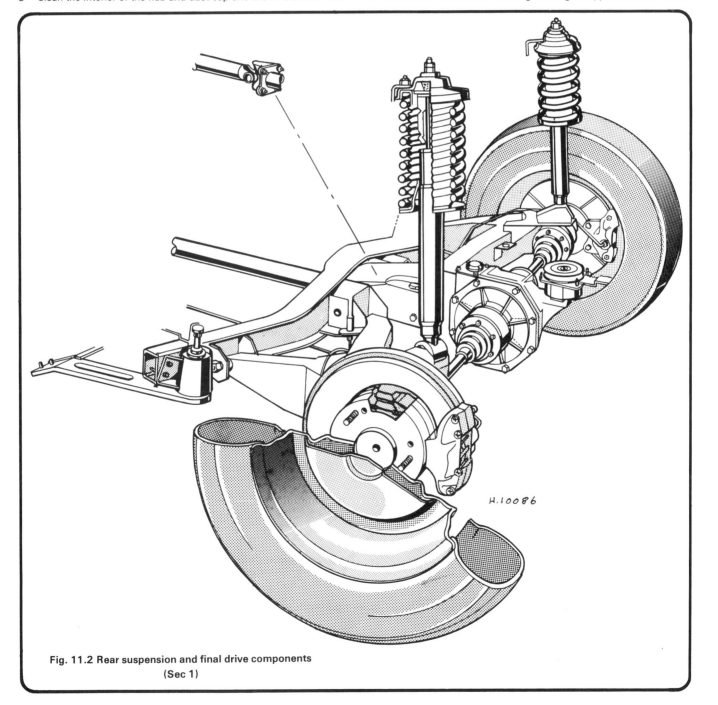

Fig. 11.2 Rear suspension and final drive components
(Sec 1)

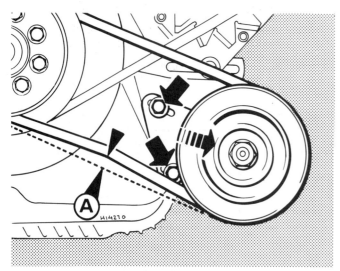

Fig. 11.3 Adjusting the power steering pump drivebelt tension
(A) (Sec 2)

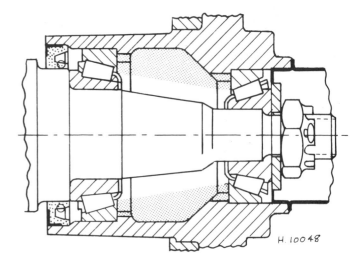

Fig. 11.4 Cross section diagram of the front hub. Shaded area
indicates grease (Sec 4)

3.2 Removing the front hub dust cap

3.3 Removing the split-pin from the front hub

3.4 Using a torque wrench to adjust the front
wheel bearings

4.5A Removing the front hub thrust washer ...

4.5B ... outer bearing ...

4.5C ... and hub/disc assembly

secures the flexible and metal hydraulic brake pipes to the suspension strut (photo).

5   Undo the two bolts securing the brake caliper. Lift the caliper away and support it from a convenient point. There is no need to disconnect any of the hydraulic pipes.

6   Remove the lower pinch bolt from the steering shaft universal coupling, and slide the coupling and column from the steering gear (photo).

7   On power steering models place a suitable container beneath the steering gear. Unscrew the union bolts and detach the hoses (photo), and allow the oil to drain.

8   Remove the lower nuts from both engine mountings, and on

automatic transmission models remove the oil cooler hose clamps.

9   Remove the suspension strut upper mounting nuts.

10 On USA models unbolt the heat shield from the right-hand side of the underbody and crossmember.

11 Take the weight of the engine with a suitable hoist.

12 Support the crossmember with a trolley jack then unbolt it from the underbody.

13 Lower the suspension assembly to the ground and withdraw it from under the car.

14 Refitting is a reversal of removal, but tighten all nuts and bolts to the specified torque. Centre the steering wheel and steering gear before connecting the shaft coupling and make sure that the pinch bolt

4.6 Levering out the front hub oil seal

5.4 Removing the brake pipe bracket from the front suspension strut

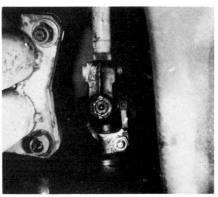

5.6 Steering shaft lower universal coupling

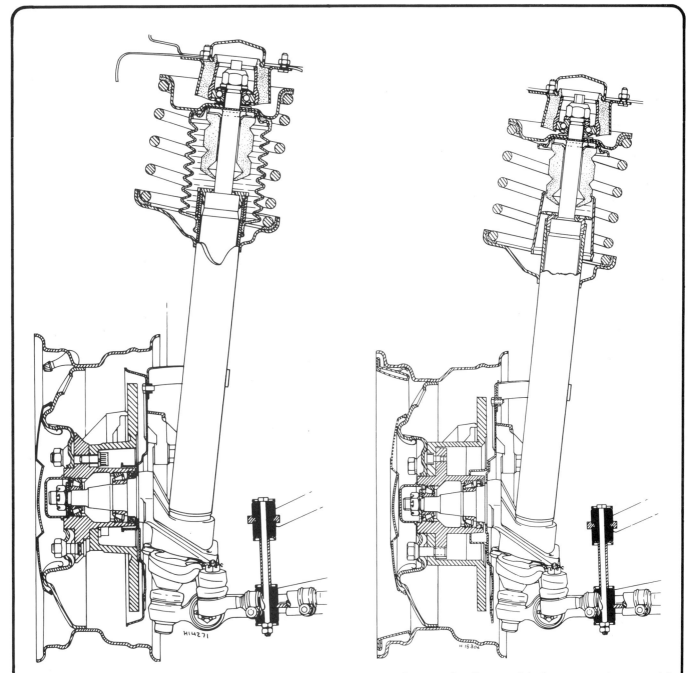

Fig. 11.5 Cross section diagram of the front suspension on models with wheel nuts (Sec 5)

Fig. 11.6 Cross section diagram of the front suspension on models with wheel bolts (Sec 5)

5.7 Power steering gear and hydraulic fluid hoses (shown with engine removed)

6.5A Outer section of front suspension crossmember

6.5B Showing middle section of front suspension crossmember

7.6 Balljoint castle nut location in the steering arm

is located in the groove. Check that the engine mounting locating pegs are located in the special holes in the crossmember. On power steering models top-up the oil level and bleed the system as described in Section 27. Check the front wheel alignment as described in Section 34.

6 Front suspension crossmember – removal and refitting

1   Remove the stabilisor bar as described in Section 9 and the radius links as described in Section 8.
2   Unbolt the steering gear from the crossmember and tie it to one side.
3   Detach the steering idler arm from the crossmember by unscrewing the nut and bolt.
4   On USA models remove the heat shield bolt.
5   Remove the bolts securing the control arms to the crossmember, and disconnect the control arms (photos).
6   Remove the lower nuts from both engine mountings, and on automatic transmission models remove the oil cooler hose clamps.
7   On USA models unbolt the mounting stops.
8   Take the weight of the engine with a suitable hoist.
9   Support the crossmember with a trolley jack then unbolt it from the underbody. Lower it to the ground and at the same time remove the idler arm pivot bolt.
10 If necessary remove the radius link roller mountings with reference

to Section 8.
11 Refitting is a reversal of removal, but tighten all nuts and bolts to the specified torque. Check that the engine mounting locating pegs are located in the special holes in the crossmember. Check the front wheel alignment as described in Section 34. Do not fully tighten the control arm bolts until the weight of the car is on the suspension.

7 Track control arm – removal and refitting

1   Jack-up the front of the car and support it on axle stands. Apply the handbrake and remove the roadwheel.
2   Unscrew the stabiliser arm link lower nuts, remove the washer and bush, and disconnect the link from the control arm.
3   Unscrew the radius link arm rear nut.
4   Remove the pivot bolt from the crossmember and withdraw the control arm. Disconnect the arm from the radius link.
5   Cut the locking wire from the three bolts at the bottom of the strut, then unscrew them and detach the steering arm from the strut.
6   Extract the split pin and unscrew the castle nut from the steering arm (photo).Using a balljoint separator tool, remove the steering arm from the control arm. Withdraw the control arm from the car.
7   The balljoint cannot be renewed as an individual unit, and if the axial play exceeds that given in the Specifications the control arm must be renewed. The rubber bush can be renewed if necessary by using a

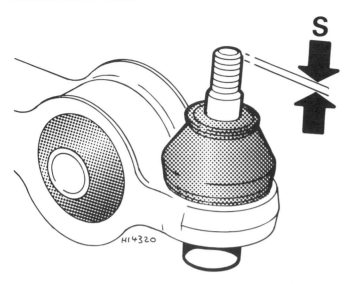

Fig. 11.7 Track control arm balljoint wear movement S – see Specifications (Sec 7)

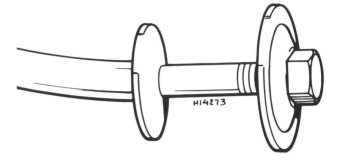

Fig. 11.8 Correct positioning of the radius link arm front mounting washers (Sec 8)

suitable metal tube, washers, and a long bolt and nut. Dip the new bush in soapy water to facilitate its fitting.

8   Refitting is a reversal of removal, but tighten all nuts and bolts to the specified torque. Do not fully tighten the control arm pivot bolt and radius link arm rear nut until the weight of the car is on the suspension. Note that the radius link arm washers must be fitted with their concave sides facing the bush. Renew all self locking nuts, and do not forget to fit the locking wire to the strut bottom bolts.

8   Radius link arm – removal and refitting

1   Jack-up the front of the car and support it on axle stands. Apply the handbrake and remove the roadwheel.
2   Unscrew the stabiliser arm link lower nuts, remove the washer and bush, and disconnect the link from the control arm.
3   Unscrew the radius link arm rear nut and remove the washer.
4   Unscrew the radius link arm front nut and remove the washer (photo).
5   Remove the control arm pivot bolt from the crossmember then move it to the rear and withdraw the radius link arm.
6   Examine the rubber bushes in the crossmember and control arm. Renew them if necessary by using a suitable metal tube, washers and a long bolt and nut. Dip the new bush in soapy water to facilitate its fitting.
7   Refitting is a reversal of removal, but tighten all nuts and bolts to the specified torque. Do not fully tighten the control arm pivot bolt and radius link arm rear nut, until the weight of the car is on the suspension. Note that the radius link arm rear mounting washers must be fitted with their concave sides facing the bush, but the front mounting washers must be fitted with their concave sides both facing forward (see Fig. 11.8). Renew all self locking nuts.

9   Front stabiliser bar – removal and refitting

1   Jack-up the front of the car and support it on axle stands. Apply the handbrake and remove both front roadwheels.
2   Disconnect the short link arms from the control arms by removing the nuts, washers and bushes (photo).
3   Unscrew the front mounting clamp bolts, unhook the clamps, and withdraw the stabiliser bar from under the car.
4   Examine the mounting rubbers and if necessary renew them.
5   Refitting is a reversal of removal, but tighten the nuts and bolts to the specified torque with the weight of the car on the suspension.

10   Front suspension strut – removal and refitting

1   Remove the front hub as described in Section 4, but place the brake caliper on an axle stand instead of tying it to the coil spring.
2   Unbolt the backplate from the strut (photo).
3   Cut the locking wire from the three bolts at the bottom of the strut, then unscrew them and press the steering arm from the strut (photo).
4   Support the strut, then unscrew the top mounting nuts within the engine compartment (photo).
5   Lower the strut and withdraw it from the car (photos).
6   Refitting is a reversal of removal, but tighten all nuts and bolts to the specified torque. Fit new locking wire to the strut bottom bolts and refit the front hub with reference to Section 4 (photo).

11   Front coil spring – removal and refitting

Warning: *Spring compressors of sound design and construction must be used for this procedure. Uncontrolled release of the spring could cause personal injury and property damage.*

1   Remove the front suspension strut as described in Section 10, however it is not essential to remove the front hub, but only the brake caliper and hydraulic lines.
2   Compress the coil spring using screw type compressors, then prise the cap from the top mounting and unscrew the self-locking nut while holding the piston rod stationary (photos).

8.4 Radius link on front mounting

9.2 Front stabiliser bar link arm location

10.2 Removing the backplate from the front suspension strut

10.3 Removing the strut to front steering arm bolts

10.4 Removing the front suspension strut top mounting nuts

10.5A Front suspension strut assembly

10.5B View of front suspension linkages with the strut removed

10.6 Fitting locking wire to the front suspension strut lower mounting bolts

11.2A Compressing the front coil spring

11.2B Front suspension strut top mounting and piston rod nut

11.6 Showing coil spring location in the front suspension strut top mounting

12.3 Front shock absorber threaded ring location (arrowed)

3   Withdraw the top mounting and washers noting their exact location.

4   Remove the upper spring retainer followed by the washer, damper and dust cover. On some models the dust cover is attached to the damper, but on other models it is convoluted and covers the damper completely.

5   Withdraw the coil spring from the top of the strut. Remove the compressors.

6   Refitting is a reversal of removal, but make sure that the ends of the coil spring locate in the special shoulders on the strut and upper retainer (photo). Also make sure that the damper cut-outs engage with the tabs on the adjacent disc. Tighten all nuts and bolts to the specified torque. Fit the washers correctly with reference to Figs. 11.5 and 11.6. Renew all self-locking nuts.

12 Front shock absorber – removal and refitting

1   To test the front shock absorbers, depress each front corner of the car in turn and check that the body rises when released and settles on the downward movement. If the body oscillates several times before settling, the shock absorber is faulty and should be renewed. Alternatively a replacement strut should be fitted.

2   To remove the shock absorber first remove the coil spring as described in Section 11.

3   Mount the strut in a soft jawed vice, then unscrew the threaded ring from the top of the strut (photo). BMW special tool No 313160 or 313150 is required to unscrew the ring, alternatively a hammer and cold chisel may be used.

4   Withdraw the shock absorber from the strut.
5   Pour the oil from the strut and discard it, then clean the strut with paraffin and wipe dry.
6   Mount the strut in the vice and pour in the specified amount of fresh engine oil.
7   Fit the new shock absorber into the strut and tighten the threaded ring to the specified torque.
8   Refit the coil spring with reference to Section 11.

13 Rear stub axle – removal and refitting

1   Remove the rear brake disc as described in Chapter 9.
2   Disconnect the driveshaft from the stub axle inner flange with reference to Chapter 8 and tie it to one side.
3   Lower the lockplate from the flange groove, then unscrew the nut while holding the flange stationary with a long bar positioned between two temporarily inserted driveshaft bolts.
4   Using a suitable puller withdraw the drive flange from the stub axle.
5   Temporarily refit the flange nut and screw it on until flush with the end of the shaft. Using a plastic mallet drive out the stub axle, removing the nut when it contacts the inner bearing.
6   Clean the components in paraffin and examine them for wear and damage. Check the oil seal spacer on the stub axle for grooving. Renew the components as necessary.
7   Refitting is a reversal of removal, but tighten the flange nut and driveshaft bolts to the specified torque. Lock the flange nut by bending the backplate into the groove.

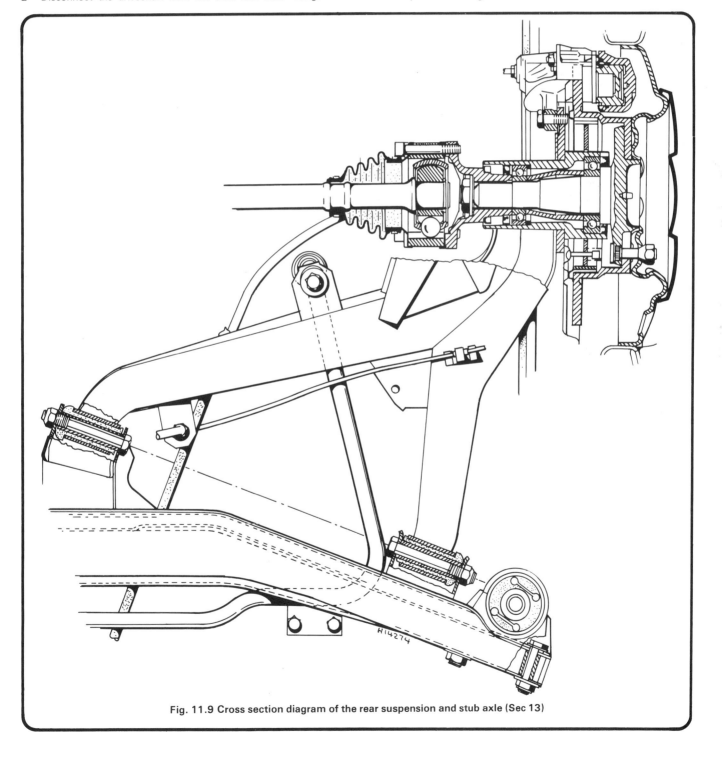

Fig. 11.9 Cross section diagram of the rear suspension and stub axle (Sec 13)

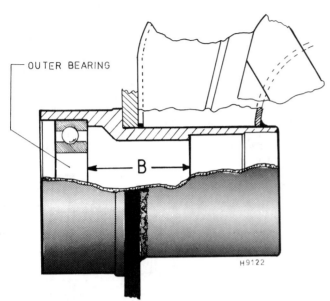

Fig. 11.10 Dimension B for calculating rear wheel bearing shim (Sec 14)

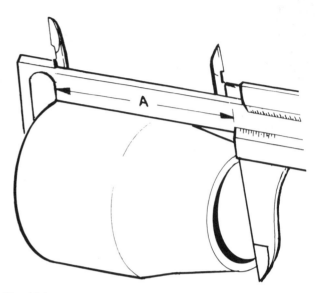

Fig. 11.11 Dimension A for calculating rear wheel bearing shim (Sec 14)

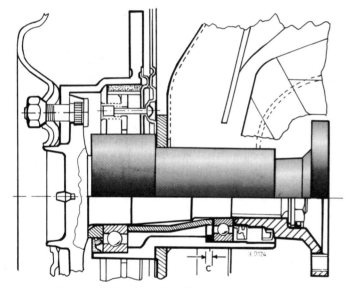

Fig. 11.12 Rear wheel bearing shim location and dimension C (Sec 14)

14 Rear wheel bearings – removal and refitting

1   Remove the stub axle as described in Section 13.
2   Using a long drift drive the inner and outer bearings from the semi-trailing arm together with the oil seals.
3   Extract the tubular spacer and shim washer.
4   Clean the components in paraffin and examine them for wear and damage. Take care not to contaminate the handbrake linings. Spin the bearings by hand and also check them for lateral movement. BMW recommend their renewal at 60 000 miles (100 000 km).
5   Using a metal tube against the outer track, drive the outer bearing fully into the semi-trailing arm. With a depth gauge measure the distance B between the seat of the inner bearing and the inner face of the outer bearing (see Fig. 11.10).
6   Measure the length A of the tubular spacer with vernier calipers.
7   Subtract B from A and from the result subtract the specified bearing endfloat. The final figure represents the thickness of the shim C which must be fitted to the inner face of the inner bearing (see Fig. 11.12).

8   Reassemble the components after packing the bearings with grease. Note that the space between the bearings and oil seals must be free of grease, but the seal lips should be coated with grease.
9   Refit the stub axle with reference to Section 13.

15 Rear suspension strut – removal and refitting

1   Jack-up the rear of the car and support it on axle stands. Chock the front wheels.
2   Using a second jack, support the suspension trailing arm otherwise the driveshaft constant velocity joints will be strained when the strut/shock absorber assembly (which acts as a check link) is released from its mountings.
3   Working inside the luggage compartment, remove the three self-locking nuts. On later models a cover ring and damper plate is secured to the strut studs.
4   From under the car remove the lower mounting bolt which secures the strut to the semi-trailing arm (photo).
5   Lower the suspension strut from the car and remove the gasket or damper from the top mounting (photo).
6   Refitting is a reversal of removal, but renew the self-locking nuts and tighten them to the specified torque. Delay fully tightening the lower mounting bolt until the weight of the car is on the suspension. On later models make sure that the spacers are located on the top mounting studs and fit the mounting so that the damper tabs face to the front and rear of the car.

16 Rear coil spring – removal and refitting

1   Remove the rear suspension strut as described in Section 15.
2   Compress the coil spring using screw type compressors.
3   Prise off the cap where fitted, then unscrew the locknut and nut beneath it.
4   Remove the mounting plate followed by the cover and damper.
5   Withdraw the coil spring together with the convoluted sleeve or upper seating (as applicable).
6   Release the compressors and where applicable remove the convoluted sleeve.
7   Refitting is a reversal of removal, but make sure that the coil spring is located correctly in its seatings. Note that where the seatings are of different thicknesses, the thicker seat must be located at the top. Make sure that the mounting plate studs are located in the upper seat cut-outs. Tighten the nuts to the specified torque.

15.4 Rear suspension strut lower mounting

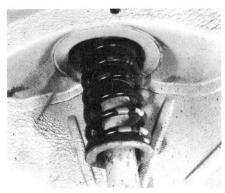

15.5 Removing the rear suspension strut

18.2 Rear stabiliser bar link location

18.3 Rear stabiliser bar mounting clamp

19.6A Rear trailing arm outer pivot bolt

19.6B Rear trailing arm inner pivot bolt

17 Rear shock absorber – removal and refitting

1   To test the rear shock absorber use the same method described in Section 12.
2   As the rear shock absorber is an integral part of the rear suspension strut, the removal and refitting procedure is as described in Section 16.

18 Rear stabiliser bar – removal and refitting

1   Jack-up the rear of the car and support it on axle stands. Chock the front wheels.
2   Disconnect the short link arms from the trailing arms by removing the nuts, washers and bushes (photo).
3   Unscrew the mounting clamp bolts, unhook the clamps, and withdraw the stabiliser bar from under the car (photo).
4   Examine the mounting rubbers and if necessary renew them.
5   Refitting is a reversal of removal, but note that the slotted end of the mounting clamp rubbers must face forward. Tighten the nuts and bolts to the specified torque with the weight of the car on the suspension.

19 Rear trailing arm – removal and refitting

1   Jack-up the rear of the car and support it on axle stands. Chock the front wheels.
2   Remove the handbrake cable with reference to Chapter 9.
3   Unscrew the brake fluid reservoir filler cap and tighten it onto a piece of polythene sheeting. Alternatively use two tapered wooden dowel rods to plug the reservoir outlets on right-hand drive models.
4   On USA models, when removing the right-hand side trailing arm unclip the brake pad wear indicator plug and disconnect it. Also unbolt the earth wire from the backplate.
5   On all models disconnect the hydraulic fluid hose from the trailing

arm and plug it to prevent loss of fluid.
6   Remove the bolts securing the trailing arm to the suspension crossmember noting which way round they are fitted (photos).
7   Disconnect the driveshaft from the stub axle inner flange with reference to Chapter 8 and tie it to one side.
8   Disconnect the stabiliser bar short link arm from the trailing arm by removing the nuts, washers, and bushes.
9   Support the trailing arm then remove the strut lower mounting bolt and withdraw the trailing arm from the car.
10   Examine the arm and bushes for wear and damage. If there is any doubt about the alignment of the trailing arm it should be taken to a BMW dealer for checking on the special jig number 333 000. The bushes may be removed by cutting off the ends and using a suitable metal tube, washers, and a long bolt and nut. When fitting new bushes make sure that the collared ends face away from the trailing arm, and dip the bushes in soapy water to facilitate their fitting.
11   If the trailing arm is to be renewed, remove the wheel bearings as described in Section 14, and also unbolt the backplate from the arm.
12   Refitting is a reversal of removal, but tighten the suspension bolts to the specified torque with the weight of the car on the roadwheels. Adjust the handbrake and bleed the brake hydraulic system as described in Chapter 9.

20 Rear suspension crossmember – removal and refitting

1   The method described in this Section is to remove the complete rear suspension and then to dismantle the various components, although it is possible to remove the components separately by referring to the relevant chapters of the manual.
2   Jack-up the rear of the car and support it on axle stands. Chock the front wheels.
3   Disconnect the handbrake cables from the handbrake lever and underbody with reference to Chapter 9.
4   Unscrew the brake fluid reservoir filler cap and tighten it onto a piece of polythene sheeting. Alternatively use two tapered wooden dowel rods to plug the reservoir outlets on right-hand drive models .

5   On USA models unclip the brake pad wear indicator plug on the right-hand side and disconnect it. Also unbolt the earth wire from the backplate.

6   On all models disconnect the hydraulic fluid hoses from the trailing arms and plug them to prevent loss of fluid.

7   Remove the rear exhaust system as described in Chapter 3.

8   Disconnect the propeller shaft from the final drive with reference to Chapter 7.

9   Adjust the axle stands so that the rear wheels just touch the ground, then support the crossmember and final drive with a trolley jack and wooden beam (see Fig. 11.13).

10   Unscrew the final drive rear mounting bolt.

11   Unscrew the crossmember side strut nuts and bolts and remove the struts (photo).

12   Unscrew and remove the strut lower mounting bolts and disconnect the struts from the trailing arms.

13   Raise the rear of the car and roll out the rear suspension assembly.

14   If necessary remove the final drive with reference to Chapter 8, and the stabiliser and trailing arms with reference to Sections 18 and 19 of this Chapter. Unbolt the mountings from the ends of the crossmember (photo).

15   Refitting is a reversal of removal with reference to the relevant chapters as necessary. Tighten all nuts and bolts to the specified torque, but delay the final tightening of the suspension bolts until the weight of the car is on the roadwheels. Adjust the handbrake and bleed the brake hydraulic system as described in Chapter 9. On completion take the car to a BMW dealer and have the rear wheel alignment checked.

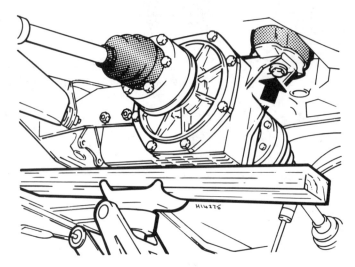

Fig. 11.13 Method of supporting rear suspension assembly. Arrow indicates final drive rear mounting bolt (Sec 20)

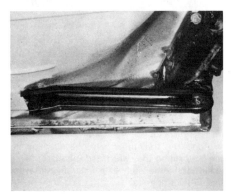

20.11 Rear suspension crossmember side strut

20.14 Rear suspension crossmember mounting bolts (arrowed)

21.1 Removing the steering wheel motif

21 Steering wheel – removal and refitting

1   Turn the front roadwheels to the straight ahead position, then prise the BMW motif (photo) from the centre of the steering wheel with a small screwdriver (late models) or unclip the cover as shown in Fig. 11.14 (early models).

2   Mark the steering wheel and shaft in relation to each other.

3   Unscrew the self-locking nut and pull the steering wheel from the shaft splines (photos).

4   Refitting is a reversal of removal, but tighten the nut to the specified torque.

22 Steering lock – removal and refitting

1   Remove the steering wheel as described in Section 21.

2   Disconnect the battery negative lead.

3   Working inside the car remove the crosshead screws and withdraw the lower facia panel from the bottom of the steering column (photo). Where applicable on USA models disconnect the wires from the electric window automatic cut-out (see also Chapter 5).

4   Unscrew the lower shroud screws, disconnect the wire and withdraw the lower shroud (photos).

5   Remove the crosshead screws and withdraw the indicator and wash/wiper switch.

6   Chisel or drill off the switch panel shear bolts, then remove the grub screw and withdraw the ignition switch.

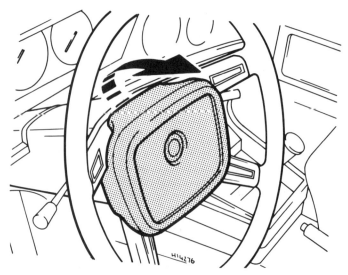

Fig. 11.14 Method of removing the steering wheel cover on early models (Sec 21)

21.3A Unscrew the self-locking nut ...

21.3B ... and remove the steering wheel

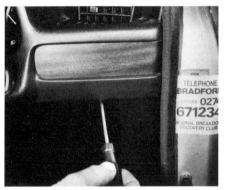

22.3 Removing the lower facia panel

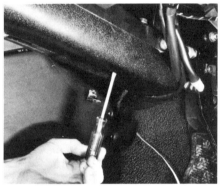

22.4A Remove the crosshead screws ...

22.4B ... and withdraw the lower shroud

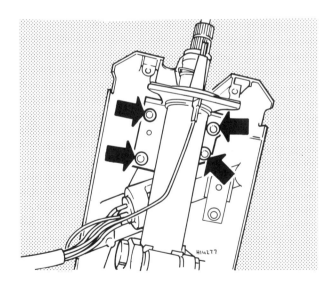

Fig. 11.15 Switch panel shear bolt locations (Sec 22)

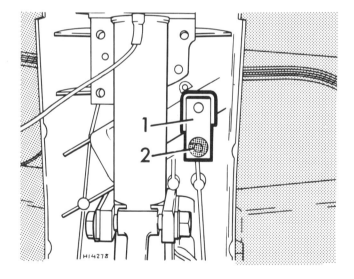

Fig. 11.16 Steering lock plate (1) and shear bolt (2) (Sec 22)

7   Chisel or drill off the shear bolt, remove the lock plate and pull out the steering lock.

8   If necessary the lock cylinder can be removed by using a pointed tool to depress the stop spring. The key number is embossed on a flat on the cylinder.

9   Refitting is a reversal of removal, but check that the lock functions correctly before tightening the shear bolts to break off the heads. Where applicable, adjust the gap shown in Fig. 11.17 to 3 mm (0.118 in) by positioning the indicator switch as necessary with the steering in the straight ahead position.

23 Steering column – removal and refitting

1   Disconnect the battery negative lead.

2   Remove the steering wheel as described in Section 21.

3   Remove the crosshead screws and withdraw the lower facia panel from the bottom of the steering column. Where applicable on USA models disconnect the wires from the electric window automatic cut-out (see also Chapter 5).

4   Unscrew the lower shroud screws, disconnect the wire and

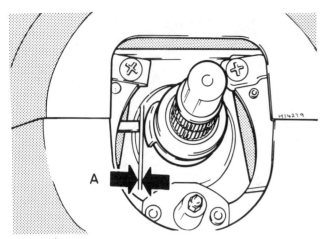

Fig. 11.17 Direction indicator cam adjustment dimension (Sec 22)

A = 3 mm (0.118 in)

withdraw the lower shroud.
5   Remove the crosshead screws and withdraw the indicator and wash/wiper switch.
6   Withdraw the inner column bearing holder followed by the collar, circlip, washer, spring and ring. Note that the stem of the ring faces downward.
7   Disconnect the footbrake pedal return spring and remove the lower column mounting bolts.
8   Disconnect the wiring plugs and horn supply lead.
9   Chisel or drill off the upper column shear bolts.
10   Using an Allen key remove the clamp bolt from the bottom of the inner column.
11   Withdraw the complete column from inside the car.
12   If necessary dismantle the column and renew any components which are worn or damaged. Mark the inner column sections in relation to each other and to the nut to ensure that the sliding torque is maintained.
13   Refitting is a reversal of removal, but make sure that the dimension shown in Fig. 11.20 is as given and tighten all nuts and bolts to the specified torque. The column bottom clamp bolt must engage the cut-out in the shaft.

---

24 Steering column joint – removal and refitting

1   Working in the engine compartment mark the steering shafts in relation to each other.
2   Unscrew the joint disc nuts noting the location of the earth spring.
3   Push up the inner column and remove the disc then unscrew and

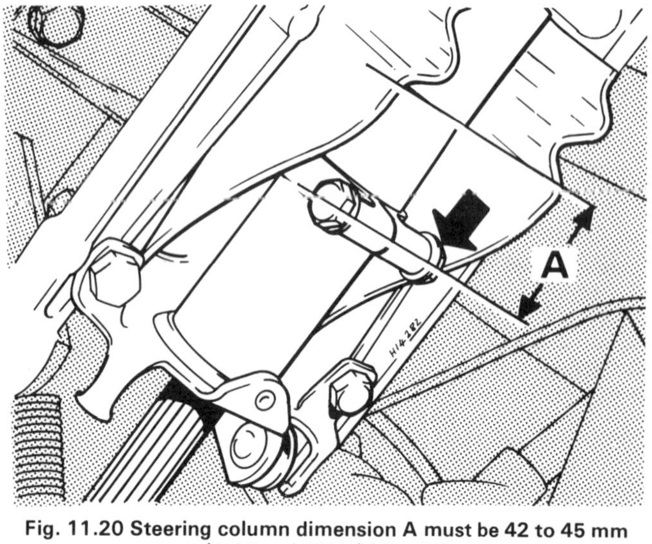

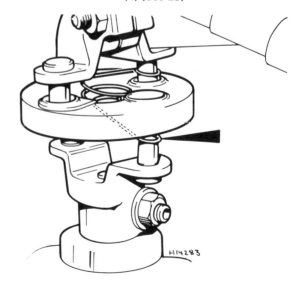

Fig. 11.20 Steering column dimension A must be 42 to 45 mm (1.65 to 1.77 in) (Sec 23)

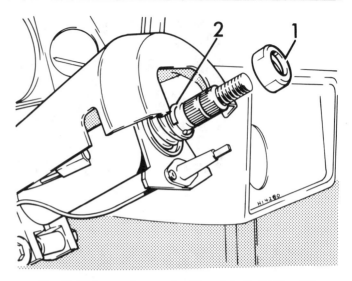

Fig. 11.18 Inner column collar (1) and circlip (2) (Sec 23)

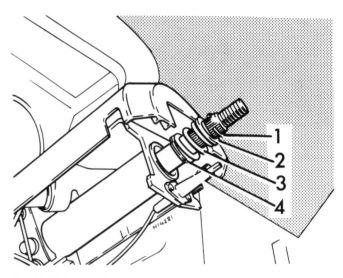

Fig. 11.19 Inner column circlip (1), washer (2), spring (3), and ring (4) (Sec 23)

Fig. 11.21 Dismantling the steering column joint, showing the earth spring (Sec 24)

remove the clamp bolts and slide the joint flanges from the shaft.
4   Refitting is a reversal of removal, but make sure that the clamp bolts engage the cut-outs in the shafts.

25 Steering gear (standard) – removal and refitting

1   Unscrew and remove the clamp bolt securing the joint to the steering gear, and slide the joint flange upwards after marking it in relation to the shaft (photo).
2   Jack-up the front of the car and support it on axle stands. Apply the handbrake and remove the front driver's side roadwheel.
3   Extract the split pin and unscrew the nut securing the track rod to the Pitman arm. Using a balljoint separator tool disconnect the track rod.
4   Unscrew the mounting bolts and lower the steering gear from the car.
5   Refitting is a reversal of removal, but tighten all nuts and bolts to the specified torque. Make sure that the bottom clamp bolt engages the cut-out in the shaft and that the flange adjustment marks are adjacent.

26 Steering gear (standard) – overhaul

1   Remove the steering box as described in Section 25.
2   Remove the steering box level/filler plug, invert the steering box and drain the oil into a suitable receptacle.

3   Bend back the tab washer, undo the nut and using a strong two-legged puller, remove the drop arm.
4   Undo the three bolts and withdraw the steering box cover and roller shaft.
5   Undo the four bolts securing the end cover and lift it away together with the shims.
6   Drive out the worm shaft from the steering box with a plastic headed hammer.
7   Undo the locknut and extract the roller shaft from the steering box cover by screwing the adjuster screw fully inwards (clockwise).
8   Remove the circlip and spacer washer and extract the adjuster screw from the roller shaft.
9   Drive out the two oil seals.
10 Clean all the parts thoroughly, examine them and renew any which are worn, scored or damaged.
11 In order to remove the outer track of the worm shaft bearing which is still inside the steering box housing it will be necessary to use a suitable expanding type extractor. This type of extractor is also needed to remove the needle roller cage bearing in the steering box cover.
12 The needle roller cage bearings in the upper part of the steering box can be extracted using a suitable size stepped drift. When fitting the new roller cage bearings it is essential that the stepped drift used to press the roller cage bearings in is machined precisely to the correct size to prevent damage to the roller cage.
13 Fitting of a new needle cage bearing in the steering box cover can be achieved using the same method as described in paragraph 12.
14 The worm shaft ball races can be drawn off using a suitable two or three-legged puller. Fit the new bearings using a suitable length of pipe.

25.1 Lower steering shaft (shown with engine removed)

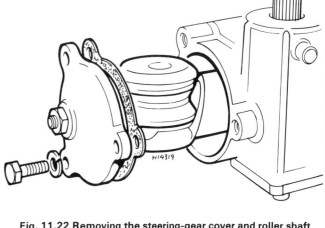

Fig. 11.22 Removing the steering-gear cover and roller shaft (Sec 26)

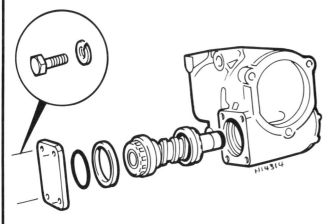

Fig. 11.23 Steering-gear end cover and worm shaft (Sec 26)

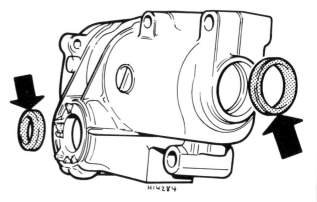

Fig. 11.24 Steering-gear oil seal locations (Sec 26)

15 Reassembly of the steering box can now commence by fitting the outer track of the worm shaft bearing.

16 Fit the oil seals, using a flat piece of wood, to avoid damaging the edges of the seals.

17 The worm shaft can now be slid into position and the outer race of the lower bearing tapped in to locate it.

18 Gather together the shims and cover plate. Note that the cover must have its machined face towards the bottom of the box. Wind a length of cord around the splined end of the worm shaft and pull the cords. As the worm is turning tighten the cover bolts. If the worm seizes, remove the cover and increase the shim thickness. If the shaft turns easily when the cover bolts are fully tightened, check the turning force. This should be between 3 and 4 ounces (85 and 113 gms) only and unless a suitable spring balance is available fit shims so that any endfloat of the shaft or bearings just disappears. The steering box should be filled with oil for this check.

19 Refit the adjuster screw, spacer washer and circlip to the roller shaft. Alter the thickness of the spacer washer if necessary so that there is no more than 0.002 in (0.05 mm) of axial play at the adjusting screw.

20 Carefully screw the threaded adjuster back into the steering box cover and screw on the locknut by a few threads.

21 Ensure that the mating faces of the steering box and the steering box cover are clean and dry. Apply a suitable jointing compound to both mating faces.

22 Before refitting the roller shaft, turn the worm shaft until the datum mark is in alignment with the mark on the steering box.

23 Refit the roller shaft so that its mark is in alignment with the gap between the two datum marks on the steering box casing.

24 Bolt the cover down and then adjust the screw and locknut to provide an endfloat of 0.002 in (0.05 mm) on the roller shaft with the gear in the 'straight-ahead' position.

25 Always align the Pitman arm and roller shaft marks before fitting a new lockplate and screwing on the securing nut to the specified torque.

26 Refit the steering box as described in Section 25 and remember to fill it with oil of the recommended grade.

27 Power steering hydraulic system – bleeding

1 Unscrew the winged nut and remove the cover from the power steering fluid reservoir. Top-up the oil level if necessary to the full mark (photos).

2 Disconnect the coil HT lead from the distributor cap and earth it to the body with a jump lead.

3 Turn the engine on the starter and at the same time keep the reservoir oil level topped-up.

4 When the oil level remains constant refit the HT lead, start the engine and let it idle.

5 Turn the steering wheel quickly from lock to lock until all air bubbles disappear from the reservoir, then finally top-up the level and refit the cover. Switch off the engine.

28 Power steering gear – removal and refitting

1 Jack-up the front of the car and support it on axle stands. Apply the handbrake and remove the driver's side roadwheel.

2 Turn the steering wheel fully to the left, then remove the steering gear drain plug and drain the oil into a suitable container.

3 Unscrew and remove the clamp bolt securing the joint to the steering gear. Mark the joint flange in relation to the shaft then slide the flange upwards.

4 Extract the split pin and unscrew the nut securing the track rod to the Pitman arm. Using a balljoint separator tool disconnect the track rod.

5 Unscrew the union bolts and disconnect the hoses from the steering gear. Hold the bolts, washers, and hose unions together by wrapping masking tape around them.

6 Unscrew the mounting bolts and lower the steering gear from the car.

7 Refitting is a reversal of removal, but tighten all nuts and bolts to the specified torque. Make sure that the bottom clamp bolt locates in the cut-out in the shaft and that the flange alignment marks are adjacent. Bleed the hydraulic system as described in Section 27.

29 Power steering gear – overhaul and adjustment

1 Due to the complexity of this unit and the need for special tools it is not recommended that the owner should attempt to dismantle or repair the steering gear, and should the owner suspect the power steering system to be malfunctioning then it is advisable to arrange for the local BMW dealer to carry out the tests and the necessary remedial action.

2 Adjustment of the sector shaft is, however, possible provided that a means of measuring a torque of 3.5 lbf in (40 Ncm) at the steering wheel is available.

3 Jack-up the front of the car and support it on axle stands. Apply the handbrake and remove the driver's side roadwheel.

4 Place the roadwheels in the straight ahead position then extract the split pin and unscrew the nut securing the track rod to the Pitman arm. Using a balljoint separator tool, disconnect the track rod.

5 Prise the BMW motif from the centre of the steering wheel or on early models unclip the cover.

6 Check that the steering wheel is in the straight ahead position by counting the number of turns to each lock.

7 Locate a socket and suitable extension on the steering wheel retaining nut, turn the steering wheel slightly anti-clockwise, and

27.1A Power steering fluid reservoir showing level mark (arrowed)

27.1B Removing the power steering fluid reservoir cover

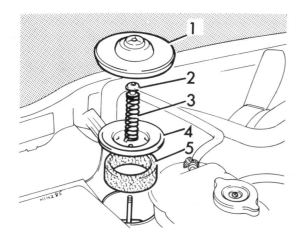

Fig. 11.25 Power steering fluid reservoir filter components (Sec 30)

1	Lid	4	Cover
2	Lockwasher	5	Filter element
3	Spring		

31.3A Power steering pump and front mounting bracket

31.3B Power steering pump rear mounting bolts

check that the frictional torque over the straight ahead position is between 2.6 and 3.5 lbf in (30 and 40 Ncm). If necessary loosen the locknut on the top of the steering gear and turn the adjusting screw to correct the frictional torque.

30 Power steering reservoir filter – renewal

1   Unscrew the wing nut and remove the lid from the power steering fluid reservoir.
2   Remove the spring and cover.
3   Withdraw the filter element and discard it.
4   Fit the new filter element and refit the cover and spring. Make sure that the element is located correctly.
5   Check and if necessary top-up the fluid level then refit the lid and tighten the wiring nut.

31 Power steering pump – removal and refitting

1   Jack-up the front of the car and support it on axle stands. Apply the handbrake.
2   Place a container beneath the power steering pump then unscrew the union nuts and disconnect the hoses. Plug the ends of the hoses.
3   Loosen the mounting bracket bolts at the front and rear, lift the pump, and detach the drivebelt (photos).
4   Remove the mounting bolts and withdraw the pump from the car.
5   If a new pump is to be fitted it will be necessary to transfer the pulley and front mounting bracket from the old unit.
6   Refitting is a reversal of removal, but before tightening the mounting bolts position the pump so that the drivebelt deflects by 5 to 10 mm (0.2 to 0.4 in) under firm thumb pressure midway between the two pulleys. Bleed the hydraulic system as described in Section 27. Make sure that the hoses are clear of the suspension crossmember or any other part of the bodywork which may chafe them.

32 Steering idler – removal and refitting

1   Jack-up the front of the car and support it on axle stands. Apply the handbrake.
2   On USA models remove the complete exhaust system.
3   On all models extract the split pin and unscrew the castellated nut securing the track rod to the idler (photo).
4   Using a balljoint separator disconnect the track rod from the idler.
5   Unscrew the nut from the pivot bolt, extract the bolt, and withdraw the idler arm.
6   If necessary press the special bearings from the idler arm using a long bolt, metal tube, washers and a nut. Use the same method to fit the new bearings. The arm can be checked for damage by checking the dimension shown in Fig. 11.27.

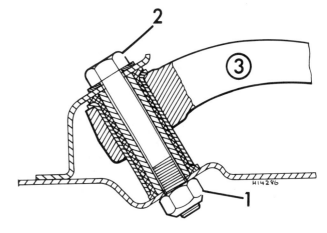

Fig. 11.26 Cross section of the steering idler (Sec 32)

| 1 | Self locking nut | 3 | Idler arm |
| 2 | Pivot bolt | | |

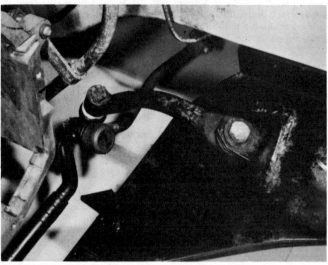

32.3 The steering idler (shown with gearbox removed)

33.2 Removing the split-pin from the track-rod end balljoint

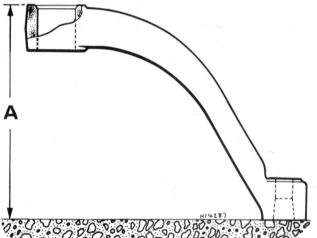

Fig. 11.27 Steering idler arm checking dimension (Sec 32)

A = 143 to 144 mm (5.630 to 5.669 in)

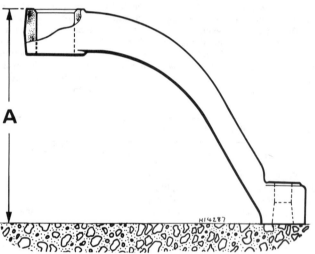

33.3 Using a balljoint separator to disconnect the track-rod end from the steering arm

7   Refitting is a reversal of removal, but lubricate the bearings with oil and tighten the nuts to the specified torque. Always use a new split pin on the castellated nut.

33 Track rod end balljoint – removal and refitting

1   Jack-up the front of the car and support it on axle stands. Apply the handbrake and remove the roadwheel.
2   Extract the split pin and unscrew the balljoint nut (photo).
3   Using a balljoint separator disconnect the track rod end from the steering arm (photo).
4   Mark the adjustment tube in line with the top of the track rod end, then loosen the outer clamp bolt and unscrew the track rod end noting the exact number of turns necessary to remove it (photo).
5   Refitting is a reversal of removal, but tighten the nut and bolt to the specified torque and fit a new split pin. The dimension between balljoint centres should be as shown in Fig. 11.28. Check and if necessary adjust the front wheel alignment as described in Section 34.

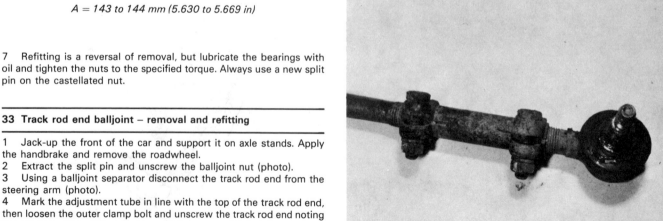

33.4 Track-rod end and adjustment tube

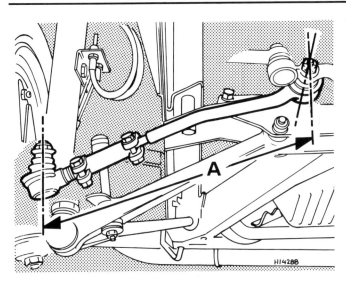

Fig. 11.28 Basic dimension between track-rod balljoint centres (Sec 33)

A = 343 to 363 mm (13.504 to 14.291 in)

34 Wheel alignment – checking and adjustment

1   Accurate wheel alignment is essential for good steering and slow tyre wear. Before checking it make sure that the car is only loaded to kerbside weight, the tyres are correctly inflated, the steering linkage and wheels are in good order, and the wheel bearings are correctly adjusted.

2   Place the car on level ground with the wheels in the straight-ahead position, then roll the car backward 12 ft (4 metres) and forward again.

3   Using a wheel alignment gauge check that the front wheel toe-in dimension is as given in the Specifications.

4   If adjustment is necessary loosen the outer track rod clamp bolts on both sides and turn the tubes by equal amounts. Note that the dimension between the outer track rod balljoint centres on each side should be equal.

5   When the adjustment is correct tighten the clamp bolts.

6   For a complete check of front and rear wheel alignment angles, the car should be taken to a BMW dealer.

35 Roadwheels and tyres – general

1   Clean the insides of the roadwheels whenever they are removed. On steel wheels remove any rust and repaint them; alloy wheels should be checked for corrosion and damage.

2   At the same time remove any flints or stones which may have become embedded in the tyres and examine the tyres for damage and splits. Where the depth of tread is at or near the legal limit, renew them. Note that the standard tyres have special tread patterns and the outer facing side is marked.

3   The wheels should be balanced every 10 000 miles (15 000 km) to compensate for any uneven loss of rubber from the tyres. At the same time they may be interchanged front to rear and rear to front on the same side.

4   Check and adjust the tyre pressures regularly and make sure that the dust caps are correctly fitted. Remember to check the spare tyre at the same time.

36 Fault diagnosis – suspension and steering

Symptom	Reason(s)
Excessive play in steering	Worn steering gear or out of adjustment Worn track rod balljoints Worn track control arm balljoint
Wanders or pulls to one side	Incorrect wheel alignment Worn track-rod or control arm balljoints Uneven tyre pressures Shock absorber faulty
Heavy or stiff steering	Seized balljoint Incorrect wheel alignment Low tyre pressures Lack of lubricant in steering gear Faulty power steering pump
Wheel wobble and vibration	Roadwheels out of balance Roadwheels damaged Worn shock absorbers Worn wheel bearings
Excessive tyre wear	Incorrect wheel alignment Incorrect tyre pressures Roadwheels out of balance Worn shock absorbers

Chapter 12 Bodywork and fittings

For modifications, and information applicable to later models, see Supplement at end of manual

Contents

1 General description

The bodyshell and underframe is of all-steel welded construction and is designed with safety 'cells' at the front and rear of the car, and also a built-in roll bar. Much design and testing work has gone into this design to make this range of models as safe as possible. The models covered by this manual have four door bodywork.

2 Maintenance – bodywork and underframe

1 The general condition of a vehicle's bodywork is the one thing that significantly affects its value. Maintenance is easy but needs to be regular. Neglect, particularly after minor damage, can lead quickly to further deterioration and costly repair bills. It is important also to keep watch on those parts of the vehicle not immediately visible, for instance the underside, inside all the wheel arches and the lower part of the engine compartment.

2 The basic maintenance routine for the bodywork is washing – preferably with a lot of water, from a hose. This will remove all the loose solids which may have stuck to the vehicle. It is important to flush these off in such a way as to prevent grit from scratching the finish. The wheel arches and underframe need washing in the same way to remove any accumulated mud which will retain moisture and tend to encourage rust. Paradoxically enough, the best time to clean the underframe and wheel arches is in wet weather when the mud is thoroughly wet and soft. In very wet weather the underframe is usually cleaned of large accumulations automatically and this is a good time for inspection.

3 Periodically, it is a good idea to have the whole of the underframe of the vehicle steam cleaned, engine compartment included, so that a thorough inspection can be carried out to see what minor repairs and renovations are necessary. Steam cleaning is available at many garages and is necessary for removal of the accumulation of oily grime which sometimes is allowed to become thick in certain areas. If steam cleaning facilities are not available, there are one or two excellent grease solvents available which can be brush applied. The dirt can then be simply hosed off.

4 After washing paintwork, wipe off with a chamois leather to give an unspotted clear finish. A coat of clear protective wax polish will give added protection against chemical pollutants in the air. If the paintwork sheen has dulled or oxidised, use a cleaner/polisher combination to restore the brilliance of the shine. This requires a little effort, but such dulling is usually caused because regular washing has been neglected. Always check that the door and sill drain holes are completely clear so that water can be drained out (photos). Bright work should be treated in the same way as paintwork. Windscreens and windows can be kept clear of the smeary film which often appears, by adding a little ammonia to the water. If they are scratched, a good rub with a proprietary metal polish will often clear them. Never use any form of wax or other body or chromium polish on glass.

3 Maintenance – upholstery and carpets

1 Mats and carpets should be brushed or vacuum cleaned regularly to keep them free of grit. If they are badly stained remove them from the vehicle for scrubbing or sponging and make quite sure they are dry before refitting. Seats and interior trim panels can be kept clean by wiping with a damp cloth. If they do become stained (which can be more apparent on light coloured upholstery) use a little liquid detergent and a soft nail brush to scour the grime out of the grain of the material. Do not forget to keep the headlining clean in the same way as the upholstery. When using liquid cleaners inside the vehicle do not over-wet the surfaces being cleaned. Excessive damp could get into the seams and padded interior causing stains, offensive odours or even rot. If the inside of the vehicle gets wet accidentally it is worthwhile taking some trouble to dry it out properly, particularly where carpets are involved. *Do not leave oil or electric heaters inside the vehicle for this purpose.*

4 Minor body damage – repair

The photographic sequences on pages 230 and 231 illustrate the operations detailed in the following sub-sections.

Repair of minor scratches in bodywork

If the scratch is very superficial, and does not penetrate to the metal of the bodywork, repair is very simple. Lightly rub the area of the scratch with a paintwork renovator, or a very fine cutting paste, to remove loose paint from the scratch and to clear the surrounding bodywork of wax polish. Rinse the area with clean water.

2.4A Clearing a door drain hole with wire

2.4B Clearing a sill drain hole with wire

Apply touch-up paint to the scratch using a fine paint brush; continue to apply fine layers of paint until the surface of the paint in the scratch is level with the surrounding paintwork. Allow the new paint at least two weeks to harden: then blend it into the surrounding paintwork by rubbing the scratch area with a paintwork renovator or a very fine cutting paste. Finally, apply wax polish.

Where the scratch has penetrated right through to the metal of the bodywork, causing the metal to rust, a different repair technique is required. Remove any loose rust from the bottom of the scratch with a penknife, then apply rust inhibiting paint to prevent the formation of rust in the future. Using a rubber or nylon applicator fill the scratch with bodystopper paste. If required, this paste can be mixed with cellulose thinners to provide a very thin paste which is ideal for filling narrow scratches. Before the stopper-paste in the scratch hardens, wrap a piece of smooth cotton rag around the top of a finger. Dip the finger in cellulose thinners and then quickly sweep it across the surface of the stopper-paste in the scratch; this will ensure that the surface of the stopper-paste is slightly hollowed. The scratch can now be painted over as described earlier in this Section.

Repair of dents in bodywork

When deep denting of the vehicle's bodywork has taken place, the first task is to pull the dent out, until the affected bodywork almost attains its original shape. There is little point in trying to restore the original shape completely, as the metal in the damaged area will have stretched on impact and cannot be reshaped fully to its original contour. It is better to bring the level of the dent up to a point which is about $\frac{1}{8}$ in (3 mm) below the level of the surrounding bodywork. In cases where the dent is very shallow anyway, it is not worth trying to pull it out at all. If the underside of the dent is accessible, it can be hammered out gently from behind, using a mallet with a wooden or plastic head. Whilst doing this, hold a suitable block of wood firmly against the outside of the panel to absorb the impact from the hammer blows and thus prevent a large area of the bodywork from being 'belled-out'.

Should the dent be in a section of the bodywork which has a double skin or some other factor making it inaccessible from behind, a different technique is called for. Drill several small holes through the metal inside the area – particularly in the deeper section. Then screw long self-tapping screws into the holes just sufficiently for them to gain a good purchase in the metal. Now the dent can be pulled out by pulling on the protruding heads of the screws with a pair of pliers.

The next stage of the repair is the removal of the paint from the damaged area, and from an inch or so of the surrounding 'sound' bodywork. This is accomplished most easily by using a wire brush or abrasive pad on a power drill, although it can be done just as effectively by hand using sheets of abrasive paper. To complete the preparation for filling, score the surface of the bare metal with a screwdriver or the tang of a file, or alternatively, drill small holes in the affected area. This will provide a really good 'key' for the filler paste.

To complete the repair see the Section on filling and re-spraying.

Repair of rust holes or gashes in bodywork

Remove all paint from the affected area and from an inch or so of the surrounding 'sound' bodywork, using an abrasive pad or a wire brush on a power drill. If these are not available a few sheets of abrasive paper will do the job just as effectively. With the paint removed you will be able to gauge the severity of the corrosion and therefore decide whether to renew the whole panel (if this is possible) or to repair the affected area. New body panels are not as expensive as most people think and it is often quicker and more satisfactory to fit a new panel than to attempt to repair large areas of corrosion.

Remove all fittings from the affected area except those which will act as a guide to the original shape of the damaged bodywork (eg headlamp shells etc). Then, using tin snips or a hacksaw blade, remove all loose metal and any other metal badly affected by corrosion. Hammer the edges of the hole inwards in order to create a slight depression for the filler paste.

Wire brush the affected area to remove the powdery rust from the surface of the remaining metal. Paint the affected area with rust inhibiting paint; if the back of the rusted area is accessible treat this also.

Before filling can take place it will be necessary to block the hole in some way. This can be achieved by the use of zinc gauze or aluminium tape.

Zinc gauze is probably the best material to use for a large hole. Cut a piece to the approximate size and shape of the hole to be filled, then position it in the hole so that its edges are below the level of the surrounding bodywork. It can be retained in position by several blobs of filler paste around its periphery.

Aluminium tape should be used for small or very narrow holes. Pull a piece off the roll and trim it to the approximate size and shape required, then pull off the backing paper (if used) and stick the tape over the hole; it can be overlapped if the thickness of one piece is insufficient. Burnish down the edges of the tape with the handle of a screwdriver or similar, to ensure that the tape is securely attached to the metal underneath.

Bodywork repairs – filling and re-spraying

Before using this Section, see the Sections on dent, deep scratch, rust holes and gash repairs.

Many types of bodyfiller are available, but generally speaking those proprietary kits which contain a tin of filler paste and a tube of resin hardener are best for this type of repair. A wide, flexible plastic or nylon applicator will be found invaluable for imparting a smooth and well contoured finish to the surface of the filler.

Mix up a little filler on a clean piece of card or board – measure the hardener carefully (follow the maker's instructions on the pack) otherwise the filler will set too rapidly or too slowly.

Using the applicator apply the filler paste to the prepared area;

draw the applicator across the surface of the filler to achieve the correct contour and to level the filler surface. As soon as a contour that approximates to the correct one is achieved, stop working the paste – if you carry on too long the paste will become sticky and begin to 'pick up' on the applicator. Continue to add thin layers of filler paste at twenty-minute intervals until the level of the filler is just proud of the surrounding bodywork.

Once the filler has hardened, excess can be removed using a metal plane or file. From then on, progressively finer grades of abrasive paper should be used, starting with a 40 grade production paper and finishing with 400 grade wet-and-dry paper. Always wrap the abrasive paper around a flat rubber, cork, or wooden block — otherwise the surface of the filler will not be completely flat. During the smoothing of the filler surface the wet-and-dry paper should be periodically rinsed in water. This will ensure that a very smooth finish is imparted to the filler at the final stage.

At this stage the 'dent' should be surrounded by a ring of bare metal, which in turn should be encircled by the finely 'feathered' edge of the good paintwork. Rinse the repair area with clean water, until all of the dust produced by the rubbing-down operation has gone.

Spray the whole repair area with a light coat of primer – this will show up any imperfections in the surface of the filler. Repair these imperfections with fresh filler paste or bodystopper, and once more smooth the surface with abrasive paper. If bodystopper is used, it can be mixed with cellulose thinners to form a really thin paste which is ideal for filling small holes. Repeat this spray and repair procedure until you are satisfied that the surface of the filler, and the feathered edge of the paintwork are perfect. Clean the repair area with clean water and allow to dry fully.

The repair area is now ready for final spraying. Paint spraying must be carried out in a warm, dry, windless and dust free atmosphere. This condition can be created artificially if you have access to a large indoor working area, but if you are forced to work in the open, you will have to pick your day very carefully. If you are working indoors, dousing the floor in the work area with water will help to settle the dust which would otherwise be in the atmosphere. If the repair area is confined to one body panel, mask off the surrounding panels; this will help to minimise the effects of a slight mis-match in paint colours. Bodywork fittings (eg chrome strips, door handles etc) will also need to be masked off. Use genuine masking tape and several thicknesses of newspaper for the masking operations.

Before commencing to spray, agitate the aerosol can thoroughly, then spray a test area (an old tin, or similar) until the technique is mastered. Cover the repair area with a thick coat of primer; the thickness should be built up using several thin layers of paint rather than one thick one. Using 400 grade wet-and-dry paper, rub down the surface of the primer until it is really smooth. While doing this, the work area should be thoroughly doused with water, and the wet-and-dry paper periodically rinsed in water. Allow to dry before spraying on more paint.

Spray on the top coat, again building up the thickness by using several thin layers of paint. Start spraying in the centre of the repair area and then, using a circular motion, work outwards until the whole repair area and about 2 inches of the surrounding original paintwork is covered. Remove all masking material 10 to 15 minutes after spraying on the final coat of paint.

Allow the new paint at least two weeks to harden, then, using a paintwork renovator or a very fine cutting paste, blend the edges of the paint into the existing paintwork. Finally, apply wax polish.

5 Major body damage – repair

Where serious damage has occurred or large areas need renewal due to neglect, it means certainly that completely new sections or panels will need welding in and this is best left to professionals. If the damage is due to impact, it will also be necessary to completely check the alignment of the bodyshell structure. Due to the principle of construction, the strength and shape of the whole car can be affected by damage to one part. In such instances the services of a BMW agent with specialist checking jigs are essential. If a body is left misaligned, it is first of all dangerous as the car will not handle properly, and secondly uneven stresses will be imposed on the steering, engine and transmission, causing abnormal wear or complete failure. Tyre wear may also be excessive.

6 Maintenance – hinges and locks

1   Every 10 000 miles (15 000 km) on UK models or 12 500 miles (20 000 km) on USA models tighten the hinge mounting bolts for the bonnet, bootlid and doors and also lubricate the hinges with a little engine oil. Smear a little multi-purpose grease around the door strikers, also on the bonnet and bootlid catches.
2   At the same time check the doors for correct operation and alignment and adjust them if necessary.
3   Do not attempt to lubricate the steering lock.

7 Door rattles – tracing and rectification

1   Check first that the door is not loose at the hinges and that the latch is holding the door firmly in position. Check also that the door lines up with the aperture in the body.
2   If the hinges are loose or the door is out of alignment it will be necessary to reset the hinge positions, as described in Sections 12 and 17.
3   If the latch is holding the door properly it should hold the door tightly when fully latched and the door should line up with the body. If it is out of alignment it needs adjustment. If loose, some part of the lock mechanism must be worn out and requiring renewal.
4   Other rattles from the door would be caused by wear or looseness in the window winder, the glass channels and sill strips or the door buttons and interior latch release mechanism.

8 Door lock (front door) – removal, refitting and adjusting

1   With the window shut, note the position of the window winder regulator handle. Prise out the plastic insert (photo), remove the screw (photo), and pull off the handle together with the washer and spring.
2   Remove the screw under the top end of the armrest and lift off the cover. Remove the exposed top screw and the base screws and withdraw the armrest (photos).
3   Twist the interior door handle plastic insert to one side, remove the screw, and withdraw the handle and washer (photos).
4   Where applicable prise the rear of the door mirror control from the trim panel, withdraw the control rearward, and disconnect the multi-plug (photo).
5   Unscrew the locking button and remove the two trim panel upper crosshead screws (photos).
6   Using a wide blade screwdriver carefully prise the trim panel and retaining clips from the door.
7   Lift the trim panel over the locking rod and withdraw it (photo).
8   Remove the plastic sheeting to expose the door lock (photo).
9   On pre-September 1977 models unscrew the nut and withdraw the lock cylinder noting the location of the metal, plastic, and rubber washers.
10 On September 1977-on models slide out the retaining clamp, disconnect the rod from the door lock, and withdraw the lock cylinder noting the position of the washers (photo).
11 On all models remove the upper cover and slacken the guide channel screw(s) located on the rear edge of the door.
12 Remove the two screws and withdraw the guide pad and plate. An Allen key will be required on later versions (photo).
13 Remove the lock retaining screws then disconnect the remote control rod or central locking switch (as applicable) (photo).
14 Withdraw the lock through the door aperture.
15 Refitting is a reversal of removal, but note that the window regulator handle should face forward with the window shut and the spring large diameter should face the trim panel. With the door shut the outer door panel rear edge should protrude from the rear door panel front edge by 1.0 mm (0.040 in). If not, loosen the striker screws on the door pillar and reposition the striker as necessary. Do not remove the screws otherwise the inside plate will drop down inside the pillar, and it will be necessary to remove the pillar trim.

9 Front door outer handle – removal and refitting

1   Remove the two crosshead screws located under the handle and withdraw the handle.

8.1A Remove the window regulator handle insert ...

8.1B ... and retaining screw

8.2A Remove the armrest top cover ...

8.2B ... and top mounting screw

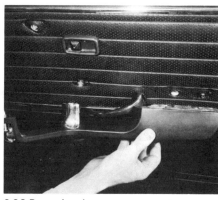

8.2C Removing the armrest

8.3A Twist the interior door handle insert to one side ...

8.3B ... and remove the retaining screw

8.4 Removing the door mirror control

8.5A Removing the locking button ...

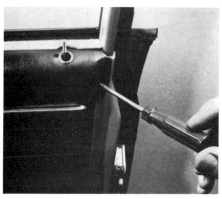

8.5B ... and upper trim panel screws

8.7 Removing the front door trim panel

8.8 The front door with trim panel and plastic sheeting removed

8.10 Front door lock cylinder retaining clamp (arrowed)

8.12 Front door lock retaining screws, and guide pad

8.13 Inner view of the front door lock

9.3 Inner view of the front door outer handle

10.2 Window regulator retaining bolt locations on the front door

11.3 Front door glass lifting rail and running rail components

11.5 Front door glass running rail lower bolt location

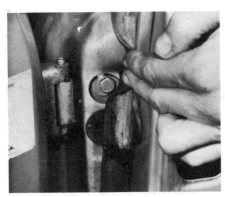

12.2 Front door upper hinge bolt location

12.3 Front door check strap

12.4 Front door lower hinge bolt location

2 Remove the interior door trim with reference to Section 8.
3 Unscrew the two self-locking nuts and withdraw the lock operating mechanism through the door aperture (photo).
4 Refitting is a reversal of removal.

10 Front door window regulator – removal and refitting

1 Remove the interior door trim with reference to Section 8.
2 With the window shut unscrew the four regulator retaining bolts (photo).
3 Hold the window then detach the regulator from the door inner skin and slide the operating arm along the lifting rod until it can be pulled through the large hole.
4 Withdraw the regulator through the door aperture.
5 Refitting is a reversal of removal, but lubricate the lifting rail with multi-purpose grease, and when inserting the operating arm make sure that the plastic discs are located on each side of the lifting rail.

11 Front door glass – removal and refitting

1 Remove the interior door trim with reference to Section 8.
2 Remove the screws and withdraw the inner sill strip then pull out the seal.
3 Position the glass so that the lifting rail is exposed in the inner skin aperture. Support the glass and unscrew the bolts retaining the lifting rail to the running rail. Remove the brackets noting the location of any shims (photo).
4 With the glass held about 17 mm (7 in) from the top of the door tilt it forward and disconnect the lifting rail from the operating arm. The glass can now be lifted from the door but take care not to scratch it on the surround.
5 Refitting is a reversal of removal, but adjust the window as follows. Loosen the running rail upper and lower bolts (photo) and position the rail so that the top edge of the window glass is parallel to the top edge of the door frame. Tighten the bolts. With the lifting rail bolts loose turn the bracket so that both pads are contacting the sliding rail then tighten the bolts. Where a stop bracket is fitted to the lifting rail adjust it so that the glass is stopped just before the upper channel.

12 Front door – removal, refitting and adjusting

1 Remove the interior door trim with reference to Section 8.
2 Support the front door on wooden blocks then unscrew the upper hinge bolts from the door. Pull back the weatherstrip if necessary (photo).
3 Using a suitable punch drive the check strap pin out from the pillar in an upward direction (photo).
4 Unscrew the lower hinge bolts and withdraw the door from the car (photo). Note the location of any shims fitted between the hinges and the door.
5 Refitting is a reversal of removal, but if necessary insert shims between the hinges and the door so that the door front edge is 1.0 mm (0.040 in) below the level of the front wing. Adjust the striker as described in Section 8.

13 Door lock (rear door) – removal, refitting and adjusting

1 Twist the interior door handle plastic insert to one side, remove the screw, and withdraw the handle and washer.
2 Unscrew the locking button.
3 With the window shut note the position of the window winder regulator handle. Prise out the plastic insert, remove the screw, and pull off the handle together with the washer and spring.
4 Press the top and bottom of the armrest cover, slide it back, and remove the front mounting screw. Remove the base screws and withdraw the armrest.
5 Remove the ashtray and unscrew the crosshead screws.
6 Remove the two trim panel upper crosshead screws.
7 On USA models fitted with electric windows prise out the switch and disconnect the plug.

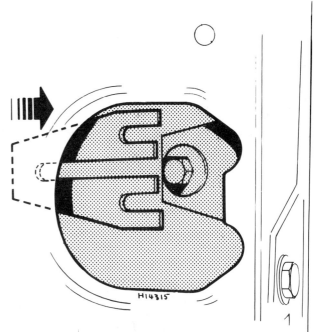

Fig. 12.1 Hinge shim location on the front door (Sec 12)

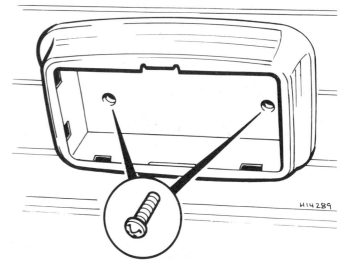

Fig. 12.2 Rear door trim panel screw locations behind the ashtray (Sec 13)

8 On all models use a wide blade screwdriver to prise the trim panel and retaining clips from the door.
9 Lift the trim panel over the locking rod and withdraw it.
10 Remove the plastic sheeting to expose the door lock.
11 Remove the two screws and withdraw the guide pad and plate.
12 Remove the lock retaining screws then disconnect the lock connecting rod.
13 On USA models fitted with electric windows remove the switch retaining screws, disconnect the linkage, and move the switch to one side.
14 On all models disconnect the remote control rod and withdraw the lock through the door aperture.
15 Refitting is a reversal of removal, but note that the window regulator handle should face forward with the window shut and the spring large diameter should face the trim panel. On USA models check that the switch is the correct way up before fitting it. With the door shut the outer door panel rear edge should be level with the rear wing panel. If not, loosen the striker screws on the rear pillar and reposition the striker as necessary. The striker can be completely removed if necessary as the mounting plate is welded in position.

This photographic sequence shows the steps taken to repair the dent and paintwork damage shown above. In general, the procedure for repairing a hole will be similar; where there are substantial differences, the procedure is clearly described and shown in a separate photograph.

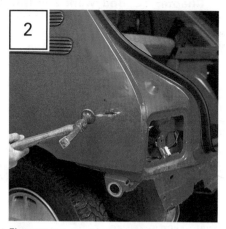

First remove any trim around the dent, then hammer out the dent where access is possible. This will minimise filling. Here, after the large dent has been hammered out, the damaged area is being made slightly concave.

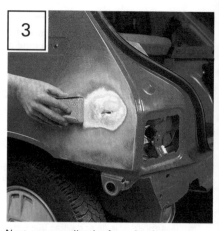

Next, remove all paint from the damaged area by rubbing with coarse abrasive paper or using a power drill fitted with a wire brush or abrasive pad. 'Feather' the edge of the boundary with good paintwork using a finer grade of abrasive paper.

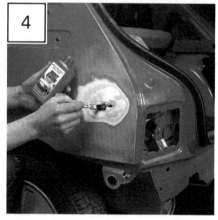

Where there are holes or other damage, the sheet metal should be cut away before proceeding further. The damaged area and any signs of rust should be treated with Turtle Wax Hi-Tech Rust Eater, which will also inhibit further rust formation.

For a large dent or hole mix Holts Body Plus Resin and Hardener according to the manufacturer's instructions and apply around the edge of the repair. Press Glass Fibre Matting over the repair area and leave for 20-30 minutes to harden. Then ...

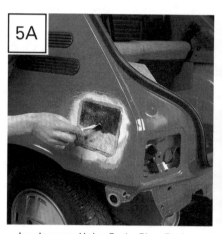

... brush more Holts Body Plus Resin and Hardener onto the matting and leave to harden. Repeat the sequence with two or three layers of matting, checking that the final layer is lower than the surrounding area. Apply Holts Body Plus Filler Paste as shown in Step 5B.

For a medium dent, mix Holts Body Plus Filler Paste and Hardener according to the manufacturer's instructions and apply it with a flexible applicator. Apply thin layers of filler at 20-minute intervals, until the filler surface is slightly proud of the surrounding bodywork.

For small dents and scratches use Holts No Mix Filler Paste straight from the tube. Apply it according to the instructions in thin layers, using the spatula provided. It will harden in minutes if applied outdoors and may then be used as its own knifing putty.

Use a plane or file for initial shaping. Then, using progressively finer grades of wet-and-dry paper, wrapped round a sanding block, and copious amounts of clean water, rub down the filler until glass smooth. 'Feather' the edges of adjoining paintwork.

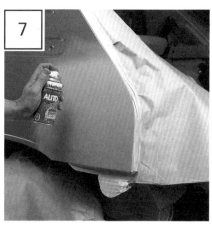

Protect adjoining areas before spraying the whole repair area and at least one inch of the surrounding sound paintwork with Holts Dupli-Color primer.

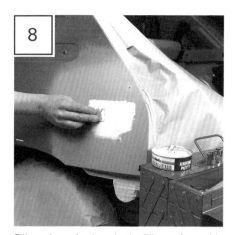

Fill any imperfections in the filler surface with a small amount of Holts Body Plus Knifing Putty. Using plenty of clean water, rub down the surface with a fine grade wet-and-dry paper – 400 grade is recommended – until it is really smooth.

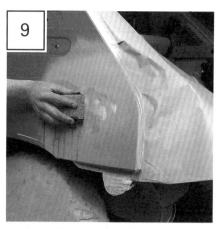

Carefully fill any remaining imperfections with knifing putty before applying the last coat of primer. Then rub down the surface with Holts Body Plus Rubbing Compound to ensure a really smooth surface.

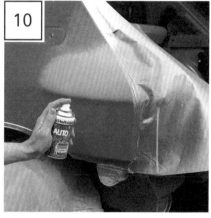

Protect surrounding areas from overspray before applying the topcoat in several thin layers. Agitate Holts Dupli-Color aerosol thoroughly. Start at the repair centre, spraying outwards with a side-to-side motion.

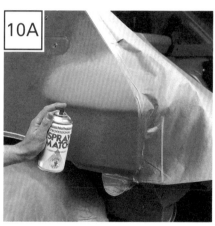

If the exact colour is not available off the shelf, local Holts Professional Spraymatch Centres will custom fill an aerosol to match perfectly.

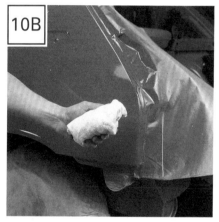

To identify whether a lacquer finish is required, rub a painted unrepaired part of the body with wax and a clean cloth.

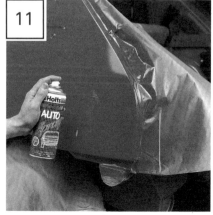

If *no* traces of paint appear on the cloth, spray Holts Dupli-Color clear lacquer over the repaired area to achieve the correct gloss level.

The paint will take about two weeks to harden fully. After this time it can be 'cut' with a mild cutting compound such as Turtle Wax Minute Cut prior to polishing with a final coating of Turtle Wax Extra.

When carrying out bodywork repairs, remember that the quality of the finished job is proportional to the time and effort expended.

14 Rear door outer handle – removal and refitting

1   Remove the two crosshead screws located under the handle and withdraw the handle.
2   Remove the interior door trim panel with reference to Section 13.
3   Unscrew the two self-locking nuts and withdraw the lock operating mechanism through the door aperture.
4   Refitting is a reversal of removal.

15 Rear door window regulator – removal and refitting

1   Remove the interior door trim panel with reference to Section 13.
2   With the window shut unscrew the three regulator retaining bolts.
3   Hold the window then detach the regulator from the door inner skin and slide the operating arm along the lifting rail until it can be pulled through the large hole.
4   Withdraw the regulator through the door aperture.
5   Refitting is a reversal of removal, but lubricate the lifting rail with multi-purpose grease, and when inserting the operating arm make sure that the plastic discs are located on each side of the lifting rail.

16 Rear door glass – removal and refitting

1   Remove the window outer moulding strip. To do this loosen the strip with a wooden wedge beginning at the rear.
2   Remove the interior door trim (Section 13) and upper moulding (4 screws).
3   Remove the window seal noting that the brush side faces the glass.
4   Position the glass so that the lifting rail is exposed in the inner skin aperture. Support the glass and unscrew the bolts. Remove the bracket and sliding pads.
5   Remove the window rear guide channel screws and where fitted the upper mounting screws. Remove the channel and guide, noting the location of any shims.
6   Lower the window and disconnect the operating arm from the lifting rail. The glass can now be lifted from the door, but take care not to scratch it.
7   Refitting is a reversal of removal, but fit the shims where necessary to position the guides against the outer panel. Adjust the door glass as follows. Loosen the running rail upper and lower bolts and position the rail so that the window moves smoothly within the channels. Tighten the bolts. With the lifting rail bolts loose, centralise the bracket over the sliding rail then tighten the bolts.

17 Rear door – removal, refitting and adjusting

1   Remove the interior door trim panel with reference to Section 13. Close the window.
2   Using a suitable punch drive the check strap pin out from the pillar in an upward direction.
3   Support the rear door on wooden blocks.
4   Working through the inner skin apertures unscrew the upper and lower hinge bolts from the door. Note the location of any shims fitted between the hinges and the door.
5   Refitting is a reversal of removal, but if necessary insert shims between the hinges and the door so that the door panel is level with the lower sill. Before finally tightening the hinge bolts make sure that the door is centralised when shut. Adjust the striker as described in Section 13.

18 Windscreen and rear window – removal and refitting

1   It is recommended that both these operations are left to professionals. Where the work is attempted however proceed in the following way.
2   Remove the wiper arms and the interior mirror or disconnect the leads from the heated rear window as appropriate.
3   Prise the trim strip from the rubber surround.
4   Run a blade around the lips of the rubber surround to ensure that

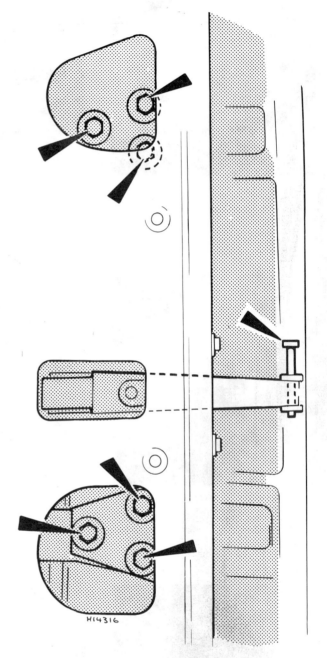

H14316

**Fig. 12.3 Rear door hinge bolt and check strap pin locations
(Sec 17)**

it is not stuck to the body.
5   Have an assistant press one corner of the glass outwards while you pull the lip of the rubber over the body flange and restrain the glass from being ejected violently. This pressure is best applied by sitting inside the car and, wearing soft soled shoes, placing the feet against one corner of the glass. To prevent scratching the glass place a piece of soft cloth between the soles of the shoes and the windscreen.
6   Unless the rubber surround is perfect, renew it. Apply black mastic or sealant to the glass channel in the rubber surround and fit the surround to the glass. It is recommended that the rubber trim strip is fitted at this stage.
7   Locate a length of cord in the rubber surround, in the groove which will engage with the body. Allow the ends of the cord to cross over and hang out of the groove at the bottom of the glass.
8   Offer up the glass and surround to the body aperture engaging the bottom groove. Push the glass downwards and inwards and have your

assistant pull the ends of the cord evenly which will have the effect of pulling the lip of the surround over the body flange.

9   If necessary the nozzle of a mastic gun can be inserted under the outer lip of the rubber surround and a bead of sealant applied all round to make a positive seal. Clean off any surplus sealant according to the manufacturer's instructions and then refit the wiper arms and interior mirror or connect the heater element on the rear window.

19 Bonnet lid – removal and refitting

1   Open the bonnet and mark around the position of the hinges with a pencil.

2   Remove the right-hand headlight rear cover and disconnect the engine compartment light wire from the loom.

3   Disconnect the windscreen washer hose at the front of the engine compartment (photo).

4   Have an assistant support the bonnet then unscrew the nuts from the bottom of the stays on each side and remove the washers and stays. Unhook the stays from the springs (photo).

5   While supporting the bonnet unscrew the bolts securing the brackets to the bonnet and withdraw the bonnet from the car (photo).

6   Refitting is a reversal of removal, but note that spring washers must be located between the stays and the body. When shut, the bonnet should be correctly aligned with the front wings and bulkhead.

If necessary loosen the hinge bolts, reposition the bonnet, and retighten the bolts. The rear edge of the bonnet can be centralised across the car by adjusting the rear runner holders. Adjust the rubber buffers so that the bonnet is held firmly.

20 Bonnet lock – removal, refitting and adjusting

1   Remove the left-hand side radiator grille as described in Section 21. Open the bonnet.

2   Mark the position of the lock bolts with a pencil then unscrew and remove them (photo).

3   Remove the headlight rear cover and withdraw the lock together with the cable.

4   Unscrew the clamp bolt and remove the lock from the cable.

5   If necessary unbolt the striker from the bonnet after marking its location with a pencil.

6   Refitting is a reversal of removal, but adjust the cable, before installing it. To do this push the operating lever inside the car fully forward and put the lock levers in the locked position. On early models insert a dowel rod through the hole shown in Fig. 12.4 – use a screw on later models. With the outer cable inserted in the lock tighten the clamp bolt onto the inner cable. The striker should be adjusted so that it is aligned with the lock.

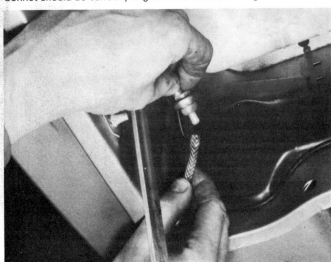

19.3 Disconnecting the windscreen washer hose to remove the bonnet

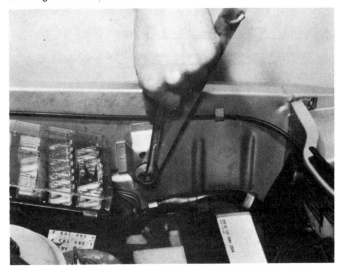

19.4 Removing the bonnet side stays

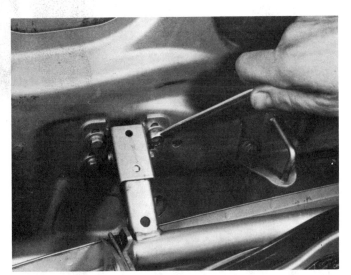

19.5 Removing the bonnet bracket bolts

20.2 The bonnet lock

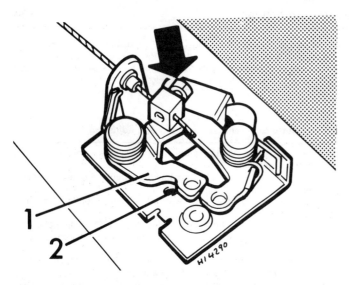

Fig. 12.4 Bonnet lock showing locking lever (1), setting hole (2), and clamp bolt (arrowed) (Sec 20)

21.5A Removing the screws ...

Fig. 12.5 Radiator grille centre section screw locations (Sec 21)

21.5B ... and the radiator grille side section

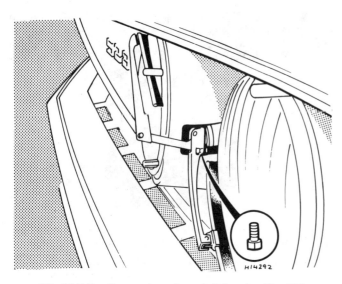

Fig. 12.6 Headlamp wiper clamp bolt location (Sec 21)

22.1 The boot lid hinge

21 Radiator grille – removal and refitting

Centre section
1   Open the bonnet and remove the two crosshead screws from the top of the grille centre section.
2   Lift the centre section from the car.
3   Refitting is a reversal of removal.

Side section
4   Open the bonnet. On cars with a headlamp wash/wipe system unscrew the clamp bolt and remove the double wiper arms and blades.
5   Remove the screws and withdraw the side section from the car (photos).
6   Refitting is a reversal of removal, but on cars with a headlamp wash/wipe system check that the wiper blades do not move past the stops. If necessary adjust the position of the arms on the shaft.

22 Bootlid – removal and refitting

1   Open the bootlid and mark around the position of the hinges with a pencil (photo).
2   Disconnect the boot illumination light wire at the connecting plug.
3   Have an assistant support the bootlid then unscrew the hinge bolts and withdraw the bootlid from the car.
4   Refitting is a reversal of removal. When shut the bootlid should be correctly aligned with the rear wings and have equal gaps on each side. If necessary loosen the hinge bolts, reposition the bootlid, and retighten the bolts. Adjust the rubber buffers on the underside of the bootlid so that the bootlid is held firmly when shut; the buffers can be turned with a large screwdriver.

23 Bootlid lock – removal, refitting and adjusting

1   Open the bootlid and remove the inner trim panel. On early models it is secured with screws, but on later models it is secured with plastic caps and spring clips.
2   Mark the position of the lock bolts with a pencil then unscrew the two bolts and withdraw the lower catch.
3   Using BMW tool 512050 remove the threaded ring and sleeve or on later models remove the bolts. Withdraw the bootlid lock.
4   If necessary mark the position of the upper catch on the bootlid then unbolt it (photo).
5   Refitting is a reversal of removal, but if necessary adjust the upper and lower catches so that the bootlid is level with the rear wings and the catches are aligned.

24 Bumpers – removal and refitting

Front
1   On UK models disconnect the wiring plugs from the rear of the direction indicator lamps.
2   On all models remove the nuts or screws securing the bumper side sections to the front wings.
3   Unscrew the front bracket nuts and withdraw the front bumper.
4   Check the condition of the mounting pads where fitted. If necessary remove the rubber strips and separate the two side sections from the centre section. On USA models the impact absorbers may be removed by unbolting the bumper brackets and removing the clamp and mounting bolts.
5   Refitting is a reversal of removal.

Rear
6   Open the bootlid and remove the inner trim panel. On early models it is secured with screws, but on later models it is secured with plastic caps and spring clips. Remove the car jack.
7   Remove the nuts or bolts securing the bumper side sections to the rear wings.
8   Remove the nuts or bolts retaining the bumper to the rear panel (UK models) or impact absorbers (USA models), and withdraw the rear bumper.
9   Check the condition of the mounting pads where fitted. If

23.4 The boot lid catch

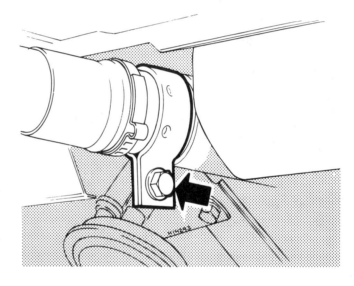

Fig. 12.7 Front bumper impact absorber clamp bolt location on USA models (Sec 24)

necessary remove the rubber strips and separate the two side sections from the centre section. On USA models the impact absorbers may be removed by unbolting the bumper brackets and removing the clamp and mounting bolts. Note that one bolt is located by removing the edge guard and seal.
10 Refitting is a reversal of removal.

25 Rear view mirror – removal and refitting

1   The interior mirror is removed by pulling towards the rear of the car, and, at the same time, bending it upwards.
2   Refitting is the reverse of the removal operation.

26 Centre tray – removal and refitting

1   Remove the crosshead screws and withdraw the lower facia panel from the bottom of the steering column. Where applicable on USA models disconnect the wires from the electric window automatic cut-out (see also Chapter 5).

Pre-January 1977 models

2   Remove the crosshead screw from each side of the tray, and on manual gearbox models unscrew and remove the gear lever knob. Remove the tray floor and the gear lever cover.

3   On automatic transmission models remove the right-hand selector lever cover (2 screws) and the tray bottom bracket nut.

4   Withdraw the centre tray to the rear, after engaging 4th gear on manual gearbox models.

5   Refitting is a reversal of removal.

January 1977-on models

6   Remove the crosshead screws from each side of the tray (photo), and on manual gearbox models unscrew and remove the gear lever knob. Remove the gear lever cover and rubber boot.

7   On automatic transmission models remove the right-hand selector cover (2 screws), and remove the surround (photos).

8   Remove the ashtray.

9   On UK models remove the screws securing the tray surround to the facia, then lift the tray floor and unscrew the bracket nut. Pull the tray rearward, remove the tray floor, and withdraw the bracket (2 screws).

10   On models with air conditioning bend up the holder in the ashtray aperture and remove the element. Disconnect the holder and bulb, remove the exposed nuts, and withdraw the bracket. Remove the radio or blanking plate, then remove the screws securing the tray surround

to the facia.

11   Disconnect the battery negative lead then disconnect the wires from the heated rear window switch, cigar lighter, and radio controls (where applicable).

12   Withdraw the centre tray to the rear.

13   Refitting is a reversal of removal.

27 Glovebox – removal and refitting

1   Open the glovebox and remove the screws securing the stays and backcloth.

2   Disconnect the return spring and unbolt the hinge (photo). Withdraw the glovebox from the car.

3   If necessary extract the clip, press out the pins, and remove the stays. Remove the screws and hinge, and the lock (2 screws).

4   Refitting is a reversal of removal.

28 Facia panel – removal and refitting

1   Disconnect the battery negative lead.

2   Remove the windscreen as described in Section 18.

3   Remove the instrument panel as described in Chapter 10.

4   Remove the glovebox light switch.

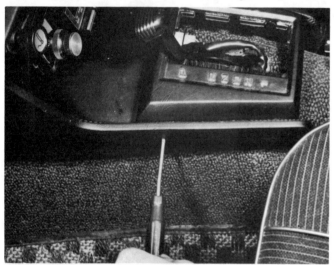

26.6 Removing the centre tray side screws

26.7A On automatic transmission models remove the selector lever cover screws ...

26.7B ... the cover ...

26.7C ... and surround

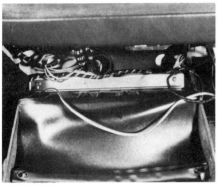
27.2 Showing the glovebox hinge location

28.8A Remove the screws ...

28.8B ... and the air distribution vent assembly

5   Pull the weatherstrips from the front pillars, remove the screws, and unclip the trim from the front pillars.

6   Remove the glovebox as described in Section 27, then remove the screws and withdraw the side trim.

7   Remove the various switches from the facia panel with reference to Chapter 10.

8   Remove the screws and withdraw the air distribution vent from the centre of the facia (photos).

9   On 1977-on models remove the centre tray as described in Section 26.

10   Remove the facia mounting screws, and pull out the instrument light holders.

11   Unscrew the mounting nuts and bolts and where applicable disconnect the loudspeaker wires and remove the trim.

12   On USA models disconnect the plug from the indicator lamp.

13   Withdraw the facia panel from the car.

14   Refitting is a reversal of removal, but refit the windscreen before aligning the facia panel with it and tightening the mounting nuts, bolts, and screws.

29 Seats – removal and refitting

Front

1   Move the seat fully to the rear on the runners and remove the front

mounting bolts.

2   Move the seat fully to the front on the runners and remove the rear mounting bolts. Note that the stop plates face forward.

3   Remove the seat through the door aperture.

4   Refitting is a reversal of removal.

Rear

5   Unscrew the centre mounting bolt in front of the rear seat cushion and withdraw the cushion.

6   Pull back the covers and unscrew the backrest side mounting bolts. Unscrew the centre mounting bolt.

7   Fold the centre armrest forward and unscrew the mounting bolts behind the backcloth.

8   Push the backrest upwards then withdraw it from the car.

9   Refitting is a reversal of removal.

30 Sliding roof – adjustment

Early version (pre-1977)

1   Open the roof by approximately 8 in (20 cm), then press off the front headlining frame and push it back.

2   Close the roof and remove the handle and escutcheon by removing the three screws.

3   Turn the removed handle fully clockwise on the escutcheon then anti-clockwise two turns. With the roof pressed fully forward, temporarily refit the handle and open and close the roof several times, finally fully closing it.

4   Remove the handle and turn it fully clockwise on the escutcheon, then refit it in the centre of the recess plate and tighten the screws.

5   Adjust the rear of the sliding roof so that it is 1 mm (0.040 in) above the level of the roof panel. To do this loosen the screw shown in Fig. 12.9.

6   Adjust the front of the sliding roof so that it is 1 mm (0.040 in) below the level of the roof panel. To do this turn the knurled nuts shown in Fig. 12.10.

7   Refit the headlining frame.

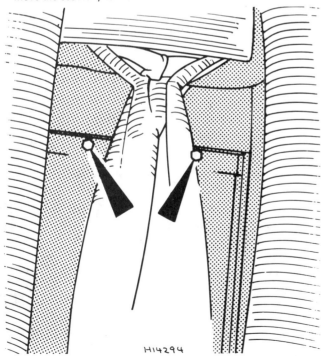
Fig. 12.8 Rear seat backrest centre mounting bolt locations (Sec 29)

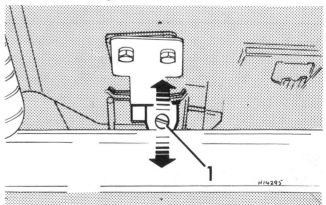
Fig. 12.9 Sliding roof rear height adjustment screw (1) (Sec 30)

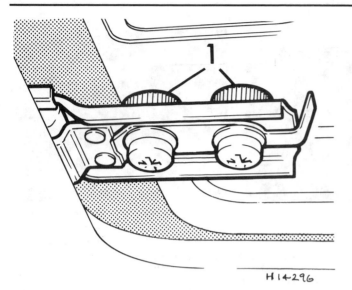

Fig. 12.10 Sliding roof front height adjustment knurled nuts (1) (Sec 30)

Later version (1977-on)

8   Open the sliding roof by approximately 2 in (5 cm) then press off the front headlining frame and push it back a little. Close the roof and push the frame fully back.

9   Adjust the front of the sliding roof so that it is 1 mm (0.040 in) below the level of the roof panel. To do this slacken the two side cross-head screws, turn the adjustment screw as necessary, then tighten the two screws while pressing them in.

10   Adjust the rear of the sliding roof so that it is 1 mm (0.040 in) above the level of the roof panel. To do this loosen the two crosshead screws on each side bracket, reposition the roof, then tighten the two screws.

11   To adjust the lift position have the sliding roof just touching the front of the roof aperture, then loosen the crosshead screws. Adjust the guide pins as necessary, then tighten the screws.

12   Refit the headlining frame and press in the retaining clip.

31   Sliding roof panel – removal and refitting

Early version (pre-1977)

1   Open the sliding roof by approximately 8 in (20 cm) and press off the front headlining frame, then close the roof and push the headlining

fully back.

2   Remove the springs and unbolt the rear guides and lockplates.

3   Note the position of the front guides then remove the screws and guides.

4   Withdraw the sliding roof forward while lifting it.

5   Refitting is a reversal of removal, but when installing the front guides note that the thick section must be on top of the guide rail. Adjust the sliding roof as described in Section 30.

Later version (1977-on)

6   Fully open the sliding roof. Remove the screws and lift out the left and right guide rails. Remove the remaining rear screws.

7   Position the roof so that it is open by approximately 2 in (5 cm), then press off the front headlining and push it back a little. Close the roof and push the frame fully back.

3   Unscrew the rear bracket nuts and withdraw the sliding roof from the car.

9   Refitting is a reversal of removal, but it will be necessary to pull the rear brackets in slightly and push the gate holder back by turning the handle. Lubricate the guides with a little vaseline. Adjust the sliding roof as described in Section 30.

32   Heater – removal and refitting

UK models

1   Remove the centre tray as described in Section 26.

2   Remove the glovebox as described in Section 27.

3   Disconnect the battery negative lead.

4   Drain the cooling system as described in Chapter 2.

5   Disconnect the heater hoses from the bulkhead in the engine compartment, also remove the sealng plate from the bulkhead.

6   Working inside the car remove the central heater control panel. To do this remove the central facia screws and the central trim, lower the panel and disconnect the plastic universal joints by depressing the lugs (photo).

7   Disconnect the wiring plug from the heater, and remove the heater cover strip by extracting the plastic plugs (photo).

8   Remove the screws and withdraw the centre air distribution grille and body.

9   Disconnect the control panel multi-plug by depressing the tabs and pull out the single wire from the centre section.

10   Unscrew the rear mounting bolt and remove the clip.

11   Working in the engine compartment unbolt and remove the bulkhead cover.

12   Unscrew the heater front mounting nuts located either side of the heater motor, and remove the spring washers, plain washers, and foam seals.

13   Remove the heater from inside the car complete with the controls.

32.6 Left-hand side of the heater showing a plastic universal joint

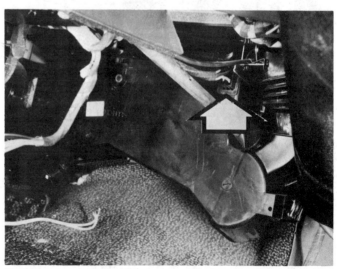

32.7 Right-hand side of the heater showing the wiring plug (arrowed)

14 Refitting is a reversal of removal. Connect the demister ducts as the heater is being installed. When connecting the universal joints, turn the control panel knobs fully anti-clockwise, turn the water valve and air flap fully anti-clockwise, then connect the shafts. Push on the heater hoses so that they press the sealing plate onto the bulkhead panel. Fill the cooling system as described in Chapter 2.

USA models

15 Remove the centre tray as decribed in Section 26.
16 Remove the glovebox as described in Section 27 then remove the side trim.
17 Disconnect the control panel plastic universal joints by depressing the lugs.
18 Remove the heater control panel screws. prise off the fresh air control knobs then unbolt the fresh air controls.
19 Remove the temperature sensor from the air conditioning evaporator housing taking care not to bend it.
20 Remove the screws and withdraw the centre air distribution grille and body.
21 Disconnect the wiring plugs from the heater and heater/evaporator control.
22 Disconnect the compressor wire in the engine compartment and remove the heater controls.
23 The air conditioning refrigerant must now be evacuated and this job must be completed by a qualified engineer. Do not attempt to evacuate the system if you do not have the special equipment and knowledge. At the same time, the engineer should remove the evaporator housing and seal the refrigerant pipes.
24 Disconnect the battery negative lead.
25 Drain the cooling system as described in Chapter 2.
26 Disconnect the heater hoses from the bulkhead in the engine compartment, also remove the sealing plate from the bulkhead panel.
27 Remove the heater cover strip by extracting the plastic plugs.
28 Unscrew the rear mounting bolt and remove the clip.
29 Working in the engine compartment unbolt and remove the bulkhead cover.

30 Unscrew the heater front mounting nuts located either side of the heater motor, and remove the spring washers, plain washers, and foam seals.
31 Remove the heater from inside the car complete with the controls.
32 Refitting is a reversal of removal. Connect the demister ducts as the heater is being installed. Have the evaporator housing refitted and charged by a qualified engineer. When connecting the control universal joints, turn the control panel knobs fully anti-clockwise, turn the water valve and air flap fully anti-clockwise, then connect the shafts. Push on the heater hoses so that they press the sealing plate onto the bulkhead panel. Fill the cooling system as described in Chapter 2.

33 Heater motor – removal and refitting

1 Working in the engine compartment unbolt and remove the bulkhead cover. Note the upper screws (photos).
2 Release the outer clips and withdraw the fan covers (photos).
3 Release the centre clip and withdraw the heater motor sufficient to disconnect the wiring. Remove the motor (photos).
4 If necessary remove the clips and extract the brushes (photo). Clean the commutator with a fuel moistened cloth then refit the brushes. Do not remove the fan wheels from the shaft as the unit is balanced as an assembly.
5 Refitting is a reversal of removal, but make sure that the motor bridge section engages with the mounting cut-out and that the flats on the fan covers face the bulkhead.

34 Air conditioning system – general description

The air conditioning system functions in a similar manner to a domestic refrigerator or deep freeze unit. A gas, termed the refrigerant (difluordichlormethane), which has a boiling point of -29.8°C (-21°F) at normal atmospheric pressure, is circulated around the system under

33.1A Remove the bulkhead cover bolts ...

33.1B ... and screws

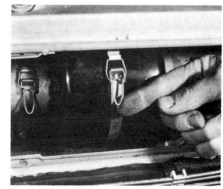
33.2A Release the clips ...

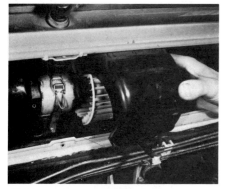
33.2B ... and remove the fan covers

33.3A Release the centre clip ...

33.3B ... withdraw the heater motor ...

33.3C ... and disconnect the wiring

33.3D The heater motor assembly

33.4 Removing a heater motor brush

the influence of a compressor unit. The compressor is belt-driven from the engine crankshaft pulley. Inside the car is a unit, termed the evaporator, which in effect has the function of a heat exchanger. The refrigerant whilst passing through this unit absorbs the unwanted heat from within the car. The refrigerant transports this unwanted heat and dispenses it to the atmosphere through the condenser unit which is mounted in front of the radiator.

The refrigerant constantly changes its state while on its cycle through the system. It enters the evaporator as a low pressure liquid, and on absorbing the heat from within the car, turns into a low pressure gas vapour. The compressor compresses this low pressure vapour and transforms it into a high pressure vapour and passes it through the condenser unit where the unwanted heat is removed and the refrigerant turns into a low pressure liquid. The low pressure liquid passes through the dehumidifier and is then recirculated.

The flow of refrigerant is controlled by a metering unit, termed the expansion valve, which senses the temperature of the refrigerant leaving the evaporator unit and controls the flow accordingly.

Dirt and moisture can foul up the system and fine filters are fitted to the expansion valve and humidifier. The main purpose of the

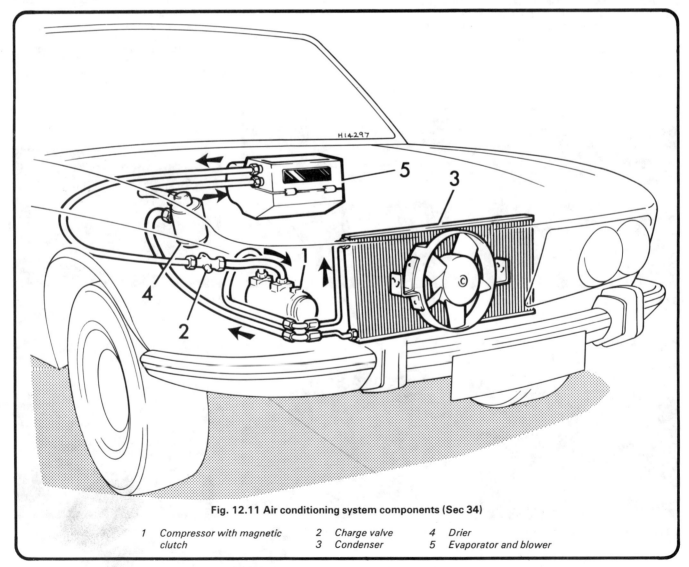

Fig. 12.11 Air conditioning system components (Sec 34)

| 1 | Compressor with magnetic clutch | 2 | Charge valve | 4 | Drier |
| | | 3 | Condenser | 5 | Evaporator and blower |

dehumidifier is to absorb any moisture circulating in the system, which would otherwise collect at the expansion valve, form as ice and block the system.

35 Air conditioning system – maintenance

Warning: Refrigerant hazards. *Liquid refrigerant can damage skin or eyes by contact. Gaseous refrigerant is harmless itself, but forms a poisonous gas when exposed to naked lights (including cigarettes).*

1   Due to the complexity of the air conditioning system, the checks and maintenance operations must be limited to the following items. No part of the system must be disconnected, due to the danger of the refrigerant escaping. Your BMW dealer or a competent refrigeration engineer must be employed to evacuate (remove the refrigerant) or recharge the system.
2   Regularly check the condition of the system hoses and connections.
3   Inspect the fins of the condenser unit, and blow out the accumulations of flies and dirt with a compressed air supply.
4   Periodically check the condition and tension of the compressor drivebelt.
5   Keep the air conditioner drain tube clear. This tube expels any condensation produced on the evaporator unit to a point under the car.

6   When the system is not in use move the control to the 'off' position.
7   During winter months, operate the unit for a few minutes every three to four weeks to keep the compressor in good order.
8   Every six months, have your BMW dealer check the refrigerant level in the system and the compressor oil level.

36 Air conditioning compressor – removal and refitting

1   If the compressor is to be removed competely the work should be completed by a qualified refrigeration engineer. However, if the compressor is to be removed from the engine and placed to one side, proceed as follows.
2   Disconnect the battery system negative lead and also the wiring from the compressor.
3   Loosen the pivot and adjustment bolts, swivel the compressor toward the engine, and remove the drivebelt.
4   Remove the pivot and adjustment bolts, withdraw the compressor from the engine, and place it to one side with the refrigerant pipes still connected.
5   Refitting is a reversal of removal but adjust the drivebelt tension so that it deflects by between 5 and 10 mm (0.197 and 0.394 in) under firm thumb pressure midway between the pulleys.

Chapter 13 Supplement:
Revisions and information on later models

Contents

2 Specifications

The Specifications given here are revisions of, or supplementary to, those at the beginning of the preceding Chapters

Engine

Torque wrench settings	lbf ft	Nm
Engine oil drain plug (small type)	24	32
Cylinder head bolts (1980-on):		
Stage 1	44	60
Stage 2 (after 15 minutes)	Tighten 33° ± 3° further	Tighten 33° ± 3° further
Stage 3 (after 25 minutes warm-up)	Tighten 33° ± 3° further	Tighten 33° ± 3° further

Cooling system

Torque wrench settings	lbf ft	Nm
Viscous fan coupling centre bolt (Holset type)	17	23

Ignition system

Spark plugs (1979-on)

Type .... Bosch W8DC, Beru 14-8DU or Champion N9YC

Clutch
Torque wrench settings

	lbf ft	Nm
Pressure plate-to-flywheel bolts (class 10.9)	21	29
Master cylinder piston rod locknut	3.5	5

Automatic transmission
Torque wrench settings

	lbf ft	Nm
Fluid filter screen bolts:		
M6	7	10
M5	4	6

Suspension and steering
Tyre pressures

	Front	Rear
528i with 195/70 VR 14 tyres:		
Up to 4 persons	2.3 bar (33 lbf/in²)	2.3 bar (33 lbf/in²)
More than 4 persons	2.4 bar (34 lbf/in²)	2.5 bar (35 lbf/in²)

1 Introduction

This Supplement contains information which is additional to, or a revision of, material in the first twelve Chapters.

The Sections in the Supplement follow the same order as the Chapters to which they relate. The Specifications are all grouped together for convenience, but they too follow Chapter order.

It is recommended that before any particular operation is undertaken, reference is made to the relevant Section(s) of this Supplement in order that any changes to procedures or components can be noted before referring to the main Chapters, thus saving time and trouble.

3 Engine

Engine oil drain plug – 2.5 litre engines
1 As from approximately June 1980, 2.5 litre engines have a smaller engine oil drain plug fitted (M12 as opposed to M22).
2 The tightening torque for the new plug has also been changed and is given in the Specifications.

Camshaft modification – fuel injected engine
3 Since February 1979, a camshaft with different cam profiles has been used on all 528i model engines.
4 This new camshaft results in a slightly higher power output (approximately 7 HP), and can be fitted to earlier engines, although no details of valve timing or other technical information was available at the time of writing.

Valves and valve seats – renovation
5 When regrinding valves, as described in Chapter 1, Section 26, it is imperative that on completion the valve rim thickness has not been reduced by more than 0.2 mm (0.008 in), and that the minimum valve head edge thickness is maintained (see Specifications, Chapter 1).
6 If the minimum valve head edge thickness is less than that given, new valves should be fitted.

Rocker shaft sealing plugs – modification (July 1979-on)
7 The sealing plugs fitted in the ends of the rocker shafts on engines built after the above date are secured in place by an angled plate.
8 This plate can be fitted to earlier engines as follows:
9 Remove the valve cover as described in Chapter 1, Section 8.
10 Loosen the two front cylinder head bolts sufficiently to allow the angled plates to be inserted between the cylinder head and the washer of the cylinder head bolts so that, on tightening the bolts, the plates will bear against the rocker shaft plugs.
11 Tighten the front cylinder head bolts and refit the valve cover.
Note: On models which have been modified by BMW or approved dealers, a white paint spot should be found on the oil filler neck of the valve cover.

Valve cover modification – 2.5 litre engines
12 From November 1979, the valve cover securing studs and nuts have been replaced by hexagon-headed bolts.

13 The thickness of the gasket used on valve covers with this modification has been reduced.

Cylinder head gasket thickness – all models
14 If the cylinder head is refinished (Chapter 1, Section 30) a thicker gasket must be used in order not to increase the compression ratio. Gaskets are available in two thicknesses, standard and +0.3 mm (0.012 in).

Cylinder head bolt tightening – 1980-on
15 Note the revised tightening torque given in the Specifications. After the Stage 1 tightening, further tightening is by angular rotation rather than torque. Make up a cardboard template to indicate the angle required, or paint lines on the bolt heads to determine their movement.

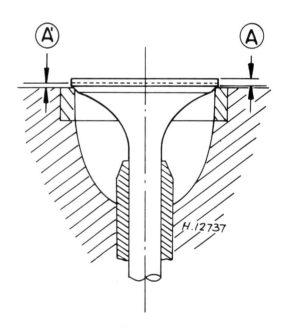

Fig. 13.1 Minimum valve edge thickness, dimension A (Sec 3)

A   Reduction due to regrinding

4 Cooling system

Viscous cooling fan (Holset type and Behr type) – removal and refitting
1 Two types of viscous coupling cooling fan may be found fitted: removal and refitting are as described in Chapter 2, Section 8, with the following additions:

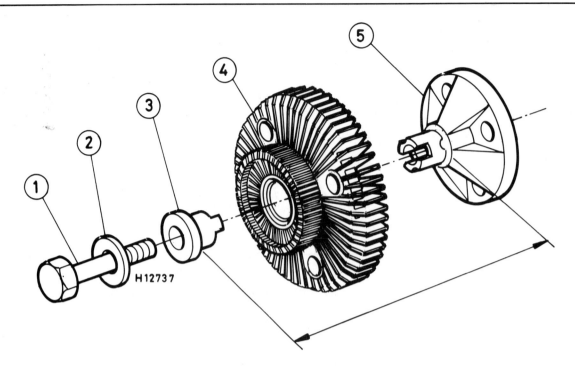

Fig. 13.2 Holset fan assembly (Sec 4)

1 Centre bolt   3 Stepped spacer   5 Support flange
2 Hardened steel washer   4 Viscous coupling

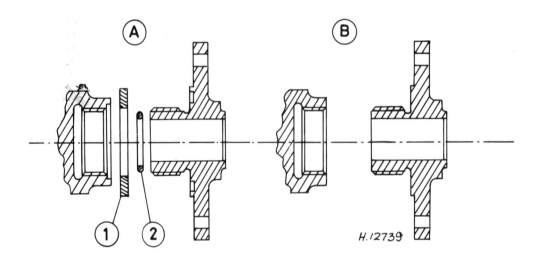

Fig. 13.3 Behr type viscous coupling with recess (A) and without (B) (Sec 4)

1 Washer   2 O-ring

Holset type

2 When refitting, the distance between the shoulder on the stepped spacer and the shoulder on the support flange should be approximately 0.5 mm (0.019 in) less than the length of the sleeve in the fan assembly (measured with the stepped spacer assembled without the fan).

3 The standard length of the sleeve in the fan is 23.8 mm (0.937 in).

4 Carefully file the ends of the stepped spacer to achieve the correct fit.

5 The spring washer under the retaining bolt should be replaced with a hardened steel washer (available from BMW dealers) and the centre bolt tightened to the specified torque.

Behr type

6 The retaining bolt has a **left-hand** thread.

7 Only 420 mm (16.5 in) diameter fan blades should be fitted.

8 On water pump hubs which have a recess (see Fig. 13.3), an O-ring and washer (obtainable from BMW dealers) must be fitted.

5 Fuel, exhaust and emission control

4A1 carburettor – modifications (September 1979-on)
TM starter – additional air control
1   In addition to the thermo valve control on the inlet manifold which senses coolant temperature, an additional air temperature valve is fitted to the carburettor cover.
2   This valve senses engine compartment air temperature and allows more air into the TM starter system, giving greater cold start control.

3   The temperature valve will open at 20°C (68°F) when the temperature is rising, and close at 14°C (57°F) when the temperature is falling.

TM starter – adjustment
4   A modified TM starter, recognisable by a thicker mounting flange (see Fig. 13.5), is fitted after the above date.
5   The modified starter cannot be adjusted as described in Chapter 3, Section 12, but can be checked in the same way; the gap being as shown in Fig. 13.5.

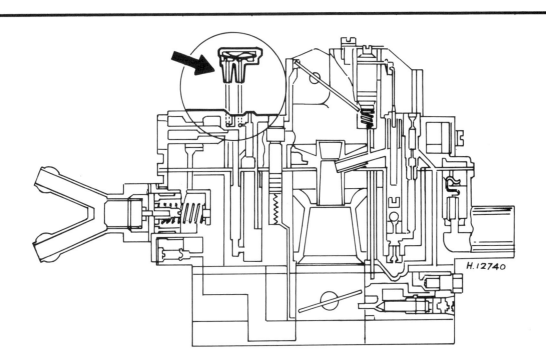

Fig. 13.4 Temperature valve (arrowed) fitted to 4A1 carburettor (Sec 5)

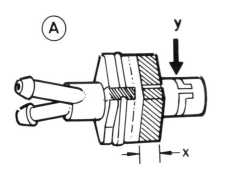
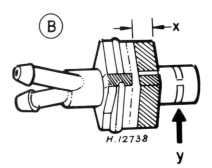

Fig. 13.5 Modified TM starter on 4A1 carburettor (Sec 5)

A (modified starter):	X = 8 mm (0.315 in)
	Y = 3.2 mm (0.126 in)
B (unmodified starter):	X = 5.5 mm (0.216 in)
	Y = 2.2 mm (0.086 in)

Thermostat valve

6 A thermostat valve is now fitted, similar to that described in Chapter 3, Section 15, paragraph 3, but operating mechanically instead of by vacuum.

7 In conjunction with this, heating of the thermostat valve is via a relay (see Fig. 13.6), which is only activated by the alternator; heating only taking place when the engine is running.

Thermostat valve – adjustment

8 Unscrew the choke housing cover.

9 Completely close the choke valve and measure the gap between the operating arm and the pull down linkage, which should be as shown in Fig. 13.7.

10 Adjustment is made by bending the connecting rod.

11 Refit the choke cover.

12 Apply a cooling spray (available from accessory shops) to the thermostat valve and check that the actuating arm moves fully out.

13 Disconnect the electrical lead from the thermostat valve.

14 Start the engine and check that the pulldown system operates.

15 Push the bi-metal spring operating arm in the direction of the arrow (rich) as far as it will go.

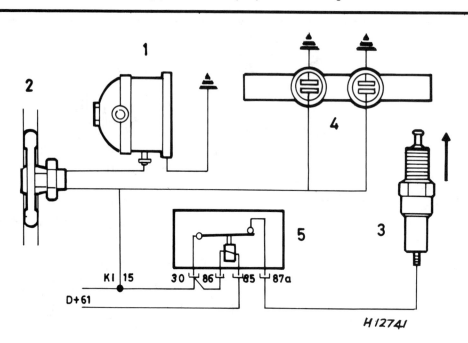

Fig. 13.6 Wiring diagram for thermostat valve on 4A1 carburettor (Sec 5)

1	Choke cover	3	Thermostat valve	5	Relay
2	Temperature switch	4	Idle shut-off valve		

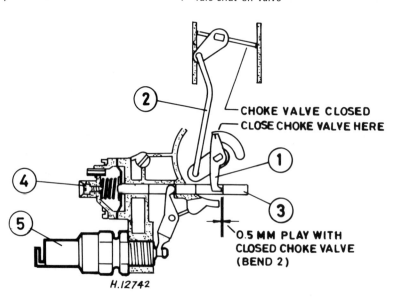

Fig. 13.7 Adjusting the thermostat valve (Sec 5)

1	Pulldown linkage	3	Operating arm	5	Thermostat valve
2	Connecting rod	4	Choke flap adjusting screw		

16 Adjust the choke gap to that specified in Fig. 13.8, by turning the thermostat valve.
17 Tighten the locknut on completion.
18 Reconnect the electrical lead to the thermostat valve and check that the actuator operates fully after about 120 seconds.
19 Push the bi-metal spring operating arm against its stop and measure the gap between the choke flap and the carburettor wall. This gap should be as shown in Fig. 13.9.
20 Adjust on the screw in the pulldown unit (Fig. 13.9).
21 On satisfactory completion, switch off the engine.

2 Over-tightening will cause distortion of the thrust rod and jamming of the master cylinder.

Clutch pressure plate bolts – revised tightening torque
3 During 1979 the class of the pressure plate bolts was uprated from 8.8 to 10.9. (The class number is marked on the bolt head.)
4 Bolts of the higher class should be tightened to the torque specified at the beginning of this Chapter. Old bolts of class 8.8 should be tightened to the torque specified in Chapter 5, or (preferably) replaced by the higher class bolts.

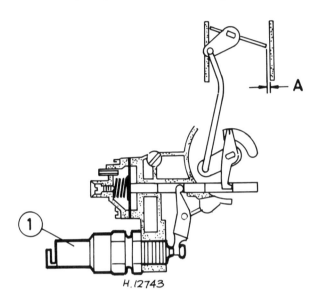

Fig. 13.8 Choke gap setting – thermostat valve disconnected (Sec 5)

1   Thermostat valve   A   = 0.7 mm (0.027 in)

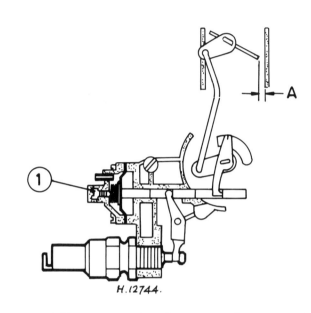

Fig. 13.9 Choke gap setting, thermostat valve reconnected and hot (Sec 5)

A = 4.2 mm (0.165 in)

---

6   Ignition system

Distributor cap and coil – protective covers
1   To decrease water ingress, later models are fitted with protective plastic caps to the distributor and coil.
2   These caps should be removed as required where operations in Chapter 4 call for the removal of the affected components or associated parts.
3   Where water ingress has been a problem in the past, causing misfiring, the distributor cap may be removed, as described in Chapter 4, Section 6, and washed in warm soapy water, then blown dry before being refitted.
4   Protective caps may be fitted to earlier distributors which do not already have them, and to modified coils introduced in August 1979 (transistorised ignition systems only).

Transistorised ignition – additional precautions
5   During checks of the transistorised ignition system, do not leave the ignition switched on without the engine running.
6   The line resistor in the system can reach temperatures of 200°C within 10 minutes under these conditions, causing burn-out of the flat pin connectors.
7   Subsequent poor contact of these connectors can lead to misfiring, poor hot start, or failure of the engine to start at all.

---

7   Clutch

Clutch master cylinder – locknut torque
1   It is important that the locknut on the eye end of the master cylinder piston rod is tightened to the specified torque (see Specifications at the beginning of this Supplement).

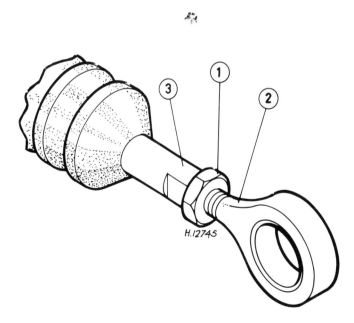

Fig. 13.10 Clutch master cylinder eye end assembly (Sec 6)

1   Locknut   2   Eye end   3   Piston rod

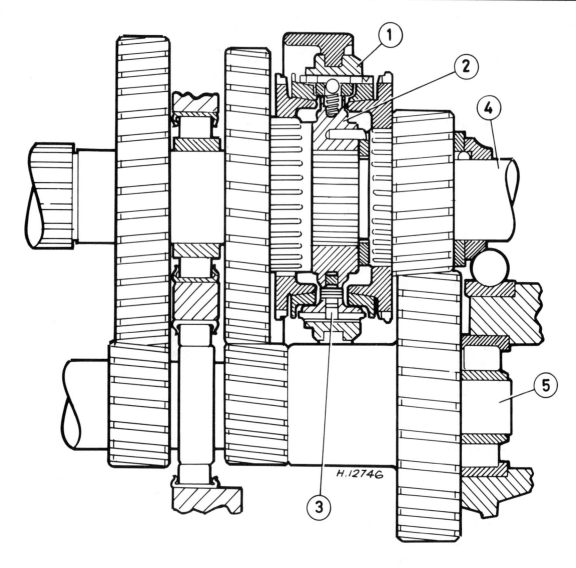

Fig. 13.11 Cutaway view of the reverse gear synchromesh assembly (Sec 8)

| 1 | Selector sleeve | 2 | Guide sleeve | 3 | Locking levers | 4 | Mainshaft | 5 | Layshaft |

---

8   Manual gearbox and automatic transmission

Gearbox, 5-speed (265 type) – reverse gear synchromesh
1   From approximately May 1980, reverse gear on the above gearbox type is fitted with a synchromesh and centrifugal locking device.
2   The centrifugal locking device prevents reverse gear being selected while the vehicle is in forward motion, and the synchromesh then provides smooth engagement of reverse gear.
3   The complete centrifugal lock assembly is incorporated in the guide sleeve.
4   A cutaway view of the assembly appears in Fig. 13.11, but no fitting tolerances were available at time of writing.

Torque converter (automatic transmission) – crankshaft location spigot
5   The diameter of the spigot on the torque converter which locates in the crankshaft has been increased from 21 mm (0.827 in) to 32 mm (1.26 in).
6   If a converter with a small diameter spigot is fitted to a crankshaft with the larger diameter hole, then a reducing sleeve (available from BMW dealers) must be fitted in order that the converter will be correctly centred.

7   The reducing sleeve should be lightly greased before being driven into the crankshaft using a soft metal drift.

Fluid filter screen (automatic transmission) – renewal
8   Drain the transmission fluid as described in Chapter 6. **Caution:** *The fluid may be very hot if the vehicle has just been run.*
9   Unscrew the dipstick/filler tube union from the side of the oil pan.
10   Remove the oil pan bolts. Be prepared for fluid spillage as the oil pan is released. Remove the oil pan and recover the gasket.
11   Remove the filter screen securing bolts (on later models these may be of the 'Torx' type) and remove the filter screen.
12   Clean any debris from the oil pan. Clean the magnet too, when so equipped.
13   Fit the new filter screen by reversing the removal operations, using new gaskets, O-rings etc as necessary. Take great care not to introduce dirt into the transmission.
14   Refill with fresh fluid on completion.

Automatic transmission (all models) – renewal
15   If an automatic transmission is renewed for any reason, the fluid cooler pipes and the cooler itself must be flushed with clean ATF. If this is not done, contaminated ATF could enter the new transmission and damage it.

9 Propeller shaft

Propeller shaft-to-gearbox coupling – 525 and 528i models (1980-on)

1 On the above models fitted with 5-speed gearboxes and produced after November 1980, a different type of coupling is used between the propeller shaft and the gearbox.

2 These new couplings (SGF flexible coupling), are not as thick as the Guibo couplings used on earlier models, and three spacer sleeves must be fitted between the coupling and the propeller shaft to take up the difference.

10 Braking system

Handbrake adjustment – rear disc brakes (1978-on)

1 Since December 1978, the holes in the rear disc assembly for adjusting the rear handbrake have been discontinued to prevent water ingress.

2 The handbrake can be adjusted by removing one wheel bolt from each rear wheel, jacking the rear of the vehicle, and turning the wheel until the bolt hole lines up with the handbrake adjustment nut, then proceed as described in Chapter 9, Section 3.

Disc pad wear sensor – all models (1978-on)

3 The disc pad wear sensor system mentioned in Chapter 9, Sections 4 and 5 (for USA models), is now fitted to all models.

4 Wear sensors are fitted to the front left-hand brake disc pad, and on the rear right-hand brake disc pad on models with rear disc brakes.

5 When the wear sensor first contacts the disc, the warning light only comes on when the brakes are applied. Further wear will break the wire in the sensor; the light will then be on continuously when driving, reminding the driver that the pads must be renewed as a matter of urgency. In this case the sensor must be renewed also.

6 If the wear warning system malfunctions, check the sensor connections, not forgetting the earth.

7 The prudent owner will not rely solely on the wear warning sensors, but will continue to inspect the pads at the specified intervals.

Brake squeal – all models

8 To eliminate brake squeal, noise suppression plates are available from BMW dealers.

9 These take the form of a metal plate in the shape of a disc pad coated with synthetic material which acts as a lubricant, preventing squeal.

10 The plates are fitted between the brake pad backplate and the piston face of the brake caliper.

Brake disc wear limits (all models)

11 Once the brake discs have been refinished to the limits given in Chapter 9 Specifications, the makers recommend that they be used for the lifetime of one further set of pads only. After this the discs must be renewed.

12 On vehicles subject to hard use (full-time towing, mountain work etc) the brake discs should be renewed before the minimum thickness is reached.

11 Electrical system

Electric door window motors – removal and refitting

1 Remove the door interior trim – see Chapter 12, Section 8. In addition the window control switch must be removed. Note the position of the switch wires.

2 Remove the quadrant stop pad.

3 On models up to 1979, remove the motor end cover and turn the end of the armature shaft until all three motor securing bolts are accessible. Support the window, remove the bolts and withdraw the motor.

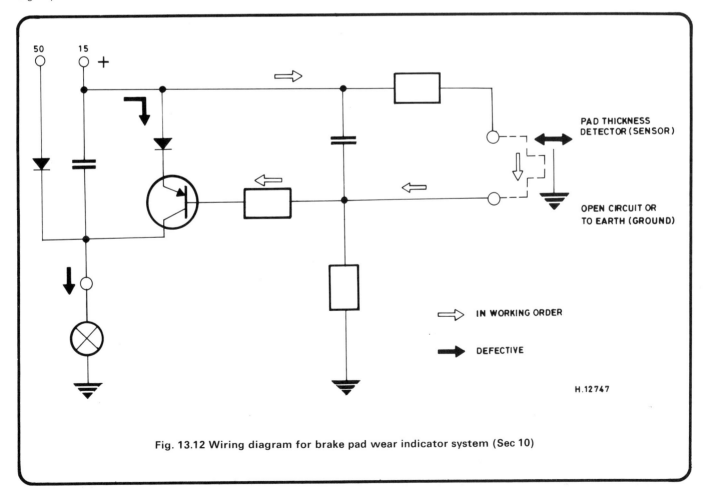

PAD THICKNESS DETECTOR (SENSOR)

OPEN CIRCUIT OR TO EARTH (GROUND)

IN WORKING ORDER

DEFECTIVE

H.12747

Fig. 13.12 Wiring diagram for brake pad wear indicator system (Sec 10)

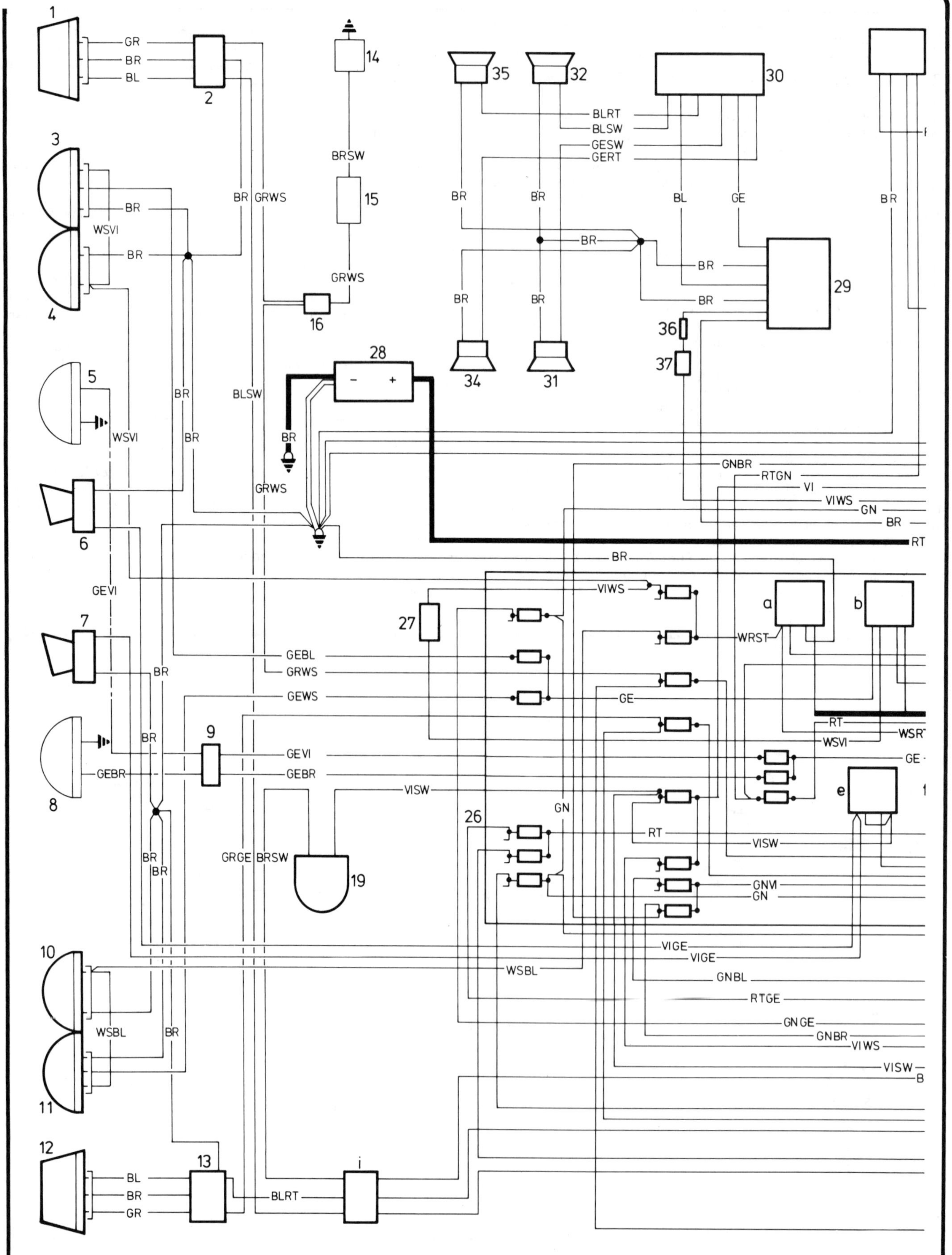

Fig. 13.13 Wiring diagram for the general electrical system – 1979-on

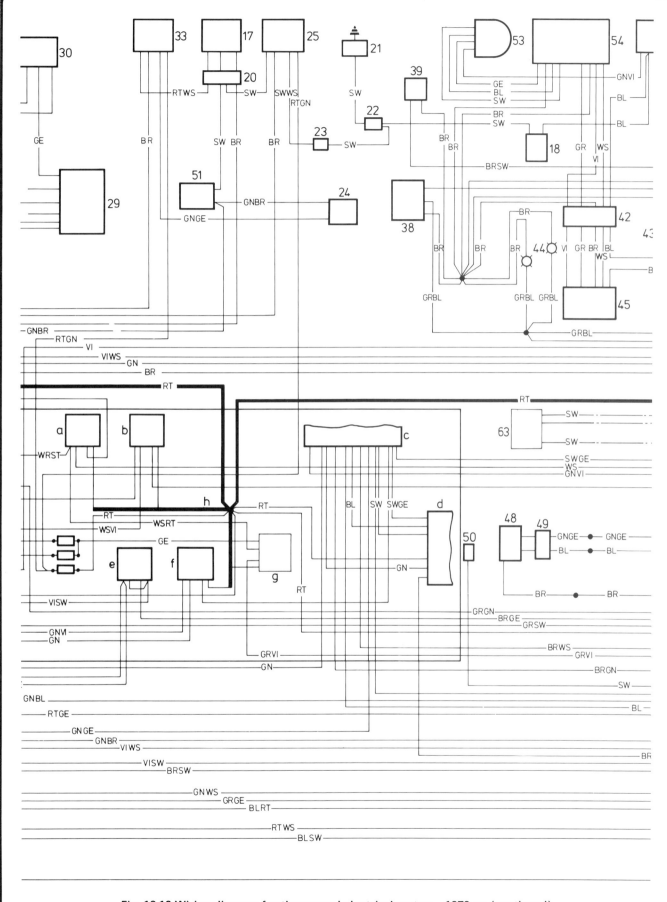

Fig. 13.13 Wiring diagram for the general electrical system – 1979-on (continued)

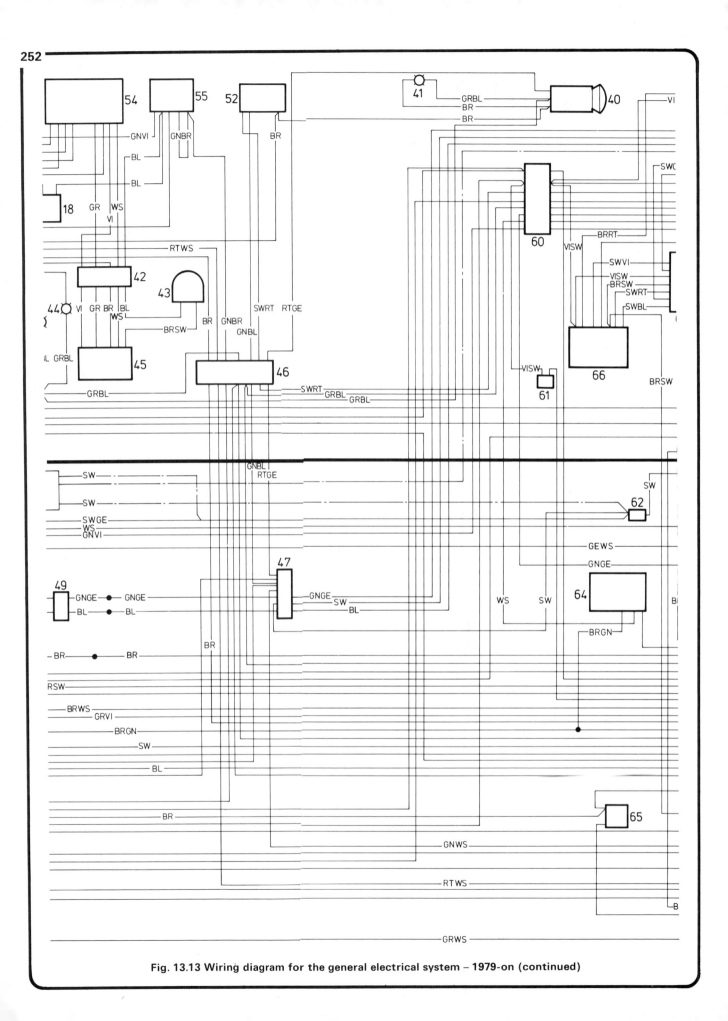

Fig. 13.13 Wiring diagram for the general electrical system – 1979-on (continued)

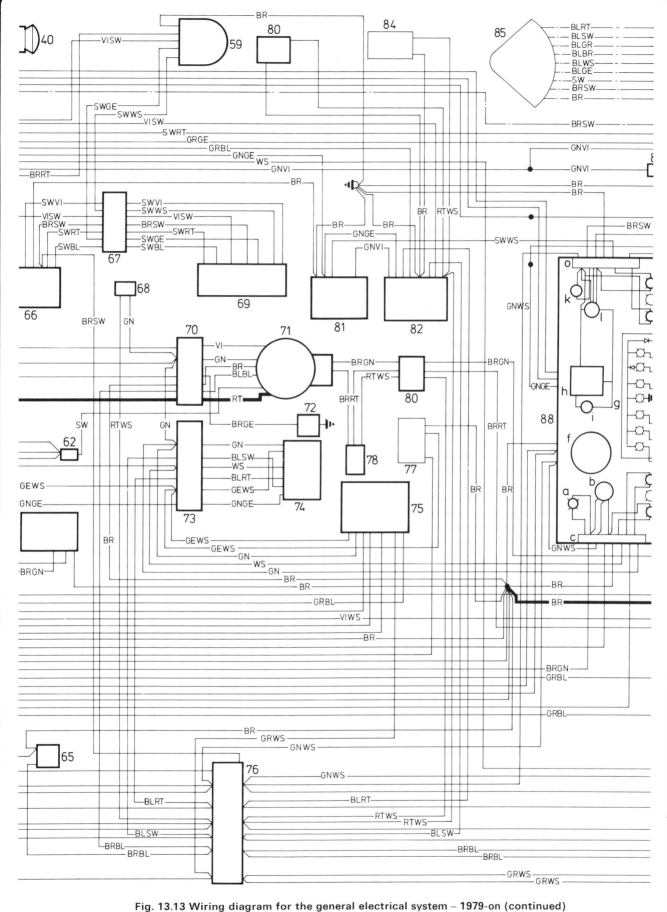

Fig. 13.13 Wiring diagram for the general electrical system – 1979-on (continued)

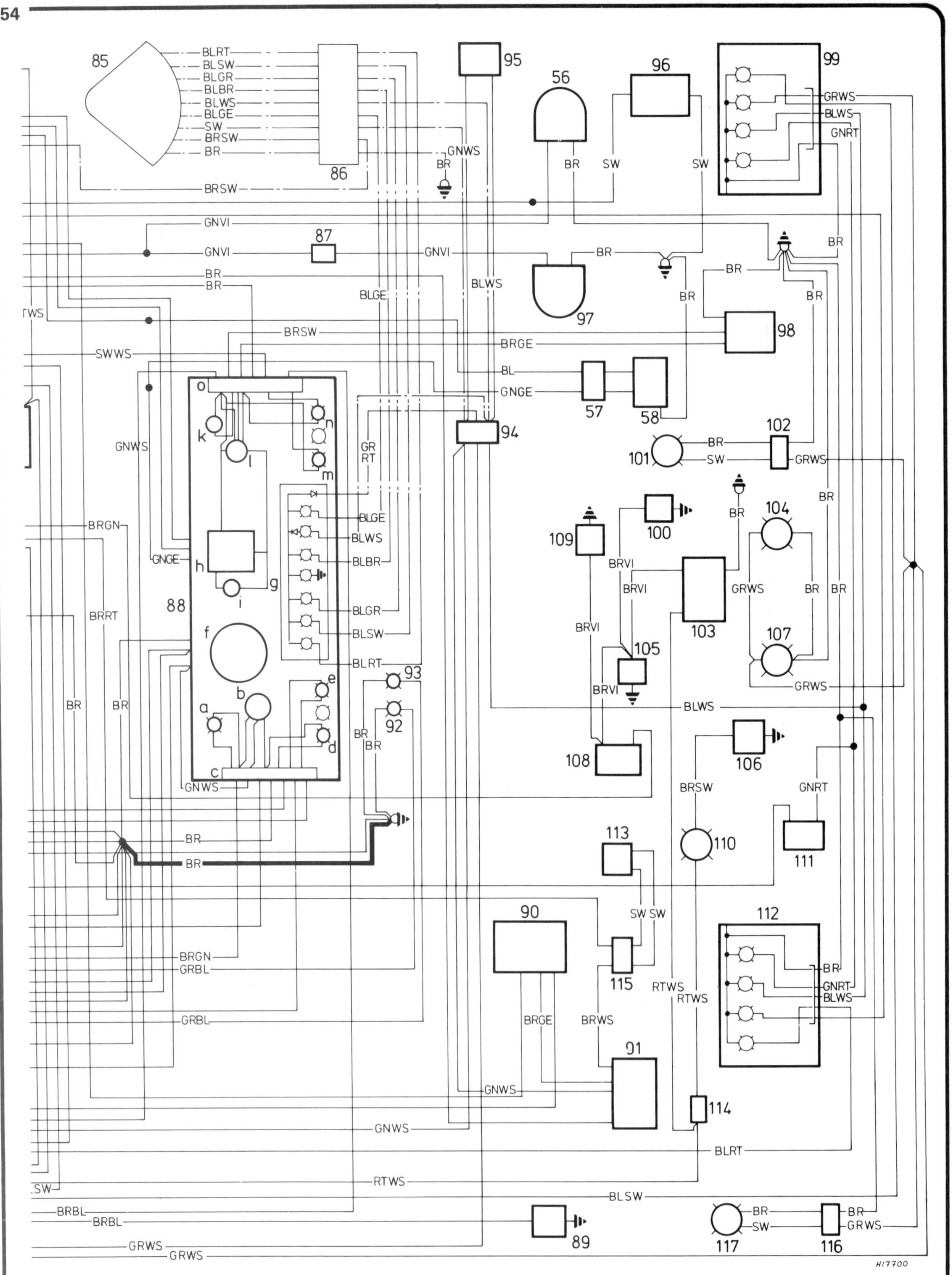

Fig. 13.13 Wiring diagram for the general electrical system – 1979-on (continued)

H17700

Key to wiring diagram Fig. 13.13 for the general electrical system – 1979-on

1   Turn signal front right with parking light
2   Plug for right front turn signal
3   Sealed beam II, front right
4   Sealed beam I, front right
5   Fog light, front right (extra)
6   Two-tone horn, right
7   Two-tone horn, left
8   Fog light, front left (extra)
9   Front fog light plug (in engine compartment front left)
10 Sealed beam I, front left
11 Sealed beam II, front left
12 Turn signal front left with parking light
13 Plug for left front turn signal
14 Engine compartment light switch (extra)
15 Engine compartment light (extra)
16 Engine compartment light plug (right headlight wire harness)
17 Extra fan motor
18 Temperature switch for compressor
19 Washer pump
20 Extra fan motor connection
21 Compressor
22 Compressor connection
23 Plug connector
24 Temperature switch 99°C
25 Relay stage I
26 Central electric board
    a   High beam relay
    b   Low beam relay
    c   Engine plug
    d   Diagnosis plug
    e   Two-tone horn relay
    f   Power saving relay
    g   Front fog light relay (extra)
    h   Power rail 30
    i   Plug connector
27 Diode
28 Battery
29 Radio
30 Speaker control
31 Speaker, rear left
32 Speaker, rear right
33 Relay stage II
34 Speaker, front left
35 Speaker, front right
36 Fuse
37 Radio connection
38 Clock
39 Microswitch
40 Cigar lighter with light
41 Ashtray light

42 A/C blower line plug
43 Evaporator blower
44 Heater light
45 Evaporator
46 Centre console plug
47 Connection for extra equipment
48 Brake pad, front left
49 Plug for left front brake pad
50 Electronic fuel injection connection
51 Temperature switch 91°C
52 Rear window demister switch
53 Heater blower motor
54 Blower switch
55 Changeover relay
56 Delivery pump
57 Plug for rear brake pad
58 Brake pad, rear
59 Windshield wiper motor
60 Plug connector II
61 Electric outside mirror connection
62 Ignition switch plug 50
63 Starter relay (automatic only)
64 Service internal switch
65 Brake fluid level control switch
66 Wipe/wash action control unit
67 Wiper switch plug
68 Connection for central locking system
69 Wiper switch
70 Ignition switch plug
71 Ignition switch with buzzer contact [1]
72 Horn contact
73 Turn signal/dimmer switch plug
74 Turn signal/dimmer switch
75 Light switch
76 Plug connector I
77 Front fog light switch (extra)
78 Buzzer
79 Buzzer plug
80 Buzzer plug
81 Hazard light flasher
82 Hazard light switch
83 Glove box light
84 Headlamp (extra)
85 Transmission switch (automatic only)
86 Transmission switch plug (automatic only)
87 Fuel pump plug
88 Instrument cluster
    a   Oil pressure indicator lamp
    b   Coolant temperature gauge
    c   Plug connector
    d   High beam indicator lamp
    e   Battery charge indicator lamp

    f   Tachometer
    g   Range indicator (automatic only)
        P = white, R = red, N = white,
        D = green, 2 = green, 1 = green
    h   Brake pad wear indicator
    i   Brake pad wear indicator lamp
    k   Fuel level indicator lamp
    l   Fuel gauge
    m   Brake fluid/parking brake indicator lamp
    n   Turn signal indicator lamp
    o   Plug connector
89 Parking brake contact
90 Fasten seat belts
91 Belt timing relay
92 Instrument light I
93 Instrument light II
94 Reversing light switch plug
95 Reversing light switch
96 Rear window demister
97 Fuel pump
98 Fuel level transmitter
99 Tail light assembly, right
    a   Turn signal
    b   Tail light
    c   Reversing light
    d   Stop light
100 Door contact, rear right
101 Side marker light, right
102 Plug for right side marker light
103 Interior light
104 Licence plate light, right
105 Door contact, rear left
106 Boot light switch
107 Licence plate light, left
108 Door contact, front left
109 Door contact, front right
110 Boot light
111 Stop light switch
112 Tail light assembly, left
    a   Turn signal
    b   Tail light
    c   Reversing light
    d   Stop light
113 Belt switch, left
114 Boot light plug
115 Belt switch plug, left
116 Side marker light plug, left
117 Side marker light, left

[1] Contact made 31 and C only when switching from "start to drive" buzzer contact closes at position R and opens when removing ignition key.

Colour codes

BL = blue	GR = grey	WS = white
BR = brown	RT = red	TR = transparent
GE = yellow	SW = black	OR = orange
GN = green	VI = violet	

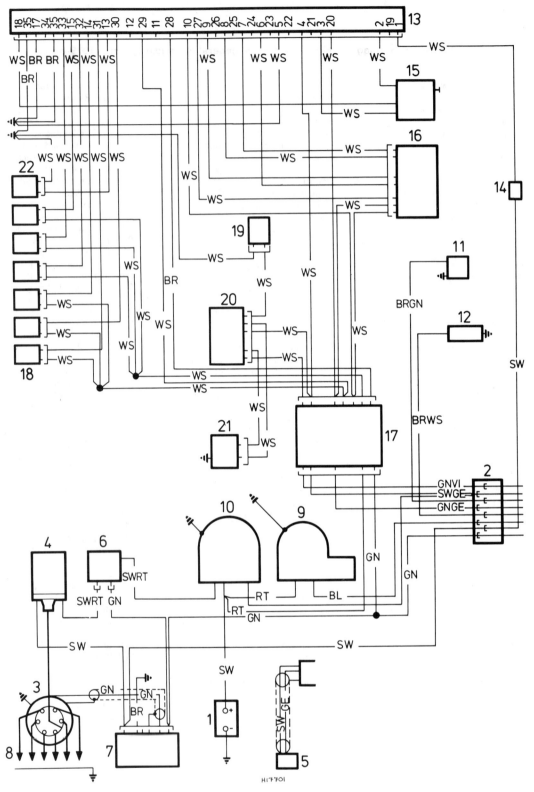

Fig. 13.14 Wiring diagram for the fuel injection system – 1979-on

1	Battery	9	Alternator
2	Engine plug	10	Starter
3	Distributor	11	Oil pressure switch
4	Ignition coil	12	Temperature transmitter
5	Position transmitter	13	Injection control unit
6	Resistor	14	Injection control unit connection
7	Transistor ignition control unit	15	Throttle switch
8	Spark plugs	16	Air flow sensor

17	Fuel injection double relay
18	Fuel injectors for cylinders 1 to 6
19	Cold start valve
20	Cold start relay
21	Temperature time switch
22	Coolant temperature sensor

For colour codes see page 255

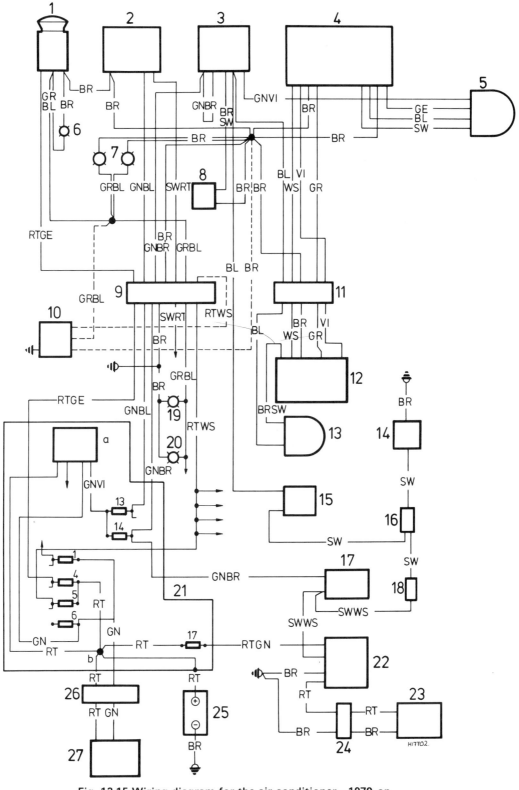

Fig. 13.15 Wiring diagram for the air conditioner – 1979-on

1	Cigar lighter with light	11	A/C blower line connection	21	Central electric board	
2	Rear window demister switch	12	Evaporator		a	Power saving relay
3	Relay	13	Evaporator		b	Power rail
4	Blower switch	14	Compressor	22	Extra fan relay	
5	Heater blower motor	15	Compressor temperature switch	23	Extra fan motor	
6	Ashtray light	16	Compressor connection	24	Extra fan motor connection	
7	Heater light	17	Extra fan temperature switch	25	Battery	
8	Microswitch	18	Diode	26	Ignition switch plug	
9	Centre console plug	19	Gate light I	27	Ignition switch	
10	Clock (extra for 518, 520)	20	Gate light II		**For colour codes see page 255**	

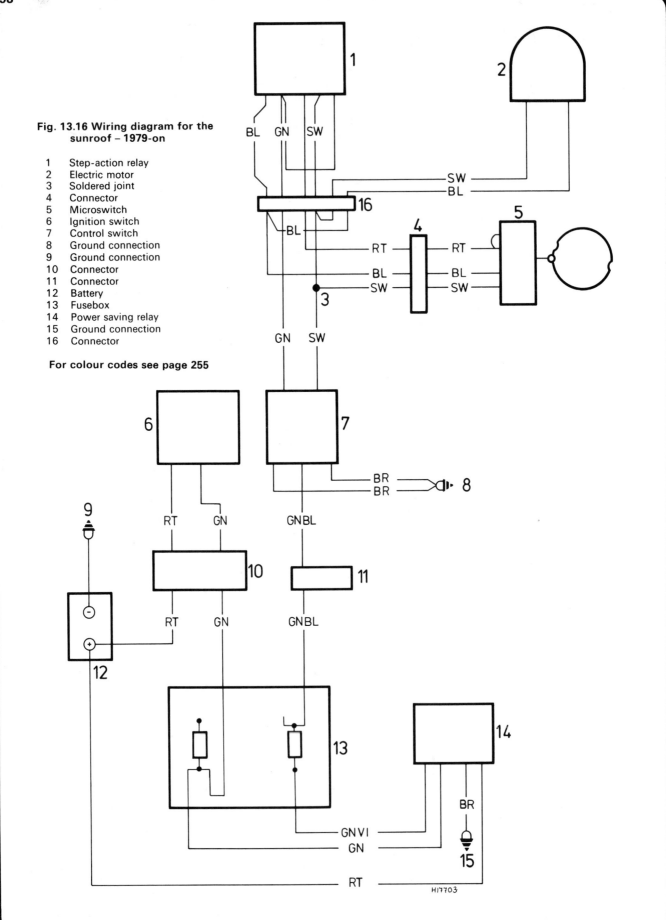

Fig. 13.16 Wiring diagram for the sunroof – 1979-on

1 Step-action relay
2 Electric motor
3 Soldered joint
4 Connector
5 Microswitch
6 Ignition switch
7 Control switch
8 Ground connection
9 Ground connection
10 Connector
11 Connector
12 Battery
13 Fusebox
14 Power saving relay
15 Ground connection
16 Connector

For colour codes see page 255

H17703

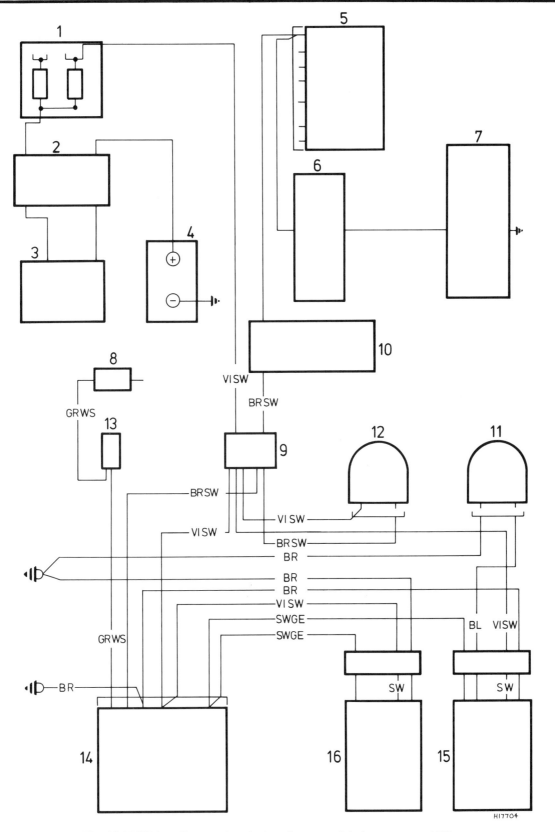

Fig. 13.17 Wiring diagram for the headlamp wash/wipe system – 1979 on

1	Central electric board fuses	7	Wiper switch	12	Windscreen washer pump
2	Ignition switch plug	8	Wire harness connection for engine compartment light	13	Engine compartment light connection
3	Ignition switch			14	Headlight cleaner control unit
4	Battery	9	Wire harness centre section plug	15	Wiper motor, right
5	Wipe/wash action control unit	10	Plug connector	16	Wiper motor, left
6	Wiper switch plug	11	Headlight washer pump		**For colour codes see page 255**

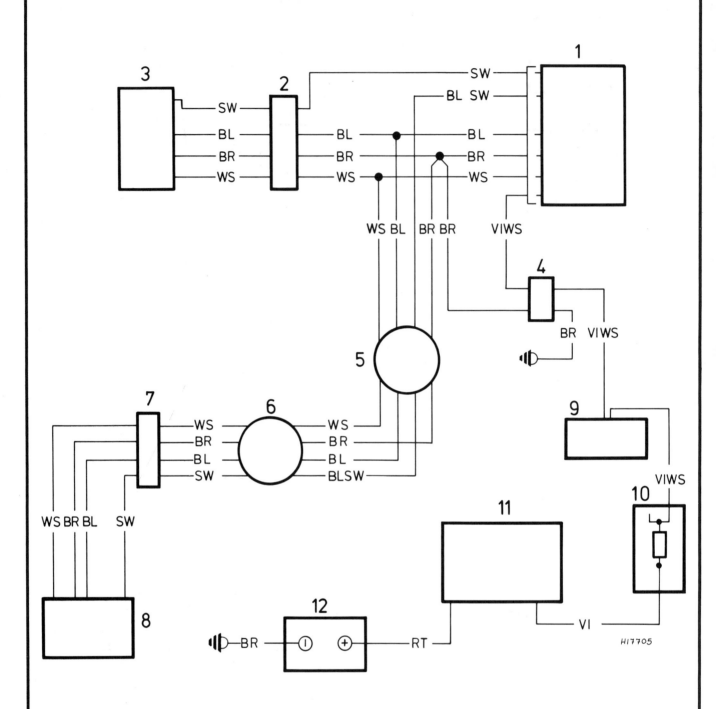

Fig. 13.18 Wiring diagram for the electric door mirrors – 1979-on

1	Mirror switch	6	Connecting wire connection	11	Ignition switch
2	Electric exterior mirror connection	7	Electric exterior mirror connection	12	Battery
3	Electric exterior mirror (driver's)	8	Electric exterior mirror (passenger's)		
4	Wire harness connection	9	Plug connector II		**For colour codes see page 255**
5	Connecting wire connection	10	Central electric board		

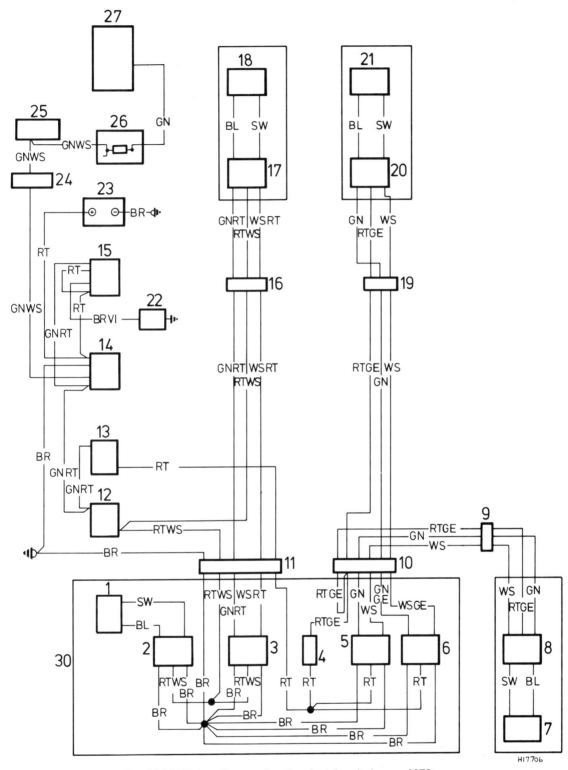

Fig. 13.19 Wiring diagram for the electric windows – 1979-on

HI7706

1	Window control motor	
2	Switch for driver's door	
3	Switch for passenger's door	
4	Safety switch	
5	Switch for rear driver's door	
6	Switch for rear passenger's door	
7	Window control motor	
8	Switch	
9	Plug connector (rear driver's door)	
10	Plug connector 2	

11	Plug connector 1
12	Automatic cut-out (front door)
13	Automatic cut-out (rear door)
14	Relay I
15	Relay II
16	Plug connector (passenger's door)
17	Switch
18	Window control motor
19	Plug connector (rear passenger's door)

20	Switch
21	Window control motor
22	Front driver's door contact
23	Battery
24	Connection for extra equipment
25	Plug connector I
26	Central electric board
27	Ignition switch

For colour codes see page 255

4 On 1979 and later models, use the emergency (manual) winder adaptor to screw the quadrant out of the pinion. Pull the quadrant further by hand and restrain it in this position using a pin in the hole provided. **Caution:** *The quadrant is spring-loaded. Uncontrolled release could cause personal injury.* Remove the three securing bolts and withdraw the motor.

5 Refitting is a reversal of removal, but the stop pad should be adjusted after installation so that the window is without tension in both the open and closed positions, and is stopped by the stop pad and not the door frame.

12 Suspension and steering

Suspension, 1980-on – general description

1 From 1980-on all models were fitted with gas-filled shock absorbers at front and rear.

2 In conjunction with this, different coil springs were fitted and the diameter of the front and rear anti-roll bars was changed.

3 If it is intended to change the older, hydraulic shock absorbers for the new gas-filled ones, then the coil springs and anti-roll bars should also be changed.

4 Removal and refitting procedures are basically the same as described in Chapter 11.

Rear wheel bearings – July 1980-on

5 Models produced after the above date are fitted with 'life-time' lubricated, grooved ball-bearings.

6 Removal and refitting instructions are similar to that described in Chapter 11, Section 14, but no greasing is necessary, and the sealing rings are omitted.

7 If new type bearings are to be fitted to older models, then both bearings should be renewed.

Rear trailing arm mounting bushes – March 1979-on

8 The rubber mounting bushes used in the trailing arm-to-subframe attachment points are now available in two patterns: normal and eccentric.

9 The eccentric bushes can be used to make small changes in rear wheel alignment.

10 Special equipment is required to install the bushes, and to measure accurately the wheel alignment; this must therefore be left to a BMW dealer or other specialist.

11 The eccentric bushes cannot compensate for distortion due to accident damage.

Rear trailing arm – revised bearing housing

12 On certain models produced after January 1980, the rear wheel bearing housing in the trailing arm has a deeper seat.

13 These trailing arms may be identified by a yellow paint mark on them.

14 Because of the deeper seat, a 2 mm (0.079 in) thick spacer is fitted in front of the wheel bearing.

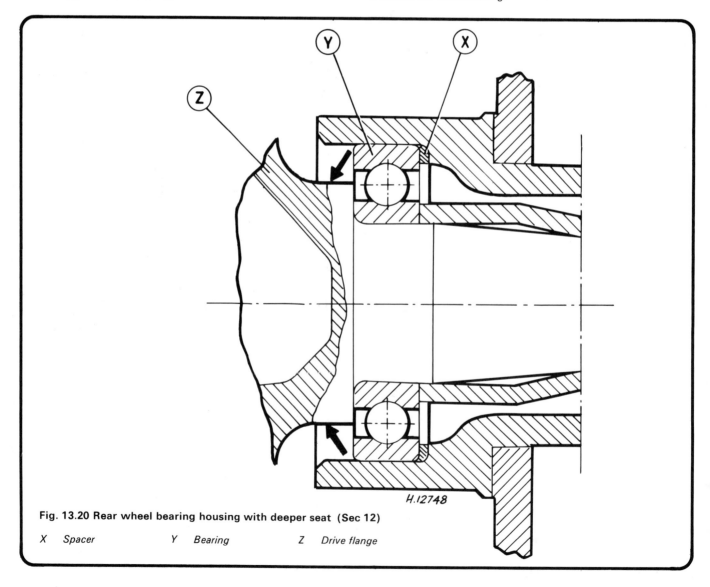

H.12748

Fig. 13.20 Rear wheel bearing housing with deeper seat (Sec 12)

X   Spacer   Y   Bearing   Z   Drive flange

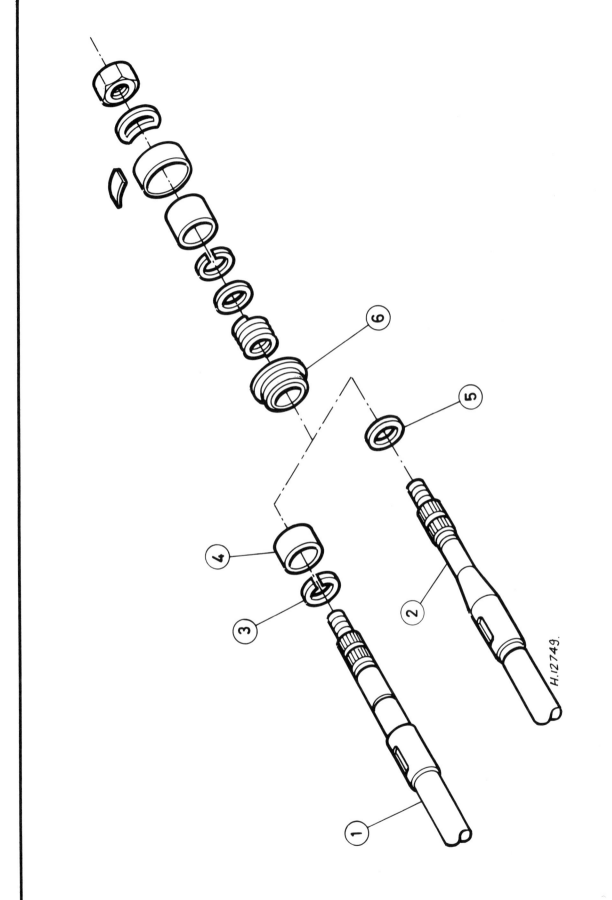

Fig. 13.21 The two types of steering column (Sec 12)

H.12749.

1 Cylindrical steering column
2 Conical steering column

3 Circlip
4 Collar

5 Washer
6 Steering column bearing

Steering column – removal and refitting (July 1981-on)

15 Two types of steering column may be found fitted, as shown in Fig. 13.21.
16 From the above date, only conical columns are supplied as spares.
17 The removal and refitting procedures given in Chapter 11, Section 23 remain the same, but if fitting a conical column in place of a cylindrical one, note that the circlip and collar are omitted, and the washer must be installed below the column bearing.

Power steering pump (all models) – renewal

18 Remove the old pump (Chapter 11, Section 31).
19 Remove the bottom bolt from the steering pump/alternator bracket.
20 Measure the gap between the bracket and the engine sump at the point where the bottom bolt passes through. Make up a shim pack of washers to fill this gap.
21 Refit the bolt, with the washers in the gap. Tighten the bolt.
22 Transfer the pulley and brackets to the new pump. Fit the pump (Chapter 11, Section 31).
23 The above procedure will ensure vibration-free operation of the steering pump, provided the drivebelt is properly adjusted.

---

13 Bodywork and fittings

Door windows – loose in holders

1 Should the door windows become loose in their holders over a period of time, the remedy is to fit an additional holder made up from suitable sheet metal, as shown in Fig. 13.22.

2 Remove the door window as described in Chapter 12, Section 11.
3 Mark the area covered by the existing holder on the back of the glass using adhesive tape.
4 Remove the holder from the window and clean all traces of adhesive from the glass and the holder.
5 Make up the additional holder, then cover it with plastic or rubber tubing as insulation.
6 Apply a suitable adhesive according to the manufacturer's instructions to the marked-out area on the glass and to the holder.
7 Refit the holder, together with the additional holder, as shown in Fig. 13.22.
8 Refit the window to the door.

Door mirrors – removal and refitting
Models up to September 1977
9 Bend back the rubber cover on the baseplate and remove the securing screw.
10 Lift the mirror from the door, disconnecting the lead if electric mirrors are fitted.
Models from September 1977
11 Prise off the plastic cover from the base of the mirror on the interior of the door.
12 Remove the mirror securing screws and lift off the mirror, disconnecting the lead if electric mirrors are fitted.
13 On pre 1980 mirrors the glass is secured by adhesive and can be removed by heating the glass with a hair dryer or heat gun, to approximately 75°C (167°F) to loosen the adhesive, then prising off the mirror.
14 Remove all traces of adhesive before fitting a new glass, using a suitable adhesive.

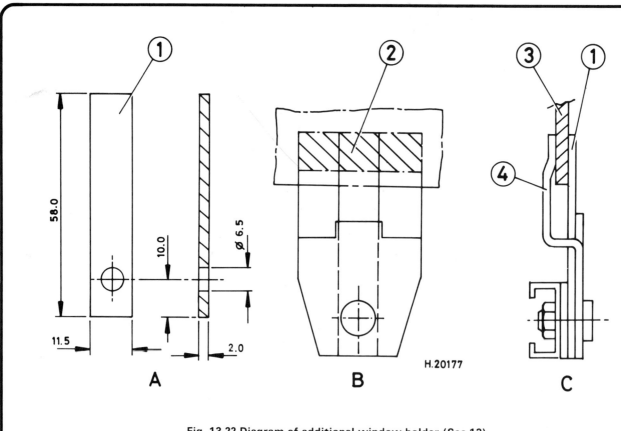

Fig. 13.22 Diagram of additional window holder (Sec 13)

A   Additional holder (1) (dimensions in mm)
B   Area to apply adhesive (2)
C   Fitting the window: additional holder (1), window (3) and existing holder (4)

15 On post 1980 mirrors, the glass is held mechanically and is released by rotating the securing ring, using a thin screwdriver inserted through the slot in the lower edge of the mirror.

All models

16 Refitting of both types of mirror is a reversal of removal.

Sliding roof panel – sealing strip

17 Should the adjustment procedure in Chapter 12, Section 30 no longer result in a complete seal due to wear in the velvet sealing strip, thicker strips are available from BMW dealers.

Heater – gurgling

18 If the heater is noisy, and gurgles, the noise can be cured by fitting a restrictor in the return hose from the heater matrix to the expansion tank.

19 The restrictor is available from BMW dealers, and should be inserted 30 to 40 mm (1.0 to 1.5 in) into the return hose connection at the heater.

Central locking system – general

20 Fitted to some later models, the central locking system allows all door locks (and the boot and fuel filler locks) to be locked and unlocked with a single turn of the key.

21 An impact switch (Chapter 10, Section 26) causes all the locks to be unlocked in the event of an accident.

22 Access to the front door lock actuator/switch unit is gained by removing the interior trim panel (Chapter 12, Section 8). After disconnecting the multi-plugs and the lock linkage, the actuator/switch unit is removed by undoing three securing nuts.

23 Access to the rear door lock actuator is similar, but there is only one multi-plug to disconnect.

24 The boot lid lock actuator is located behind the boot inner trim. See Chapter 12, Section 23.

25 The fuel filler lock actuator is also located behind the boot inner trim; the flap can be released manually if required.

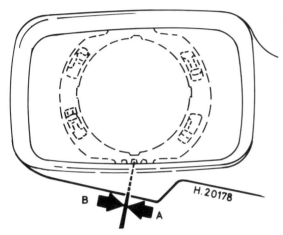

Fig. 13.23 Rotate the mirror glass securing ring in direction A to release, B to secure (Sec 13)

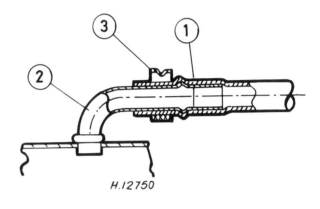

Fig. 13.24 Heater restrictor fitting position (Sec 13)

| 1 Restrictor | 2 Return hose | 3 Pipe clip |

Conversion factors

Length (distance)

Inches (in)	X	25.4	=	Millimetres (mm)	X	0.0394	= Inches (in)
Feet (ft)	X	0.305	=	Metres (m)	X	3.281	= Feet (ft)
Miles	X	1.609	=	Kilometres (km)	X	0.621	= Miles

Volume (capacity)

Cubic inches (cu in; in³)	X	16.387	=	Cubic centimetres (cc; cm³)	X	0.061	= Cubic inches (cu in; in³)
Imperial pints (Imp pt)	X	0.568	=	Litres (l)	X	1.76	= Imperial pints (Imp pt)
Imperial quarts (Imp qt)	X	1.137	=	Litres (l)	X	0.88	= Imperial quarts (Imp qt)
Imperial quarts (Imp qt)	X	1.201	=	US quarts (US qt)	X	0.833	= Imperial quarts (Imp qt)
US quarts (US qt)	X	0.946	=	Litres (l)	X	1.057	= US quarts (US qt)
Imperial gallons (Imp gal)	X	4.546	=	Litres (l)	X	0.22	= Imperial gallons (Imp gal)
Imperial gallons (Imp gal)	X	1.201	=	US gallons (US gal)	X	0.833	= Imperial gallons (Imp gal)
US gallons (US gal)	X	3.785	=	Litres (l)	X	0.264	= US gallons (US gal)

Mass (weight)

Ounces (oz)	X	28.35	=	Grams (g)	X	0.035	= Ounces (oz)
Pounds (lb)	X	0.454	=	Kilograms (kg)	X	2.205	= Pounds (lb)

Force

Ounces-force (ozf; oz)	X	0.278	=	Newtons (N)	X	3.6	= Ounces-force (ozf; oz)
Pounds-force (lbf; lb)	X	4.448	=	Newtons (N)	X	0.225	= Pounds-force (lbf; lb)
Newtons (N)	X	0.1	=	Kilograms-force (kgf; kg)	X	9.81	= Newtons (N)

Pressure

Pounds-force per square inch (psi; lbf/in²; lb/in²)	X	0.070	=	Kilograms-force per square centimetre (kgf/cm²; kg/cm²)	X	14.223	= Pounds-force per square inch (psi; lbf/in²; lb/in²)
Pounds-force per square inch (psi; lbf/in²; lb/in²)	X	0.068	=	Atmospheres (atm)	X	14.696	= Pounds-force per square inch (psi; lbf/in²; lb/in²)
Pounds-force per square inch (psi; lbf/in²; lb/in²)	X	0.069	=	Bars	X	14.5	= Pounds-force per square inch (psi; lbf/in²; lb/in²)
Pounds-force per square inch (psi; lbf/in²; lb/in²)	X	6.895	=	Kilopascals (kPa)	X	0.145	= Pounds-force per square inch (psi; lbf/in²; lb/in²)
Kilopascals (kPa)	X	0.01	=	Kilograms-force per square centimetre (kgf/cm²; kg/cm²)	X	98.1	= Kilopascals (kPa)
Millibar (mbar)	X	100	=	Pascals (Pa)	X	0.01	= Millibar (mbar)
Millibar (mbar)	X	0.0145	=	Pounds-force per square inch (psi; lbf/in², lb/in²)	X	68.947	= Millibar (mbar)
Millibar (mbar)	X	0.75	=	Millimetres of mercury (mmHg)	X	1.333	= Millibar (mbar)
Millibar (mbar)	X	1.40	=	Inches of water (inH₂O)	X	0.714	= Millibar (mbar)
Millimetres of mercury (mmHg)	X	1.868	=	Inches of water (inH₂O)	X	0.535	= Millimetres of mercury (mmHg)
Inches of water (inH₂O)	X	27.68	=	Pounds-force per square inch (psi, lbf/in², lb/in²)	X	0.036	= Inches of water (inH₂O)

Torque (moment of force)

Pounds-force inches (lbf in; lb in)	X	1.152	=	Kilograms-force centimetre (kgf cm; kg cm)	X	0.868	= Pounds-force inches (lbf in; lb in)
Pounds-force inches (lbf in; lb in)	X	0.113	=	Newton metres (Nm)	X	8.85	= Pounds-force inches (lbf in; lb in)
Pounds-force inches (lbf in; lb in)	X	0.083	=	Pounds-force feet (lbf ft; lb ft)	X	12	= Pounds-force inches (lbf in; lb in)
Pounds-force feet (lbf ft; lb ft)	X	0.138	=	Kilograms-force metres (kgf m; kg m)	X	7.233	= Pounds-force feet (lbf ft; lb ft)
Pounds-force feet (lbf ft; lb ft)	X	1.356	=	Newton metres (Nm)	X	0.738	= Pounds-force feet (lbf ft; lb ft)
Newton metres (Nm)	X	0.102	=	Kilograms-force metres (kgf m; kg m)	X	9.804	= Newton metres (Nm)

Power

Horsepower (hp)	X	745.7	=	Watts (W)	X	0.0013	= Horsepower (hp)

Velocity (speed)

Miles per hour (miles/hr; mph)	X	1.609	=	Kilometres per hour (km/hr; kph)	X	0.621	= Miles per hour (miles/hr; mph)

Fuel consumption*

Miles per gallon, Imperial (mpg)	X	0.354	=	Kilometres per litre (km/l)	X	2.825	= Miles per gallon, Imperial (mpg)
Miles per gallon, US (mpg)	X	0.425	=	Kilometres per litre (km/l)	X	2.352	= Miles per gallon, US (mpg)

Temperature

Degrees Fahrenheit = (°C x 1.8) + 32   Degrees Celsius (Degrees Centigrade; °C) = (°F - 32) x 0.56

*It is common practice to convert from miles per gallon (mpg) to litres/100 kilometres (l/100km), where mpg (Imperial) x l/100 km = 282 and mpg (US) x l/100 km = 235

Index

Printed by
J H Haynes & Co Ltd
Sparkford Nr Yeovil
Somerset BA22 7JJ England